Elizabeth Murphy was born in Liverpool and has lived in Merseyside all her life. When she was twelve, her father gave her a sixpenny book from a second-hand bookstall, *Liverpool Table Talk One Hundred Years Ago*, which led to her lifelong interest in Liverpool's history.

Throughout her girlhood, she says, there was an endless serial story unfolding in her mind with a constantly changing cast of characters, but it was only in the 1970s that she started to commit the stories to paper. Her first novel, *The Land is Bright,* was shortlisted for the Boots Romantic Novel of the Year Award in 1989 and the continuation of the story of the Ward family, *To Give and to Take* and *There is a Season* (both available from Headline) won even more readers and gathered critical acclaim:

'Hard to beat for good old-fashioned Northern common sense . . . real "muck and brass" stuff tracing the fortunes of two sisters' *Manchester Evening News*

'The whole-heartedness of Liverpool people shines through in a refreshing tribute to Merseyside' *Liverpool Daily Post*

'As heartwarming as it's sincere, this is storytelling at its best' *Best*

A Nest of
Singing Birds

Elizabeth Murphy

HEADLINE

First published in 1993
by HEADLINE BOOK PUBLISHING PLC

First published in paperback in 1993
by HEADLINE BOOK PUBLISHING PLC

10 9 8 7 6 5 4 3 2 1

ISBN 0 7472 4010 8

Printed and bound in Great Britain by
HarperCollins Manufacturing, Glasgow

HEADLINE BOOK PUBLISHING PLC
Headline House
79 Great Titchfield Street
London W1P 7FN

For our grandchildren, Andrew, Sarah, Paul, Helen, Catherine, Laura, Peter, Stephanie and Eleanor, with love.

I would like to thank Janet Jenkins and Jean M. Williams, of the Reference Library, and other staff of Crosby Central Library, also the staff of the Local History Department, Central Library, Liverpool, for their help; and the members of Crosby Writers Club, Shelagh Richardson, and other friends and relatives, and my husband Ted and all our family, for help and encouragement for which I am deeply grateful.

'Sir, we are a nest of singing birds.'
Samuel Johnson (of his friends
at Pembroke College, Oxford),
Boswell's *Life of Dr Johnson*

Chapter One

The big kitchen was warm and quiet with a bright fire burning and a black kettle on the hob beside it, purring like a contented cat.

Although the spring morning was dull and the room shadowy, the flames struck gleams of light from the polished fire irons, and from the glass of a framed photograph which stood on the dresser opposite the fireplace.

The child playing with her toys on the hearthrug left them and climbed on to a chair to reach the photograph which was of her dead brother, Patrick. She was kissing the smiling face of the little boy when her mother came through from the back kitchen.

'Anne, be careful child,' she exclaimed. 'You could get a nasty cut from the glass if you fell.'

'I'm just telling Patrick I'm starting school after Easter,' she explained. Her mother took the photograph from her and sighed as she looked at it.

'The years go past so fast,' she murmured. 'Already you're nearly the age he was when we lost him.'

She replaced the photograph and lifted Anne down from the chair. 'Put away your toys now, love,' she said. 'They'll all be in in a minute for their dinners.'

Anne went obediently to pick up her toys. Her big sister Maureen had told her that Patrick had gone to heaven when he

1

was six years old. 'I was three and Tony was six months old,' Maureen said. 'But it was a long time ago, love. Patrick would be a young man now if he'd lived.' But to Anne he was always the little boy of the photograph, and the dream playmate who accompanied her in all her imaginary adventures.

Anne was the youngest of the eight Fitzgerald children. She was loved and petted by her elder brothers and sisters, yet she would have been lonely without her dream companion. Since her brother Terry had started school two years earlier in 1923, she had played alone during the day.

Now a noise drew her to the window overlooking the back yard and she saw three of her brothers, shouting and laughing as they scuffled to kick a ball of newspaper tied with string.

Fourteen-year-old Tony was a tall, well-built boy with dark curly hair, and Stephen, four years younger, very like him. Joe who came between them in age was more slightly built but he fought as strongly for the ball, and all showed the same energy and high spirits.

Suddenly they saw Anne peeping through the window and waved to her, then kicked the ball into a corner and trooped into the kitchen. A few minutes later seven-year-old Eileen arrived, holding Terry by the hand. He was carrying a paper lantern he had made in school and rushed to show it to his mother.

'Isn't that grand?' she said in her gentle voice. 'You're a clever lad. I'll put it up on the mantelpiece for your daddy to see when he comes home.'

Tony was throwing Anne up into the air and Stephen was trying to tickle her. Their mother said firmly, 'All of you now, go and wash your hands and come to the table.' Although naturally gentle Julia Fitzgerald was strict with her children and they obeyed her immediately.

Their main meal was eaten in the evening when their father and Maureen returned from work. Now their mother placed a boiled egg at each place. Three large plates piled high with slices of bread and butter were on the table as well as a large fruit cake.

Joe put a cushion on the chair beside him and lifted Anne on to it, then he took the top off her egg and made 'soldiers' for her with a slice of bread and butter. Anne beamed at him. She loved all her brothers and sisters but thought that she loved Joe and Maureen best. They and Patrick and herself were like their mother, with clear pale skin, smooth dark hair and very dark brown eyes.

A poster advertising the opera *Carmen* with a picture of a toreador had been displayed in Crane's music shop, and when Anne had pointed to it and said 'Joe', Maureen had explained that the toreador was a Spaniard.

'Some of us look Spanish, even though we live in Liverpool,' she said. 'You and me and Joe and Patrick, and Mummy because she came from the West of Ireland. Some of the sailors from the Spanish Armada hundreds of years ago were washed up on that coast and married Irish girls, and we're descended from them.'

Anne had been too young to understand at the time, but in later years she felt proud of her Spanish ancestry and was interested in anything about Spain which came into a History or Geography lesson.

Now Tony said, 'Your last day at home, Anne, and my last day at school. You'll like school, y'know.'

'Will you like work, d'you think, Tony?' Stephen asked.

Tony shrugged. 'I think so,' he said. 'I'll soon know, anyway.'

'You'll like it, son,' Julia said. 'Benson's Engineering has the name of a good employer, and you'll finish up with a trade that'll always stand to you.' She had been pouring tea. Now she put down the teapot and smiled at Anne.

'Your last day at home with me, love. We'll make the most of it, and divil take the ironing.'

'What will we do, Mummy?' Anne asked eagerly.

'We'll do a bit of visiting, and you can wear your Sunday coat,' her mother promised.

Tony had been eating quickly, with frequent glances at the clock. Now he said, 'I've got to be back early, Mum, to finish clearing my books and put things away in the classroom, seeing as it's my last day.'

'Yes, all right,' Julia said absently. She was piling dishes on to a tray held by Joe and followed him to the scullery, telling him to be careful. Tony stood for a moment looking after her, then shrugged and picked up his cap, and went out unnoticed.

He was soon followed by the other children, then Mrs Fitzgerald damped down the fire and changed her own blouse and Anne's pinafore.

All their relations lived near to them in the Everton district of Liverpool, and they went first to visit Mrs Fitzgerald's mother, who lived in a tiny house squeezed between two larger ones in a street off West Derby Road.

Anne was fascinated by her Grandma Houlihan's house. Their own house in Magdalen Street was a big old place with four bedrooms and a bathroom with attics above, and a scullery, kitchen and two parlours downstairs. It was set back from the street with a small garden beside a path, with four steps to the front door, and cellars beneath the house.

Her Aunt Carrie's house was even larger, and although her Aunt Minnie and her Grandma Fitzgerald both lived in four-roomed houses, they seemed large compared to Grandma Houlihan's tiny house. Anne thought it was like a doll's house.

Grandma Houlihan was like a doll too. A small woman always dressed in black with a black lace cap on her white hair, she seemed to fit the house but she could be very severe.

Anne enjoyed walking through the busy streets wearing her best coat and hat and holding her mother's hand, but she was nervous about the visit.

4

Grandma was so *very* holy, and so easily shocked by the most innocent remark. Her mother had warned Anne not to chatter and she hoped she could remember not to speak.

When they reached the house Grandma opened the door and said, 'Oh, it's yourself, Julia, and Anne. Come in. I'll make you a cup of tea but I'm fasting this day. I'm only taking bread and water.'

'We won't have tea, thanks, Ma,' Julia said quickly. 'We're just after having our dinners and seeing the children back to school.'

Anne sat looking about her at the tiny room. Every inch of the wallpaper was covered with holy pictures and every flat surface held statues of saints or framed pictures of the Sacred Heart or the Pope. The horsehair stuffing of the chair she sat on pricked the back of her knees, but she was afraid to move lest she knock over a statue or a picture.

She smiled nervously as her grandmother's gaze rested on her. 'So Anne is to start school after the Easter holidays? You'll miss her, Julia – the last one left at home.'

'I will,' Julia agreed. 'It's a long time since I was without a child in the house with me during the day.'

'God has been good to you,' her mother said in a melancholy voice. 'Eight children and only one lost to you. I was never able to rear a boy. When Patrick died I thought you were going to be like me but you were spared that sorrow.'

'I grieve for him still,' Julia said in a low voice. 'There's only Maureen remembers him out of all the children. She was three and Tony only six months when we lost him.'

'I remember Patrick,' Anne announced. 'He talks to me and I talk to him.'

'Don't be telling lies now, child,' Grandma exclaimed, horrified. 'Sure the lad was dead years before you were ever born.'

'She looks at the photograph on the dresser and makes up her little daydreams about him,' Julia said apologetically.

'Then you shouldn't encourage her,' her mother said.

'It must have been very hard for you, Ma, losing all those children,' Julia said in an obvious attempt to change the subject, and her mother gave a deep sigh.

'It was indeed, but it was a cross sent to me by God and I tried to bear it willingly,' she said. 'Five little ones I left under the sod in Ireland and then Declan that was born in Liverpool died when he was two years old. Only you and Minnie and Carrie that I was able to rear, but sure it was the will of God. And your poor da taken from me too.'

Anne was relieved when a little later her mother said that they must go. 'I want to see Pat's mother, and maybe Minnie and Carrie too before we go home,' she explained. She rose and placed some money and some snuff and tea on the sideboard, then her mother accompanied them to the door.

'Don't even be thinking those lies now, child,' she said to Anne. 'Pray that God will make you a good girl, and a help to your mammy. I'll say a prayer for you too.'

She sprinkled Anne with Holy Water from the stoup which hung inside the front door and the child sighed with relief as she walked away with her mother.

It was only a short distance to the house where her father's mother and sister lived, but their reception there was very different. A tiny hallway opened into the living room where Grandma Fitzgerald sat.

As soon as her daughter Bridie opened the door Grandma called, 'Come in, come in, Julia, and Anne too. Come to Grandma, darlin', and give me a kiss. Weren't we just saying, Bridie, we hoped Julia would call?'

Grandma Fitzgerald was a huge woman who suffered from dropsy, and Anne felt as though she was sinking into a feather bed as her grandma hugged and kissed her. Bridie bustled about and within minutes a cup of tea and a piece of her favourite short-bread were produced for Julia, and a slice of bread for Anne sprinkled with the tiny multi-coloured sweets known as hundreds and thousands.

Bridie was a chain smoker and Anne watched with fascination as her aunt blew elaborate smoke rings. Bridie had told Anne that one of her boyfriends had taught her this trick. Now she said, 'So you'll soon be going to school with the others, Anne? I'm sure you'll be clever like them and quickly learn to read and write. You'll like it, Anne.'

'Mummy said I'll have lots of little girls to play with,' she said.

'You will indeed, love,' said Bridie, picking up the teapot to refill their cups. 'Do you know, I was grown up when I learnt to read and write? I never had much schooling because I was delicate, but one of the lads who courted me taught me.'

On previous occasions Bridie had told Anne that she had been taught to paper a room and to fit a gas mantel by other boyfriends, and now Anne said admiringly, 'You must have had a lot of boyfriends and they were very useful, weren't they, Aunt Bridie?'

'Indeed, and wasn't it lucky for me that she didn't decide on any one of them?' Grandma said. 'And she's here with me still. What would I do without Bridie at all? And Pat's a good son to me too. Sure his hand is never out of his pocket for us, God bless him.'

Anne pictured a younger Aunt Bridie surrounded by young men. She was rather like a man herself, Anne thought, with her large hands and feet and the dark hair on her upper lip, but Anne loved her dearly.

Now Bridie brought out a game called The Road to Berlin and sat down with Anne to play, while Julia talked to her mother-in-law. Anne hung over the board, her tongue caught between her teeth in concentration as she moved the counters up the board, successfully evading shell holes and tank traps to arrive triumphantly on a picture of Kaiser Bill, complete with curling moustaches and an open mouth.

'There, you've won again,' Bridie exclaimed. 'You have a talent for the game, childie.'

Anne was sorry when her mother said they must go, especially as they went next to visit her mother's sister, Minnie Connolly. She was a widow with an eighteen-year-old daughter named Dympna, and a son, Brendan, who had been born six months after his father was killed in an accident. That was fifteen years ago. Minnie was a thin woman with a whining voice and a talent for saying whatever would wound or cause trouble.

When she heard that Julia had just visited Grandma Fitzgerald she said spitefully, 'Is Bridie still telling those yarns about her imaginary boyfriends? Her mother should put a stop to it. They're downright lies.'

'Poor Bridie. She's only dreaming her dreams,' Julia said in her gentle voice. 'Why shouldn't her mother encourage her if it keeps her happy and does no one any harm? She's very good to her mother.'

'She'll feel it when the old lady goes,' said Minnie. 'No one else will put up with her nonsense and her mother isn't long for this world, I'm sure. All that water is bound to go to her heart and kill her.'

Julia nodded warningly towards Anne. 'Grandma has had the dropsy for years now and it doesn't seem to trouble her. She's always very cheerful. Is Dympna's chest any better with the milder weather?' she said.

'Not much,' Minnie said. 'You're looking frail yourself, Julia. It's a wonder Pat doesn't make Maureen stay home and help you, with the long family and the big house you've got to look after.'

'I'm not going to keep Maureen at home just because she's the eldest girl,' Julia said firmly. 'I've seen it too often, a girl kept at home and becoming the family drudge. No life of her own.

Looking after younger children then still waiting on them when they're grown up. Being left to look after the parents when they're old and all the others have gone off and got married. No, I want Maureen to meet people and make friends, not be stuck at home.'

Minnie sniffed. 'Well, *I* think it's her duty to stay home and help instead of working in that wool shop. Pat can afford to keep her and he should make her stay home if he doesn't want to see you kill yourself with hard work.'

'No danger of that. They all help, boys and girls. Pat sees that they do,' Julia said firmly. She stood up. 'I'll have to go. I want to call into Carrie's next.'

'You never stay here very long,' Minnie whined. 'Of course there's not the comfort here like in Carrie's house. I can't afford it.'

'I only stayed a few minutes in Ma's and in Pat's mother's because I wanted to get round to see everyone. The last day I'll have alone with Anne,' Julia said, smiling at the child.

'And Tony leaving school today. You'll soon have them all off your hands and working. He's lucky to get that apprenticeship in Benson's, and lucky you can afford to leave him there for seven years. My poor Brendan had to take anything he could get to bring some money into the house.'

Julia pressed her lips together angrily as she bent over Anne and buttoned her coat, but only said, 'We'll have to hurry. I want to be back for the children coming in from school.'

Minnie came to the door with them. 'I hope Anne can sit still in school or she'll be in trouble with the teacher,' she said. 'She's never stopped fidgeting while you've been here. Do you think her nerves are bad?'

'There's nothing wrong with her nerves,' Julia snapped, and Minnie said huffily, 'I'm sorry I spoke, I'm sure. I'm only showing concern for your family.'

'Say ta ra to your auntie, Anne,' Julia said. She hurried her daughter away, walking with such quick angry steps that Anne had to trot to keep up with her until they reached the home of her mother's other sister, Carrie Anderson. They were warmly welcomed by Carrie and two-year-old Carmel who flung herself at Anne with screams of delight.

'She loves Anne,' Carrie said fondly. She took off her niece's coat and gave her a biscuit. Anne went to play in the corner of the kitchen with Carmel.

As soon as she sat down Julia burst out, 'I've just been to our Minnie's and I don't know why I ever go there. She makes my blood boil. Making nasty remarks about Bridie who wouldn't hurt a fly and saying I look ill and Pat should keep Maureen at home to help me!'

'Don't let her upset you,' Carrie said soothingly. 'You know she's never happy unless she's causing trouble.'

'I tried to keep my temper but it was one nasty remark after another. She finished up asking if Anne's nerves were bad because she was fidgeting, then tried to make out she was only concerned about my family.'

'The wicked faggot,' Carrie said. 'The truth is, she's eaten up with jealousy. You've known her ways long enough, Julia. Don't let her get you down.'

'I'm a fool to let her annoy me,' Julia agreed. 'I'm sorry I raved on before I even said hello properly.' She smiled. 'When I said I had to go she said it was because there was more comfort in your house.'

'There's more comfort in *anybody's* house than in hers,' Carrie declared. 'And it's got nothing to do with the furniture either. It's because of her vicious tongue. I'd never go there but imagine the carry on if we didn't. She'd be right down upsetting Ma.'

'You're right, Carrie,' Julia said. 'I suppose really we should pity her for her bitter nature. Where are the twins?'

'Out in the back garden making the most of it before they start school,' Carrie said. 'They'll be filthy dirty, the scallywags.'

She had been making tea and pouring a glass of milk for Anne as she talked. Julia became calmer as she sipped her tea. 'You won't know yourself when the twins start school,' she said. 'Will Theresa take them?'

'Yes, and she won't stand any nonsense from them for all she's only ten,' Carrie laughed. 'She's a proper bossyboots.'

'Like our Eileen,' said Julia, then sighed. 'She won't have any trouble with Anne though.' She looked fondly at her youngest child as she played with the baby. 'I'll miss her out of the house.'

'You will,' Carrie agreed. 'She's full of life for all she's so good.'

There was a sudden commotion at the kitchen door and two small boys erupted into the room, struggling with each other. 'Mum, he's got my stone,' one cried. 'I dug it up and he's took it.'

'Taken it,' Carrie said, pulling their soil-covered hands apart. 'Give it to me and behave yourselves. Say hello to Auntie Julia and Anne.'

Beaming smiles replaced the scowls and they chorused, 'Hello, Auntie Julia. Hello, Anne.'

'Desmond, you've lost a tooth,' Julia exclaimed.

'Yeth, the tooth fairy took it and left me thixpence,' he said. 'Dom tried to pull his out but it wouldn't come.'

'Never mind. You shared your sixpence with Dominic and he'll share his with you when his tooth comes out,' his mother said.

'Theresa said she only got threepence when her teeth came out, and Shaun said he only got a penny,' Dominic announced.

'The tooth fairy must be getting better off,' Julia said with a smile at Carrie. She glanced at the clock. 'I'll have to go. I wish I could stay longer but I want to be in when they come home as it's Tony's last day.'

11

'Is he pleased about the apprenticeship?' her sister asked.

'Made up,' replied Julia. 'Benson's is a good place to work and engineering will just suit him. He's always messing about with old bikes.'

'I think it's important for a lad to like his job because he's in it for life,' Carrie said. 'Not like a girl who's only there until she's married. And Tony should do well. He's a hard-working lad.'

'I nearly forgot!' Julia exclaimed. 'And it was one of the reasons I came. Tony told the milkman he won't be able to help on the round when he starts work and Mr Meadows asked him to recommend a reliable lad. Would Shaun like to do it?'

'But what about Joe? Doesn't he want it?'

'He can't. He's on the list of servers for Mass at six o'clock in the morning and he's got the choir three nights a week. If Shaun would like it, he could go with Tony to see Mr Meadows tonight or tomorrow.'

'He'd be made up but I might be sorry,' Carrie laughed. 'If he gets any money he's right round to the pet shop for more hamsters or white mice. I'll send him round tomorrow.'

'It's hard work but good money for a lad,' Julia said. 'Six shillings for six days. Meadows' son does the Sunday round with him.'

She took Anne's hand and moved to the door just as a burly man wearing a leather apron came through from the garden and greeted her.

'Hello, Fred,' she said. 'I'm hopping round everyone today like a hen on a griddle, and I'm just off again.'

'Wait till I get my apron off and I'll walk down with you,' he said. 'I've got to call into the shop.'

Fred Anderson always described himself as a cobbler. He owned a small shop where two elderly men worked repairing the shoes that were brought in, but his chief income was from the skilled work he did with leather in the hut in his garden.

There he made shoes for customers who could afford to have them hand made, and designed and made handsome desk fittings and bags and purses in supple leather. He also repaired harness and it was his proud boast that he could mend anything that was brought to him, even small objects from the Museum.

Fred's house was bigger than the Fitzgerald house in Magdalen Street with larger and more luxuriously furnished rooms and a garden front and rear. Carrie and Fred had five children, Shaun and Theresa born before the war, and the twins and Carmel when Fred returned from the trenches.

'Carrie thinks wars are a good idea,' he often joked. 'Gave her a break to get her strength up before she had the twins to deal with.'

Julia felt that it was tactless of Fred to make this joke before people who had lost family or friends in the war and often thought of dropping a hint to him or Carrie but the opportunity never arose. She was too fond of both of them to risk hurting their feelings.

Now he took off his apron and put on a jacket while Carrie kissed Anne and gave her some sweets and the twins shouted: 'See you at school.'

'I pity the teacher who has those two in her class,' Fred said as they walked away, but Julia said soothingly, 'I'm sure they'll soon settle down, and they'll have each other to ease them in.'

'Anne won't give any trouble, and she'll do well at school,' Fred said, smiling down at the little girl.

'These young ones have a big advantage,' Julia said. 'With the others going through the school before them. Yours and mine have all been well behaved so the teachers will be well disposed towards these younger ones. They'll have brothers and sisters in the school to look after them, too.'

'Aye, that's true,' Fred agreed, then suddenly laughed. 'Des and Dominic might break the mould as far as behaviour goes, and queer the pitch for Carmel.'

'Now don't go borrowing trouble, Fred,' Julia said firmly, 'I'm sure they'll behave very well.'

'Aye and pigs might fly, but they're most unlikely birds,' Fred laughed. They had reached the shop and he bent down and put a threepenny bit in Anne's hand. 'Get an ice cream or some sweets, love,' he said. 'Ta ra then, Julia. Tell Pat I'll be in the Mere about eight o'clock if he feels like a pint.'

He went into his shop and Julia hurried away, an anxious frown creasing her forehead as a nearby church clock struck four-thirty.

'Dear God, I'll have missed seeing Tony and no potatoes done or anything. I don't know where the time's gone,' she murmured as she sped along with Anne trotting beside her.

Chapter Two

When they reached home Julia was relieved to find that Eileen and Stephen had laid the table and Joe had peeled the potatoes. 'Aren't I well blessed with such good children?' she said, thankfully sinking into her chair and changing her shoes. 'Is Tony long gone, Joe?'

'No, Mum, only about twenty minutes,' he said. 'He's got things to show you, but he'll tell you about it when he gets back.'

'Ah, God, I wanted to be here when he got in from school but the time just flew away from me,' she mourned. Joe made tea and brought a cup to her. 'Thanks, son,' she said. 'I'll have five minutes before I start, seeing you've all helped me.'

Eileen had taken off Anne's coat and told her to hang it on one of the hooks which were across the middle of the door. 'You'll have to do this yourself when you start school so you might as well start practising now,' she said. 'She took a piece of chalk from the dresser. 'Come on and I'll show you a new game.'

'Will you teach me how to whistle too, Eil?' Anne asked as the two little girls ran out to the backyard.

'No, because I'm always getting told off for it in school,' Eileen said, but she began to whistle the merry notes of a jig, The Blackbird.

'Will you listen to her?' her mother said. 'Sure she sounds as sweet and clear as a blackbird herself.'

The evening meal was ready when their father and Maureen

15

returned from work, and Tony from the milk round. Pat Fitzgerald was a big man with a weatherbeaten face and a hearty laugh. He was a bricklayer by trade with his own small building business, and was a loving but strict father to his children.

When he came home the children gathered round him as he sat in his armchair, and Terry showed him the paper lantern he had made while the other children chattered to him until Julia called them to the table. Maureen helped her mother to serve the meal of liver and bacon, cabbage and potatoes, then Pat said Grace before they began.

Anne sat next to her father and he said fondly, 'And what have you been doing today, queen?'

'I went to Grandma's with Mummy,' she said. 'And Grandma Fitz's and Aunt Minnie's and Aunt Carrie's.'

'You had a full day be the sound of it,' Pat said looking down the table at his wife.

'We only dashed round this afternoon,' she said. 'We couldn't stay long anywhere but I wanted to make the most of Anne's last day at home with me.'

'Long enough at a couple of places, I suppose,' he said meaningfully.

'Indeed,' she said with a smile, but when Eileen said: 'I don't like going to Grandma Houlihan's. She's so *holy*,' her father checked her sharply.

'That's no way to talk about your grandma, Eileen. Some of that same holiness wouldn't do you any harm.'

'I like going to Grandma Fitz's and Aunt Carrie's,' Anne said.

'That's because Uncle Fred gave you threepence,' Stephen teased her.

'No, it isn't,' Anne said indignantly, and Maureen said, 'We know it isn't, pet. Stephen was only joking.'

'So you finished at school today, Tony?' Pat said. 'How did you go on?'

16

'It was the gear, Dad. Father Magee came in and gave us a talk, then he gave all the lads who were leaving a Missal and a shilling. Then Mr Bolton gave us our references and said he wished us success in life on behalf of all the staff. The class gave us three cheers.'

'Well, you got a good send-off, anyway,' said Pat.

The dinner plates had been cleared away and Julia was taking a huge rice pudding from the oven. 'Let's see your character, Tony,' Pat said. 'Before your mother starts on the pudding.' Tony took his reference from the dresser and handed it to his father, who read it and handed it back with a pleased smile. 'That's very good, son. Have you seen this, Julia?'

'No, I missed Tony after school,' she said, busily serving the rice pudding. 'I'll look at it when we've finished.'

Tony looked downcast but folded the reference and put it back on the dresser without comment.

'You did well, lad,' Pat said. He looked round the table at the other children. 'I hope you're all going to work hard and leave with a good character like Maureen and Tony. See how they've both got good jobs while other boys and girls are out of work or in dead-end jobs.'

'We could work for you, Dad,' Stephen said, but his father shook his head. 'No. I don't want any of you to go into bricklaying if you can avoid it. It's too chancy. You never know when you're going to be rained off.'

When the meal was finished and cleared away, Pat asked if Eileen and Joe had done their practising. Neither had and he said, 'Right, Joe. Into the parlour and get yours done and leave the way clear for Eileen.'

Joe obeyed and soon the sweet strains of the violin floated from the parlour. He played some exercises first, then his mother's favourites: The Snowy-breasted Pearl and The Londonderry Air.

Tony had shown his mother the Missal he had been given and

his reference and been praised by her. Now he sat at one end of the table sorting cigarette cards while his father sat at the other end.

Pat had taken a thick notebook and a stub of pencil from his pocket. He was studying the book and writing in it with a frown on his face.

'Leave the old sums and rest yourself, Pat,' Julia said. 'Let your tea settle before you start worrying about them.' He looked up and smiled ruefully. His lips and tongue were dyed purple from the indelible pencil he had been sucking. 'I think I'd better go back to school meself,' he said. 'Can't get me sums to turn out right.'

'Never mind. Sit down and have your smoke and they might work out better when you're rested,' she said.

Pat sat down in his armchair with Julia sitting opposite knitting, her feet on a stool.

'Our Minnie was going on again about Maureen staying home to help,' she said quietly while all the family were occupied. 'I told her we wouldn't dream of it. I said Maureen was happy in the wool shop, and anyway all the children helped with the work. We've good children, thank God, Pat.'

He was pressing tobacco into his pipe with quick angry movements. 'What the divil has it got to do with Minnie?' he demanded. 'It'd suit her better to be looking after her own. Keeping an eye on young Brendan.'

Julia looked up in alarm. 'Brendan?' she exclaimed. 'What's the matter with him?'

Pat turned his head and looked into the fire. 'Nothing,' he said hurriedly. 'He's just – just a bit wild, that's all. Me and Fred had a word with him. He'll be all right now.'

'Minnie said nothing. She doesn't know there's anything wrong, I'm sure.'

'She doesn't need to know. It was nothing,' Pat said. 'I'm sorry

18

I spoke.' He put his pipe in his mouth and began to light it as a sign that he would say no more.

Julia said with a sigh, 'Minnie doesn't show him much example with that bitter tongue of hers. And no father to guide him, poor lad.'

Pat took the pipe from his mouth. 'Aye, poor Francis,' he said. 'It's for his sake me and Fred tried to guide the lad.'

Anne had come to stand by her father and he lifted her up on to his knee. 'Ah, me baby's a baby no longer,' he said. 'Here you are a big girl nearly ready for school before I knew what was happening.' She nestled against him.

Joe had come from the parlour and Eileen was about to go in to start practising, but Tony said quickly, 'Can we have prayers before she starts, Dad? I want to go to the Boys' Club for a game of ping-pong.'

'Right, we will so,' said Pat, lifting Anne from his knee and taking Rosary beads from where they hung on a nail beside the fireplace.

The family knelt down and Pat began. Their voices rose and fell as he recited the first half of the Hail Mary and the family responded with the second part. He then prayed for the people they knew who were ill or in trouble, and concluded with a prayer for: 'All those who have gone before us, O Lord. My father and my brothers and sisters, and Julia's father and brothers and sisters, for Francis Connolly, and for our beloved son, Patrick. Eternal rest grant unto them, O Lord, and let perpetual light shine upon them. May they rest in peace. Amen.'

The family replied, 'Amen.'

Anne leaned against her father listening to the rise and fall of the voices as they prayed. Too young to analyse her emotions, she only knew that she felt safe and happy, surrounded by her family. Even Patrick was present, she felt, as her father prayed for him.

When the prayers were finished the family stood up and Tony snatched his jacket from behind the door and sped off to the Boys' Club. Eileen went into the parlour but as soon as she began to play Joe and Stephen stood outside the parlour door and began to sing in falsetto voices: "'Nelly Bly, Nelly Bly, blinks her little eye".'

Eileen burst out of the parlour just as her father shouted, 'Cut that out now, lads. Leave Eileen in peace for her practising.'

Joe and Stephen retreated into the kitchen, laughing as Eileen belaboured them with rolled-up sheet music, and Julia said soothingly, 'Take no notice, Eileen. Go on with the music. It sounded grand.'

It was true that Eileen played well. Although she was a well-built girl, a tomboy who was always ready to join in the boys' games of football or cricket, she had long, slim fingers and a delicate touch on the piano.

Maureen went upstairs to change her dress, taking Anne with her to put her to bed. When the little girl was tucked into the bed she shared with Eileen, she begged Maureen to tell her a story.

'I can't tonight, love,' Maureen said. 'I've got to get ready for the social. I'll tell you one tomorrow night. Go to sleep now.' She went into the bathroom and when she returned Anne was fast asleep.

Maureen changed into a pale green dress with a white embroidered collar, then she took a tiny jar of Tokalon vanishing cream from a drawer and smoothed a little on to her face before passing a powder puff lightly over it.

She went into her mother's bedroom to look at herself in the long pier glass there, examining her face carefully to be sure that the cream and powder would not be evident to her father. Maureen was now seventeen, a tall slim girl with large brown eyes and dark hair cut with a fringe and a middle parting. She was attractive but knew that it was unlikely that she would be asked to dance by a young man at the social.

One reason was her shyness and the other that there would be few young men there. The Great War had claimed many of the lads who might have been her partners. When it ended one hundred and eighty of the men of the parish lay beneath the sea or buried in foreign soil.

Girls a little older than Maureen told her wistfully of the days before the war when young men outnumbered girls at the socials, but it seemed that those days would never return.

The few men who were present were discouraged by Maureen's air of reserve and her friend Hannah said in exasperation, 'You'll never click, Maureen, if you don't smile at fellows and encourage them.'

'I can't,' she said. 'I can't stand the way some girls throw themselves at fellows.'

'But there's no need to go to the other extreme,' Hannah said. 'Willie Stone was looking over here but you just looked away.'

'I'd rather dance with you, Hannah,' Maureen said. 'You haven't got two left feet and bad breath like Willie Stone.' Hannah laughed and Maureen felt conscience-stricken because she had been unkind.

When Willie Stone looked at her again she smiled at him, and then had to endure two dances with him. I'm a fool, she thought. He didn't even know I'd said that to Hannah.

Most of the couples were girls dancing together and Maureen was happy to spend the rest of the evening dancing with other girls. Her head was full of romantic dreams but she was realistic too, and knew that the young men at the social were very far from her ideal man.

Someday he would appear, she was sure, and meanwhile she was happy. Most of her social life was centred round the church and she had many good friends among the members of the clubs and confraternities to which she belonged.

She liked her job in the wool shop and was very happy at home.

Close to her mother, she enjoyed helping her with the younger children, especially Anne. Maureen was twelve when Anne was born and just old enough to enjoy cuddling and dressing the baby.

Anne loved Maureen too. Her mother was constantly busy, cooking and cleaning for her large family, but Maureen was always willing to answer Anne's questions or to tell her stories and play with her.

All the Fitzgeralds were happy together. The children rarely quarrelled, and when they did their parents insisted that they made friends with each other before bedtime. Their father quoted: '"Never let the sun go down on your wrath."'

Their mother told them, 'Don't keep up quarrels. Just think how you would feel if God took your brother or sister in the night and you had gone to bed bad friends.' All the children but especially Maureen saw the force of this argument. She was always quick to make up a quarrel and the younger children followed her example.

Carrie Anderson often complained to Julia that her family were always quarrelling. 'I think we should be called the fighting Andersons,' she said. 'The twins are always trying to murder each other and —'

'But they stand up for each other if anyone else attacks them,' Julia interrupted. 'They only squabble with each other.'

'And our Theresa and Shaun,' Carrie went on, 'it's like a red rag to a bull when they see each other. I tried that about going to bed bad friends, but Theresa said she wouldn't care if anything happened to Shaun and he said the same about her.'

'Oh, Carrie, I'm sure they didn't mean it!' Julia exclaimed. 'They must just have been mad at each other at the time.'

'They're *always* mad at each other,' Carrie said. 'I don't know what it is. They just seem to rub each other up the wrong way . . . And Des and Dom fight and you'd think they'd be good friends being twins. Now even Carmel's joining in. She bit Dominic's leg yesterday.'

'Maybe our boys don't fight so much because they're near in age and they're all so mad on football,' Julia said. 'They even took Terry to Everton on Saturday in the boys' pen.'

They were sitting in Carrie's kitchen. Carrie poured tea for them then laughed suddenly.

'The tea reminds me,' she said. 'I can't talk about the kids. We're as bad, Fred and I.' She showed Julia a stain on the wallpaper near to the door. 'I got mad at him the other night and flung my cup of tea at him. He ducked and it went all over the wallpaper.'

'Good God, I'd be afraid of harming him or breaking the cup!' Julia exclaimed.

'Oh, the cup was only a muggan one from the market,' Carrie said carelessly. 'I suppose if it had been one of my china cups it would have been in smithereens.'

'Good job Fred ducked all the same,' Julia laughed.

Carrie smiled too. 'We got over the row anyway,' she said. 'I just burst out laughing when I saw the look on Fred's face and he had to laugh too. The cup just bounced along the floor.'

Later Julia told Pat about the episode. 'Carrie was complaining about the way their kids fight and then she showed me the stain on the wallpaper where she'd thrown a cup of tea at Fred and missed.'

Pat laughed. 'The first word was always a blow with Carrie,' he said. 'I remember her from when I was courting you, the way she'd let fly.'

'She just throws the first thing that comes to her hand,' Julia agreed, 'but the rows are soon over.'

'Aye, they're both a bit fiery, but it dies down as quick as it flashes up with Fred and Carrie,' Pat said. 'There's no malice in either of them.'

'Indeed there isn't,' Julia agreed. 'I wish I could say the same

23

for our Minnie.' She seemed about to add more but instead said, 'Did any more happen about Brendan?'

'No. I told you, me and Fred put the wind up him,' said Pat. 'Just forget it will you, Julia? I'm sorry I ever mentioned it.'

She said no more but she was curious about the episode. Fred was less discreet than Pat and a few days later Carrie told Julia what had happened.

Brendan was employed as a messenger boy by the owner of a small grocery business where Carrie shopped. He had occasionally been left in charge of the shop for brief periods and on one occasion the owner, Mr Woodward, had returned suddenly to the shop and found Brendan helping himself to money from the cash drawer.

Carrie was a valued customer at the shop and Woodward decided to inform Fred before sending for the police. He had gone immediately to the shop where he found Woodward furious and Brendan snivelling. The boy said that it was the first time he had taken anything but Woodward said he had suspected him for some time. 'You know I'm not on a big scale, Mr Anderson, and I've noticed me takings were down for a while now, and biscuits and such like missing from the stock.'

Fred had asked how much was involved and the shopkeeper said he was not sure. 'He only took a little bit at first but then he got more hardfaced when he thought I hadn't noticed anything,' he said. 'I know he's your nephew, Mr Anderson, but I've got to say he's a real bad penny. I've been good to him and this is how he repays me.'

Fred had apologised to the man and made his loss good.

'It's a shame that Fred had to go through that when Brendan's not even a blood relation,' Julia said. 'I don't tell Pat half the things our Minnie says or the trouble she causes, y'know, Carrie. To tell you the truth I'm ashamed for him to know my own sister behaves like that.'

'I feel the same,' said Carrie. 'And I'm like you, Julia. I'm ashamed for Fred to know some of her tricks, and yet if I told him and he said anything about her, I'd stick up for her.'

'So would I with Pat,' Julia said with a smile. 'I suppose blood's thicker than water.'

'I just hope she behaves herself on Saturday, that's all,' said Carrie.

On Easter Saturday Carrie and Fred always gave a party for all the family, and everyone felt that this was the real start of spring. The Fitzgeralds and the Connollys were invited, and Pat's mother and sister, Fred's two brothers and their families, and numerous cousins.

Fred always concealed Easter Eggs around the garden for the children if the weather was sunny, or around the attics where they were sent up to play if it was wet. The children enjoyed playing in the attics. They could slide down an old mattress propped against the wall or swing from a rope that hung from the ceiling, and they knew that they could scream and shout as much as they pleased and not be heard downstairs in the well-built old house.

On Easter Saturday although he had left school Tony still went upstairs to play with two Anderson cousins who were also fourteen years old and Shaun and Joe who were twelve. Brendan mooched alone round the damp garden.

'I'm not staying downstairs with *him*,' Tony had whispered to Maureen. The other children welcomed Tony, but they were all pleased that Brendan had decided that he was too old at fifteen to mix with them. He had always cheated about his turn on the slide and given sly kicks and pinches to the smaller children.

Maureen and Dympna and two of Fred's nieces of the same age sat in the small back parlour while the adults gathered in the parlour. Maureen felt that she would rather be with them, or even up in the attics with the children.

Minnie's daughter Dympna was a lumpen girl with thick

glasses and a perpetual cold in the head. She constantly complained 'It's not fair', no matter what happened. Fred's nieces giggled together about boys they knew, shrieking with laughter when Maureen failed to understand the double meaning of some of their remarks.

Dympna ignored them and slumped in her chair biting her nails. Maureen felt ready to scream with boredom. At length they were called into the kitchen where two long tables were spread with a lavish meal. When it was over Bridie washed the dishes and Maureen dried them, pleased to have an excuse to escape from Dympna and the other girls.

Carrie and Julia laid the tables again for the children's meal, and when Brendan appeared scowling at the door from the garden, Carrie said quickly, 'Oh, I was just going to call you. Come on, love, get some food before we're overrun.'

The next moment there was a noise like thunder as the children clattered down the stairs and into the kitchen and Carrie said laughingly to him, 'What did I tell you? Like the charge of the Light Brigade.' But she drew no answering smile from Brendan. She left him alone and helped the younger children with their food instead.

Minnie had stood by as Pat helped his mother from the parlour to a chair in the kitchen, saying, 'Oh dear, oh dear,' and shaking her head mournfully. When Pat helped his mother back to the parlour Minnie was there again, sighing and shaking her head. Carrie had followed to make sure that old Mrs Fitzgerald was comfortable and she said sharply, 'What's the matter, Minnie? Have you got a pain?'

Anger replaced the melancholy expression on her sister's face and she looked even more cross when Pat's mother said with genuine sympathy, 'Try bi-carbonate of soda, girl. It does wonders for me.' Carrie went back to the kitchen humming cheerfully.

When the children had been fed and the table cleared, everyone assembled in the big parlour and the party took its usual course. Most people had a party piece which the others urged them to perform.

Fred sang The Road to Mandalay in a powerful baritone accompanied on the piano by Eileen, and followed it with The Lost Chord. Joe played a selection of Irish airs on the violin, and his cousin Shaun played The Londonderry Air on the flute. The company ignored the mistakes made by the young musicians and applauded them warmly.

Julia had a sweet voice and sang as she worked about the house, but she was too shy to sing in public. Pat sang The Irish Emigrant and followed it with The Miner's Dream of Home which drew tears from some of the older women.

Terry and Stephen and some of the other boys had gone back to the kitchen to play games with cigarette cards or tiddley-winks, but Anne sat on her mother's knee sucking her thumb.

Maureen was sitting beside her mother and she leaned over to take Anne's thumb from her mouth, but her mother said gently, 'Leave her, Mo. It's a comfort to her.'

'But she doesn't *need* comfort, Mum. It's just a bad habit,' Maureen protested. 'You're happy, aren't you, Anne?'

She nodded and smiled, and Fred who was moving about filling the men's glasses said heartily, 'Isn't she always happy? Happy Annie, I call her. You've got the pick of the bunch there, Julia.'

She looked up to protest, but Pat's mother who was nearby said quickly, 'Aren't they all good children? One as good as the other. You've a grand family, thank God, Julia, but sure the youngest is always the pet of the family.'

'The older children are not the baby for long because the others come crowding after them,' another woman said. 'But the youngest is the baby all her life. Remember Baby Hanson? Over fifty when she died but she was still called Baby.'

Fred's brother began to sing Phil the Fluter's Ball, and everyone joined in the lively chorus. There was laughter and an air of gaiety, and Anne snuggled close to her mother, looking around her with delight.

Presently she drifted off to sleep, and knew nothing more until she was lifted in her father's strong arms from the sofa where she had been placed.

'A grand "do", Fred, one of your best,' she heard her father say, then still half asleep she was carried home through the dark streets.

'It was a grand do, wasn't it?' she murmured as she was slipped into bed. She heard her father laugh and her mother exclaim, 'Ah, the darlin' child,' and she smiled at them and fell sound asleep, still smiling.

Chapter Three

Julia told Pat that Carrie had told her about Brendan's stealing and asked him to tell her more about the incident.

'Let's hope he's learnt his lesson,' she said.

'Time will tell,' said Pat grimly. 'God knows we did our best to cure him. I talked to him about taking his father's place and not disgracing his mother and his sister, but I think he took more notice of Fred.'

'What makes you think that?'

'Fred knows the Governor of the main Bridewell. He arranged to take Brendan in there and the bobbies showed him the cells and the birch. Even got a lad who'd been birched for stealing to talk to him. Frightened the life out of young Brendan, I can tell you.'

'I hope it did. That's probably the best way to cure a lad like him,' said Julia. 'Mind you, Pat, I feel sorry for those children for all they're such an unlikeable pair. No father to guide them and only a bad example from Minnie.'

'Do you know, that lad didn't know how his father died or anything about him?' Pat said.

'Never!' exclaimed Julia.

'As true as God. When I spoke about Francis he said he knew nothing about him. His mother started crying and carrying on if he asked.'

'Wouldn't you think he'd have asked one of us?'

'To tell you the truth, Julie, I think he had the idea that there was something shameful about his dad. When I talked about Francis and what a good man he was, the lad seemed surprised.'

'God forgive Minnie!' Julie exclaimed.

'Aye. I told the lad the way Francis worked every bit of over-time he could get and rode that old bike all the way to the South Docks to save the fare.'

'You didn't tell him it was because of Minnie nagging about money?'

'Give me credit for *some* sense, girl. I told him the way the bike wheel went in the tramlines and poor Francis was thrown off and cracked his head open, Lord rest him.'

'I wonder will it make a difference to Brendan, knowing about his dad?' said Julia. 'Perhaps he'll be a better lad from now on.'

'Maybe,' said Pat. 'Maybe.' But he looked doubtful.

Soon after the Easter party the time came for Anne to start school. Terry had moved up to the Junior Boys' School and had decided that he was now too old to be taken to school by a girl, but Anne was happy to go off to school every day clutching Eileen's hand.

She liked school. The teacher of the infant class was a young woman whose fiancé had been killed late in the war. She was a gentle girl who poured out the love she would have felt for her own children on the little ones in her charge.

This made the transition to school easy for Anne. She dearly loved Miss Anstey and liked most of the children in the class too. She enjoyed playing with them at playtime. The junior girls' play-ground was to one side of the infants' patch of ground and she could see Eileen playing boisterously there with her own friends and wave to her.

A new world seemed to open for Anne now that she was a

schoolgirl. Soon after Easter the church May procession took place and she was now eligible to walk in it. All the Fitzgerald family walked in the procession.

Pat carried a banner for the Men's Sodality to which he belonged, and Julia walked with the Women's Confraternity. Tony walked with the Young Men's Society, and Maureen, wearing a white dress and veil and a blue cloak, walked with the Children of Mary. The boys who were at school wore sashes over their white shirts, and Eileen and Anne had new white dresses and wreaths and veils.

There was tremendous bustle and excitement as they all dressed and made ready, but before they left the house Pat said, as he said every year, 'Remember now, all of you, this isn't just a matter of dressing up. The procession is to honour Our Lord and His Blessed Mother, and don't any of you forget that.'

The family all promised but Anne found it hard to remember her father's instructions in the excitement of forming into lines for the procession and walking round the church grounds.

Next they walked along the aisles of the crowded church, singing hymns, and finally the statue of the Virgin Mary was crowned with a wreath of flowers by the girl chosen to be May Queen. Most of the children carried bunches of white narcissi, and even when she was old the scent of the narcissus Cheerfulness would recall to Anne those days of happy innocence.

The school outing to Ainsdale took place next on 29 June which is the feast day of Saints Peter and Paul and was a school holiday. Anne thought it was all wonderful, from the excitement of watching for a red sky the night before as a sign of good weather to the return home, dirty, sticky, exhausted but happy.

The children travelled by special train to Ainsdale and Anne was speechless with excitement as it drew into the station to squeals of delight from the children and shouts of 'Hoky Cokey, a penny a lump' from a man on the platform.

Eileen had been told to keep Anne with her, and several of her friends had younger sisters to watch over too. The younger girls played happily together making sandcastles while their elders raced about the shore playing tick or rounders, then they all paddled at the edge of the waves.

A handbell was rung to summon the children to a meadow where trestle tables had been set up. They sat on wooden forms and were given a cup of milk and a bag containing a cheese sandwich, an apple and a sticky bun. It was like nectar and ambrosia to the hungry children.

Anne and Eileen had been saving pennies for weeks for the day out and their father had made their savings up to two shillings each. Most of this was spent at the funfair which had been set up, and the girls were determined to win or buy a present for their mother.

They were successful and a gaudy brooch and an incredibly ugly statuette were received with profuse thanks by their mother. She wore the gaudy jewellery about the house for months and put the statuette on the mantelpiece. Both girls were delighted.

Now that the twins and Anne were at school, Julia and Carrie often went to the shops in town together. The distance was short and Carmel walked between them or rode in a folding go-chair.

They managed to conceal these jaunts from Minnie. 'I feel mean leaving her out,' Julia said. 'But we've got to watch our tongues so carefully since that business with Brendan.'

'And she'd do her best to spoil the day for us anyway,' Carrie said forthrightly. Minnie still had not been told of her son's trouble.

Mr Woodward had refused to take him back, but before Minnie knew he had left there Brendan had found another job. He told his mother that it was a delivery job, and his uncles that he was helping a man who sold goods from a handcart and needed help to wheel it round. He was actually employed as a look-out man, watching for the approach of policemen as most of the goods were stolen. But he was good at the job and it introduced him to people who operated on the fringes of the law.

Pat and Fred were surprised that the job paid so well and that Brendan seemed flush with money, but he told a plausible story and though they were sometimes troubled by doubts, they accepted it.

For Anne the weeks seemed to fly past and soon it was time for the school to break up for the summer holidays. Now she was allowed to go to the park with Eileen and Terry and Stephen, with Joe in charge of the family. They took parcels of bread and jam and penny bottles of lemonade, supplemented by lemonade powder which they mixed with water from the tap in the park for extra drinks. Sometimes they went further afield. It was possible to buy a ticket known as a penny return which actually gave four rides for a penny.

They travelled to the Cast Iron Shore in the south end of the city, to the farmlands of Kirkby and Knowsley, and to Seaforth Sands in the north of Liverpool.

The red letter days of the holidays were those when their father and mother took them out for the day. Pat Fitzgerald's small building firm only employed ten men and a boy, and occasional casual labour, but they worked to a high standard. Most of their work came from recommendation by satisfied customers, and their order book was always full. The business provided a comfortable living for Pat and his family and a good rate of pay for the men. Pat was known as a good employer. The days of paid holidays had not yet arrived for most people but he allowed his men two days off each year without loss of pay, in addition to Bank Holidays. He took three days off himself, and used two of them to take the family out during the school holidays. They always had one day at New Brighton and the other day was always to a surprise destination.

One year it was a day trip to Llandudno, when they were able to go on the tiny railway up the Great Orme, and another year they went to Chester and their father took them on the Dee in a rowing boat.

Anne had always enjoyed being hoisted on her father's shoulders to watch for the ferryboat approaching for the New Brighton trip, and being able to see over the heads of the crowds the shipping in the river, but this year she felt that it was wrong. She was a big girl now and she refused to grip her father's hair as she usually did, and clasped her hands round his forehead instead.

Pat noticed nothing and when the gangway came down marched on to the ferryboat with Anne still perched on his shoulders, but for her it was a milestone. It was the first time she had ever felt too old for anything, and the first time she had ever felt critical of her father. Why did he have to shout 'You OK, baby?' and make everyone look at her and laugh.

Anne soon forgot her unusual feelings about her father and watched wide-eyed with admiration when he went on the 'Try your Strength' machine in the fair. Pat took off his coat and rolled up his shirtsleeves before picking up the hammer and bringing it down with a force that sent the marker to the top of the pole.

There were murmurs of amazement from the crowd and the man in charge shouted, 'Well done, sir. Any prize on the stall.' Pat pushed Anne forward. 'You pick, love,' he said and she chose a black doll which she treasured for years.

He was determined that his children should have a good time, and bought ice cream and toffee for them and allowed them to go on all the different attractions. Later they all went to a café in Victoria Road and enjoyed a meal of fish and chips, followed by sticky cakes.

When Pat gave the children pennies to get chocolate from the Nestlé's chocolate machine, Julia protested, 'Pat, they'll be sick,' and in a lower voice, 'and you won't have a penny left to bless yourself with.'

'It's only once a year,' he laughed, 'and they've got stomachs like horses.'

When they reached home, Maureen and Tony had eaten the cold meal left for them by their mother, and were preparing to go out for the evening. Pat gave each of them half a crown. 'You couldn't come today and I'd have spent that on you,' he said.

The first year at school was a happy one for Anne and she was sorry when the class moved up at the end of the year and gentle Miss Anstey was left behind.

The new teacher was more strict but she was an excellent teacher, and Anne enjoyed learning to form the letters she had been taught into words, and writing simple sentences. With a shock of pleasure she recognized some words in a book that Maureen was reading. By the time she moved into the Junior School she could read and write fluently.

In this class she was told to share a desk with a silent girl, Kathleen O'Neill, who seemed to be unwilling to speak or be friendly. She was a pretty girl, always neatly dressed, with long fair hair carefully combed into ringlets. Anne saw her walking to school every day with her mother and brother.

Kathleen was left as near as possible to the entrance gate to the school then her mother went off to deliver her brother to the entrance to the Boys' School. Anne was always friendly and chattered away to Kathleen who would only say, 'Mammy says I have to keep myself to myself.' Eventually Anne stopped trying to talk to her.

Even at playtime Kathleen shunned the other girls and stood by the railing which divided the boys' and girls' playgrounds, holding her brother's hand through the railing.

Anne was puzzled by Kathleen's behaviour but it mattered little to her because so often she was far away in spirit, weaving dreams and paying no attention to what was happening around her. This caused trouble for her one day during a music lesson.

Anne sat quite still as usual, with her arms folded in the regulation manner and her mind far away, dreaming of rescuing Miss Anstey from terrible danger.

Suddenly the sound of her own name woke her from her dream. 'Why can't you behave like Anne Fitzgerald instead of fidgeting and talking?' the teacher was scolding the girl who sat at the next desk. 'She hasn't moved or spoken once during this lesson, and you'd better follow her example. Do you hear me?'

'Yes, Miss,' muttered the girl, Hannah Brady. When the teacher turned back to the blackboard, Hannah put out her tongue at Anne. Her friend who sat next to her did the same and the two girls muttered together.

Suddenly the teacher swooped on them. 'Don't think I can't see you just because my back's turned,' she said sharply. 'You, Hannah Brady, and you, Kitty Mullen, are a bad influence on each other.'

The next moment she had tweaked Anne from her seat and thrust Hannah into it then told Anne to sit by Kitty.

'We'll see if you can behave if you're separated,' she said grimly. She returned to the blackboard and Kitty promptly pinched Anne's leg. She as promptly pinched her back and Kitty squealed and put up her hand.

'Miss, Anne Fitzgerald pinched me,' she cried.

'That's enough,' the teacher snapped. 'Another word and you'll *all* go to Sister Assumpta.'

'Teacher's pet,' Kitty whispered to Anne when the teacher was again busy with the class. 'We'll get you at playtime.'

At playtime the two girls grabbed Anne and dragged her to a corner near the toilets. They pulled her hair and kicked her, and although she tried to fight back, she was no match for the two hefty girls.

The next moment Eileen appeared like an avenging angel. She grabbed both girls and shook them until their hair ribbons fell off, then she smacked their legs.

'Don't you ever dare to touch my sister again or I'll kill you,' she shouted, then gave each of them a hearty smack on the bottom as they ran away.

Eileen hugged Anne and dried her tears, then helped her to straighten her clothes and pull up her socks. Finally she spat on her handkerchief and wiped the tear stains from Anne's face. 'Don't let them see they've hurt you,' she said. 'Don't give them the satisfaction, the bullies. Tell me if they ever threaten you again.'

Anne slipped her arms round Eileen and kissed her, trying to show her gratitude to her sister.

Later when Maureen took her up to bed Anne told her of her rescue by Eileen. 'You're lucky,' Maureen said, 'I was bullied when I was at school but I had no one to stand up for me. That's where you're fortunate being the youngest instead of the eldest.' And Anne could only agree.

Maureen also explained something that had puzzled Anne. 'How could Miss Holden see what we were doing when she had her back to us?' she asked. And Maureen explained that there was a picture hanging on the wall near the blackboard and the teacher could see the class reflected in it.

'That's good. I thought she might be a witch,' Anne confessed, but Maureen only laughed and tucked her up.

A few weeks later Anne thought that she was not only lucky to be the youngest but also to be born into the Fitzgerald family. Family gatherings were sometimes held on Sunday evenings either in the Andersons' house or the Fitzgeralds'.

Minnie and her children were invited but often Minnie came alone. Grandma Fitzgerald and Bridie and Grandma Houlihan also attended. One Sunday the gathering was held in the Fitzgerald house. Minnie had arrived with Dympna and Brendan shortly before Fred and Carrie arrived with their family. Fred pretended to fall back in surprise when he saw Minnie's children.

'We *are* honoured tonight,' he said with a loud guffaw. 'Are you giving the courting a miss tonight, girl?' Dympna scowled at him and turned away but Fred was unabashed. 'Have you turned over a new leaf, Brendan? Being the model son now.'

Minnie suddenly wailed loudly and Carrie snapped at Fred, 'When are you going to learn to keep your big mouth shut, Fred Anderson? It's not just a button you need on your lip, it's a hook and eye too.'

His face grew red. 'It was a joke, for God's sake,' he said. 'Why the hell is everyone so touchy?'

Julia was trying to soothe Minnie, who was pretending to have hysterics, and Carmel became alarmed by the angry voices and began to cry loudly. Maureen picked her up and ushered Anne and Terry and the twins into the small back parlour, while Pat tried to act as peacemaker between Fred and Carrie.

Julia told Eileen to make a fresh pot of tea and Pat produced beer for Fred and himself, but Minnie continued to weep. Carrie sat down beside her. 'I don't know what you're making such a fuss about, Minnie,' she said. 'You know Fred didn't mean any harm. It was just a joke.'

'Everyone picks on my two,' Minnie whined. 'Just because they've got no father to defend them.'

'For God's sake, Minnie,' Carrie said in exasperation, 'why do you always have to drag poor Francis into it? He'd have been the last man to look for trouble. He wouldn't have taken offence at Fred's joke and neither would anyone else.'

'Oh, everyone's perfect except me and mine,' Minnie said with more tears.

'I think enough has been said,' Julia said firmly. 'Here's Eileen with fresh tea so let's have a cup and forget all the unpleasant-

ness.' Maureen and Carmel followed Eileen. Carmel carried a
bowl of tiny wafer biscuits known as Dinky Wafers for the children and Maureen a plateful of buttered fruit loaf which she
handed to her mother.

'Carmel's the biscuit monitor,' she said cheerfully. 'Come on,
love. We'll go and see the kids in the back parlour.'

The back parlour was unfurnished and used as a playroom by
the Fitzgerald children on wet days. A joiner who worked for Pat
had made a few wooden toys and stools for the children to keep
there, and a pile of wood blocks to be used for building. Desmond
and Dominic were cheerfully pushing a cart back and forth when
Maureen went in but Anne, who had been as frightened as Carmel
by the sudden row, was hunched on a stool looking out of the
window.

She forced a smile and took a biscuit from Carmel, but her face
was pale and Maureen crouched down beside her and put her arm
round her.

'Don't worry, love,' Maureen whispered. 'Everything's all right
now. It was only a storm in a teacup.'

'But why, Mo? Why was everyone shouting?' Anne asked.

'It was over nothing,' Maureen said, putting her finger to her
lips and looking warningly at Carmel and the twins. Terry was
sitting in a corner reading a comic and when Maureen asked: 'Do
you want to stay here, boys, or come in the other room?' the three
said in unison, 'Stay here.'

'Right,' Maureen said. She took the bowl of biscuits from
Carmel and put three equal piles on the shelf. 'Come in to me if
you want a drink.' She gave Anne a quick kiss and took her and
Carmel back to the parlour. More visitors had arrived including
Grandma Fitzgerald and Bridie, and all was now peace and
harmony.

Anne was still troubled about the row and the following day
spoke to Maureen about it again. 'Why do the Andersons fight,

Mo? They're all so nice and yet they fight with each other. We don't fight like that, do we?'

'They're just more lively,' Maureen said soothingly. 'Aunt Carrie is a bit excitable and so they're all the same. In our house, Mum is very quiet and calm and she sets the pattern for us. It's nothing to worry about. The Andersons understand each other and they know they don't mean the things they say when they are in a temper.'

Anne smiled at her. She was not absolutely sure that she understood what Maureen meant, but she trusted her sister and if Maureen said it was all right, it must be so.

Anne never worried about anything for long. There was always so much to do, and so much to see in the busy streets: the pavement artists who drew wonderful pictures in chalk and the street singers and buskers who entertained the queues outside the theatres and cinemas; the escapologist who stood on his head in a bucket; and the many hawkers. There was the man who sold salt from a handcart filled with large blocks, another who rode a bicycle with a grindstone attached to sharpen knives, and the Mary Ellens who walked with stately tread through the streets with baskets of fish or flowers balanced on their heads and their linsey petticoats swinging about their ankles.

Even on Sundays women cried their wares in the back entries. Lightcakes and muffins, shrimps and cockles, and a woman with a particularly piercing voice who screeched 'Kewins, luverly kewins' every Sunday.

Even more interesting to Anne were the ragmen who would give a balloon or a small toy for a few rags or jamjars, and the merry-go-round pulled by an ancient horse on which children could have a ride for a halfpenny or two jamjars. The fact that it was so rickety made the ride even more exciting.

But best of all was the Pier Head, with the Mersey full of shipping and the seamen of many colours and nationalities who could be seen near the docks.

The Lascars went immediately to Paddy's Market when they came ashore and could be seen walking in single file with two or three hats on top of each other on their heads, and their arms full of unmatched shoes and other oddments.

Tony told her that the men walked in single file because they were used to walking on narrow paths through the jungle, and Anne thought this must be true. Many of them were marked with tribal scars and they were all pitifully thin.

As well as the rich life of the streets there was always something interesting nearer home. There were few children in Magdalen Street, but Anne enjoyed visiting her older neighbours. The Misses Dolan, two maiden ladies, lived next-door, and had a noisy parrot brought home by a seafaring brother, now dead. Nothing could cure the bird of using the bad language learnt on ship, and Anne was always delighted to be greeted by a squawk of: 'What the hell's that?' as she walked in. She also visited another neighbour, Billy Bolten, an old man with a wooden leg. He had sailed the seven seas, but now lived in a rented room a few doors away.

His room was full of curios and he allowed Anne to dust them and told her tales about them. There was a long boat with eight rowers all carved from black wood, with even the tiny faces of the rowers etched to show the strain and effort as they rowed, and an elephant of the same wood with brilliantly coloured trappings correct in every detail.

At home every day was interesting too, with Maureen and Tony talking of what happened at work and frequent visits from relations. Anne heard far more gossip than she was intended to hear as she sat unnoticed on a stool or in a corner of the sofa.

One day she was sitting on a stool trying to use a wool bobbin known as a Knitting Nancy while her mother and her Aunt Carrie sipped tea and talked. Aunt Carrie was talking again about Shaun and Theresa's quarrels and Anne was paying little attention until she heard her mother mention Patrick.

'Losing him was a terrible grief to us, Carrie,' she said. 'But sometimes I think it has drawn the family closer together.'

'But there's only Maureen remembers him and she was only a baby herself, really. Only three years old,' Carrie said.

'Yes, but we talk about him, and Pat always mentions him in the nightly prayers. We don't want to make the mistake we made with Maureen.'

Carrie sighed. 'If only I hadn't been bedfast with the sciatica at the time, I'd never have let Minnie clear all trace of the child away while you and Pat were out of your minds with grief.'

'She did it with good intentions,' Julia said. 'Leaving nothing that could remind us. But sure how could we ever forget him? And Maureen, poor child. It was years before I realised she was blaming herself. She screamed when we sent her to Ma when Patrick took ill, and when she came back he'd disappeared and so had all his toys and clothes. She thought it was because she'd been naughty and she was afraid to ask.'

'How can you fathom the mind of a child?' Carrie said. 'But at least you found out and put it right in time.'

'Yes, and we talk about Patrick and have his photograph on the dresser. I don't want him to be forgotten. Anne made him her little imaginary friend before she went to school, but she has plenty of real friends to play with now.'

They looked fondly at Anne as she sat with her head bent and her tongue caught between her teeth in concentration, pulling the wool through the bobbin.

'Happy Annie, Fred calls her,' Carrie said. 'He never spoke a truer word.'

Chapter Four

When Joe left school in 1927 at the age of fourteen job prospects were bleak. There was no hope of an apprenticeship for him, and his father was unable to take him into the business.

'I know I always said I didn't want any of you lads to go into the building trade, but I'd take you on now for the sake of a job for you if things weren't so bad.'

'I know, Dad,' he said. 'I'm sure I'll get something. I'm trying everywhere.'

'I think it's just a bad patch,' his father said. 'But I've only managed to keep all the lads on because they've taken a cut in wages. It was Billy Joyce who suggested it and his lad's our can lad. I can't sack him and take you in his place.'

'I wouldn't want you to sack Freddie,' Joe said. 'I'll get something, Dad.'

Eventually, after much searching, he managed to secure a job in a men's outfitters as an assistant. The hours were long and the pay poor but at least it was a job, Joe felt, and he was relieved to find it.

In the late summer of 1927 Grandma Houlihan fell downstairs and broke her leg. She lived alone and had no one to look after her, and when she confessed that the fall was caused by a dizzy spell which she was subject to, it was decided that it would be wise for her to give up her house and live with Carrie and Fred.

For many years Pat and Fred had each put aside a small weekly sum to be divided between Grandma Houlihan and Minnie to supplement their meagre pensions, and Pat also helped his own mother and sister.

He and Julia decided that these obligations must be met even though they were having to economise because of the difficult times. When Julia's mother went to live with Carrie and Fred, Pat offered his brother-in-law the weekly amount but Fred brushed the offer aside.

'No, Pat,' he said. 'I'm saving what I used to give towards her rent and you know yourself, what's one extra mouth in a big family? Especially when Grandma's on black tea and dry bread half the time.' He laughed loudly.

Julia and Pat were visiting the Andersons at the time and both protested but Fred and Carrie were adamant.

'If Dympna and Brendan shaped themselves, you wouldn't need to pay Minnie's rent either,' Carrie said. 'Most of what Dympna earns goes on her back – not that it makes her look any better. She's such an awkward lump of a girl. And God knows what Brendan gets up to with his money.'

Fred looked at Pat and jerked his head towards the door and they went out to the shed.

'Is Ma settling in all right?' Julia asked Carrie.

'She is,' said her sister. 'Of course, she'll be bedbound for a few weeks yet, but she's happy enough with her statues and holy pictures around her. She bears her pain very bravely.'

'It won't be easy for you, Carrie,' Julia said. 'We'll take a turn if it gets too much for you, or even if it doesn't.'

'Ma's no trouble at all,' Carrie said. 'It's only the fasting days that worry me. I've told her that it's not expected of her and she needs to build up her strength, but she's determined to fast on Tuesdays and Thursdays and sometimes an extra day too.'

'If it's what she wants – and it hasn't done her any harm, when you think of the hard life she's had and she's with us still, thank God,' said Julia.

'Yes, but imagine how I feel when we're sitting down to a good dinner and I take a cup of black tea and a slice of dry bread up to her.'

'But you know she'd rather belong to the Third Order and take dry bread than eat a hearty dinner. At least she's upstairs in her room and not sitting there while you're eating,' Julia consoled her sister. 'It'll be a while yet before she can come downstairs.'

'I see Anne's going to be a Maid of Honour in the May procession,' Carrie said. 'Ma will be made up to hear that. I didn't tell her. I thought I'd leave that to you. Do you want to go up now and I'll bring a tray up in a minute?'

'Is it dry bread and black tea today?' Julia asked with a smile.

'No. You're all right. It's an eating day today,' Carrie smiled in return.

Julia found her mother propped up in bed with her leg supported and the room full of statues and pictures brought from her old home. She seemed quite resigned to the move and told Julia that Carrie and Fred had done all they could to make her comfortable.

Carrie had brought up a tray with tea and cake, and Julia told her mother that Anne had been selected to be a Maid of Honour in the May procession.

'That's grand. It shows she's a good well-behaved girl to be chosen for such an honour.'

'It's a pity you'll miss the procession, Ma,' Julia said. 'But the children will come to see you and tell you all about it.'

'And Joe has a job, I hear. I wish he'd gone for the priesthood,' Grandma sighed. 'Sure he has all the makings of a priest, serving Mass and singing in the choir the way he has all these years.'

'Joe has no vocation for the priesthood, Ma,' Julia said. 'It was just chance about the serving. Maureen had to give up coming to the six o'clock Mass with me in the morning because of her job so Joe came with me because he was an early riser too. Father Cooksey noticed him and put him on the waiting list for the servers, and as for the choir – it was just a couple of them were picked out in school for it.'

'I never reared a lad I could offer to God but I hoped I'd have a grandson a priest,' Mrs Houlihan said. 'Still, if none of them has a vocation it must be the will of God.'

They chatted for a while and when there was a noise downstairs Julia rose to her feet. 'I'll have to be going, Ma,' she said, but the next moment Pat and Fred came into the room.

Pat greeted his mother-in-law and Fred said to Carrie, 'Have you had a good gossip?'

'Yes. Have you?' she said swiftly.

'Men don't gossip,' Fred said. 'We talk.'

'And so do we, don't we, Julia?' Carrie said. Fred laughed heartily and put his hand on her shoulder.

'We've got a right suffragette here, Ma,' he said. 'She'll be chaining herself to the railings next.'

Before Carrie could speak Julia said quickly, 'Goodbye then, Ma. The children will be round to see you. Come on, Pat.' She led the way from the room followed by Pat and Fred, and Carrie fixed her mother's pillows before following them.

'You won't mind the children popping in?' Julia asked her sister when she came downstairs.

'No, of course not. I'll be glad to see them. They'll keep Ma's mind off the pain.'

Later, as Julia and Pat walked home, she said quietly, 'Our Carrie has a heart of gold and so has Fred, but I'm always waiting for an explosion when they're together.'

'Aye, Fred's not very tactful,' Pat agreed. 'But he's a good fellow. And Carrie's very kind too. Your ma seems happy enough with them anyway.'

They walked in silence for a while then Pat said forcefully, 'I think Carrie was right about Brendan. Fred said he'd heard that the boy was hanging round billiard halls, very flush with money and dressed to the nines. Fred collared him and tried to talk sense into him, but he said he was wasting his time. That lad's as slippery as an eel.'

'But how can he be flush with money? Where does he get it from?' said Julia.

'That's what Fred wanted to know but he was no wiser when he'd talked to Brendan. I think that lad's got funny friends.'

'Well, Minnie can't see any of the money because she's still crying poverty,' Julia said.

'I know. I don't begrudge the bit we give her, Julia, but it makes me mad that that lad's throwing money around and leaving his mother short when it's such a bad time for us.'

'Are things no better, Pat?'

'No sign of them getting better, girl,' he said heavily. 'There's just no money about at all. I'm just hanging on be the skin of me teeth.'

'But you're hanging on, that's the main thing,' she comforted him. 'God's good. Something will turn up.'

'When I think of the order book I had,' he groaned. 'Now the lads are nearly at the end of a job before I get another one on the book, and then I've nearly got to cut someone's throat to get it.'

'But you always manage another order,' Julia said. 'Times are bad for everyone but we're keeping our heads above water and the children are happy, thank God.'

'It's a good thing we've got three of them working anyway,' Pat said, and Julia agreed.

'We had the good years when we needed them,' she said. 'When all the children were small.'

Julia and Pat concealed their worries from the family as far as possible, and he managed to keep the business going.

* * *

When Stephen left school in 1929 it was almost impossible to find a job, but he had a stroke of luck. One of the teachers at his school heard of a place in a small factory and recommended him for it. He would be a general 'dogsbody' for the first two years but if he worked hard and proved suitable would be apprenticed at sixteen. He seized the chance eagerly.

Joe was still working in the men's outfitters, but wondering how much longer he could stand the job. He hated having to accept the rudeness and arrogance of some of the customers and the bullying of the manager.

Uriah Heep, Joe thought scornfully as he watched the manager fawning on customers, bending low and rubbing his hands together, but dared not let his feelings show. 'The customer is always right,' the manager told him and Joe had to agree or lose his job. He knew there were no others to be had.

He was friendly with a boy who had been at school with him who now went to sea as a cabin boy. All Ben's family were seafarers and Joe enjoyed listening to their tales and often repeated them at home. Ben was home from a trip in the summer of 1929 and Joe spent most of his spare time in his friend's company.

All the family knew how unhappy Joe was in his job, and no one was surprised when he asked his father if he could leave it and go to sea. Pat agreed, but warned Joe that he might find the life very hard.

'I don't care, Dad,' he said. 'I don't care how hard I have to work. Anything's better than creeping round in that shop.'

Julia was tearful but Pat told her it was better for Joe. 'He hates that shop, Julie, you know that, and this is a good chance for him.'

'I know,' she wept. 'I've expected this ever since he got so friendly with Ben. The sea's in that family's blood though and our Joe mightn't like it. I don't want him to go away from home, Pat.'

'He doesn't want to leave home, girl, but there's nothing for him here. Perhaps in a little while things will pick up and he'll find something in Liverpool. Don't let him see you crying.'

The family tried to hide their distress when Joe left but Anne wept bitterly when he had gone. It was hard for her to understand that he was going because there was no work to be had in Liverpool.

The years of her childhood were desperate ones for the country and there was great hardship in Liverpool, but immersed in her own small concerns Anne was unaware of this and perfectly happy.

Since babyhood she had seen groups of ragged out-of-work young men on street corners, passing a solitary cigarette from hand to hand or filling their empty hopeless days by playing marbles on waste ground. She was used to seeing gaunt shabby women and hungry barefoot children and was unaware that their number had increased, and destitution and misery stalked her native city.

In the school the classes were divided into A, B, and C streams, and the poorer and the more ill-nourished children were mainly in the C class. Anne in the A class was surrounded by girls who were reasonably well fed and poorly but neatly dressed.

As Anne moved up the school she still shared a desk with Kathleen O'Neill who remained an enigma. Anne's attempts to become friendly with her still received the same reply: 'Mammy says I mustn't speak to people. I must keep myself to myself.' Kathleen worked hard and received good marks, but she never put up her hand to answer a question that was put to the class, although if directly asked she could always answer correctly.

Cormac O'Neill was now in the Senior Boys and a different playground, but Kathleen still made no attempt to play with other girls. She stood alone watching them. Occasionally a teacher on playground duty would notice her and make her join a group, but she always left it as soon as possible.

Eileen was scornful when Anne spoke about Kathleen. 'It's a pity about her and her old mammy and sissy brother,' she said. 'Nine years old, and her brother's older, but *Mammy* still brings them to school and meets them at dinnertime. Then brings them back and meets them again at four o'clock. They're pathetic.' Anne was sure that Eileen was right but she still felt sorry for her strange deskmate.

Anne was still happy at school although on one occasion she staged a small rebellion. She was in the Junior Girls by that time and the class had been told that they must forfeit their swimming lesson because some of the girls had been fighting in the school playground.

The rest of the class meekly accepted the punishment but Anne stood up and protested. 'That's not fair,' she said. 'The rest of us weren't fighting so why should we have to give up our swimming?'

The class, less malleable now than when they were infants, showed signs of supporting Anne and the teacher acted swiftly. 'Anne Fitzgerald, how dare you speak to your teacher like that?' She snatched up the strap which lay on her desk. 'Come out here and hold out your hands.' She struck twice on each hand with the heavy strap, and Anne went back to her desk struggling to keep the tears in her eyes from falling.

No one else spoke and the lesson was resumed but Anne was surprised to feel a nudge from Kathleen O'Neill. She blinked away her tears and looked at Kathleen, then realised that her deskmate was holding out a piece of chocolate under cover of the desk.

Anne smiled at her and as soon as she thought they were unobserved, whispered her thanks.

'You were right,' Kathleen whispered, 'and she knows it.' The teacher looked over at them and there was no opportunity to say more. At four o'clock Anne was called to the teacher's desk and given a note to take home, and when she came out of school Kathleen was walking away with her mother.

Anne was more worried about the note for her parents than the pain in her hands, and gave it to her mother timidly without saying anything about the incident. Her mother read the note and put it on the mantelpiece.

'If you're impudent to your teacher, Anne, you must expect to be punished,' she said.

Anne's father said the same and told her that she must tell her teacher she was sorry. 'You're the first one in the family to bring a note like that home,' he said sternly.

Anne hung her head and wept. She had always been so loved and petted by her father that she was disproportionately upset by his disapproval.

Uncle Fred called later when Pat had gone to see one of his workmen, and he took a different view. 'A storm in a teacup,' he said breezily. 'We're forever getting notes like this about the twins.'

He crouched down before Anne. 'What a sad little face,' he said. He took a penny from his pocket. 'Here, love, buy some sweeties.' When Julia protested he said, 'Nonsense, Julia. It's a crime to upset a child like that and all over nothing.'

Anne's brothers and sisters agreed with Fred. Maureen was horrified when she saw Anne's hands and spread ointment on them and wrapped them in pieces of old sheeting.

Tony was furious. 'Why do parents always think the teacher's right?' he said angrily. 'That damn' woman knew she'd gone too far, that's why she sent that note – to cover herself in case Mum complained. The bitch!'

They asked Anne what had actually happened and Tony told her that she had been quite right to protest. 'It wasn't fair to punish the whole class like that, and I'm glad you had the courage to say so,' he said, but Maureen looked at him warningly.

'But you mustn't stand up and say so in front of the whole class, love,' she said. 'Just say it to her quietly at her desk, then she can't say you're being cheeky.'

Tony was about to protest but he looked at Maureen and smiled, acknowledging her calm good sense.

Anne was given a note by her mother to take to the teacher the following day, and Miss Derby read it and smiled at her. 'Very well, we'll say no more about it,' she said graciously. 'It was quite out of character for you, Anne.'

She went quietly to her desk, thinking cynically that Tony was right. The teacher had looked relieved.

The incident seemed to bring Kathleen out of her shell a little and now she sometimes walked about with Anne in the playground. She still refused to join in any of the boisterous games played by the other girls, saying that her mother would be vexed if her clothes got dirty. Anne suspected she was afraid to show any sign that she played with others, disobeying her mother's orders, but said nothing to Kathleen.

Girls who lived near her had told Anne that she never played out after school and neither did her brother. They went out with their mother but the three O'Neills were never seen apart.

Gradually Kathleen became more and more friendly with Anne during school hours and listened wistfully when her friend talked about her family. She told Anne that her mother had told her that she and Cormac had Royal blood and were descended from the Kings of Ireland.

She knew a great deal about Irish history and told Anne that her mother read aloud stories about Queen Maeve and Deidre of the Sorrows and of the great Hugh O'Neill, Earl of Tyrone. 'He was a brave man but he was defeated at the Battle of Kinsale and driven from Ireland,' Kathleen said. 'That's why we live in England now.'

Anne thought it was all very romantic, and felt rather ashamed of her own humdrum family, but Kathleen told her that the Fitzgeralds were also noble Irish. 'Norman Irish,' she corrected herself. 'They were very powerful, and at the beginning of the sixteenth century they were known as the House of Kildare.' Anne was very pleased to hear it.

Although so friendly during school hours, Kathleen was still met at the gates by her mother and never dared to show any sign of friendship with Anne before her.

Anne told Maureen about Kathleen, and her sister advised her to be friendly with Kathleen but not to speak to her while her mother was there. 'You might get her into trouble,' she said.

'Why, what's wrong with me?' Anne asked indignantly, but Maureen said that Mrs O'Neill had strange ideas.

'I know,' Anne said. 'She says they have Royal blood and are descended from the Kings of Ireland, but it doesn't mean they can't make friends, does it?'

'It does as far as Mrs O'Neill is concerned,' Maureen said. 'One of her neighbours comes in the wool shop and she says Mrs O'Neill won't let the children mix at all. She calls them her King and her Queen, and they only go out when they go out with her. Mind you, she's a good mother. She works her fingers to the bone so that they go short of nothing, Mrs Williams said.'

Miss Derby had noticed the friendship developing between Anne and Kathleen too. 'I'm very pleased that you have become friendly with Kathleen O'Neill, Anne,' she said graciously.

Anne looked down at the ground and said nothing and the teacher walked away. Anne still had not forgiven her for sending the note to her parents, and Tony kept her resentment alive by asking: 'How's the bitch, Anne?'

'Still bitching,' she said one day, feeling very daring. Tony laughed but warned her not to let their parents hear her using the expression, and it became a small private joke between them.

When Anne was a young child she loved all her family

indiscriminately, but as she grew older she began to see them as individuals. She realised that she and Joe and Maureen not only resembled their mother in appearance but were like her in character. Tony, Stephen, Eileen and Terry were like their father, tall and well-built, with brown eyes and thick curly dark hair.

At first she thought they were all extroverts like their father too, but gradually Anne realised that though Tony was big and boisterous and made friends easily, there were times when he was quiet and withdrawn.

Tony's glooms, the family called them, but no one was aware of the reason for these moods of melancholy and silence which seemed to descend on him. He would watch his mother anxiously, especially when she talked in a low voice to Joe, and try to cheer her if she seemed sad.

Life had never been the same for Julia since Patrick's death. Often she seemed to retreat into a world of her own. Then Tony would bring her a small treat like some sweets, or would put out a stool for her feet. Although Julia always rewarded him with a vague smile it was clear that her thoughts were far away, and she was not really aware of Tony. No one connected these times with his dark moods. He had once heard his Aunt Minnie say: 'Patrick's death destroyed Julia. You'd have thought the baby would have consoled her, Tony was only six months at the time, but she just wasn't interested in him. Of course he was just like his father over again. It was only when Joe was born, the image of Patrick, that she got over his death, and Joe's her favourite still.'

Tony had never forgotten these words. He was usually happy and cheerful, but these thoughts were like a dark current beneath the surface. He felt that he had never been loved as much as the rest of the family, especially as like many eldest sons he often clashed with his father.

He loved Joe and would have indignantly denied that he was jealous of him, but even his private little jokes with Anne had only happened since her beloved Joe had gone away.

There was nothing complex about Stephen or Terry. They were typical boys, mad on football and both given to sudden enthusiasms for fishing or swimming or other sports. Both preferred the company of other boys and regarded girls, and sisters particularly, as a nuisance although they were always kind to Anne.

She was fond of Eileen but at this stage in their lives they had little in common. Eileen was a big, boisterous girl, good at any kind of sport, but did not share Anne's love of books as Maureen and Joe did.

The difference in their ages and interests caused divisions between the Fitzgerald family which would close as they grew older, but there was still a strong bond of love between them. For Pat and Julia their children were a comfort and consolation in the troubles which now beset them.

Chapter Five

After the Wall Street Crash in America there was even more hardship and distress in Liverpool and many firms were forced to close down. Pat Fitzgerald managed to keep his building firm going, mostly with repairs and small jobs which he would not have taken in better times.

When it was clear to him that the business was not simply going through a bad patch but that he was fighting for survival, he called the men together and told them.

'You know we're just hand to mouth with the jobs now, lads,' he said. 'We've got the repairs to the houses in Beelow Street, and after that, God knows. I tried hard for that funeral parlour job and for *anything* with the Corporation but no luck so far. We couldn't have gone this far if we weren't all pulling together, you lads taking a cut in wages and me taking next to nothing. I'll try and keep you all on, lads, because you've stuck by me, but if you get a chance somewhere else – well, I've told you how things are. I wouldn't stand in your way, but I'd be glad to see you back if things pick up.'

He stepped down, mopping his forehead, visibly upset. Billy Joyce the foreman looked round the men then stepped forward.

'I reckon we'll all sink or swim together, boss,' he said. 'We're all keeping our eyes open, and some fella on the wireless said things are going to get better.'

'I hope he's right,' said Pat. 'Thanks, lads.' He wiped his handkerchief over his face again, and turned away.

It was true that Pat was taking as little as possible from the firm, and while he worried about the business Julia's worries were the day to day ones of keeping her family clothed and fed on little money. Fortunately no one seemed to notice the economies. If bread and jam replaced more ample meals it was still sufficient for their hearty appetites and they knew that jam butties were the staple diet of many of their friends.

Maureen could make a small contribution from her wages, and Tony and Stephen earned their own pocket money so Julia felt that they were more fortunate than most families.

Even though she and Pat sometimes spent sleepless nights, worrying about the business and the future, they managed to conceal their worries from the family.

In addition to their cut in wages Pat's workmen had agreed to take only one day off instead of two, and he decided to forgo his usual three days altogether.

Fred Anderson's business was not affected by the slump. His most profitable work was for the luxury trade and although there was so much distress in Liverpool there was wealth too. The 'carriage trade' still shopped in Bold Street and rich women could be seen followed by chauffeurs or ladies' maids with their arms full of parcels, or else sitting regally in their cars while obsequious shopkeepers took their orders.

The leather desk fittings made by Fred had suddenly become very fashionable and he had difficulty in keeping up with the demand.

Grandma Houlihan was still living with Carrie and Fred. Her broken leg had healed but she walked with a limp and needed a stick. She spent much of her time in her own room, and the Fitzgerald children were often sent to visit her. A visitor from the church had left her a small book entitled *The Lives of the Saints*, and Anne was sent to read aloud from it to her grandma.

'Why can't she read it herself?' she said rebelliously one night when she had to go to the Andersons' and wanted to visit the cinema instead.

'Because Grandma can barely write her own name and she can't read,' her mother said. 'Not everyone has had your advantages, remember. Grandma was brought up on a farm in Ireland where it was just work from the time they got up until they went to bed. No time for schooling or any pleasure.'

Anne went more willingly to read to her grandma after hearing that. Imagine not being able to read! It was true that there were not many books in her own home but all the family were able to read. Since Joe had gone away there was no one who shared her own deep love of books.

Maureen read mostly romantic novels, and her mother read magazines from the church such as *The Messenger of the Sacred Heart* or *The Far East*. Her father and the rest of the family read magazines and newspapers but rarely a book. Anne had never thought of this before and suddenly realised how much she took for granted.

When she was ten she brought home the application forms which her parents had to sign before she could enter for a scholarship, which would enable her to attend a Grammar School.

'Do you want to go in for this?' her father asked doubtfully. 'You're happy enough where you are, aren't you, queen?' Anne nodded. She was not sure whether she wanted to enter for the scholarship or not. Sister Assumpta had sent for her and told her that she had a good chance of passing the examination, and it would open up a whole new world for her, but as her father said, she was perfectly happy at her present school. On the other hand, she was tempted by the prospect of spending more time on the subjects she enjoyed, and of wearing the Grammar School uniform.

Her parents discussed it further when she had gone to bed. Forms were only sent to the parents when the teachers considered that a pupil had some chance of passing the examination, and only Joe had previously brought them home.

'The same thing applies to Anne as it did to Joe,' Pat said. 'We don't want her mixing with different people instead of being where her brothers and sisters are there to look after her.'

'It wasn't so much that Joe couldn't look after himself,' Julia said. 'It was more that we didn't want him drawn away from the family, and that we didn't want to do for one what we hadn't done for the others.'

Pat agreed but said, 'That's another thing. All the others have done well at the parish school and been satisfied there. I don't want to make flesh of one and fowl of another. I like to keep them all equal.'

'I've sometimes thought though, Pat,' said Julia, 'if Joe had gone to College, he might have got a decent job and not had to go away.' But Pat disagreed.

'There's plenty of College lads walking the streets looking for jobs. I think we'll leave her where she is. It's a waste of time for a girl anyway. She'll only go off and get married.'

'And Eileen's got that nice little job without any scholarship or anything,' Julia said. The forms were returned with a polite refusal, and Anne heard no more of the matter.

Eileen's 'nice little job' was in the office of the engineering firm where Tony worked. He had heard of the vacancy and she had immediately applied and been successful.

Julia thanked God daily that all her children were working when she saw the queues of young people wherever a job was advertised and the dispirited crowds at the Labour Exchanges.

There were plenty of books in the Misses Dolan's house next-door and Anne was often allowed to borrow them. The old ladies thought that she should have tried for the scholarship.

'Education is never wasted, dear,' Miss Louisa said. 'I know it is only an extra two years, but you would have received a smattering of knowledge of various subjects, enough to have encouraged you to seek further knowledge.'

'Dad thinks it's not important for a girl,' Anne said. Miss Louisa's face grew red and Miss Ellen said quickly, 'Louisa thinks that girls have as much right to an education as men. She was much cleverer than our brothers, but our dear father sent them away to public school and kept us at home.'

'That was all a long time ago, Ellen,' Miss Louisa said repressively. 'You must foster your love of books, Anne. A world of knowledge can be found between the covers of a book. Why don't you join the Public Lending Library? You're very welcome to borrow any of our books, but you will find many more there.'

Anne found that a girl in her class belonged to the Kensington Library and she went with her on Saturday morning to join. It looked very imposing to Anne with the lamps at either side and the wide flight of steps leading to the door. Inscribed in the stone above the door were the words: 'Reading maketh a full man.' She stood gazing at them for so long that Sadie pulled her arm impatiently. 'Come on,' she said. 'It'll be closed before we ever go in.'

Anne spent the rest of the day curled up on a chair in the parlour weeping or smiling as she read *Little Women* and *Anne of Green Gables*. Her mother exclaimed at her red eyes when she called her to eat her meals and do the messages and other jobs, which Anne did in a daze.

'It was the Dolans who told her to join the Library,' Julia told Pat. 'I was talking to Ellen this morning. They think she should have gone in for the scholarship. Perhaps we should have let her, Pat.'

'What do they know about it, a pair of old maids?' he said scornfully. 'No, we did the right thing, girl. A feller was telling me there's a lot of expense with it even if they get the scholarship, and this isn't the time for anything like that, the way things are.'

'I suppose so,' Julia said. 'Miss Ellen was really chatty this morning. She was on her own because her sister's twisted her ankle. She said her sister thinks that it's wrong that only rich people can send their sons to University. She says poor boys should be able to go there if they're clever enough.'

'Easy said,' Pat said. 'Where's the money to come from? I suppose she never thought of that. Women!'

'It's a funny thing,' Julia mused. 'I know they've come down in the world and they haven't got two ha'pennies to knock together but no one ever calls them anything but Miss Dolan or Miss Ellen and Miss Louisa. You've got to respect them.'

'Aye, it's not like them to meddle,' Pat said. But Anne was very glad that they had.

The new world which Sister Assumpta had spoken about now lay for her on the shelves of Kensington Library and she was a frequent visitor there. She also went more frequently to visit the Misses Dolan and talk about books with them. Louisa taught her to write in the copperplate handwriting that she had been taught, and Anne began to get comments like 'Handwriting excellent' on her essays. But no one asked her why it had improved so much.

She still went to read to her grandmother and tried to introduce different books, but Grandma Houlihan never tired of *The Lives of the Saints*.

She was still in excellent health despite her spartan lifestyle, but Grandma Fitzgerald was now unable to rise from her bed. She was as cheerful as ever, and was devotedly nursed by Bridie. Many of their neighbours were pleased to be able to repay past acts of kindness by Bridie and her mother by helping them now.

All the Fitzgerald family frequently and willingly visited Grandma Fitzgerald and Bridie, and Pat and Julia and their children did all they could to make life easier for them.

There was great sorrow for all who knew her when Grandma Fitzgerald died peacefully in the spring of 1931. Bridie, who had been so tireless, always ready day or night to minister to her mother, suddenly collapsed. She lay in her bed sleeping, waking only to weep bitterly then sleep again.

'Nature taking over,' the doctor told Pat. 'She's managed to keep going while her mother needed her, but it's taken its toll. She'll be all right. She's a brave woman.'

Pat made all the funeral arrangements and on the day Bridie welcomed the mourners with great dignity. The previous day Julia had gently persuaded her to get up and dress, and had gone with her to choose mourning clothes. 'Ma always said mourning clothes didn't matter,' Bridie told Julia. 'But I'll feel better in black.'

'It shows respect,' she agreed, and Bridie said quietly, 'It's the way I feel. Black's right for me.' Julia pressed her arm in silent sympathy.

After the funeral was over, Pat and Julia spoke to Bridie about her future. 'We don't want to rush you, girl,' Pat said gently. 'We just want you to know there's a home with us if you want it.'

'And you know you'll be as welcome as the flowers in May,' Julia interrupted.

'If you'd rather stay on here, Bridie, we'll see that you're all right for money. Just do what *you* want to do,' said Pat.

'Perhaps you'd like one of the girls to stay with you, Bridie?' Julia offered.

Bridie sat pleating her dress between her fingers. 'I don't want to leave here,' she said finally. She began to weep. 'I feel close to Ma here.'

Julia put an arm round her. 'Don't decide anything in a hurry, love,' she said. 'No one should decide anything right after a bereavement. You can't think straight. Me and Pat just wanted you to know that whatever you want to do is all right with us, and we'd all be glad to have you if you decide to come to us.'

'And don't worry about the rent if you want to stay here,' Pat said.

'I was glad that Joe was at home for the funeral,' Bridie said, it seemed at random, but she rose and went to the dresser and came back holding a five-pound note.

'I found this under the runner on the dresser after he'd been in to see me,' she said. 'I don't want to take it, Pat. It must be best part of his pay-off.'

'He got a good pay-off,' Julia said. 'It was a long trip this time, thirteen months. You keep it, Bridie.'

'But with your business – you could do with it yourselves,' she said.

'No, Joe saw us all right. You keep it,' Julia repeated.

'Joe has plenty in his pocket,' Pat said. 'He doesn't drink his pay. Can't. The smell of a barman's apron and he's legless.'

They all laughed and Bridie said more cheerfully, 'Speaking of drink – I've never asked you if you had a mouth on you.' And Pat poured beer for himself and port wine for Bridie and Julia.

Before they went Julia asked again if Bridie would like one of the girls to stay with her, but when she refused Julia did not press her. She realised her sister-in-law wanted to be alone with her memories of her happy years with her mother.

It was a consolation to all the family that Joe was home at this sad time. They could see little change in him. He was taller and more muscular, as quiet as ever, yet with the same ready laugh and dry comment, and as fond as ever of his family and home.

He looked for a shore job but it was impossible to find one in the short time before he had to go back.

'Do you hate the life then, lad?' Pat asked, but Joe said cheerfully, 'No, I don't, Dad, not really. I get fed up at times but I'm with a good crowd of mates and there are times I wouldn't be anywhere else. I miss the family though.' He looked round with a grin. 'I don't know why I do, but there it is.'

Tony pretended to aim a punch at him and Julia said quietly, 'And we miss *you*, son. I'm storming Heaven, Joe, for a shore job for you.'

'Thanks, Mum,' he said, giving her a quick hug.

'I'll pray for it too, Joe,' Anne said. 'And when I have to read to Grandma Houlihan, I'll offer it up as a penance for you to get a job.'

Joe thanked her gravely and the rest of the family hid their smiles.

'What a thing to say about your grandma,' Julia said in a shocked voice. 'You should be glad you can do something for her.' But Anne was unabashed.

All too soon Joe had to go back to sea, but for a shorter trip this time, and his family promised to keep looking for a job for him while he was away.

Chapter Six

Bridie quickly recovered from her collapse after her mother's death, and through a neighbour found a job in a greengrocer's shop on the corner of the street. The wages were small, but the company of the customers was as helpful to Bridie as the money.

Her mother's small pension had died with her, and Pat tried to insist that Bridie allow him to pay her rent but she told him she could manage.

'You know, Ma's insurance policies paid for the funeral and a bit over so I'm all right. I've got a good stock of coal and plenty in the cupboard, so my wages will be more than enough for me. Thanks all the same, lad.'

'I wanted to pay for the funeral,' Pat said.

'I know you did, Pat, but Ma paid the coppers all those years so she wouldn't be an expense to anyone when she went. You know how independent she was, never wanting to be a trouble, but she was grateful for all you did for her and so was I, Pat. You've been a good son and a good brother.'

They both had tears in their eyes and he gave her a quick hug. 'And you were a good daughter, Bride, none better,' he said gruffly. 'I only hope my girls turn out like you.'

'Don't let them hear you,' Bridie said with a watery laugh. 'No, I was glad of your help, Pat, while I had to stay home with Ma, but you've got your own troubles now. It's time I stood on my own two feet anyhow.' She looked down at them and added with a rueful smile, 'God knows, they're big enough.'

As Pat walked home he passed Brendan with another flashily dressed young man and stopped to speak to him. But his nephew said 'Good evening' and walked on quickly, leaving Pat staring after him.

'You should have seen the cut of him,' he told Julia later. 'His hair greased down like patent leather, and the suit! A double-breasted waistcoat with *lapels*, and the coat looked as though the hanger was left in. That feller's up to no good, Julia. Does Minnie ever say anything to you about him?'

'Don't talk to me about Minnie,' Julia said angrily. 'You should have heard her carrying on at Ma's today. She came here yesterday, it seems, and I was out and I'd locked the back door.'

'You don't often do that,' he said.

'I know I don't but they were talking in the shop about the hatchet man. I didn't want to come back and find him under the bed or something.'

Pat roared with laughter but Julia was not amused. 'It's all very well for you to laugh,' she said. 'I've had a terrible day with Minnie going on: "Walking through the teems of rain to your house and finding it locked and barred against me, and me soaked through. Not welcome in my own sister's house." Carrie said it was only a drizzle so how did she get soaked through? And that set her off even more. Then Ma took Minnie's part just to be awkward.'

'Poor Carrie's got her own share there,' Pat commented and Julia agreed. 'I don't know how she puts up with it,' she said. 'But she keeps her sense of humour. Minnie was saying that all the girls are after Brendan and Carrie said to me at the door, "They must all have white sticks".'

'I don't care if our Minnie does take the huff,' said Julia. 'I'm not risking any of us getting murdered just for her.'

She warned her sister that the back door would be locked if

she was out, and the reason, and was surprised when Minnie agreed with her.

'I can see now why your door was locked against me,' she said. 'I've told Dympna to be careful when she's out late. A young girl wouldn't stand a chance against a maniac like the hatchet man.'

They were in Carrie's house at the time, and Julia and she looked at each other expressively.

'She could always fall on him and crush him to death,' Carrie whispered when she went to the door with Julia, and Julia walked away smiling.

Julia was in a happier frame of mind now and so was Pat because he had managed to secure a good order, in spite of the fact that the country was in dire straits. He had secured a contract to build two pairs of semi-detached houses on the site of an old house in West Derby. One day he and the men were all in the yard sorting out supplies for the new job.

Suddenly the gate was thrust open and a man who had been on an errand burst in. 'I've just seen something terrible,' he gasped. 'Remember Jimmy Getty did casual work for us, boss? A roofer.'

'Jimmy Getty? A thin fair lad?' Pat said.

'He was thin all right,' the man said. 'Half-starved he was, and so was his missus and kids. He didn't have no stamps for dole and they were on the parish. They just told him it was cut by two shillings and he come home and hung himself.'

'Oh, God, no!' Pat exclaimed, and there were horrified exclamations from the other men.

'His missus found him. She run out and got the bobby on the beat and he cut him down. Terrible it was. His missus was screaming then she just crumpled up like. I'd run in when I heard the screams but there wasn't nothing I could do. The bobby was shook up too. He said Jimmy made a mess of the hanging. He must of taken half an hour to die.'

'It's a wonder he told you that, Eddie,' another man said.

'Well, like I said, he was shook up too. When Jimmy's missus come round the bobby said he went quick. Poor Jimmy. The two shillings must've been the last straw like.'

'It's a crying shame,' Billy Joyce said. 'He was a good worker too and a nice quiet lad, lived for his family.'

'He wasn't thinking of them when he done that,' a younger man said.

'What do you know about it?' Billy Joyce said angrily. 'His mind must've give way, just cracked like. He couldn't have done that if it hadn't been for listening to his kids crying with hunger and his missus wore away to a shadow, and not being able to do anything about it.'

'Maybe he thought they'd do better without him, get more help like?' the older man said.

'A terrible death, the copper said. He'd have been better putting his head in the gas oven, but I suppose he didn't have no pennies for the gas.'

'I wouldn't let them beat me,' the younger man said suddenly. 'I'd steal before I'd let my family starve. Kill even.'

'That's wild talk, Jed,' the older man said reprovingly.

'I mean it,' he said. 'I'd kill before I'd let my family starve. What could they do? Only top me. And old Pierrepoint might make a better job of it than Jimmy done. Blimey, not even a penny for the meter to die decent.'

Pat had paid no attention to the excited talk, standing as though struck dumb. Billy Joyce touched his arm.

'All right, boss?'

'Oh, God, if only I'd known,' he said with anguish. 'He'd been to me for work, but there was nothing. If I'd known.'

'There wasn't nothing you could do,' Billy said. 'All the casual fellers are desperate, scratting and scraping to live. It took you all your time to keep your regular fellows going.'

'But two shillings, Billy. I could have found him two shillings' worth of work,' Pat said, shaking his head.

The man who had brought the news was still talking excitedly but the other men were in a subdued mood as they finished their work and left.

Pat said nothing to Julia until the younger children were in bed, although she had glanced at him several times with a worried frown.

'What's the matter, Pat? What's happened?' she asked as soon as the children had gone upstairs.

When he told her, Julia exclaimed in horror, and crossed herself. 'Lord have mercy on him, the poor lad. Was he married?'

'Aye, and some little kids too. That's what made him crack up, the lads reckon. Seeing them very near starving with the bit they got from the parish and then he was told it was cut be two shillings.'

'God forgive them,' she exclaimed.

'But two shillings, Julie, and he hanged himself. I could have found him work for two shillings.'

'But you didn't know, Pat. Don't blame yourself. There's plenty of others with more reason to feel guilty – them on the Board of Guardians and higher up still in London. You've done the best you can for your workmen.'

'That's what Billy Joyce said. He said there's plenty more like Jimmy. Young Jed said he wouldn't put up with it. Said he'd steal or kill even before he'd let his family starve.'

Tony had been sitting on the sofa reading and he looked up. 'Jed's right,' he said forcefully. '*I* wouldn't let people walk on me and starve my family. I'd fight back. I wouldn't lie down under it.'

'That's daft talk,' Pat said. 'What could you do? Do you think Jimmy hadn't tried everything? You young fellas know nothing.'

'I know I wouldn't stand for it,' Tony said. 'That's what they

71

count on, people being afraid to stand up to them. I wouldn't care if I *did* break the law.'

'Are you making out the lad was a weakling?' Pat snapped. 'There was nothing weak about Jimmy, but he wouldn't break the law. He was a decent lad.'

'And look where it got him,' Tony said. 'Anyway the law is only made by men to protect their own interests. Do you think it's God's law to drive a man to suicide?'

'Tony, Tony,' Julia said. She rose to stand before him and lay her hand on his shoulder. 'Don't argue with your dad now, son. He's upset.'

Tony looked up and seemed about to say something but his mother's expression made him change his mind. He closed the magazine and went upstairs.

Julia turned back to Pat who was sitting slumped in his chair, with his head in his hands. 'I feel as though I've been kicked in the stomach, Julie,' he said. 'A lad I know – a lad I've talked to. Not much older than me own.'

'Well, his troubles are over now, poor lad,' she said, but she too put her hands over her face and wept.

The following day Billy Joyce told Pat that the men had had a whip round for the widow. 'It's only a couple of shillings, that's all the lads have got, but it might help her.'

Pat had just been paid for a small repair job and he handed the money to Billy, with another two shillings from his own pocket. 'I suppose it's the easy way out, to make us feel better, isn't it, Billy?'

'The way I look at it, it's the best we can do. And poor Jimmy didn't die for nothing if she gets some help.'

It was some time before Pat could stop thinking of Jimmy and blaming himself for not finding work for him, but commonsense told him that there had been no work to give.

The men were all very quiet and subdued for a while after the tragedy, but gradually their good spirits returned, helped by the fact that Pat had secured another good order for repairing and extending a mansion which had been empty for some time. It was to become a private school.

It took longer for Julia to recover from the tragedy. She said nothing about Jimmy's death to the younger children, but her temper was unusually short for some weeks. Unfortunately Anne chose this time to refuse her dinner. She had been picking at the food and finally pushed her plate away. 'I don't want my dinner,' she said. 'I don't like cabbage anyway.'

She was taken aback when her mother jumped to her feet and leaned over her menacingly. 'Eat it,' she hissed. 'Don't you dare to waste good food while there are children in this city crying with hunger. And their poor parents driven desperate because they've nothing to give them, God help them.'

Anne hurriedly picked up her fork again, shocked and frightened to see that her mother's eyes were full of tears. The Fitzgerald children had always been taught that food must not be wasted, and their plates must be cleared, but her mother's rage on this occasion frightened and impressed Anne.

It was many years before she knew the reason for it.

Chapter Seven

Anne soon recovered from her fright at her mother's strange behaviour and was her usual cheerful self again. She looked forward to the autumn and winter. Aunt Carrie had said that as Anne and Terry were the only Fitzgeralds of school age, she would have a Duck Apple Night party in her house where they could join the twins and Carmel in bobbing for apples and making toffee apples.

The idea had grown and now it was to be a Hallowe'en party with all the older members of the family included. It was a party that was long remembered. Theresa had hollowed out turnips and put candles inside them and Aunt Carrie supplied a feast of spareribs and pasties and gingerbread.

The children bobbed for apples with much advice and screams of laughter from their elders, then the mess was cleared away and the party games began. They tended to involve kissing and scuffling behind doors but most of the guests were of the age to enjoy them.

Finally everyone sat round in the shadowy candlelit kitchen and told ghost stories. Anne enjoyed the ghost stories while she was in Aunt Carrie's kitchen surrounded by people, but was terrified later when she had to go to bed alone.

Fortunately she was soon joined by Eileen, and could clutch her when she came to bed. With her sister Eileen beside her Anne felt safe. No intruder, earthly or ghostly, would be a match for Eileen, Anne felt.

Fred had always refused to allow fireworks in his house or to allow his children to attend bonfire night parties. 'I seen a lad lose his life with a rocket,' he once told them. 'The bottle fell over and the rocket went straight into his eye and killed him. I swore I'd never let my children take any chances like that.'

Instead of buying fireworks he always gave half a crown each to his own children and to the Fitzgeralds, and this money had been invaluable to them for buying Christmas presents.

Anne had gone for several years with Eileen to do the shopping for presents, and they had spent happy hours carefully choosing something suitable for each member of the family. Fred's half crown was supplemented by saving their Saturday penny for a few weeks and adding coppers earned by running messages for the neighbours.

Eileen lit fires for a Jewish family on Saturdays and when she started work the job passed to Anne. The threepence a week was added to her savings. She was fascinated by the Goldsteins who lived above their business premises, and by their luxuriously furnished home. Mrs Goldstein was very kind to her and explained the origin of the orthodox customs and told her about the Jewish faith.

Anne listened entranced and Mrs Goldstein smiled and patted her head one day. 'You listen with the eyes and the ears,' she said. Anne often called to see the Goldsteins and four-year-old Becca grew very fond of Anne and clung to her, demanding that she should stay with them.

The days never seemed long enough for Anne with all she wanted to do. Two of her classmates lived in Cresswell Street and she often went there to play with them but continued to visit the Misses Dolan frequently.

Miss Ellen was teaching her to do macramé work which Anne

hoped to use to edge a small altar cloth for Grandma Houlihan. Often she went to borrow or return books or to tell Miss Louisa about those she had out from Kensington Library.

'I hope Anne's not being a nuisance,' Mrs Fitzgerald said when she met the Misses Dolan in a local shop.

'No indeed. We are always pleased to see her,' Miss Louisa said.

'She's shy till she gets to know people, but then she doesn't stop to think people might be busy,' Mrs Fitzgerald said. 'She likes going in to see you but if she's going too often . . .'

'No indeed. We are always pleased to see Anne,' Miss Louisa repeated. 'She has charm. There are people who light up a room when they enter it and Anne is one of those people.'

'But she's a sensible girl too,' Miss Ellen said. 'The two things don't always go together.'

'She's never been any trouble,' Julia said. 'And she's always very happy.'

'Let us hope she always will be,' Miss Louisa said graciously.

Anne was eagerly looking forward to Christmas, especially now that she had more money to spend on presents, although this year she would not be able to shop with Eileen.

She arranged to go to town with Carmel and they went immediately to Woolworth's in Church Street where Anne had always done her Christmas shopping. They had usually budgeted three-pence each for presents for their brothers and sisters, and sixpence each for their parents, and had spent happy hours choosing from the array of gifts at those prices.

Shopping with Carmel was not nearly as enjoyable, Anne found. Carmel had grown into a stolid child, never showing much interest in what happened around her, and chose her own gifts with little thought for those who would receive them.

She simply shrugged when Anne asked her opinion about the suitability of any of the goods displayed, and finally, when Anne was trying to decide between a tie and a fountain pen, each priced at sixpence, for her father, Carmel said impatiently, 'It doesn't matter. They always say they like them anyway.'

Anne and Eileen had always finished their Christmas shopping with a visit to the herb shop for a glass of Vantas, but Anne decided not to suggest it to Carmel.

She felt she had had enough of her cousin, and told her mother when she returned home that Carmel was a pudding.

'I don't know why. She was great when she was a baby,' she said.

Her mother agreed. 'You'd never think her and Theresa were sisters,' she said. 'Theresa's like quicksilver.'

Theresa's numerous boyfriends were a byword in the family, and Fred declared that she changed them as often as she washed her face. It was all lighthearted and Theresa made no enemies, even among the discarded boys.

Anne enjoyed collecting her Christmas Club more than the shopping. The Fitzgerald children had always saved pennies and halfpennies in the shop on the corner of the street for their Christmas Clubs. The girls usually chose Squirrel Selection boxes, and the boys 'Pay what you like, have what you like', which meant that they assembled their own selection up to the value of what they had saved.

Eileen's favourite in the Squirrel selection was the section of Cherry Lip Gums, crescents of hard red jelly. Anne preferred the cachous, and hung over the box sniffing rapturously when that section was opened.

'They remind me of the exotic East,' she said to Eileen.

'You say that about the Dolans' house,' her sister scoffed.

'That's only because Miss Louisa smokes Turkish cigarettes,' Anne retorted. 'But this smell stays on my breath.'

She tried to make the cachous last as long as possible, and breathed out hopefully after sucking them, expecting someone to comment on her scented breath.

This year she decided to have 'Pay what you like, have what you like' and spent a happy hour in the shop choosing what she would have. She had saved three and sixpence and felt immensely rich as the Squirrel selections had only cost a shilling. The shopkeeper was remarkably patient, allowing her to change her mind several times, and then assembling her purchases in a cardboard box.

'You've got enough to last you for a while there,' he remarked, but Anne smiled ruefully.

'I don't suppose it will, Mr Hicks,' she said. 'We always say we won't open our Clubs until Christmas Eve, but we can't resist dipping into them.'

'You've got a good selection anyhow,' he said as he put them in the box. 'Sherbet dabs, Tiger Nuts, cinder toffee, pear drops, Spanish laces and licorice pipes, creamy whirls, Fairy Whispers – are you going courting then?' Anne laughed obligingly and the shopkeeper picked up a packet of sweet cigarettes and a packet of sweet tobacco. 'Smoking too. I'll have to keep my eye on you.'

'They're for the little Delamere boys,' Anne explained.

'Oh, aye, your Auntie Bridie's been very good to those poor kids and so was your poor grandma, RIP. No joke growing up without a mother, Anne. I know I had to do it, and my dad wasn't like Jack Delamere. He was more fond of the drink than he was of me.'

'Never mind, you're happy now, Mr Hicks, aren't you?' Anne said, and he smiled at her.

'Can't grumble, girl.'

She took the sweet tobacco and cigarettes to her Aunt Bridie's house. The door from the backyard to the narrow entry which ran behind the house was faced with a similar door to the backyard of a tiny house in the next street. Bridie had become friendly with Maisie Delamere who lived there, and when after years of disappointment Maisie's first child was born, she often brought the baby to visit Bridie and her mother.

Shortly after Maisie's second son was born, she developed the tuberculosis from which she died when the boys were aged two and four respectively. During Maisie's illness Bridie and her mother had often cared for the little boys and had done all they could to help Jack Delamere.

His own family had disapproved of the marriage and stayed away, even after Maisie's death, but her mother decided to move in and take charge. She was a quarrelsome woman and immediately stopped the children from running across the entry and into the Fitzgeralds' house.

Before long she had quarrelled with most of the neighbours, but Jack continued to visit Bridie and her mother and to do jobs around the house for them.

'We're always glad to see you, Jack,' Mrs Fitzgerald said. 'But don't come, lad, if it causes trouble.'

'I don't care about her. Let her try,' Jack always said, but the tiny houses were close together and they often heard raised voices when he went home.

While Jack was at work his mother-in-law often locked the children in a dark cupboard and threatened worse if they told their father, but one day the youngest one was in such distress when Jack came home that he finally learned the truth and had a showdown with his mother-in-law, ending by putting her out.

This was shortly before Mrs Fitzgerald's death and later he came to offer condolences to Bridie.

'Your ma was one in a thousand,' he said. 'I'll never forget how kind she was to us when Maisie was ill.'

'The children brought Ma a lot of pleasure,' Bridie said, weeping.

'I'm just sorry I let that cow stop them from coming,' he said.

'What could you do? You had to have her there and go along

with her. How are you managing now, Jack?'

'The neighbours have been good,' he said. 'And anything's better for them than being at that old cow's mercy. If I'd only known what was going on!'

'Well, I hope you'll let them come and see me when – when everything's over,' Bridie said. 'I suppose they've forgotten me.'

Other people came to offer condolences and Jack left, but after the funeral the children came to see Bridie. There was a bad moment when they looked for her mother but Carrie was there and distracted their attention by giving them sweets, and they never asked again about Mrs Fitzgerald.

They were now aged five and seven and were at school. They stayed with neighbours until Jack returned from work, and often went to see Bridie when she was not in the greengrocer's shop.

Anne had been to see Bridie one Sunday and was surprised and not very pleased to see young Dan and Teddy sitting with her and playing The Road to Berlin. She hid her feelings and Bridie said cheerfully, 'Remember when you used to play this, Anne? Your grandma used to love to watch your face when you won.'

'I think you let me win,' Anne said.

'Only at first. You got very good at it,' Bridie said.

'I won the last one, didn't I, Auntie Bridie?' Teddy said, and she smiled at him.

'You did,' she agreed. 'You're a clever lad.'

Anne listened in disbelief. Auntie Bridie! she thought, and made an excuse to leave as soon as possible.

Tony was alone sitting reading a newspaper when she went home and Anne sat down on a stool beside him. Since Joe had gone away and Maureen was out more often she sometimes confided in Tony. Now she said to him, 'I've just been to Aunt Bridie's. Those Delamere children were there.'

'Teddy and Dan?' Tony said. 'Poor little beggars, they've been through a lot in their short lives, haven't they?'

Anne scarcely listened. 'They were calling her Auntie Bridie and playing The Road to Berlin and they had butties with hundreds and thousands on. I think I was jealous, Tony.'

She expected a few soothing platitudes from him and was amazed when he put down the newspaper and said forcibly, 'Don't, Anne. Nip it in the bud now. Jealousy can poison your life, love.'

'Well, I'm not usually jealous,' she said defensively.

'I am,' he said with a sigh. 'At least, I suppose it must be jealousy. We're the odd ones out, Anne. Me at one end of the family and you at the other.'

She looked at him with such amazement that he flushed and hastily picked up his newspaper. 'Only joking, Anne,' he said. 'Take no notice.'

Later, in bed, she thought about Tony's words. She felt sure they were not intended as a joke. Was she the odd one out as the last of the family? she wondered. And Tony? Perhaps he felt left out because Maureen and their mother were so close, especially now that Joe was away from home.

Eileen and Terry, with only eighteen months between them in age, had always done things together, and Stephen and Terry were united in their love of football and fishing. Anne came back to thinking of her own position. Was she the odd one out?

Maureen had been to the cinema with a girlfriend. Anne heard her return and a little later come upstairs to bed.

'Mo,' she called softly. Eileen was fast asleep when Maureen tiptoed into the bedroom. Anne sat up with her arms round her knees.

'Mo, do you think I'm the odd one out at the end of the family?' she asked.

'Now what put that in your head?' Maureen whispered.

'I was just thinking about the family,' she said, 'and me being the youngest.'

'You're the spoilt baby,' Maureen whispered with a smile. 'Me and Tony are breaking the ground for you younger ones. You'll all get away with murder. Go to sleep now.'

Anne knew what her sister meant. Some years earlier Pat had seen Maureen with her small jar of Tokalon Cream and box of Phul Nana face powder, and had been furious.

'No respectable girl wears that muck on her face,' he had roared. 'Painting your face like a – like a woman of the streets. Give them here. They're going behind the fire.'

Maureen had wept and her mother had intervened in her quiet voice. 'Sure it was only a touch. She's used it for years and you haven't noticed, Pat. All the girls use it now.'

'Not my daughter. Not respectable girls,' her father said, but their mother insisted: 'Respectable girls. You don't think I'd have allowed it otherwise?'

Her father had given in with much grumbling and Maureen had kept the cream and powder and continued to use them discreetly.

A few years later when Eileen produced a jar of cream and a powder compact, he had said nothing about them.

I suppose I'm lucky really, being the youngest, Anne thought, and soon forgot Tony's words. But she bought the sweet cigarettes and tobacco to make her feel better about her jealousy of the Delamere children.

Christmas was a happy time for the Fitzgerald family, marred only by the fact that Joe was away at sea. Trade had improved steadily since the order for the semi-detached houses and in spite of bad times for most small businesses, Pat now had orders for several months ahead.

He unobtrusively helped Jimmy Getty's widow and children, only bitterly regretting that the improvement in his business had not come in time to save the young man.

Even the bad weather was not too much of a problem to him, now that he had paid off his debts and was paying cash for supplies, so he had no worries.

Terry left school at Christmas 1932 and went to work in the grocer's where he had been employed as a Saturday lad. Julia often said that God had been very good to them, with everyone having found work.

There was plenty of fun and laughter especially when all the family were at home in the Fitzgerald house, but Julia's gentle tranquillity made the home calm and peaceful too.

It was different in the Anderson household. Something exciting seemed always to be happening there. The twins were never out of trouble. They climbed lamp-posts, fell off roofs, sat down on newly painted seats, and never seemed to be without bandages.

Anne always liked visiting the Andersons, and enjoyed the high drama and even the frequent rows, but she thought she preferred her own quiet home. It was never dull even though there was not the excitement of the Anderson household.

The Delamere children were often in Bridie's house when the family called to see her, and sometimes Jack was there too. No one was surprised when he came to see Pat and asked if he had any objection to a marriage between Bridie and himself.

'I'd take good care of her, Mr Fitz,' he said. 'She's a heart of gold and I value her. My little lads love her and they'd be made up too.'

'I've no objection,' Pat said. 'As long as it's what Bridie wants. She deserves to be happy.'

'I'll see that she is, Mr Fitz,' Jack said earnestly, and Pat told him to drop the Mr Fitz. 'It'll have to be Pat and Jack if we're family.'

Julia was delighted. 'The best thing that could happen,' she declared. 'It's just what Bridie needs – someone to look after. And Jack and the lads have had such a miserable time with that mother-in-law they'll appreciate Bridie all the more.'

They went to see Bridie and found her very happy and full of plans. 'I know Dan and Teddy will be glad,' she said. 'Remember last October when Jack went on that chara from his work to see the Blackpool lights? The little lads stayed with me then. I slept in Ma's bed and they had my bed in the back room, and the next morning they looked over at their own house and said they wished they could stay here.'

Julia and Pat glanced at each other and she said gently, 'There's not just the children to think about though, is there?'

Bridie blushed. 'I'm very fond of Jack,' she said. 'And he's not just marrying me for the sake of the boys.'

'We know that, Bridie,' Julia said hastily. 'It was just your side of it I was thinking about. We're all made up about it. You deserve to be happy, love.'

'And so does Jack,' Bridie said. 'Not only losing Maisie and all the years she was ill, but that time with Maisie's mother – the bitch!'

'I like him,' Pat said, 'and I like the straightforward way he came to me. You'll be all right there, girl.'

There was a tap at the kitchen door and Jack came in. 'Speak of the devil!' Bridie exclaimed. 'Where are the lads?'

'Both asleep,' he said. 'Can I sit here, Bridie, and keep my eye on the window in case they want me?'

'That's handy, being back to back,' Julia said.

'Aye, if they wake up they can look out of the back bedroom window and I can see them from here,' Jack explained.

'Where will you live?' Pat asked.

Jack answered. 'We thought we'd live here,' he said. 'There's no happy memories in my house for the lads. Their mam sick from when they were babies and then the years with that – that —' Bridie laid her hand on his.

'Forget her now, Jack. What's done is done.' She turned to Pat.

'Jack did a bit of decorating when Ma was still here, and he'll do a bit more now, then we'll sort out the furniture.'

Everyone in the family was pleased at the news except Minnie. She seemed to feel that all her years of sneering at Bridie's fantasies had ben nullified now that there was to be a marriage. 'He's only marrying her for someone to look after those boys,' she told Julia.

'You wouldn't think so if you saw Bridie and Jack together,' Julia said. 'We're made up the way things have turned out.'

Minnie changed tack. 'Her mother not cold in her grave,' she said. '*I* won't be going to the wedding, I can tell you.'

'Maisie's mother won't be either, but she won't be missed,' said Julia.

'And I won't either, I suppose you mean?' Minnie said, but Julia only replied calmly, 'I'm doing the wedding breakfast in our house. Pat will give Bridie away and Jack's foreman will be best man.'

Bridie's house was in St Francis Xavier's parish, and there was a simple wedding ceremony at the side altar of the magnificent church. Everyone rejoiced in the evident happiness of Bridie and Jack and the two little boys, and afterwards at Julia's house Carrie warmly congratulated the groom. 'You're a lucky man, Jack,' she said. 'You've a jewel in Bridie.'

'An uncut diamond,' Fred guffawed, but was quelled by a look from Carrie. Jack was oblivious.

'I know,' he said, smiling fondly at his wife. 'I'll do my best to make her happy.'

Fred raised his glass. 'We'll drink to that,' he said heartily. 'A long life and a happy one for you both.'

Chapter Eight

Tony and Stephen often made dates with girls, and Tony sometimes made a foursome with a friend from work and two girls, but they were always casual dates, usually invitations to the cinema. Neither Tony nor Stephen had ever brought a girl to visit their mother, which was regarded as a sign of serious courtship.

One night as they were all having their meal Maureen said casually, 'Do you know a girl named Bernadette Brady, Tony?'

'Yes, I went to the pictures with her last week. Do you know her?'

'I do now,' Maureen said, smiling. 'She came into the shop today and told me she knew you.'

'You'd better watch yourself, Tony,' Stephen said with a grin, and their mother said sharply, 'She sounds rather bold.'

'Just because she went into the shop?' Tony said. 'She probably wanted some wool.'

'I think you're all daft,' Terry said. 'Girls are useless. They don't even understand football.'

'I know more about football than you,' Eileen told him, 'And *you* needn't worry about girls. Who'd have you?'

All the Fitzgerald boys were Everton supporters and the talk soon turned to the team's prospects for the FA Cup.

Later Maureen said to Tony, 'I'm sorry I mentioned Bernadette at the table when they were all there. I just didn't stop to think.'

'That's all right, Mo,' he said. 'There's nothing secret. She's only a friend.'

'Does *she* know that?' Maureen said, half joking and half in earnest. Obviously it was not the impression that Bernadette had given, but Tony only laughed so she said no more.

In March Everton won the Football Association Cup and brought it home in triumph to Liverpool. All the Fitzgerald boys went to join the crowds welcoming the footballers home, and Eileen and Anne went with them to share in the excitement. They found a good vantage point, with Tony, Stephen and Terry forming a guard round the girls in case they were crushed.

Anne shouted and cheered as loudly as anyone and thoroughly enjoyed the occasion. She was unaware that her future husband was among the crowds lining the streets.

She still shared a desk with Kathleen O'Neill and on Monday morning told her about the excitement when the coach appeared, with the manager holding the Cup high, and the jokes made by the crowd. She felt that she had been tactless when she saw Kathleen's sad face, and said impulsively, 'Why don't you ask your mam if you can come out with us sometimes?'

But Kathleen shook her head. 'She wouldn't let me,' she said. There was no time to say more, but later as she walked around the playground with Anne, Kathleen told her more of her strange home life than she had ever done before.

It was as though Anne's suggestion had opened a door in Kathleen's mind, and she poured out all the bitterness that had been building up behind it.

'Remember that doll I won in Miss Lawson's class?' she said. 'I loved it. I'd never had a doll before, but one night I said I wanted to play with her instead of listening to Mammy reading and she went mad. She said the stories were the history of my family and that I should want to listen to them more than anything. Then she said I loved the doll more than her and she snatched it off me and threw it in the fire.'

Anne was horrified. 'What happened? Was it burnt?' she asked.

'Yes. I tried to snatch it out but she pushed me away and held it down with the poker.'

'Was Cormac there?' Anne asked, and when Kathleen nodded, said indignantly, 'Why didn't he try to help you? If there were two of you —'

'*Help* me?' Kathleen exclaimed bitterly. 'Not him. He said I shouldn't vex Mammy. Well, he's finding out for himself now.'

'What do you mean?' Anne asked.

'He found a rabbit in the back yard. He didn't know where it came from but the back gate was open for the binmen. He made a hutch for it and called it Binny.'

'Did – did your mother mind?' Anne said.

'She didn't say so then. Maybe she remembered how I'd carried on about the doll. She let him build the hutch, then she opened it one night and let Binny run away.'

'Oh, Kathleen, are you sure?' Anne said. 'After all, it had run away before, hadn't it?'

'Yes, but the hutch was open and the back gate shut and bolted. It couldn't have got out unless she'd opened the gate then shut and bolted it again. She didn't realise that Cormac would know she'd let Binny out – or maybe she wanted him to know.'

Anne was silent, horrified and not knowing what to say, but the whistle for the end of playtime put an end to Kathleen's revelations. She never spoke so freely to Anne again but sometimes made a scornful remark about her brother.

She was still met at the school gates by her mother and unemployed brother, and walked away submissively with them, but in the classroom she had become a different girl.

She had been made a class monitor, and had proved to be good at swimming and netball. Her mother had sent a note asking for Kathleen to be excused swimming and games as she was too delicate, but the headmistress had replied firmly that the school doctor had passed her as perfectly fit. Swimming costumes were provided by the school so Mrs O'Neill could do nothing.

'Cormac was excused swimming and games,' Kathleen told Anne. 'But he didn't want to do them anyway.' She glanced at Anne's expressive face and said defensively, 'It's only because Mammy loves us so much, and wants to keep us safe.'

Anne said nothing.

Tony was nearly twenty-one years old when he finished his apprenticeship and was ready to become a tradesman. Many firms sacked young men when they became eligible for tradesman's wages, but Tony was fairly confident that he would be kept on at Benson's Engineering.

His birthday was on the last Saturday in July and shortly before that he was told that his job was safe.

'We'll have a party,' his father said when Tony told his parents his news. They were in the kitchen and Pat slapped his hand down on his order book which lay on the table. 'We've got plenty to celebrate with the way the business has picked up as well.'

'And best of all, our Joe should be home then too,' Julia said with delight.

Tony felt the familiar bitterness rising in him and said unsmilingly, 'Yes. All right.' He turned and went upstairs immediately, and Pat said angrily, 'What's he got that gob on for? There's no pleasing that fellow.'

'God knows,' Julia said. 'I thought he was getting over these moods.'

'I tell you what, Julia,' her husband said, 'if I'd tried any moods with my da, he'd have damn' soon knocked them out of me. We've been too soft with that fellow.'

Tony had regretted his surly words and jealousy as soon as he reached his room. He turned and came downstairs to put things right.

His parents were still standing in the kitchen and as Tony reached the kitchen door, his father turned and picked up the photograph of Patrick from the dresser. They were too intent to see Tony and he stood frozen with shock as his father said loudly, 'Here's the one who'd have been a proper eldest son to me. No moods out of him. I could have talked to him about me worries too.'

'Don't Pat, don't,' Julia said, bursting into tears.

He put his arm around her. 'I'm sorry, girl. It never gets better.' His voice was thick with emotion. 'Why, Julia? Why did we have to lose him? What did we do wrong?'

She said nothing but wept bitterly, and Tony turned, still unnoticed, and rushed upstairs again. He dived into the bathroom and sat on the edge of the bath, shaking with shock.

All the feelings of bitterness and jealousy that he had tried to suppress for so long burst over him in a despairing flood. He sat crouched with tears rolling between the fingers covering his face.

He had been right: his mother and father had never loved him. They wished he had died and Patrick had lived. He felt worse than he had ever done in his life. Before he had suspected but not really believed: now he had heard it in his father's own words.

He had no idea how long he had been there when he was roused by a banging on the door, and Eileen's voice calling cheerfully, 'Come out, come out, whoever you are. Are you making your Will?'

Tony jumped to his feet. 'Just a minute,' he called, sluicing cold water over his face and opening the door with the towel still held to it.

'I thought you'd died in here,' Eileen said breezily, darting past him into the bathroom, and he was able to slip up to his attic bedroom.

He examined his face in the mirror, looking at his blotchy skin with disgust. Whingeing like a girl, he thought. Terry came leaping up the stairs two at a time, shouting, 'Tea's ready, Tony. Aye, it's great about your job, isn't it? Good place, Benson's.'

He mumbled something in reply then waited until Terry came out of his bedroom and went down with him. He felt strange and lightheaded but the family sitting round the table seemed to notice nothing different.

There was a chorus of congratulation about his job, then they all began to talk about the party. Tony glanced furtively at his parents. His mother looked paler than usual but composed as she served the huge steak and kidney pie. His father showed no sign of his earlier distress.

Presently Julia said mildly, 'You'll have to go and see Aunt Carrie, Tony, and tell her your news.' Before he could speak Eileen announced that she was going out in a foursome with Theresa later.

'What's your feller like?' Stephen asked.

'I don't know yet. He's one of Theresa's, really. I get the ones she throws back. The crumbs that fall from the rich man's table,' said Eileen.

'That was a real crumb you were with outside the Futurist,' Stephen told her.

'He wasn't one of Theresa's,' Eileen said indignantly. 'He was one of my own.'

'"A poor thing but mine own",' Anne quoted.

'Anne's courting now,' Eileen said. 'She gave the milkboy a Fairy Whisper that said "will you be mine?"'

'I didn't!' Anne exclaimed. 'It was a mint imperial that Billy Bolten gave me.'

'Billy Bolten now,' Eileen teased her. 'You're going to be like Theresa.'

'Billy's about a hundred and he's got a wooden leg,' Anne retorted.

'Sounds like one of Eileen's,' Stephen said, but their father said loudly, 'That's enough now. Don't be putting ideas in the child's head.' He smiled fondly at Anne. 'There's many a long year yet before any sprig comes to take you away from us, queen.'

'The years are flying,' Julia said with a sigh. 'And that's another thing, Anne. It was all right when you were only a baby saying Billy – he thought it was funny – but you should show more respect now. I hope you don't call him Billy to his face?'

'I don't call him anything,' Anne said. 'Do you know, he landed off his ship at an island one time. They'd put in for water and he was walking about and talking to some people he met on the beach and was surprised because the captain thought it was uninhabited. A bit later on a priest came off this little hill and he told Billy it was a leper colony.'

'It's a wonder he didn't realise just by looking at them,' Stephen said.

'He said natives are often mutilated because of accidents or tribal customs,' Anne observed.

'The priest was a brave man. Was he English?' Maureen asked.

'I don't know. Billy didn't say, but he could talk to him – properly, I mean, not just sign language like with the natives. Billy's had a very interesting life.'

Tony had barely spoken and the meal was nearly finished. His mother said again that he should go to see Aunt Carrie.

'I will, Mum,' he said, surprised to find that he sounded normal and that no one had noticed any difference in him.

'I think you'd better tell Aunt Minnie as well,' Julia said, but Tony made no promises. Minnie's words of so long ago had started all this, he felt, and he had no desire to see her.

As soon as the meal was over he washed then changed his collar and went to see the Andersons. Carrie and Fred were delighted at his news. 'I knew you'd be kept on,' she declared. 'You've a knack for that sort of thing, and you're hard-working and trust-worthy.'

Tony smiled. 'I'll come to you if I want a reference,' he told her. He had always felt close to Carrie, who was his godmother, and stayed to talk to her even after Fred had gone out to his shed to finish a job and Shaun had gone to see a boxing match.

Carmel was playing at a friend's house and Theresa only looked in briefly before she went to meet Eileen and their escorts. Tony was alone with Carrie, and suddenly it seemed the right moment to ask her something which he had long wanted to know.

'What happened when Patrick died, Aunt Carrie?' he said. 'I've never liked to ask Mum or Dad.'

'He was only ill for forty-eight hours,' Carrie said. 'I was laid up myself at that time with sciatica but I believe it just started with a cold. Your mother kept him in bed and gave him black-currant drinks because his throat was sore, but then suddenly he got worse. Maureen and you went to Grandma Houlihan and they got the doctor for Patrick.'

'What was wrong with him?' Tony asked.

'They never really found out, but a lot of children died the same way at that time. Forty-eight-hour fever, it was called.'

'Dad seemed to think they did something wrong,' Tony said in a low voice.

'People always think that if they lose someone, especially a child,' Carrie said. 'They think they should have called the doctor sooner or something, but with Patrick I don't think it would have made any difference. Your mum had kept him in bed and dosed him, and the doctor couldn't have done any more.'

'So you don't think medicine could have saved him?' Tony said.

'No, even if the doctor had been called right away, and you don't call one every time a child has a cold,' Carrie said.

Tony was silent for a few minutes, wondering if he could ask what he really wanted to know. Finally he said gruffly, 'Aunt Minnie said Mum didn't start to get over it until she had Joe.'

'Your mum's never got over it, love, and neither has your dad although I think it hits women harder than men,' Carrie told him. 'It's a terrible thing for a mother. It's like losing part of herself. I know women who've lost three or four, but it hits them as hard every time. They never get over it, and they get a look about them. I thank God I've never had to face it.'

'But Aunt Minnie said Mum started to get over it when Joe was born,' Tony persisted.

'Aye, well, that was two years after and the first shock had worn off, then she had a bad time with Joe and that made her pull herself together, I suppose. She had her hands full with three of you to look after, one a new baby,' Carrie said.

She glanced at Tony who was sitting with his head bent, staring down at his clasped hands. 'What else did Minnie say?' she asked. 'It wouldn't be her if she didn't have a bit more to say.'

Tony hesitated then he said in a low voice, 'She said I was no consolation to Mum because I looked more like Dad, but when Joe was born he was like Patrick and that's why he helped her to get over it, and he's still her favourite.'

Carrie drew in her breath with a hiss. 'The bad bitch! She probably knew you could hear her and that's why she said it,' she said angrily. 'I hope you weren't daft enough to take any notice of her?'

'It seemed feasible,' he said with a wry smile.

'It was nonsense, Tony. Your mum doesn't have any favourites. She loves you all for different reasons, the same way as I do mine,' his aunt insisted. 'Just think. She often goes to Benediction with

Maureen and she goes to the pictures with her because your dad's not keen on them. Do you think she loves Anne, for instance, any less because she's so close with Maureen?'

Tony thought for a moment then lay back in the chair and smiled wholeheartedly at Carrie. 'I think I *am* daft, Aunt Carrie,' he said. 'Or at least I have been.'

'You should have known better than to take notice of Minnie,' she said forthrightly. 'If she lived in one of these places abroad she'd have had her tongue cut out by now. Do you ever see anything of Brendan these days?'

'I haven't seen him for months,' Tony said, glad now to change the subject. He had definitely decided not to go to see Minnie, and soon said he must be off.

'I'm made up about your job,' Carrie declared. 'You've got a place for life there, Tony.'

'I hope so,' he said. 'Dad's talking about having a party to celebrate, and for my twenty-first.'

'That's great. I just feel like a good party,' Carrie said. She had walked to the door with him and suddenly he turned and gave her a hug. 'Thanks, Aunt Carrie,' he said. They both knew it was for the questions spoken and unspoken that she had answered for him.

Tony walked home with a light step, and as soon as he went in said cheerfully, 'They were made up about the job. I told Aunt Carrie about the party. Is that all right?'

'Yes, of course,' Pat said, with a surprised glance at Julia and she asked Tony if he had been to see Minnie.

'I couldn't be bothered tonight, Mum,' he said. 'Anyway, she'd only say something to take the shine off it. Aunt Carrie's so different.'

'Isn't that the truth?' Pat said. 'To the devil with Minnie anyhow. The lad's right. She'd only have one of her nasty remarks to make.'

'But she'll have a cob on because she hasn't been told,' Julia said nervously.

'Let her,' Pat said. 'I know she's your sister, Julie, but I don't think she'd be the way she is now if everyone hadn't given in to her moods all her life.'

Tony went to the bathroom then went out for a long walk to think over his conversation with his Aunt Carrie. It had been a queer day, he thought. First the elation when he heard that his job was safe, then the scene in the kitchen and his feelings of despair, then the talk with Aunt Carrie when so much had been cleared in his mind.

He walked for several hours along Low Hill and up Kensington and Prescot Road until he came to Green Lane then back in a semicircle down to West Derby Road and home. He felt physically tired when he arrived home, but his mind was at peace.

Joe arrived home on the following Thursday and the party was held on the Saturday, which was Tony's twenty-first birthday. It was a great success. Although it had been arranged at short notice almost everyone who had been invited came: all Tony's friends from the cycling club, a few friends from work, as well as friends of other members of the family and the usual aunts and uncles and cousins.

The exceptions were Dympna and Brendan. Minnie simply said that they were busy, but later she told Bridie that Dympna was out with her young man. 'She wouldn't bring him here,' she said. 'They're such a lot of skits.'

'It's only fun, Minnie,' Bridie said. 'They don't mean any harm.' But Minnie sniffed and pursed her lips.

Bridie seemed to glow with happiness as she proudly introduced Jack to various people. The two little boys were with them, but they had fallen asleep soon after arriving and been put to bed in Maureen's room which was near the bathroom. Most people who visited the bathroom peeped in on them, but they slept soundly curled up close to each other.

Julia had made a cake and iced it but hidden it away from Tony. After supper Maureen and Eileen slipped away and put twenty-one candles on the cake, then put it on the trolley with an array of clean glasses.

Eileen stepped into the parlour with a cry of 'Attention!' then she and Maureen wheeled the trolley in with a flourish amidst cries of 'Happy Birthday, Tony' from the guests.

Fred and Pat filled the glasses with wine and everyone cheered when Fred proposed a toast of 'A happy birthday and many more to follow' to Tony as he cut the cake.

His mother, Maureen, Eileen and Anne kissed him, and his father and brothers shook his hand and clapped him on the shoulder, but Tony was amazed when Bernadette, who was there with the cycling club members, suddenly pushed through his family and pulled his head down to kiss him passionately.

An ironic cheer went up from the young people but his friend Jerry said quickly, 'That's from all of us, Tony. Best wishes from the club, mate.'

Tony's face had gone red, but he gave Jerry a grateful glance and said, 'Thanks, everyone.' Jerry was a cartoonist on a local paper and now he asked Tony to stand between his parents while he did a lightning sketch of them.

They stood smiling, Tony with his arm round his father and his mother holding his other arm, Pat's arm round Tony's shoulders. Tony caught Aunt Carrie's glance and smiled at her whole-heartedly. The sketch was a good likeness and someone said jovially, 'Better keep that, Tony. Might be worth something one day when Jerry's famous.'

'It's worth a lot now as far as I'm concerned,' he said. 'Thanks for the souvenir, Jerry.'

The older people drifted into the kitchen, but before they went

Tony heard Minnie say to Maureen, 'You never had a "do" like this for your twenty-first, did you?'

'I didn't want one,' she said cheerfully. 'I was made up to get this watch though.' She held out her hand with the tiny gold watch on her wrist. 'Times were bad for Mum and Dad, so I know they must have had a job to afford it.'

Tony felt a stab of shame. I wish I was more like Maureen, he thought. Minnie's tongue has no chance against her. Later he heard his aunt talking to Fred and thought that he was another who was impervious to Minnie's spite.

Dominic and Desmond now attended St Edward's College in Sandfield Park. Desmond had passed the examination for a scholarship to the College, and Fred had decided to pay the fees so that Dominic could accompany him there. They had both come to the party wearing their purple blazers and caps, and Minnie's eyes gleamed with malice as she looked at them. 'It's no wonder your Shaun's always falling out with them,' she said to Fred. 'I suppose he feels it, that you do for them what you wouldn't do for him?'

'You've got the wrong end of the stick there, Minnie,' Fred said heartily. 'I thought if anyone could tame that pair it'd be the Christian Brothers, but Shaun was happy in the Parish School. He's doing well now working with me – a real flair for it he's got.'

Tony smiled to see the disappointment on her face, but thought he would have a word with his cousin Shaun in case Minnie succeeded in dropping any poison in his ear. Not many people are as daft as me though, he thought ruefully. Shaun would take as little notice as Fred had.

Tony had gone into the kitchen to talk to Aunt Carrie, but Eileen was now playing the piano in the parlour and he could hear laughter and singing from the young people there. He soon left Carrie and went back to the parlour.

As soon as he walked in Bernadette claimed him, slipping her hand through his arm and reaching up to kiss him. They were in a crowd by the door so few people saw her. Although Tony made no move to return the kiss she slipped her arm around his neck and drew his head near to her.

'I thought you would have chosen tonight to settle things,' she whispered. 'Then we could have made the announcement when you cut the cake.'

'What announcement?' he asked in genuine puzzlement.

'Oh, Tony, don't tease. Our engagement, of course.'

'Engagement? I couldn't – I'm – I'm only just out of my time,' stammered Tony, his face scarlet.

'Yes, but you'll be on tradesman's money now. We can save up,' Bernadette said.

Tony pulled away from her clutching hands. 'But, Bernadette,' he began, 'it's – it's not that.' Before he said any more Jerry suddenly grabbed his arm and pulled him through the crowd, leaving Bernadette behind. 'Where've you been, birthday boy?' he said, laughing. 'We've been looking for you. Eileen's found some old music.'

'"Can You Dance the Polka?"' Eileen said, jumping up from the piano stool. 'Come on, Tony.' A young man took her place and a space was hastily cleared then Eileen and Tony danced the Polka with abandon, finishing with Eileen giving a high kick and falling back into his arms. There was loud applause, but Bernadette stayed glowering in the doorway.

As soon as there was an opportunity Jerry drew Tony into a corner. 'I saw you were being waylaid there, Tony. Watch yourself, mate, that's a tarantula if ever I saw one.'

'But I don't know why,' Tony said in bewilderment. 'Honestly, Jer, I've never given her any encouragement. That sounds lousy, but what I mean is, I've never even thought of an engagement, let alone mentioned it. How could I? I haven't been earning enough to keep a flea.'

'Is that what she's after?' Jerry said. 'I thought it might be. Listen, son, I'm afraid it's not your handsome face that's bowled her over. It's the thought of those tradesman's wages you'll be getting.' He grinned and Tony grinned back. 'Careful, you'll be giving me a big head if you're not careful,' he said, but Jerry added seriously, 'Be warned, though, old son. Better men than you have been caught like that.'

Jerry was called to organise a game of Chinese numbers, and Tony joined Maureen and two girlfriends she had invited to the party. He had decided not to avoid Bernadette but to make it quite clear that she had made a mistake. He thought of Fred's phrase to Minnie, that she had got hold of the wrong end of the stick, and smiled to himself as he thought he might try it with Bernadette if she tried to corner him again.

Whether by accident or design Tony's friends seemed to surround him all evening and Bernadette sulked in a corner.

Joe was backwards and forwards between the kitchen and the parlour all night as all the older relations in the kitchen wanted to see him, but he came back as often as possible to the festivities in the parlour.

'Anne's growing up fast, isn't she?' he said to Tony. 'This is what I hate about being away.' They both looked at Anne who was talking to one of the boys surrounding her pretty cousin, Theresa.

Anne had grown taller and her dress of cream silk patterned with brown pansies showed that her figure was beginning to develop. Her cheeks were pink with excitement and her eyes sparkled. 'She's going to be a beauty, isn't she?' Tony said.

And Joe replied, laughing. 'What do you mean? Going to be? She is already.'

A game of Forfeits was played later and Anne chose Joe and gave him a hearty kiss. 'Hey, that's not right,' one of Tony's friends called. 'You should have chosen Tony. He's the birthday lad.'

'I can kiss Tony anytime,' Anne said, hugging Joe. 'Our Joe's not home often.'

Tony joined in the laughter, pleased to feel only pleasure in Anne's words and no trace of his old jealousy of Joe.

Everyone agreed that the party was a big success, and Pat continued to secure orders to keep his business going. Joe was still unable to find a shore job, but said he was determined that this was the last time he would go back to sea. The family agreed but all knew that in spite of the fact that Pat's business had improved, the general employment position was worse if anything.

Chapter Nine

Anne's friendship with Kathleen O'Neill continued. The time was approaching when they were due to leave school, but Anne had never been able to see her after school hours. Although she sometimes tentatively suggested outings, Kathleen always refused, saying that her mother would not allow it.

None of the teachers seemed to Anne to show any interest in individual pupils, and she was amazed one day to be told to stay behind by the teacher in charge of the top class, Miss Woods.

When the class had gone and Anne was standing by Miss Woods' desk, the teacher told her that she was pleased to see that she was friendly with Kathleen O'Neill.

'Kathleen seems to enjoy the swimming lesson,' she said. 'Do you know if she ever goes to the baths out of school hours?'

'I don't think so,' Anne said. 'Her mother . . .' She had been about to say that Mrs O'Neill would not allow it but thought it might be disloyal to Kathleen to say so.

The teacher probed gently. 'Does Kathleen talk about her life at home, dear? I know her mother has rather unusual ideas.' Anne was torn, not wanting to betray confidences but feeling that the teacher was truly concerned about Kathleen.

At last she said in a subdued voice, 'Kathleen doesn't go out on her own. The three of them go together, but Kathleen says it's because her mammy loves them and wants to keep them safe.'

'Poor child, poor loyal child,' Miss Woods said. She looked down at her desk and Anne heard her murmur, 'So sad. Obsessive love against the pull of normality.'

She sighed deeply and looked at Anne. 'Will Kathleen be allowed to go to work, do you think?'

'If she can get a job, Miss,' Anne said. 'We know it won't be easy. We've talked about it.'

'You have? I'm pleased to hear that, Anne. Do you know whether her brother is seeking employment?'

'Cormac. No, I don't think so. He doesn't really want to and his mother has three jobs now so she says he doesn't need to.'

'Three jobs!' the teacher exclaimed.

'Yes, she cleans offices before Kathleen and Cormac get up in the morning, and she mends umbrellas, and she has another job she goes to at night.'

Miss Woods closed her eyes as though in prayer and Anne shuffled her feet uneasily. Was she betraying Kathleen? she wondered, but Miss Woods opened her eyes and said gently, 'You were right to tell me what you know of the family so that I know how to help Kathleen. Try to keep in touch with her when you leave school, Anne. Kathleen needs a friend. Now this is all in confidence, dear, but you're a sensible girl and won't mention it to anyone else, will you?'

Anne promised, but wondered how she could ever see Kathleen, let alone be her friend, if she could never escape from her mother.

Very occasionally teachers heard of jobs for girls leaving school and were able to recommend one of their pupils for the position. A few weeks before the girls were due to leave Miss Woods gave Kathleen a note to take to her mother. 'There is a letter of recommendation enclosed in it, Kathleen,' she said. 'It's for a position as a clerk in a coal merchant's office which is very near your home. The wages are small but there is an opportunity for promotion if you suit.'

Kathleen told Anne the next day that her mother had been to look at the coal merchant's office and it was only five minutes' walk away from their house. 'Nearer than school,' Kathleen said, 'so I'm going today to see the man with Mammy.'

Anne wondered whether Cormac would be taken too, but she said nothing about him and wished Kathleen success in getting the job. As soon as she saw her friend's face the following day she knew that all had gone well, and was sincerely pleased for Kathleen.

'The money will be a help for Cormac's clothes,' she told Anne innocently. 'He's growing so fast, you see.' Anne was pleased to hear it, if that was what had swayed their mother to allow Kathleen to take the job.

Anne had applied for several jobs without success so she felt that she was very lucky when she obtained a job in a cake shop in Kensington, within walking distance of her home.

Anne enjoyed school and in many ways was sorry to leave but she looked forward to the excitement of the new job and of earning a wage. She said goodbye to Kathleen in the classroom and asked her to keep in touch.

'Perhaps we could go to the pictures together sometimes now that we'll both be working? I mean, if your mother will let you go to work . . .'

Kathleen agreed eagerly, 'Yes. Mammy might feel differently if I'm working. I'd like to go to the pictures with you, Anne.'

'I'll look out for you at Mass,' she promised.

Anne started work on the following Monday and soon changed her mind about the pleasures of working. Her employers were Australians. In theory Mrs James was in charge of the shop and Mr James of the bakehouse, but in practice Mrs James paid only fleeting visits to the shop. While she was there she seemed to prefer talking to the customers to working, which left far too much work for Anne and the senior assistant, Jessie.

Mr James was a small swarthy man with a large paunch and a rough aggressive manner. He was never satisfied, no matter how hard his staff worked, and his constant cry was, 'Carm on, jump to it.'

The bakehouse was behind the shop and he had a habit of suddenly appearing in the shop when Mrs James was absent. Anne felt nervous and clumsy with his beady eyes fixed on her, and thought he must put the customers off too.

He always wore a stained singlet and cotton trousers with a belt slung low under his paunch, and gave off an unpleasant smell. The other assistant, Jessie, was his favourite and often he told her that she could go as soon as the shop closed at six o'clock, even though the window might be only half cleared.

Anne was often left to finish clearing the window and cleaning the shelves and counters while Mrs James appeared only to cash up the money in the till. Often Anne felt almost too tired to eat her meal when she arrived home, but none of the family realised how hard she was working.

Her mother thought that she was finding it hard to adjust to the longer hours after the short school day, and that she would soon become accustomed to them. At that time of high unemployment a job was not lightly surrendered and Anne struggled on for several months, thinking that all employment was like this.

Saturday was always a busy day at the shop and Anne and Jessie came in at 7.45 a.m. to fill up the shelves and window before the shop opened. One Saturday was particularly hard for Anne.

There had been a noisy row between Mr James and one of the bakehouse girls the previous day, culminating in the girl's demanding her insurance cards and walking out. Jessie had been in the bakehouse filling custards and blackcurrant tarts, and helping to weigh dried fruit and other ingredients, all Saturday morning.

Mrs James had leaned indolently on the counter gossiping while Anne had scurried about trying to serve several impatient customers at once.

Jessie came back into the shop briefly then went for her lunch. When she returned Mrs James said to Anne, 'You're not going home, are you? You can manage with half an hour for lunch. I'll have to go out when you get back.'

Anne stayed to lunch on Saturdays because she was too tired to walk home and back, but realised that she was not going to gain by staying that day. She sat in the storeroom to eat her sandwiches and drink from her flask of tea, and when she returned to the shop after half an hour Mrs James immediately departed and was not seen again.

The shop was still full of customers at six o'clock and when the doors were finally closed at six-twenty Anne felt as though there were lead weights on her feet. The shop was a daunting sight as there had been no time between serving to tidy it.

Jessie had taken only a few of the empty glass dishes from the window when Mr James appeared. He was obviously in a furious temper but said to Jessie, 'You can go. You've done your share, helping in the bakehouse. Pity I haven't got more like you instead of these lazy cows.'

Jessie departed with a smug smile and he said roughly to Anne, 'Carm on, carm on, jump to it. Get them dishes washed and this place cleaned.' Anne was near to tears but she took the dishes to the sink in the bakehouse and washed them, then cleaned the window and replaced them.

All the bakehouse staff had gone home long ago and Anne was alone with Mr James who was banging furiously about the bakehouse, swearing and cursing. She nervously wiped down the shelves and counters then mopped the floor.

Just as she finished Mr James appeared. 'Don't put that bucket away,' he ordered. 'Change the water and mop out the bakehouse.'

When she went in to the bakehouse he was cursing again and flung some baking tins in the sink. 'Get them washed,' he shouted. 'Wait 'til I see that bloody Dolly! Look at those bloody corners. Bloody sodding women! Shift yourself. Clean them out and get right in the corners. Plenty of bloody soda, you hear me?'

Anne was terrified and plunged her arms into the hot water and scrubbed frantically at the tins, her tears dropping on to them as she worked. After his outburst James had become quiet, and soon Anne's tiredness was forgotten in her fear of the man.

He had moved to stand behind her, his paunch pressing against her so that she was pushed against the sink. His arm came round her, brushing against her developing breasts as he took the tins and pretended to examine them.

A sound at the door made him move away swiftly as Mrs James came in. She looked at Anne's tear-stained face and demanded suspiciously 'What's going on?'

'That bloody Dolly. Left the tins half washed,' he blustered. 'Be just the bloody time an inspector'll come.'

'And why is *she* still here?' Mrs James questioned.

'*Somebody* had to wash the bloody tins, didn't they? Although she's no bloody good either.' He snatched the tin from Anne. 'Go on, beat it,' he ordered, and she ran through for her coat and flask and thankfully escaped.

It was nearly eight o'clock as Anne stumbled home, feeling drunk with fatigue. As she turned into Magdalen Street Tony was setting out. He stared at her in horror and put his arm around her. 'Anne, what's happened? Where have you been?' he said.

'At work,' she said. Her tongue felt thick and her words were slurred. 'Cleaning.' She could say no more and Tony put his arm more firmly around her and almost carried her home. He burst into the kitchen with her, his eyes blazing. 'Look at her,' he cried. 'Half dead. Couldn't put one foot in front of the other. I'm going down there. I'll kill that Aussie.'

Pat and Julia had jumped to their feet in dismay, and her mother rushed to Anne as Tony lowered her onto the sofa. 'Anne love, what happened? Where have you been?'

'In that shop,' Tony shouted angrily. 'Cleaning, she said. I'm going down there.'

'Hang on, hang on,' Pat said, clamping his hand on Tony's shoulder. 'We'll get the whole story first then *I'll* see the fellow. It's my place.'

'Oh, Mum,' Anne said, putting her arms around her mother's neck and bursting into tears. 'I thought he'd never let me come home.' The relief of being at home was almost too much to bear. Tony's anger was blazing again but his father restrained him. 'No, lad,' he said grimly. 'We'll hear it all first. You be off now. Don't worry. He won't get away with it.'

After Tony had gone, Pat mixed a spoonful of brandy with hot water and sugar and held the cup to Anne's lips. She pulled a face but he said firmly, 'Drink it, queen. It'll do you good.' She drank obediently.

The brandy seemed to run through her body like fire and she sat up, feeling stronger. 'Now tell us what happened, love,' her mother said. 'We thought you must have called into Aunt Carrie's.'

Between her tiredness and the brandy Anne found it difficult to tell her story coherently but her parents were able to gather how hard she had worked and how callously she had been treated.

'And that Jessie just went off and left you to it, a little girl like you?' her mother said angrily. And her father said, 'But tell us, queen, what about when you'd done the shop? What were these tins?'

'The baking tins,' Anne said. 'Mr James said Dolly hadn't cleaned in the corners and he made me do them. He kept saying "bloody" all the time.' She shuddered. 'It was horrible. He was pressing his stomach against me while I was washing the tins . . .'

'*What?*' her father shouted. 'What do you mean?' His face had suddenly become red and congested and Anne said nervously, 'I was standing at the sink and he was behind me and his stomach was pushing me against the sink. I was frightened.' She began to cry and her mother took her in her arms and rocked her, saying frantically over her head, 'Pat, Pat, have sense! Don't go now!' But her father had snatched his coat and was roaring, 'I'll kill him! By God, I'll kill him!'

He rushed out and Julia clutched Anne. 'Oh, merciful God, he'll go berserk,' she exclaimed, then crossed herself and began to pray. 'O Lord, stay his hand,' she prayed. 'Watch over him and keep him from damaging the man.'

'Oh, Mum, I shouldn't have told him,' Anne said fearfully.

Julia looked at her terrified face and tried to smile reassuringly. 'Don't worry, lamb. Your dad's bark is worse than his bite. He'll just give that fellow a fright!'

She gave Anne a quick kiss and stood up. 'Now how about something to eat?' she said briskly.

'I couldn't, Mum,' Anne said, but when her mother brought her a bowl of barley broth she was able to eat and enjoy it.

'Now off to bed,' Julia said, 'and I'll bring you a cup of tea.' Anne would have liked to wait to see her father but she was too weary, and when Julia went up with the tea a few minutes later, she was fast asleep.

In a surprisingly short time Pat was back, his temper restored. 'That feller's had a fright he won't forget in a hurry,' he said with satisfaction. 'He'll bully no more little girls.'

'Pat, what did you do?' Julia said fearfully.

'Don't worry, girl. I didn't leave a mark on him,' he said. 'I nearly battered the door down and the wife came down and opened it. She knew who I was and why I was there the minute she laid eyes on me. Took me upstairs and he was there shaking like a jelly. I stood over him and he wet himself. It's the God's truth, Julia, he wet his trousers.'

'He *must* have been frightened,' she gasped.

'Aye, and I frightened him a bit more. I told him his fortune, I can tell you. You should have heard them, blaming each other. Him saying she was always clearing off and her saying he didn't make Jessie pull her weight, but I think she's the boss there.'

'It's often the way with a bully like that,' Julia said. 'Did you say – about what Anne said he'd done?'

'I did,' Pat said grimly, 'and that really put the cat among the pigeons. She flew at him, tried to scratch his eyes out, and she said something. I didn't think much of it at the time, too busy trying to stop her murdering him, but I thought about it afterwards.'

'Why, what did she say?'

'Something about him at his old tricks. Did he want to have to run away from here too? I wonder was he run out of Australia or got out in case because he'd been up to these tricks?'

'And our Anne's been with a fellow like that?' Julia said in horror.

'Mind you, I'm only guessing,' Pat said. 'But it might be why she's got the upper hand.'

'Thank God she came back when she did,' Julia said, looking white and shaken.

'I told him we'd had to restrain our Tony from coming after him. Said he was a big lad and didn't know his own strength, and he might still go there. Told him I'd report him to the Factory and Shops Inspector too.'

'I've never heard of him,' Julia said, and Pat said with a chuckle, 'Neither have I. I just made it up but he believed me.'

'It sounds as if he was frightened enough without that, but no more than he deserved,' Julia said. 'I hope you told him he wouldn't see Anne again.'

'I did. He gave me her cards and a week's wages for her,' Pat said. 'He was really entitled to a week's wages in lieu of notice from her, but I wasn't going to argue.'

Julia looked in on Anne from time to time, but she still slept all night and on Sunday even while Eileen got up and went to Mass. The family went to Mass and returned and still Anne slept until nearly six o'clock on Sunday evening.

'I've missed Mass, Mum,' she exclaimed when she woke.

'No sin. You needed that sleep,' her mother said calmly. 'If you get up now you'll sleep better tonight.'

Remembrance flooded over Anne. 'What happened with Dad?' she asked fearfully.

'He was back just after you went to sleep,' Julia said cheerfully. 'Dad told him off and said you wouldn't be going back there. He gave him a week's wages and your insurance cards.'

'But I'd had my wages. I might have to give them back if I leave without notice. He was keeping Jane's wages, he said.'

'Don't worry, Dad's sorted it all out,' Julia said. 'And you got an extra week's wages out of it.'

Julia decided that Anne could stay at home for a few weeks before looking for another job, and one evening she decided to walk along to the coal merchant's office to meet Kathleen. She was waiting across the road when she saw Mrs O'Neill and Cormac turn the corner and quickly dodged back out of sight, feeling shocked and dismayed.

She had been so sure when Kathleen was allowed to take the job it meant the start of a different life for her, but even to go the short distance home she was not allowed to be alone evidently.

Anne peeped round the corner. Cormac and his mother stood close to the door of the office. He was still wearing short trousers even though Anne calculated he must be nearly seventeen. A group of school leavers, swaggering along in their first pairs of long trousers, were whistling derisively at him.

Cormac and his mother ignored them and the next moment Kathleen emerged from the office. She looked pale but otherwise much as Anne remembered her. She was still very neatly dressed with her hair now hanging in a plait down her back, and she walked away submissively with her mother and Cormac.

Anne came home, feeling depressed and worried about Kathleen. It wasn't the sort of life her friend wanted, she was sure, when she remembered how lively Kathleen had been in class. Although it might suit Cormac.

In bed at night she pondered on the O'Neills and wondered how she could help Kathleen, but always she came to the conclusion that she could do nothing. Kathleen would have to help herself.

Although Anne told herself that Kathleen didn't *have* to walk home with her mother and she could just tell her not to meet her, she knew that it was not really so simple. Something that Maureen told her confirmed this.

The O'Neills' next-door neighbour was a keen knitter and was often in Maureen's wool shop. She told Maureen that a doctor and another man had been to see her. 'They told me I hadn't got to say nothing to no one, but I can tell you because I know you won't talk,' she told Maureen.

Maureen suspected that the same words had been said to most people in the neighborhood, but she was too intrigued to refuse to listen.

'They wanted to know if I ever seen anything of them,' the woman said. 'Did I ever see the boy or girl on their own? I told them the three of them went round as if they was glued together.'

'But the girl goes to work,' Maureen said.

'Aye, but they go with her and fetch her home like jailers,' the woman said triumphantly. 'It was the lad they really wanted to know about, though. I told them I seen him one time in the yard, dressed up in a kilt with a cloak over his shoulder fastened with a big brooch. I was sitting out on the sill cleaning me windows.'

'What did they say?' asked Maureen.

'They went on an' on about it but I told them he was like one of them Irish dancers or the band that come over from Ireland one time.'

'Perhaps he does Irish dancing?' Maureen said.

'No. He'd have to practise and we never hear no music there. Not that we listen like but the walls are thin,' the neighbour said. 'We only ever hear talking or her reading out to them.'

'It's a pity the boy can't get a job,' Maureen said.

'*She* wouldn't let him, and he wouldn't be no good anyway. He was in the same class as my lad. Stan says he was awful mardy. Cried if they came near him. The whole class got the strap one day because they'd been having a bit of a laugh with him and his mother complained, so they left him alone after that.'

'Did you tell the doctor that?' Maureen asked.

'Yes, and he said, "You've been very helpful, Mrs Norton,"' the woman said proudly. 'That's when he said not to say nothing, so you won't tell anyone, will you?'

Maureen promised but when Anne said that she was worried about Kathleen she told her about the doctor's visit to the neighbour. 'So someone is trying to do something,' she consoled Anne.

Chapter Ten

Anne had been at home for several weeks and had fully recovered from her experience at the cake shop. She had started again to apply for jobs, but without success, when Eileen came home one night and said that she had heard of one.

'The only thing is, it's another cake shop.'

'A cake shop!' Anne exclaimed in dismay.

'They're not all like the last,' Eileen said. 'This one's nearer home, in West Derby Road, and the manageress seems very nice. She's related to Phil Maddan and I met her at their house. Mrs Maddan had told her about you and that James fellow and she said they're getting busy for Christmas and if you have cake shop experience you might suit.'

Anne looked at her mother. 'It's a chance, love,' Julia said. 'You know now what they *can't* ask you to do, and if you don't like it you can always leave.'

'I told Mrs Burroughs that you'd go to see her at the shop tomorrow anyway,' Eileen said. 'Mrs Burroughs says it's up to Mr and Mrs Dyson who own the business, but it's worth a try, Anne.'

She went nervously to the shop on the following morning and Mrs Burroughs took her through to the bakehouse to see Mr and Mrs Dyson. They were busy but both smiled at Anne and Mrs Dyson said, 'I believe you've got some experience, love?'

She could only whisper shyly, 'Yes,' but Mrs Dyson said

briskly, 'It's up to you, Mabel. You know what you need in the shop.'

'I think we should give it a try. Anne does have some experience,' Mrs Burroughs said and Mrs Dyson said, 'Right. You fix it up, Mabel.' To Anne she said, 'Mabel will look after you, love, and tell you what to do.'

It was arranged that Anne should start the following morning, and she knew immediately that she would like the job.

Mrs Burroughs, or Mabel as she told Anne to call her, was a tall, bony woman with large hands and feet and Anne was immediately reminded of her Aunt Bridie. Mabel had the same warm manner and sweet smile.

The other assistant was a girl of about the same age as Anne with large blue eyes and glossy chestnut-coloured hair. She seemed shy but very ready to help Anne and to make her feel welcome. Mabel introduced her as Sarah.

The shop was busy with the morning trade of bread and scones and barmcake, but Anne found the work easy with Sarah prompting her unobtrusively about prices and Mabel and Sarah doing most of the serving. As soon as the rush slackened a girl came through from the bakehouse with three cups of tea.

'Before the pies come out,' she said to Anne with a smile. Sarah explained that they did a roaring trade in hot meat pies, mainly to men from banks and offices nearby, or people from other shops.

'Some women buy them to save cooking too,' she said. 'We have a cup of tea before the rush starts, then we have our dinners after it.'

Anne was amazed at the amount of food brought through from the bakehouse and the number of customers queuing for the hot savoury pies, full of rich gravy. When the rush slackened Mabel told Anne she could go for her lunch. Her mother was waiting anxiously for her.

'How did it go, love?' she asked. 'Do you think you'll like it?'

'Oh, *yes*, Mum,' she said fervently. 'Everyone's so nice. Mrs Burroughs told me to call her Mabel and showed me what to do but she's not bossy or anything. The other girl in the shop is lovely and really friendly. She told me all the prices and names but in a nice way. Didn't make me look soft in front of the customers, and they're nice too.'

'What about the bakehouse?' Julia asked, putting a plate of bacon and eggs in front of her.

'We don't go in there,' Anne said. 'The bakehouse boy brings the trays through and the only other one I saw was a girl who brought us a cup of tea each before the rush started for the pies. Oh, I do hope I suit and they keep me on.'

'Well, do your best, love. You can do no more,' Julia said. 'I'm glad you like it anyway. There aren't many places like that other shop, you know.'

In the late afternoon Mrs Dyson came into the shop. 'We're off now, Mabel,' she said. 'Is everything all right?'

'Yes, fine,' said Mabel. 'Anne's done very well. You can tell she's been used to tying cake boxes.'

Mrs Dyson smiled at Anne. 'That's a good girl,' she said in motherly tones. 'See you tomorrow, girls.'

As the day's stock of bread and cakes was sold, Sarah and Mabel gradually gathered what remained on a few shelves and trays and put the cleared trays and dishes at one end of the shop. Mabel cleared the window and brushed it out with a tiny brush and dustpan, then put a large plant in the centre and ruffled silk around it.

'Looks classy, doesn't it?' she said with satisfaction. Anne agreed and asked if she should wash the glass display dishes.

'Oh, no. A woman comes in to do them and clean the bakehouse,' Mabel said. 'We'll just sweep the floor before we go, and put out more bags and tissue paper.'

Promptly at six o'clock they left the shop and Sarah walked part of the way home with Anne. Mabel had told Anne that she was pleased with the way she worked, and thought that they would all get on like a house on fire. Anne was almost skipping home.

'Do you think you'll like it then?' Sarah said, smiling at her.

'I'm *sure* I will. Do you think I'll be kept on?'

'I'm *sure* you will,' Sarah said, in exactly the same tone as Anne, and they laughed together. 'Seriously though, Anne, we really need you, because we're so busy now and Mabel says we'll be frantic when we start the Christmas stuff. Mince pies and bunloaves and puddings.'

'People *buy* bunloaves and Christmas puddings?' Anne said in amazement.

'I know. My mum couldn't believe it either,' Sarah said, smiling. They parted at the corner and Anne hurried home unable to keep a beaming smile from her face. She told her mother how different the routine was in this shop and that Mabel had praised her and Sarah told her that she was really needed.

Julia was delighted, and later told Pat that she was sure that Anne would be happy in Dyson's. 'She'll appreciate it all the more after what she had to put up with in that other place,' she said.

Anne was surprised by the number of people who knew about her experience at the first cake shop, and wished her well in her job in the second one. Anything that happened was like a stone thrown in a pond, she thought, with ripples spreading out in all directions.

Her brothers and sisters had been so indignant that each had talked about Anne's ordeal in the different places where they worked and to their own circle of friends, and Julia had told Carrie and Bridie who had talked about it.

'That's the thing about a big family,' Anne told Sarah. 'And, honestly, it's not that important. I've almost forgotten about that horrible man and his job.' But she shivered and Sarah said sympathetically, 'I don't think you have, but you will when everyone stops talking about it.'

Anne liked Sarah more and more, and felt that they thought alike about almost everything. Sarah too belonged to a loving family, with two brothers and a sister, and her grandparents living just across the road from her home.

When Anne had said at home that Sarah's name was Sarah Redmond and she lived in Egremont Street, her father had exclaimed, 'She must be Lawrie Ward's grand-daughter,' and her mother added, 'She comes from a good family then, love. She'll be a nice friend for you to have.'

Fred had called in and her father said immediately, 'What do you think, Fred? Anne's working with Lawrie Ward's grand-daughter.'

'Is she? She's in good company then if the girl's anything like her grandfather *or* her grandmother. Salt of the earth, Lawrie and Sally Ward,' Fred said.

'Aye, Lawrie Ward's done more for the poor than all the councillors put together,' Pat said. 'Or the rich people who open soup kitchens and such like.'

'Well, he's a working man himself,' said Fred. 'One of the cobblers that works for me – y'know, Wally, the little humpbacked fellow – he told me that when he was down on his luck it was Lawrie Ward helped him. He said he knew Lawrie didn't have much more in his pocket than he had himself, but he did all sorts to help him. Found him a room and went to see people to get justice for him, was the way Wally put it.'

'I've heard that he'll tackle anyone, the Lord Mayor even, and write to nobs in London to get things done too,' Pat said. 'He'll put his hand in his own pocket and leave himself short to help people as well, and Sally Ward's always the one people send for when they've got sickness or death in the house.'

Anne listened eagerly, planning to tell Sarah what had been said about her grandparents. At the first opportunity the following day she told Sarah how much her father and uncle admired Sarah's grandparents and the girl said with a smile, 'That's how I got this job really. My grandma helped Mabel when her husband died, and when Mabel heard I was looking for a job she recommended me for this.'

'My Uncle Fred said she's the salt of the earth and so is your grandfather,' said Anne. 'I was surprised at how much my dad knew about him too.'

'I'm surprised too,' Sarah said, 'because he does everything very quietly. Grandad says working men should stick together and help each other, but he doesn't say anything about what he does.'

'Probably people he's helped talk about him,' Anne suggested, and Sarah thought this was likely.

Among the people who queued for pies were several young men from offices and banks nearby. They were still formal with Anne but had known Sarah for some time, and several of them flirted with her, although she was only a few months older than Anne.

One of them was a bank clerk named Dennis who always managed to spend some time in the shop looking at Sarah and waiting to be served by her. Anne willingly cooperated in this, but within a week or two of Anne's starting work in the shop, another young man seemed to single Sarah out.

Michael Rourke was a handsome young man with dark hair growing in a widow's peak and blue eyes with thick dark lashes, and Sarah confided to Anne that she thought she had fallen in love with him.

Anne thought it was all wonderfully romantic, and Mabel did all she could to encourage the romance. 'I think he's lovely,' she declared. 'If you married him, Sarah, and you'd nothing to eat, at least you'd have something to look at.' The girls laughed. Marriage was still in the remote future.

Michael seemed very shy, but with a gentle push from Mabel he plucked up courage to ask Sarah to the cinema. Anne and Mabel waited eagerly to hear her account of the night out, but she had little to tell them.

'It was very nice,' she said. 'It was lovely being out with him, and his manners were very good.' It seemed to be all she intended to say but Mabel asked bluntly, 'Did he kiss you?'

'Er – no. He shook hands with me. I suppose that's better than being too pushy,' Sarah said, but Anne thought that she seemed disappointed, and when they were alone later, Sarah admitted that she was right.

'A girl I know said you shouldn't let a boy kiss you on a first date in case he thinks you're cheap,' she said. 'It says so in *Peg's Paper*.'

She sounded doubtful and Anne said with a grin, 'But you'd have liked the chance to say no.' They both laughed and Anne said, 'He's bound to ask you out again, and it'll probably be quite different then.'

'Not too much, I hope,' Sarah said, laughing.

Anne had not been to the coal merchant's office again to try to see Kathleen O'Neill, and sometimes her conscience was troubled by her neglect.

The shop was closed on Wednesday afternoons and she decided that she would try again to speak to Kathleen on the following Wednesday. She went early to the corner opposite the coal merchant's and when she saw Kathleen leave the office and be met by her mother and brother, Anne dashed through back entries and emerged in time to be walking up the street where the O'Neills lived just as they turned the corner.

She planted herself in front of her friend and said loudly, 'Hello, Kathleen.'

She smiled nervously and said, 'Hello, Anne,' but her mother pulled at her arm and propelled her past. Kathleen glanced back over her shoulder at Anne but her mother hustled her and Cormac to their door and almost pushed them indoors.

Anne had to walk away, but felt that at least she had made some contact with Kathleen. She told Maureen about the incident, and a few weeks later her sister told Anne that the O'Neills' neighbour had been in the wool shop again.

'She said a priest and a doctor had been to the O'Neills'. She couldn't properly hear what they were saying but she thinks they had a job for Cormac. After they'd gone Mrs O'Neill was what Mrs Norton called "yisterical". She was screaming and saying she wouldn't let Cormac demean himself to work as a porter. He had Royal blood in his veins and was descended from the Kings of Ireland. I think Mrs Norton must have had her ear to the wall,' said Maureen.

'Mrs O'Neill must be mad,' Anne said in amazement. 'Poor Kathleen. She must hate her.'

'But she doesn't,' Maureen said. 'Mrs Norton said Kathleen and Cormac were both crying and saying, "Don't cry, Mammy. We love you. We'll never leave you." I wonder what the doctor and priest had been saying?'

'What can they do, Mo? *Someone* should help Kathleen. She doesn't want to live like that, I'm sure, although Cormac seems to like it.'

'Not much anyone can do, love, I'm afraid.'

'Why not?' asked Anne.

'Because Kathleen and Cormac are not children,' Maureen said. 'Kathleen's fifteen and the boy nearly eighteen. Then Mrs O'Neill seems normal enough to most people. She does two cleaning jobs and mends umbrellas so she just seems a hard-working woman, a bit overprotective of her children. You notice she did all that screaming *after* the priest and doctor had been.'

'Kathleen told me how hard she works to keep them,' Anne

said. 'Her mother does everything in the house too and just waits on them. She won't let them wash dishes or anything.'

'And when she dies they'll be helpless,' Maureen said with a sigh. 'Poor children – and poor woman. How long has she been a widow, Anne?'

'Years and years. Their father was drowned at sea when they were only babies, I think.'

'I'll say a prayer for them,' Maureen said, and Anne hugged her.

'I'm glad I live here, Mo. In this family, I mean.'

'Yes, we're very lucky,' Maureen said gently.

When Anne went to bed, her mind was full of Maureen's story about the O'Neills and pictures of Kathleen's sad face passed constantly through her mind. She thought of all the other families she knew and decided that none were as happy as her own and some were nearly as strange as the O'Neills.

Before she fell asleep Anne decided that the only thing she could do for Kathleen was to go as often as possible on Wednesdays to see her leave work and to say hello, even if Kathleen was rushed away by her mother afterwards. At least she would know that Anne had not forgotten her.

Anne had settled very happily in to her work in the shop and had become even more friendly with Sarah Redmond.

'You're a pair well met as far as giggling goes,' Mabel told them, but she smiled as she spoke. As long as the girls did their work and customers were not kept waiting and treated politely, Mabel was an indulgent superior. In the lulls between customers the three chatted together, and Mabel often gave the girls her views on life.

As Anne became known the young men in the queue began to flirt with her as they did with Sarah, and Mabel pretended to be shocked.

'If I'd been flirting at your age my mother would have had my life,' she declared. 'I don't know what you young girls are coming to.'

'I'll bet you did it without your mother knowing, Mabel,' Sarah teased her. 'You wouldn't encourage us otherwise.'

Michael Rourke still came every day for pies, but he had not asked Sarah out again and Mabel told her she should encourage him. 'He's just shy,' she said. 'He wouldn't have asked you out the last time if I hadn't tipped him the wink about that film.'

'I wouldn't have gone if I'd known,' Sarah exclaimed and Mabel told her she was foolish. 'Anne would've encouraged him, wouldn't you, Anne? You'd tell him you like George Raft.'

Anne still felt a little insecure and nervous of losing the job because she liked it so much, but she contradicted Mabel.

'No, I wouldn't. Not to the extent of telling him about a film and saying I wanted to see it,' she said. 'I think if he wants to ask Sarah out he should conquer his shyness to do it.'

She waited nervously for Mabel's reaction but Mabel only said, 'You two are living in a dream world. You'll learn.'

A few days later Sarah had gone to the other counter with a woman who had bought pies, then kept changing her mind about the cakes she wanted. Mabel came round to help Anne with the pie queue and seized the opportunity to have a few words with Michael when he reached the counter.

Anne was horrified to hear her telling him that *Rumba* was on in Crosby, and Sarah loved George Raft. Michael hung back and when Sarah came back to the pie counter asked if he could take her to see the film.

Anne was tempted to warn Sarah, but when her friend told her, starry-eyed, that Michael had asked her out, and soon afterwards confided that her mother and father had started courting when her mother was fifteen, Anne was unable to spoil her joy.

I'll make sure Mabel doesn't do it to me, Anne thought. I'm

not getting involved with any of these lads.

The shop was becoming busier every day and there was little time to talk as Christmas drew nearer, but Anne still enjoyed working there, even though on Fridays and Saturdays she and Sarah and Mabel stayed to lunch. They stayed in the storeroom only long enough to eat a pie and drink a cup of tea before returning to help the two in the shop deal with the hordes of customers, but on the first occasion this happened Anne was pleased to find an extra five shillings in her wage packet.

Mrs Dyson told Mabel to put three boxes of cakes away for the staff, and on Saturday Mr Dyson made a rare appearance in the shop to say gruffly, 'Ta, girls. You done well to manage that lot.'

To Anne the praise and the extra money in recognition of their work were all the sweeter because she still compared Dyson's with her last job.

'Catch Mr James doing that,' she told Sarah and Mabel. 'He thought we were kangaroos. All he ever said was "Jump to it".'

They laughed and Mabel said, 'All his slavedriving hasn't done him much good. His shop's closed, y'know.'

Anne's mother was alone when she reached home and Anne said in surprise, 'Where's everybody, Mum?'

'All at the pictures except Eileen and she's gone to the Roller Rink. Dad's at a parish meeting,' Julia said.

She spoke wearily and Anne asked if she was tired. 'I'm all right, love. I've been making the mincemeat,' she said. 'Your dinner's in the oven. Are you ready for it?' She made to rise but Anne stopped her.

'I can get my own dinner out,' she said. 'Look, Mum, Mrs Dyson told Mabel to make up a box of cakes for each of us before they all went, and Mabel asked what we liked. I asked for a cream horn for you. I know they're your favourites.'

'That's a good girl,' Julia said. 'I'll make a cup of tea when you've finished your dinner, and I'll have it then.'

She leaned back in her chair and closed her eyes, and Anne looked at her with a worried frown. She thought that she had never seen her mother look so exhausted but then she realised it was only on rare occasions that she and her mother were alone together. Perhaps her mother had looked tired on other occasions but she had failed to notice because other people were there?

As soon as she finished her meal Anne jumped up and insisted on making a pot of tea. 'Let me wait on you for a change,' she said.

'But you've been working hard all day, child,' her mother said. 'It's not right.'

'And I suppose you haven't?' Anne said. 'You do too much, Mum. We sell mincemeat in the shop, you know.'

'Oh, God bless us, that's only for people who are ill or unable,' her mother exclaimed. 'I haven't come to that yet, buying shop mincemeat.'

Afterwards Anne lay on the sofa, while her mother sat with her feet on the footstool, knitting, and they talked. Anne told her mother about the shop and about Mabel scheming to arrange dates for Sarah, and her mother said dubiously, 'I hope she's not doing anything like that for you, Anne?'

'Chance would be a fine thing,' Anne said, laughing. 'No, don't worry, Mum. I've been warned by seeing her in action for Sarah. She means well, though.'

'No doubt, but I don't think Sally Ward would thank her to be interfering like that,' Julia said. She told Anne some anecdotes of Sarah's grandmother, then went on to talk about the Misses Dolan.

'They miss you, love. Try to slip in to see them, Anne.'

'I'll go tomorrow,' she promised. 'And I'll go to see Billy Bolten too. I mean to go and see them, but the time just goes.'

'They know you haven't as much time now you're working,' her mother said. 'But their lives haven't changed even if yours has.'

Anne went to see the Misses Dolan the next day and spent an hour with them, admiring the lavender bags they were making and sniffing rapturously at the aroma of the Turkish cigarettes Miss Louisa smoked.

She realised that the sisters were looking at her and laughed. 'I'm sorry. I must look like one of the Bisto Kids,' she said. 'I love the smell of those cigarettes.'

Miss Louisa glanced at the fat oval cigarette which she smoked through a cigarette holder. 'I had to get a special holder for them,' she said. 'But I've always enjoyed them. My brother disliked the smell. He smoked gaspers.'

'Tony smokes Gold Flake, and Stephen and Maureen smoke Capstan Medium,' Anne said.

'Your father doesn't object to Maureen smoking?' Miss Dolan asked.

'I don't think so,' Anne said. 'After all, she's twenty-seven and all her friends smoke. When I start I'll smoke Turkish, I think.'

When she left the Dolans Anne went to see Billy Bolten. She found him greatly changed in the short time since she had seen him, and pathetically grateful for her visit.

Mrs Cullen, in whose house Billy had a room, told Anne that the old man had failed quite suddenly. 'Mind you, it's just weakness,' she said. 'He's not in any pain. It's just like a clock running down.'

Anne went again to see her old friend a few days later, taking him a quarter of a pound of his favourite humbugs and some of her mother's fruit cake. She was glad that she did when two days later she heard that he had died in his sleep.

Billy had never had any visitors or spoken of any family, so Mrs Cullen was astounded when a few days after his death a man and a woman arrived with a horse and cart.

'We've come for my poor uncle's things,' the woman said, dabbing her eyes with a black-bordered handkerchief.

'Your uncle?' Mrs Cullen gasped. 'He never spoke of a niece. No one ever came to see him.'

'He fell out with me dad,' the woman said glibly. 'But we're his next of kin and we want his stuff.'

'You can't just walk in and take his things,' Mrs Cullen protested.

'Why not?' the man said aggressively, and the woman added, 'I suppose you had your eye on them?'

'Indeed I didn't,' Mrs Cullen said, but another man had appeared, and before she could gather her wits, the cart was swiftly loaded with Billy's furniture and goods and driven away. Too late she realised that she had no proof that they had any connection with her lodger. The undertaker told her that this form of theft had happened to others also.

Chapter Eleven

Anne watched her mother anxiously, wondering that others in the family were not more worried about her. Her hair had gone grey at the front, and to Anne it seemed that she had never before looked so tired and drawn.

She mentioned it to Eileen one day when they were stoning raisins for the bunloaves and their mother had gone upstairs.

'Don't you think Mum looks ill and tired, Eil?' she asked, but Eileen shrugged.

'It *is* Christmas after all,' she said. 'There's a lot more to do.'

'I'm surprised Maureen hasn't noticed it,' Anne said.

Eileen laughed. 'Our Maureen's in a world of her own these days,' she said cheerfully. 'I think she must be in love.'

'Who isn't?' Anne said. 'Sarah from the shop is in a dream world – although she still pulls her weight at work,' she added hastily.

'*I'm* not and you're not, are you?' Eileen said.

'No, but I thought you might be, all the boyfriends you've got.'

Eileen laughed again. 'That's just what they are, friends who happen to be boys,' she said. 'Except when I go out in a foursome with Theresa and two lads. Then it's all romantic and lovey dovey.'

'I can't imagine you being romantic,' Anne said frankly.

'Watch it!' Eileen exclaimed. 'I can be as romantic as the next if I want to. It's in the air when I'm out with Theresa.'

Anne felt comforted by Eileen's attitude. Perhaps her mother *was* just tired because of the extra work at Christmas, and surely her father and Maureen would have noticed if she was ill? Until Eileen spoke of it she had not noticed how dreamy Maureen was at times, but when she made a joking remark about it to her sister she was amazed by her reaction.

She had spoken to her twice and Maureen seemed too lost in thought to hear her, but when Anne said flippantly: 'What is it, Mo? Love's young dream?' Maureen blushed and said furiously, 'What's that got to do with you? Mind your own business.'

Anne could never recall being spoken to like that before by Maureen, and said huffily, 'All right, keep your hair on. It was only a joke.'

Maureen put her hand on Anne's arm. 'Sorry, love. I'm touchy these days,' she said.

'That sounds more like you,' Anne said, smiling at her, but she thought that Eileen must be right. Only being in love could account for Maureen's changes of mood, from dreamy happiness to sadness.

Sarah was also sad, as her affair with Michael made no progress, but on Christmas Eve he came into the shop and gave her a Christmas card and a brooch. Sarah was delighted to receive them but told Anne that she wished she had known about them sooner so that she could have bought a gift for him.

'Pity he didn't have the nous to give it to her sooner,' Mabel said to Anne, out of Sarah's hearing, and Anne agreed.

'Michael seems a bit of a wet Echo, doesn't he?' she said. 'I think Sarah deserves better. I like Dennis more.'

'Yes, but bank clerks can't get serious too soon with a girl,' Mabel said. 'The bank won't let them marry until they're twenty-six, in case when they have a home to keep they get the bank's money mixed up with their own.'

Anne admired Sarah more and more and felt that only the best was good enough for her. A few days before Christmas an ex-servicemen's band stood in the road outside the shop to play. There was one man playing a mouth organ, another badly scarred playing a flute, and a blind man and a man with one leg singing.

The weather was bitterly cold and Sarah said impulsively, 'Can I take pies to them, Mabel? I'll pay for them.'

'Take them damaged ones. You can have them for nothing,' she said, but Sarah looked doubtful.

'I wouldn't like them to think they were getting the throw-outs.'

Mabel answered impatiently, 'For God's sake, Sarah, they'd have to break them to eat them.'

Sarah smiled but Anne noticed that she dived into the store-room for her purse and carefully selected pies with only the rim of the crust broken. She put them in separate bags and the men received them gratefully and went round the corner to eat them. Mabel gave an expressive shrug. 'That's her grandfather's influence,' she said.

'My dad and uncle know him and they say he's a very good man,' Anne said.

'He is,' Mabel said emphatically. 'But I'm just saying that's why Sarah's like that. Her grandad always made them call a man "Mister" if he was out of work and down on his luck, she told me once.'

'I always called Billy Bolten "Billy",' Anne said guiltily. 'I suppose it wasn't very respectful.'

'I don't suppose he minded,' Mabel said. 'Did you hear any more about those people who took his furniture?'

'No. Mrs Cullen was blaming herself, but everyone said it wasn't her fault. They just took her by surprise and the police said they were professional thieves. It didn't matter anyway because Billy knew nothing about it. He was already dead so it couldn't hurt him.'

Sarah came back into the shop and went through to the storeroom with her purse and Mabel whispered to Anne, 'She'll have given them what she saved by not paying for the pies. No use trying to help her.'

On Christmas Eve the shop was never empty from opening time until just after five o'clock when everything had been sold. Mr and Mrs Dyson came into the shop and Mabel said, 'I didn't think we'd shift all that. I didn't think there was the money about but it'll be people's Christmas Clubs and Tontines.'

'Nothing left on our hands anyway,' Mrs Dyson said with satisfaction. She produced a bottle of port and glasses. 'We had a drink with the bakehouse staff and now we'll have one with you,' she said, and also gave them each a Christmas card containing a ten-shilling note.

A combination of tiredness and port wine made Anne feel quite lightheaded as she walked home, and Sarah, who was with her, carrying the card and brooch from Michael, seemed speechless with happiness.

Most of the family were in when Anne arrived home and the house was filled with the savoury aroma of roasting pork. Mrs Fitzgerald always ordered a turkey and a leg of pork for Christmas for her large family, and cooked the pork on Christmas Eve.

When Anne arrived and showed her gift of ten shillings, her mother said, 'I don't doubt you've worked hard today, love. Why don't you go and lie down and I'll call you for Midnight Mass?'

Anne agreed to go and Stephen said jokingly, 'I think I'll do the same. Take myself out of temptation. The smell of the pork is driving me mad.'

Christmas Eve was a day of fasting and abstinence and the Fitzgeralds were unable to eat meat, but always had some of the pork when they returned from Midnight Mass. Anne said, 'I'm sure I'll enjoy it more when we come back from Mass. I'm too tired to eat now anyway.'

She fell asleep as soon as she lay down, but with the resilience of youth felt completely refreshed when Maureen woke her at eleven-thirty.

It was the first time that all the family had attended Midnight Mass. In previous years the younger children had gone to Mass on Christmas morning with their mother, even after Anne as the youngest had stopped believing in Father Christmas. This year Anne felt that she was now accepted as an adult by the family.

Even Uncle Fred who was at Midnight Mass with Shaun and Theresa and the twins made no comment on the fact that Anne was with the family, except to say, 'You're able to come to this Mass now, Julia. Carrie still has to stay back with Carmel and Grandma. We'll see you all on Boxing Day.'

Pat always provided ale for the males in the family to drink with their Christmas dinner and cherry wine for his wife and daughters, and this year for the first time Anne was included.

Her father poured her a glass of cherry wine mixed with water then raised his glass. 'To the family' he said. 'All of us here and the two who are not with us, Patrick and Joe.' Anne saw the momentary sadness on her mother's face and leaned forward and clinked her glass against her mother's, smiling at her and receiving a smile in return.

'Will you look at that now?' her father exclaimed. 'To the manner born. I hope that's the first drink you've ever had, queen.'

'No, I had a glass of port in the shop last night,' Anne said with a blasé air that caused laughter from everyone.

After the dinner was cleared away and the dishes washed and put away presents were exchanged among the family then Julia lay down on the sofa and Pat went up to lie on his bed.

The others went into the parlour where a bright fire was burning. Eileen drifted over to the piano but she played softly, so that her parents were not disturbed. The rest of the family were content to lounge about, examining their presents and talking. One of

Anne's presents was a box of chocolates and she opened it and passed it round, but everyone said it was too soon after dinner.

'No Selection Box this year, Anne,' Tony teased with a smile.

'No, all that seems a long time ago,' she said.

'Hark at Methuselah,' Stephen broke in. 'I suppose methylated spirits is more your taste now.'

'It's true,' Anne said indignantly. 'It does seem a long time since I left school. I said that in my letter to Joe and when he wrote back he said it was because so much has happened to me this year.'

'That's right,' Maureen agreed. 'Did you manage to see Kathleen O'Neill again, Anne?'

'Twice,' she said. 'But she was with her mother and brother every time, so we just said hello.'

'I wonder what Joe's doing just now,' Stephen said idly.

'Probably working hard,' Terry said. 'Rob Sykes' father is on a cruise ship like Joe and he says there's all sorts of festivities for the passengers but it just means more work for the crew.'

'I wish he could have got home for Christmas,' Maureen said with a sigh.'

'I tell you what,' Stephen said, 'it's strange Brendan didn't come home for Christmas. He's a real mystery man, isn't he?'

'He just seems to have vanished into thin air,' Tony agreed. 'Perhaps he'll turn up for the party tomorrow.'

'I think that's the last place he'd want to show up,' Stephen said. 'Imagine the comments from Uncle Fred.'

'I'm looking forward to the party,' Eileen said, leaving the piano and coming to sit on the rug before the fire. 'It's always a good do at the Andersons', and I'll be able to use my Christmas presents.'

She had received bath salts and soap from Maureen, Californian Poppy perfume from Tony, and an embroidered blouse from her parents, among other presents. 'I'll look like a gypsy and smell like a flower garden,' she declared amid laughter.

Maureen slipped away into the kitchen after a while and came back to beckon Anne and Eileen. 'Mum's asleep,' she whispered. 'I think she needs it so we'll get the tea ready quietly before she wakes up.'

The three girls crept about laying the table with pickles and celery and bread and butter and bunloaf and mince pies. Pat Fitzgerald came downstairs and Maureen met him in the hall and spirited him through to the back kitchen to cut platesful of turkey and pork and ham.

Just as the preparations were completed Julia woke up, declaring that she felt better for the sleep and delighted that everything had been done.

After tea she was installed in an armchair near the parlour fire with a footstool for her feet while the family gathered round the piano. They sang Silent Night and Away in a Manger, then the Irish ballads that their mother loved.

When they sang Kathleen Mavourneen Anne thought of Kathleen O'Neill and remembered her saying that the Kathleen of the song was not a girl. 'It's about Ireland really, Kathleen na Houlihan, from the days when people daren't sing songs praising their country.'

What sort of Christmas was Kathleen having? Anne wondered. She had hoped to see the family at Midnight Mass, but thought it more likely that Mrs O'Neill had taken them to the six o'clock Mass, to have them safely home before most people were about.

She looked over at her mother who was lying back with her eyes closed, looking white and tired, but as though she felt Anne's eyes on her Julia opened her eyes and smiled and Anne was reassured.

Hailstones beat against the windows but Anne felt warm and happy safe in the circle of her family. Maureen's arm was around her waist and her father's hand on her shoulder. I like being grown up, she thought suddenly, looking ahead to her growing friendship with Sarah, to flirting with the young men in the shop, and being included in more outings with the family.

The family were all due to return to work the day after Boxing Day, but Maureen woke Eileen and Anne to tell them she was staying at home. 'Mum's had a bad night and her temperature is 101,' she said. 'Dad's gone for the doctor. Will you take a note to the shop for me on your way to work, Anne?'

She had to leave for work before the doctor arrived, and spent a miserable morning. Mabel had spent a happy Christmas with relatives of her late husband, and Sarah declared that her Christmas was the happiest she had ever known.

They told Anne not to worry about her mother, she was probably just rundown, and asked about her Christmas.

Anne knew that they were trying to be kind and to take her mind off her worry about her mother. She tried to remember items to tell them but found it hard to concentrate, or to serve customers.

Mabel sent her to the storeroom to cut squares of tissue paper, and Anne was free to think. To keep her mind from her fears she thought back over Christmas. It had been strange, she thought. On the surface very enjoyable, but with the worry about her mother like a dark undercurrent beneath.

At times she had felt grown up, at other times like a child again. I'm just betwixt and between as Mum would say, she thought, but that brought her mind back to her fears again.

She was glad when her lunch hour came and she could race home for news of her mother. Maureen said that the doctor had been and there was some internal trouble causing pain, but mainly she was simply overtired.

'He said that she must have felt unwell but struggled to carry on normally, and now Nature was taking its toll,' Maureen said. 'She has to stay in bed and rest.'

'He's sure it's not TB, isn't he?' Anne asked fearfully.

'Of course not. What put that in your head?' Maureen exclaimed.

'That's what most people die of, isn't it?' Anne said, and Maureen said crossly, 'Don't talk soft. Mum's not going to die.'

'A woman in the shop said her daughter had a high temperature and I know she died of TB,' Anne said.

Maureen looked at Anne's worried face and slipped her arm round her sister's waist. 'Lots of things can cause a high temperature, love,' she said gently. 'The doctor said Mum's a bit anaemic as well so she'll have to have lightly cooked liver.'

'She hates liver, doesn't she? But at least she can have it cooked,' Anne said. 'A girl in our class had pernicious anaemia and she had to eat platesful of raw liver.'

'Did it cure her?' Maureen asked.

'I don't know. She left to go into hospital and didn't come back, at least not before I left,' Anne said.

She crept in to see her mother but Julia was deeply asleep and Maureen said that the doctor had told her that sleep was the best medicine for her mother at present. Anne went back to work feeling much more cheerful.

Later when Julia awoke she seemed to be in pain and asked Maureen to bring her a bottle labelled Female Complaints which was in the cupboard in the bedroom.

Maureen hesitated. 'The doctor asked what you took, Mum, and when I told him he told me to throw it away.'

'You didn't, I hope?' Julia said in alarm.

'Not without telling you,' Maureen said. 'But the doctor gave me pills for you to take instead. He said the medicine was only opium and you could get addicted to it.' Her mother's face suddenly twisted with pain. 'Get me the medicine, love,' she said. 'I'll try the pills later.'

Maureen brought the black bottle and measured out a dose into a glass. Her mother drank it thankfully. 'There's three more bottles in the cupboard, Mum,' Maureen said with a worried frown when her mother had taken the medicine and was lying back on her pillows.

'I know. The fellow's not always in the market, so I get some whenever I see him,' Julia said. 'Sometimes these quacks just disappear and I don't want to be without it.' Maureen still looked worried and her mother patted her hand.

'Don't worry, Mo,' she said. 'Never mind what the doctor says. I know what eases me and I only take it when I need it. Don't say anything to Dad or anyone.'

Maureen promised. Her mother slept again and when she woke said that she felt much better, but the doctor had insisted that she must rest. Carrie had called and said that she would come the next day so that Maureen could return to work, and Dora Duggan had been engaged to come for the following weeks.

Dora Duggan was a tiny person with a curved spine which gave her a hump on her back, but she was a sweet-natured woman and an efficient housewife. She had run the house for a few weeks before, when Julia's babies had been born. She and Julia greeted each other like old friends. 'I wish it was a baby you were in bed with,' Dora said, and Julia laughed and agreed with her.

As soon as Pat's business had improved Julia had been able to send out most of the family washing, and now a woman was engaged to come in for the rough cleaning.

Julia was able to get up after two weeks and rest on the sofa while Dora ran the house, and after three weeks when Dora had to leave for a maternity case she had been booked for, Julia was able to resume her place in the household.

Anne was in the kitchen one evening when Maureen came in and said that her Aunt Minnie had said that she should stay at home and help her mother, instead of working in the wool shop.

'Is she on that tack again?' Julia exclaimed. She took Maureen's hand and said earnestly, 'Pay no attention, love. I wouldn't let you. You're entitled to live your own life and I'm all right. I only want you to be happy, pet.'

She was looking into Maureen's face and Anne could see tears trembling on her sister's lashes. She said tremulously, 'I *am* happy, Mum.'

Anne felt that more was implied than was spoken, especially when her mother said gently, 'Half a loaf is better than no bread at all, love.'

Anne was sure there was some mystery, but before anything more was said Terry and Stephen came in.

All the family were doing as much as possible to help their mother, but Stephen grumbled to Maureen one day, 'I've never worked so hard in my life. I didn't know having a cleaning lady meant that you had to clean the house before she came.'

Anne laughed, knowing that Stephen was only joking, but Maureen flared at him: 'So it's too much trouble to pick things off the floor in your bedroom? I suppose you'd like Mum to go back to doing it even if it kills her.'

'Hold on,' Stephen said indignantly. 'It was only a joke, for Godsake.' Anne expected Maureen to smile and apologise but she only said sharply, 'I don't like your idea of a joke, then,' and walked away.

'What's eating her?' Stephen asked Anne. 'One minute she's as nice as pie and the next she bites your head off.'

'Perhaps she's just worried about Mum,' Anne said.

'We've *all* been worried about Mum, but she's better now, isn't she? I heard her singing The Rose of Tralee in the kitchen last night,' Stephen said. 'You knew I was only joking about Mrs Bennet, didn't you?'

'Yes, but I think you were right,' Anne said with a grin. 'Eileen and I have never been so tidy. Sometimes I think I'm in the wrong bedroom when I walk in.'

Although Anne joked with Stephen she wondered what was wrong with Maureen. It wasn't worry about her mother. As Stephen said, their mother was better now, and whatever it was with Maureen her mother knew about it. It was a mystery, Anne thought, and gave up trying to solve it.

Chapter Twelve

Although Anne was happier about her mother's health she was distressed about Sarah's unhappiness. Her grandfather Lawrie Ward had been ill since New Year's Day, and had become steadily worse.

On the night of 10 January there was one of the worst gales in living memory. Anne picked her way to work through broken slates and chimney pots and debris of every kind. Mabel was late in arriving at the shop, and Sarah even later.

When she arrived she told them that her grandparents had been awake for most of the night. 'Grandad was much worse,' she said. 'And Grandma was up nearly all night with him. She came over for my dad to go for the doctor as soon as it was light this morning.'

'He'll be all right,' Mabel comforted her. 'A night like last night would upset anyone, sick or well.'

'I wish she'd come over sooner instead of having the worry on her own all night. We're only across the street,' Sarah said. 'I went to see them before I came here and Grandad was asleep. The doctor increased his tablets and said he must be kept warm and quiet.'

'He could have no better nurse than your grandma,' Mabel said. 'He'll be all right, you'll see.'

Sarah seemed comforted but the following day a message was

brought to the shop that Sarah's grandfather had died during the night. Mabel was in tears and Anne wept for Sarah's sorrow, although she had not known Lawrie Ward. She was surprised to see Mrs Dyson and the bakehouse girls in tears too.

'The world will be a poorer place without Lawrie Ward,' Mrs Dyson wept, and Mabel cried with her.

'No one knows how much good he's done,' she said, and the bakehouse girls both told of people Lawrie had helped.

'A woman in our street got her parish stopped, and he went with her to the Board of Guardians and got it back for her,' one girl said. The other girl told how he had helped her grandmother.

'My nin said she'd have gone out of her mind without him,' she said. 'My grandad dropped dead and she was left with five little children and not a ha'penny in her pocket. She didn't know where to turn but someone fetched Lawrie Ward and he done everything for her.'

'And Sally too,' Mabel said. 'God comfort her the way she's comforted others. When my poor Willie died . . .' She could say no more but turned away, sobbing.

The news had spread and Anne was surprised at the number of customers who were distressed by it. Even the topic of the storm which had seemed so important was forgotten as people talked of Lawrie Ward and all he had done.

'All done on the quiet. No fuss,' several people said to Mabel, and she said, 'Aye. He let his deeds speak for him.'

Anne, Mabel, the bakehouse staff and the Dysons contributed for a wreath, and Dennis the bank clerk collected among the customers for one. The fact that it was Dennis and not Michael made Anne angry, and she hoped Sarah would not be hurt that he had not made the effort.

Mabel said she was going to the house to offer condolences, and Anne would have liked to see Sarah to add hers but was too shy.

'Tell Sarah she can stay off for as long as she can help at home,' Mrs Dyson said. 'You can manage without her while we're slack, can't you, Mabel?'

She agreed and Mrs Dyson added, 'Tell her her wages will be here just the same. In fact, take her wages with you, Mabel. There's all sorts of expenses at a time like this.'

People are good, Anne thought, then it occurred to her that it was the goodness of Lawrie Ward and his wife which had spread to touch everyone with some of their compassion.

Anne was left in charge of the shop while Mabel went to attend the funeral with Mrs Dyson and one of the bakehouse girls.

'Just call Albert if you can't manage, love,' Mrs Dyson said, but Anne found that it was easy to serve the small number of customers. She wondered if Michael had gone to the church service or followed the cortège to the cemetery, but Mabel said she had not seen him.

'I've never seen such a crowd,' she said. 'And on such a bitter cold day too. Everyone from real nobs to the poorest of the poor. It must have been a consolation to the family to see how he was respected. That poor lad, the grandson, looked brokenhearted.'

'You mean John?' Anne asked. 'Sarah said he thinks the world of his grandad. He lived with his grandparents during the war while his dad was in the trenches.'

'Sally Ward looked sad but very dignified,' Mabel said. 'It'll be hard for her. Someone said they've been married for forty-five years.'

Sarah came back to the shop wearing a black dress and looking pale and sad. Anne suspected that to add to her misery about her grandfather's death she was also disappointed by Michael's behaviour. He still came for pies, but Anne never heard him say anything to console Sarah and she seemed to be trying to avoid him.

The other young men who came in the shop joked with Sarah

143

to try to cheer her up, but they seemed more at ease with Anne. A young man who worked nearby as a carpenter came for pies every day, and always manoeuvred to be served by her.

He told Anne that his name was Tom Dodd and that he knew her brothers, and several times brought sweets or hot chestnuts to her. Anne was pleased and flattered by his attention, and although he had red hair and freckles, and was not nearly as handsome as Michael, told herself that character counted for more than looks in a man.

She said nothing to Sarah about Tom while Sarah was so unhappy and Mabel, usually so eagle-eyed, was preoccupied by what was happening in London.

She arrived at the shop with her eyes red from crying after the death of King George V on 20 January.

'I cried all night,' she told Anne and Sarah. 'I thought it was lovely the way the man on the wireless said: "The King's life is drawing peacefully to its close." I loved my King.'

Anne felt sorry for Mabel who seemed to have few people to love, and Sarah was grateful for her kindness in her own sorrow, so both girls listened sympathetically to Mabel's outpouring of grief for the King.

The following week Tom brought Anne hot chestnuts from a nearby barrow and a photograph frame which he had made for her. He asked her to go to the cinema with him on the following Saturday and Anne joyfully agreed.

When she announced at home that she was going to the Futurist with a boy her father said sternly, 'What do you mean, you're going with him? You haven't asked me, and I'll have something to say about that. A lad we know nothing about.'

'He knows our lads and he comes in the shop,' she said. 'I've known him for ages.'

'Ages? You haven't been at the shop for ages,' her father said. 'No, you're far too young to be going out alone with any

Tom, Dick or Harry who asks you.'

'I'm nearly sixteen,' she protested.

'That's what I mean. You'll be a lot older than that before I consider any of these capers,' her father said grimly.

When her father spoke in that tone the family knew that it would be impossible to make him change his mind, and Anne went to Maureen for sympathy.

To her surprise she found that her sister agreed. 'Dad's only concerned with what's best for you,' she said. 'You *are* too young to go out alone with a boy. You should go round in a crowd.'

'Sarah went out with Michael on his own,' Anne said sulkily.

'Yes, and it's only brought her unhappiness from what you say,' Maureen said. 'And she's older than you.'

'Only a few months,' Anne said. 'I'm going to feel such a fool, having to say I can't go. My dad won't let me.'

'If he's a decent lad he'll respect you all the more because your family look after you,' Maureen said. 'It's easy to get a bad name if you go out with just anyone.'

'Tom's perfectly respectable,' Anne said indignantly. 'Our lads know him, but Dad didn't even ask them about him.'

'Dad still thinks of you as a little girl,' Maureen said, smiling.

Anne dreaded telling Tom why she was unable to keep the date, and she was amazed when he only said, 'I didn't realise you weren't sixteen yet. Your Dad's right to watch over you. I'll get your Tony to put in a word for me when you're older.'

Although Anne was angry with her father she was amused by his efforts to console her. On Friday night he brought her a whipped cream walnut, her favourite sweet, and two pink sugar mice.

'Sugar mice!' Anne exclaimed to Maureen. 'Are they supposed to make up for a date with Tom?'

'Take them in the spirit in which they were given,' Maureen advised. 'What did Tom say?'

'He agreed with Dad,' Anne admitted. 'He said he'd ask me again when I was older. He didn't realise I wasn't sixteen yet, but I know a girl who was *married* when she was sixteen. Do you honestly think it's too young, Mo?'

'Yes, I do,' Maureen said. 'People often marry too young and for the wrong reasons, and it's a life sentence. They pay all their lives for their mistake and so do others.' She stared unseeingly out of the window, so Anne went quietly away.

In normal circumstances Julia and Carrie visited each other several times a week. Partly because of the bad weather but chiefly because of Julia's illness and Carrie's need to be with her mother, they had scarcely seen each other since Christmas.

Eileen went frequently to the Andersons' house because of her friendship with Theresa and she told her mother that Grandma Houlihan often criticised her and Theresa and told them that they would come to a bad end because of their dates with boys.

'You know what Theresa's like,' she said. 'She doesn't take any notice, but sometimes Aunt Carrie has been crying because of Grandma's remarks.'

Pat confirmed this one night. 'I saw Fred in The Volunteer,' he said. 'Your ma's turned out cantankerous, he says, and he'd come out for a bit of peace. The old lady's nearly driving them mad.'

'Eileen says she's getting at them about Theresa,' Julia said.

'She's getting at them about *everything*, it seems,' said Pat. 'Fred says he can see where Minnie gets her character from.'

'Dear God, I'd better go down there tomorrow,' Julia said.

'Get yourself well wrapped up if you do, and watch your step. It's still bitter out and icy underfoot,' Pat advised her, but she said that Anne would go with her. 'It's the half day closing tomorrow.'

The next day Anne and her mother carefully picked their way

to Carrie's house. They found Grandma Houlihan sitting close to the fire wrapped in two crocheted shawls.

'How are you, Ma?' Julia asked, and for the next hour her mother told her. The list of complaints seemed endless, and when Anne stood up to help her aunt who was making tea, her grandma said sharply, 'Mannerly children you're rearing, Julia, God knows, that walk away while their grandmother's talking.'

'She's going to help Carrie,' Julia said.

'Oh, Carrie, Carrie, that's all I hear,' her mother said. 'I'm of no account, but our Blessed Lord said: "The last shall be first". I've lived too long to suit them, Julia, but never mind. The draughts in this house will soon kill me and I'll be glad to go to my reward.'

'That's foolish talk, Ma,' Julia said. 'If you feel the cold why don't you stay in bed? It's the warmest place with the weather we're having. Pat says we should all hibernate until the spring.'

'All very well if you've got a comfortable bed,' her mother said. 'It's like lying on a bed of nails on that mattress and the draughts from the door and window enough to cut the head off you.'

'It's the worst weather for I don't know how long,' Julia said. 'D'you know the sea froze at Southport and there were icicles three foot long from a broken gutter on a house in Low Hill?'

'I thought you hadn't been out,' Grandma Houlihan said suspiciously. 'Carrie said you were ill and that's why you haven't been to see me.'

'I *have* been ill,' Julia said. 'But I'm better now, thank God. I'd be better still if only the weather would pick up.'

Grandma drank the tea that Carrie brought and then fell asleep, and Julia and Carrie and Anne crept out to the back kitchen and gathered round the bright fire there.

'Honest to God, Julia, I don't know what's got into Ma lately,' Carrie said. 'She's always had her odd little ways, but now she's impossible. Nothing suits her and she's always causing trouble in the family.'

'Pat said you're having your own share with her,' Julia said sympathetically.

'I heard her going on to you about her bed,' Carrie said. 'She'd always said it was very comfortable but when she started complaining Fred bought her a new mattress but then she said the old one was more comfortable. Luckily we'd put it in the attic so Fred and Shaun brought it down again.'

'You're very patient and so is Fred,' Julia said. 'For so many years too. I'm sure she appreciates it really.'

'But she never stops picking on the young ones. I know we always had our tiffs in the family but this is different. Of course it's like water off a duck's back with the twins, and our Theresa says she doesn't care but I'm sure she does. Shaun just bangs out and Carmel answers her back and that's another fault. I'm nearly distracted one way and another,' said Carrie.

As Anne and her mother walked home, Anne said, 'Aunt Carrie seems at the end of her tether, doesn't she?'

'Yes, I think it's time we took our turn with Grandma,' said Julia. 'I haven't been well enough lately but I'm grand now, thank God.'

Soon preparations were being made for Grandma Houlihan to come to live with the Fitzgeralds. Julia had talked to Pat when she returned home after her visit and he had agreed that Carrie and Fred had done their share and that he and Julia should assume the care of her mother.

Carrie had not been so easy to persuade. She felt that Julia was not yet strong enough, and that her mother might be hurt if she was suddenly asked to leave the Andersons' after so many years, no matter how diplomatically it was suggested.

The perfect excuse came when Carrie became bedridden with sciatica, especially as it was caused by her mother.

A window cleaner usually did the outside of the Andersons' windows but because of the bad weather he had not been for several weeks. Grandma Houlihan had decided to stay in bed for most of the day, and complained constantly about the state of the windows.

'Bad enough to have to stay in this bed, but to have nothing to look at but those dirty windows all day . . . I'd have been ashamed to let my windows get in that state. If only I had my health and strength I'd do something about them.'

Goaded beyond reason by her moaning, Carrie sat out on the windowsill to clean the outside of the window. The stone of the windowsill was icy, and the cold seemed to strike through to her flesh while a bitter wind froze her fingers and face.

Within hours she was suffering with earache and then her old enemy sciatica struck. She lay in bed unable to move and in agonising pain.

Fred and the rest of her family were furious when they found out the reason for her affliction. 'You sat out on the windowsill in this weather?' he said. 'Carrie, you must be mad.'

'I was driven mad,' she said, moaning with pain as she attempted to move.

Fred told Julia and Pat about it when they came to see Carrie, alerted by Eileen.

'I can't speak civilly to that old faggot,' he said forcefully. 'I'm sorry, Julia. I know she's your mother but when I see the pain Carrie's in I can't help it.'

Julia went to see her mother and told her that while Carrie was in bed it would be better if she came to stay with her family.

'We'll bring all your statues and anything you want, Ma, and we've got a warm bedroom ready for you,' she said.

She said nothing of the shift round that had been necessary to make room for her mother, and her mother asked no questions but simply decided that she would be more comfortable with Julia.

She said nothing to Carrie or Fred about the ten years of care she had received from them, only said that the sciatica was a judgement on Carrie for her laxness with Theresa.

'It's people like her who get religion a bad name,' Fred said, but Julia said softly, '*We* appreciate what you and Carrie and all your family have done for her, Fred,' and Pat shook his hand.

'You've been a trouper,' he said. 'I only hope we can be half as patient.'

When the time came for Grandma Houlihan to leave the Andersons' Fred relented and kissed her and told her that she would be welcome to come back when Carrie was better.

'I think this winter has got us all down,' he said, and later to Pat when they were in the pub he said that Grandma was 'not a bad old bird, really.'

'I still say that you and Carrie have been Trojans,' Pat said. 'It won't be so bad for us because we've come fresh to it, but you've had nearly ten years.'

'We used to get on like a house on fire, in spite of her religious mania,' Fred said, laughing heartily. 'It's only this last year or so we've rubbed each other up the wrong way. She'll enjoy the change of scene with you and she's very fond of all your family.'

'She hasn't lived with them at close quarters yet,' Pat said with a grin.

Anne still felt resentful about being forbidden to go out with Tom but enjoyed the repartee with the other young men. Sarah was upset because Michael had asked her to go to the cinema only a few weeks after her grandfather's death.

'He knows I'm in mourning,' she said to Anne. 'My grandma says my grandfather didn't think people should feel obliged to mourn, but I *want* to. I certainly don't feel like going to the pictures and I thought he'd understand that.'

'Perhaps he thought it would cheer you up?' Anne suggested.

'He doesn't know me very well then,' Sarah said. 'It's as bad as Mabel with her daily dose of news about deaths in the neighbourhood.'

Anne smiled. 'She does it for the same reason,' she said. 'She thinks it might make you feel better to know that others are bereaved too. I know it's daft but as my Grandma Fitzgerald used to say: "There's nowt so queer as folk." At least it gives us a break from Royalty.'

Sarah smiled ruefully. 'Do you know, she's been five times to see that Pathé News where they showed the King's funeral?'

'Everyone in Everton must have heard her tell about the cross falling from the State crown as the gun carriage bumped over the tramlines.'

'And Gypsy Rose Lee's prediction that the Prince of Wales or rather King Edward VIII would be King but would never be crowned.'

'I suppose if he has so much as a cold they'll expect him to die,' Sarah said.

'I can't understand why Mabel's so obsessed with Royalty,' Anne commented, but Sarah said tolerantly, 'She hasn't much else in her life. Hardly any relations.'

Anne talked to Maureen about Mabel that evening. 'Strange how some people have hardly any relations and others have almost too many, like us,' she said. 'Even Sarah hasn't many. Her father was an only child, and her mother only has one sister who lives in America. Sarah doesn't like her.'

'How does she know, if the aunt lives in America?' Maureen said.

'Apparently she came home last year. Sarah liked her husband but said her aunt was very vain and selfish.'

'She won't see much of her anyway if she lives in America,' Maureen said. 'Do you think Sarah's getting over her loss?'

'It's a bit soon, isn't it?' Anne said. 'She was upset because

ELIZABETH MURPHY

Michael asked her to go to the pictures. Not very sensitive, is he?
And she said her brother was very bitter about all the fuss about
the King's funeral. He says his grandfather was more worthy of
all that palaver.'

'I thought his grandfather had a wonderful funeral,' Maureen
said. 'From what I've heard, I'd be proud if I was shown half
that respect when I died.'

'Oh, don't, Mo!' Anne exclaimed. 'Don't talk like that.'

'Let's talk about something nice instead,' her sister said.
'Bridie came to see Mum today and gave her a lovely bit of news.
She's going to have a baby.'

'Bridie is? I'm made up,' Anne said joyfully.

'So am I,' said Maureen. She looked doubtfully at Anne. 'I
suppose you understand about babies?'

Anne blushed. 'I thought they came in the nurse's bag until
just before I left school,' she said. 'But a girl in the class told me
that they grow inside their mother. I thought she was having me
on at first.'

'I didn't know until after I left, and neither did Eileen,' Maureen
said. 'That girl must have been very forward.'

'She said her *mother* told her,' Anne said. 'Imagine Mum
telling us.'

'Don't tell her I told you,' Maureen said. 'She's very reserved
about such things. She only told me for – for a special reason.'

Anne guessed that the special reason had something to do with
the mystery she sensed surrounding Maureen, but her sister said
no more. The news about Bridie had cheered Anne, and she told
Sarah hoping it would have the same effect on her but warned
her not to mention it to Mabel.

'I don't know whether Bridie wants everyone to know,' she
said. 'My mum doesn't know that I know. She hasn't mentioned
it to me – she might think I don't know anything about babies.'

'Mabel would probably say she was forty when she found out,'

Sarah said with a grin. 'I'm made up for your aunt though, Anne. She deserves to be happy, doesn't she?'

'Yes. It's nice to hear some cheerful news, isn't it? This winter seems to be lasting forever. I'm really fed up.'

A few days later she felt even more despondent. The firm where Tom worked closed down, and he stopped coming to the shop for pies.

'I suppose that's the last I'll see of him,' she told Sarah. 'He didn't even come to say goodbye.'

'He didn't have any warning though, did he?' Sarah said. 'Their cards and wages were sent to them on Sunday.'

A few days later Tom called at the shop and told Anne that he was searching for another job, but so far without success. 'The firm played a dirty trick on us, I think,' he said. 'We got no warning at all, but they must have known it was closing before we left work at midday on Saturday.'

He continued to call into the shop at intervals, seeming more and more depressed about his prospects of finding another job. Eventually he told Anne that the only job he had been able to obtain was in Scotland and he would have to move there.

'I don't want to leave Liverpool, but anything's better than being out of work,' he said.

'You'll feel at home there with your red hair,' Anne joked, hoping to cheer him up, but he still looked gloomy.

He asked her to write to him, and said he would wait for her to grow up, which annoyed her, but she replied to his letters when they came.

The bitter weather continued and everyone seemed down-hearted. Trade was slack and Mrs Dyson said it was always the same. 'You do well before Christmas,' she said, 'then afterwards nobody has any money and the shop's empty.'

'And the customers we *do* have, every one of them leaves the door open,' Mabel grumbled. 'In the summer they close it and in the winter they leave it wide open.'

Anne and Sarah agreed, but while Mabel and Mrs Dyson talked Sarah said to Anne, 'My grandma gave me Grandad's books last night. I was reading one of the books of poetry and I came across "The West Wind" by Shelley. Do you know it?'

'Not off by heart,' Anne said. 'But I remember some lines from it.'

'Do you remember the last line?' Sarah asked. '"If Winter comes, can Spring be far behind?" It really cheered me up to read that.'

'I suppose so,' Anne said rather doubtfully. 'Except that spring *does* seem far behind this year. I don't ever remember being so fed up. The cold, and slipping and sliding to work, and chilblains, and then at home Grandma Houlihan sitting there. We've got to watch every word we say and we can't get near the fire. If I didn't love this job I'd shoot myself.'

Sarah grinned. 'You *are* in a bad way,' she said. 'I thought your grandma stayed in bed.'

'No, she says she can't get used to the strange room,' Anne said. 'I know I shouldn't grumble about her but I'm sure she comes down and sits there for spite. Mum used to sit in that chair by the hob and Dad on the oven side of the fire and we could all gather round, sitting on the rug or on stools.'

'That's how Mum and Dad have their chairs,' Sarah exclaimed. 'But we sit in them if they're not using them.'

'So did we, but there seemed plenty of space. Now Grandma seems to spread right across in front of the fire with all her wrappings, and if we stand close she says we're distracting her from her prayers. Our Stephen says he's saying his prayers backwards when she talks like that. I think he means he's swearing under his breath,' Anne said. 'And she finds fault with everything we say.'

'Perhaps it'll get better as she settles in,' Sarah tried to console her.

'It must do,' Anne said. 'I'm sure the Andersons couldn't have put up with this for all those years.'

'The weather's bound to get better soon, and then it won't matter about the fire,' Sarah said, and Anne smiled ruefully.

'I'm sorry. I sound a right moaner and I haven't got much to moan about really. It's funny though, sometimes I feel really miserable and the next minute I feel happy and don't know why.'

'That's funny. So do I,' Sarah said.

'I wonder if it's because we're what my mum calls betwixt and between?' Anne said.

'Probably,' Sarah agreed.

'You'll have to ask your friend what it says in *Peg's Paper*,' Anne said, laughing, but mention of the magazine made them both think of Michael.

'I'm sure he'll ask you out again when you're out of mourning,' Anne said. 'He really cares for you, Sarah. I know by the way he looks at you.'

'He puzzles me,' she said. 'We've been talking more in the shop lately and sometimes he seems as though he really likes me then he seems to go all formal. As though he likes me but thinks he shouldn't.'

'You don't think Michael could be married?' Anne asked Sarah one day when she had seen them talking together and thought she saw the sudden stiffness in Michael's manner that Sarah had spoken of.

'I'm sure he's not.'

'Perhaps he's just shy then as Mabel says,' Anne said. 'You'd think with looks like that he'd have plenty of experience with girls, though, wouldn't you?'

They were interrupted by customers, and Anne decided that Michael's behaviour was just one more mystery. I feel as though I'm surrounded by them, she thought.

She had heard no more about the O'Neills. It was too cold to

ELIZABETH MURPHY

hang about waiting to see Kathleen leave work, and Maureen had heard no more because the O'Neills' neighbour had sprained her wrist in a fall on the icy pavements and had been unable to knit.

Maureen was spending more time than ever at church and seemed moody, but Anne sensed at times that she was very unhappy. It was impossible to ask Maureen or her mother why, and no one else seemed to be aware of the mystery.

Anne passed a wayside pulpit outside a small church on her way home, and one night there was a fresh poster there saying: 'Be not afraid. In due time all will be revealed'. She took it as a sign and decided to stop wondering about all that puzzled her.

Chapter Thirteen

At last spring arrived, with a warm west wind melting the snow and ice which still lingered in places. Everyone was suddenly more cheerful, and Anne told Sarah that it felt like a new lease of life.

'Even Grandma seems different,' she said. 'Although that's got less to do with spring than with Father Monaghan.'

'Why? What did he do?' asked Sarah.

'He came to see her. The priests often visit her and Mum leaves them to talk to her. I don't know what he said but Mum told us that Grandma said to her, "You won't hear me grumbling again, Julia. I'm going to keep a still tongue in my head and offer up my sufferings and the annoyances I have for the Holy Souls in Purgatory."'

'It'll be a relief for all of you, but especially for your mum,' Sarah said.

'Yes, she's borne the brunt of it and never moaned like the rest of us,' Anne admitted. 'I think I'll offer to stay with Grandma tomorrow so that Mum can go to see Aunt Carrie. Strike while the iron's hot and Grandma's more likely to agree.'

Grandma Houlihan agreed and Julia was able to go the following day, which was Anne's half day. No one expected visitors during the extremely cold weather, and although the Fitzgeralds had visited Carrie while she was confined to bed, it was several weeks since anyone but Eileen had been to the Anderson house.

It was longer still since they had seen Minnie but Julia said she would only visit Carrie on this occasion.

She came home full of news which could not be mentioned until her mother had retired for the night, but as soon as the evening meal and the family prayers were over, Grandma was settled in bed.

Tony, Stephen, and Terry were getting ready to go out but the rest of the family had gathered in the kitchen when Julia began, 'Carrie was so glad to see me. She hasn't been across the door while the weather's been so bad, but what a lot has been happening! Brendan's turned up again.'

'When?' everyone asked in unison.

'A few days ago,' Carrie said, 'and dressed up to dolrags. Fred said his policeman friend told him Brendan hadn't been in gaol but he thinks he's been in trouble with a gang and lying low.'

'In Liverpool?' Eileen exclaimed.

'No, it was a London gang. Brendan did something for another fellow from London and that's why he was in trouble. Carrie didn't know the ins and outs of it, but anyway Brendan's back home as large as life.'

'Has Aunt Carrie seen Auntie Minnie?' Maureen asked.

'No, but Theresa has. She met her face to face and Minnie said in a nasty way, "Tell your mother my son's home again and very prosperous. It's not what she wants to hear but it'll stop her wondering about him",' said Julia.

'What did Theresa say?' exclaimed Eileen.

'Nothing. She was too flabbergasted, but our Carrie's furious. She says when she sees Minnie she'll tell her she doesn't care whether he's here or in Timbuctoo.'

'He must think he's out of danger then,' Pat said, puffing thoughtfully at his pipe. 'That lad's a bad lot and always will be.'

'But that's not all,' Julia went on excitedly. 'Dympna must be getting married! Minnie said to Theresa that there might be wedding bells for Dympna before there were any for her. That's all Theresa told her mother but she whispered to me in the hall that Minnie said, "There'll be wedding bells for our Dympna before there are any for you, for all you've been passed from one lad to another like an old handrag." Our Carrie'd kill her if she heard that.'

'What a thing to say!' Maureen said, looking shocked. And Eileen exclaimed, 'But Dympna! I'm dying to see the fellow who would marry her.'

'Did you know Theresa was getting engaged?' Julia asked Eileen.

'Yes, I did,' she admitted. 'But I didn't want to steal her thunder. I thought it was Theresa's privilege to announce it.'

'Well, Carrie told me so it's all right to talk about it now,' Julia said. 'They'll get engaged at Easter. Carrie and Fred like the lad.'

'Jim's a nice fellow,' Eileen said. 'I think they're well suited, and Jim's a printer so they'll be all right for money.'

'And you'll be a bridesmaid, Eileen, you and Carmel,' Julia said.

She nodded. 'I wonder what Minnie has to say about our family if she's saying that about Theresa?' she said. 'She'll be asking about wedding bells for me and Maureen.'

Maureen blushed but before anyone else could speak Julia said quickly, 'If that bold Bernadette had her way our Tony would have been married long ago.'

'I know. Jerry said the lads sing "A hunting we will go" when they see her coming,' Eileen said.

'And she hears them!' Julia exclaimed.

'Oh, no. They just sing it quietly to tease Tony but Jerry says he should watch out. He's seen persistence win with other fellows,' said Eileen.

Maureen's blush had faded and she said nothing, but Anne felt sure that her mother had deliberately diverted attention from her. Tony chose that moment to look in and announced that he was going out, and was amazed when everyone laughed.

'Mind yourself, son,' his mother said. And Eileen added, 'Yes. Watch out for arrows.'

'Arrows? What are you talking about?' he said. 'Who's firing arrows?'

'Cupid,' Eileen declared with a laugh, then she and Anne collapsed in giggles on the sofa.

'You're nuts,' Tony said. 'Ta ra, Mum.'

'You shouldn't tease him, Eileen,' her mother said, but she was smiling.

A few days later Sarah asked Anne if she would like to go to the pictures with her.

'I'd love to,' Anne said eagerly. 'If you feel all right.'

Sarah looked down and said in a low voice, 'Grandma suggested it and Mum thinks it's all right too. You know she goes to work for a catering firm? She says the women are so funny it's the same as going to the pictures.'

'I'll see what's on,' Anne said. 'I saw a newspaper in the storeroom.'

The girls thoroughly enjoyed their night out and the opportunity to talk as much as the film. As they walked home Anne said, 'Isn't it lovely not to be slipping about on ice? I'm really looking forward to the summer.'

'So am I,' said Sarah. 'I don't want to forget Grandad, but it's true that it gets easier to bear as time goes on.'

Anne pressed her arm in silent sympathy, and the next moment Sarah exclaimed, 'There's our John.' She called his name and a tall young man crossed the road to them. Sarah introduced him to Anne, and he smiled and raised his hat then shook her hand firmly.

They were near a street lamp and Anne stole a look at him.

She had a swift impression of a handsome face with a cleft chin and dark wavy hair falling across his forehead. He looks nice, she thought, not a bit like the moody youth Sarah talks about.

John asked about the film, and they confessed that they had spent as much time talking as watching the programme.

'I love Charles Boyer though,' Anne said, and that led to a discussion about their favourite film stars, until Anne realised that the Redmonds were making a detour to take her home to Magdalen Street.

'You shouldn't have come out of your way to see me home,' she exclaimed, and John said, smiling at her, 'We had to know what you thought about Joan Blondell and Henry Wilcoxen.' Anne saw the flash of his white teeth as he smiled.

The following day she took the first opportunity to tell Sarah that she thought her brother was very nice. 'He was all right last night,' Sarah said. 'But he's a moody beggar sometimes. Most of the time, in fact, although he's been a bit better lately.'

'I didn't think he looked moody,' Anne said. 'Perhaps it's because he's so upset about your grandad.'

'Perhaps,' Sarah said doubtfully. 'They were very close but it's no excuse for the way he speaks to Dad. He's always been like this anyway, thinking he knows everything.'

Anne said nothing and Sarah glanced at her and said, 'He's mad about politics. You know that thing that was on the Pathé News last night, about Herr Hitler invading the Rhineland? It was in the *Echo* and John was ranting on about it and about Signor Mussolini invading Abyssinia. He says they're Fascists. Are your brothers like that?'

'Not really,' Anne said. 'Tony goes on about things sometimes, but they don't take much interest in politics. There's so much else going on in Liverpool that's interesting, isn't there?'

'It'd be more peaceful in our house if John thought like that,' Sarah said ruefully. 'He's forever arguing with Dad. He can't argue with Mick because he's interested in nothing except aeroplanes.'

Anne felt that Sarah was being unfair to John, but also wondered whether she was trying to warn her not to become too interested in him. She had hinted several times that John was too obsessed with politics to be interested in girls.

Joe came home at the end of April and seemed shocked by the change in his mother. He sat beside her talking until Maureen said, 'Don't you think you should go to bed now, Mum, and be fresh to talk to Joe tomorrow? I'm sure he needs an early night too.'

She looked meaningfully at Joe and he said immediately, 'Good idea, Mo. I'm looking forward to a night in my own bed and not being called to go on watch.' His mother went to bed soon afterwards, and Maureen took cocoa up to her and Grandma Houlihan.

Pat and the rest of the family were gathered in the kitchen and Joe said sombrely, 'I didn't realise Mum had been so ill.'

'She was bad after Christmas but she's fine now, thank God,' his father said. 'She's a bit tired with looking after the old lady but it'll do her good to see you, Joe.'

No one disagreed with him, and Anne wondered whether they were deliberately deceiving themselves or whether they truly believed that their mother was well again. She thought that her mother looked years older than before her illness at Christmas.

Joe sat down beside her and put his arm round her. 'Here's another change I hadn't bargained for,' he said, smiling at her. 'I didn't recognise you at first, Anne. I thought we had a strange young lady in the house.'

Everyone laughed and she blushed. 'I told you in my letter that I felt quite grown up now,' she said.

Stephen was fiddling with the wireless, and some dance music came on.

'Come on, Eileen, try this,' he said. 'It's a quickstep.' He seized her and they began to dance, bickering as Stephen trod on her toes or she fell over his feet.

Anne hugged Joe. 'I *have* missed you,' she said.

'I've missed you too, pet,' he said, and sighed. 'This is the worst part, being away while everything's happening.'

'What are you two whispering about?' Eileen asked. 'Come on, Joe, let's try a waltz.'

He told Anne that the American papers were full of reports that the King was going to marry an American divorcee, Mrs Herbert Simpson, but when Anne told Mabel she indignantly dismissed the news.

'Another tall story from America,' she scoffed. 'They'll write anything to fill the papers over there. No, he'll marry an English girl or a foreign princess. She'll be a lucky girl, whoever she is.'

Sarah also refused to believe the story. 'It'd be in the papers here too,' she said, and when Anne told her that Joe said Mrs Simpson had been divorced from her first husband and planned to divorce her second to marry the King, Sarah laughed. 'No wonder Mabel said it was a tall story,' she said.

'Joe was only saying what was in the papers in America,' Anne said defensively, and Sarah said quickly, 'Yes, I know that.'

'We were hoping he might get a job while he was home this time,' Anne said sadly. 'Everybody's been looking out for one for him, now that trade's picking up again, but no luck. The trouble is you have to be on the spot to grab a job when it comes up.'

'Couldn't he work for your dad?' Sarah said.

'No, he's not a tradesman, and the labourers have all been with Dad for a long time. Maureen told me that Dad would have to lay a man off to take Joe on because he's just keeping going and can't expand the business yet.'

The usual Easter party had not been held at the Andersons' but now that the weather was better and Carrie had recovered they decided to give a party to celebrate Theresa's engagement. Joe had to go aboard his ship the day before the party but Anne told Sarah that it might help to cheer the family after he left. 'We always feel so downhearted when he goes so I suppose the party has come at a good time for us,' she said. 'It's just such a pity that he's missing it.'

Fred had told Eileen to bring the young man she was currently going out with and Stephen, Tony and Terry were all taking girls there. 'The more the merrier,' Fred said, and invited Anne to bring Sarah and Maureen to bring her friend Mary Mullen.

Theresa had brought her fiancé to meet Grandma Houlihan, and those of the Fitzgeralds that he had not already met, and everyone had liked the quiet young man. Grandma Houlihan had blessed the young couple and sprinkled them with Holy Water, and Theresa had declared afterwards to Eileen and Anne that she would keep Jim away from her grandma until after the wedding.

'I don't want him dead of pneumonia before he even gets to the altar,' she said. She was a slim vivacious girl who seemed to dance through life, and a favourite with all the family. She was a hairdresser and could copy any hair style that she saw on film stars so was in great demand.

On the night of the party the Andersons' house was filled with Jim's relations as well as the usual Andersons and Fitzgeralds and many friends, but the young people still managed to find room to dance, either to records on the gramophone or Eileen playing the piano.

Fred's speech was as embarrassing as Theresa had predicted it would be, but by the time it was made everyone was in high good humour. A toast was drunk and the cake cut, and Fred's speech received loud applause. Theresa and Jim looked blissfully happy as they stood smiling at each other and clinking their glasses.

Afterwards the party separated, the older people gathering in the kitchen and the younger ones in the parlour. A friend from the church had offered to sit with Grandma Houlihan, who had refused to go to the party, so Julia was able to go. She wore a brown silk dress with the cameo brooch which had been Pat's wedding present to her, and Anne was delighted to see how much better she looked.

'Mum looks awfully well tonight, doesn't she?' Maureen whispered to her. She nodded, realising that Maureen too had been worried about their mother.

Sarah was thrilled. 'I've never been to a party like this before,' she said to Anne. 'We always have a family gathering for Christmas, but there's only a few of us. We had a sort of party when my aunt was home from America but not like this.'

She was fascinated by the fun and games. Stephen and Anne danced an Apache dance, with Stephen wearing one of the girl's berets and Anne with a brightly coloured scarf around her shoulders. It finished with her falling flat on the hearthrug after Stephen had inexpertly whirled her around, and Tony called, 'It'd be better if you could dance, Steve.'

'Oh, la la,' Anne said. And Stephen said, 'Eez that so, Monsoor?'

'Oh, very Latin Quarter,' Tony said, laughing. They played games of Forfeits and Postman's Knock which involved a lot of scuffling and kissing in the hall. Everyone was sorry when the party was over, and then someone said tactlessly, 'Work tomorrow.'

'Only half day,' someone else replied.

For Anne and Sarah Saturday meant a full day's work, but they looked forward to seeing each other then and talking over the party.

'I thought it was wonderful,' Sarah said. Her eyes were still bright with excitement and Mabel laughed.

'It sounds as though *you* enjoyed yourself, anyway.'

'We all did. Anne's family are such *fun*, Mabel. Anne was the life and soul of the party too.'

'You might as well enjoy yourselves,' Mabel said tolerantly. 'You're only young once. I suppose there were plenty of lads there?'

Anne and Sarah looked at each other and laughed. 'We've made a date with two of them for tonight,' Anne said. 'They're Jim's cousins. You know, Mabel, Theresa's fiancé.'

'You should be safe enough with them, they're almost family,' she said. And Anne replied gaily, 'We were spoiled for choice, weren't we, Sar? I think our Terry was sorry he'd brought a girl. I think he fell for Sarah.'

'Has he been going out with his girl for long?' Mabel asked.

'No, only a week or two,' Anne said. 'He doesn't bother much with girls usually. He's just football mad, and goes with a crowd to the wrestling and sometimes plays billiards in the club.'

'It's a pity that your brother Joe missed such a good party, isn't it?' Sarah said, and Anne said impulsively, 'I *do* wish you'd been able to meet Joe, Sarah. His time ashore seemed to go in a flash but I thought you'd meet him at the party.'

'When did he go aboard?' asked Mabel.

'Only the day before. I'm sure you'd have liked him, Sarah.'

'I'm sure I would,' she agreed. Neither of the girls realised how much heartache a meeting then would have saved Sarah in later life.

The girls enjoyed their visit to the cinema with Phil and Charlie, and arranged to go out with them again. The boys were cousins, Phil who was Anne's escort as dark as Charlie was fair. The next morning Sarah and Anne compared notes. 'Was it just a handshake?' Anne asked quizzically and Sarah laughed. 'No, but he did ask permission before he kissed me.'

'Phil didn't,' Anne said. 'You must inspire more respect than I do.'

'Tell me how to cure it,' Sarah giggled. 'Preferably before Saturday night.' She was to see Michael again then.

Tom Dodd wrote to Anne from Scotland and she replied, but gradually the intervals between the letters became longer until they petered out altogether.

'He's probably found a wee Scots lassie,' Anne said to Sarah. 'I can't say he's broken my heart.'

'I don't know when you'd find time to write anyway,' Sarah said, laughing.

Anne's brothers and Eileen were keen cyclists and Anne and Sarah decided to buy bicycles for five shillings deposit and two shillings and sixpence a week. As the evenings lengthened they cycled through the farmland which surrounded Liverpool or beside the Mersey.

Anne was invited to Sunday tea by Sarah's mother and dressed very carefully for it, hoping to see John again, but she was disappointed. When she had been introduced to the rest of the family, Sarah's mother said casually, 'I'm sorry our eldest son isn't here to meet you. He belongs to a rambling club and they go out on Sundays.'

'It's all right, Mum. Anne met John when we were coming home from the pictures one night,' Sarah said.

Anne's mother had been pleased by the invitation and interested in hearing all about the family when she returned home.

'They're all very nice,' Anne said. 'I felt as though I knew them already because Sarah's told me so much about them. Her mother's lovely and really made me feel at home. Her father did too but he's very quiet and doesn't talk much. He's got a lovely deep voice though and an awfully nice smile.'

'Was Sarah's grandmother there?' her mother asked.

'Yes. She's like Sarah, tall and thin with blue eyes, but her hair's white now. She's very dignified and yet very welcoming. Sarah's brother Mick was there. He goes to the College and Sarah said he's very clever, but he seems a case. A bit like Dom and Des. I didn't like her sister Kate very much.'

'Why not?' Julia asked.

'I think she's very vain. She *is* pretty. She's got fair curly hair and brown eyes and a straight little nose, but she doesn't half know it! The old man who lodges with Sarah's grandma pays for dancing lessons for Kate.'

'Sarah's a nice friend for you to have, Anne,' her mother said. 'Especially when you're working together all day. You must ask her to tea next Sunday.'

Anne said nothing about John Redmond. She often thought of him and pictured his face, but she had an uneasy feeling that on the walk back from the cinema he had only seen her as his young sister's friend.

Sarah and Anne were often invited out by various young men now, but no one that Anne had met seemed to her as interesting or as handsome as John Redmond.

Chapter Fourteen

Sarah came to tea the following Sunday. She seemed shy and rather overwhelmed at first by the large crowd of young people, but before long she was joining in the repartee.

All the Fitzgeralds except Maureen owned bicycles and it was arranged that the following Sunday Sarah would join them for a ride on the Wirral, if the weather was good.

Sunday was dull but warm, and after early Mass they set off with flasks of tea and parcels of sandwiches in their saddlebags, to take the ferry across the Mersey and ride to Thurstaton, a beauty spot on the Wirral.

This was the start of a regular pattern. Nearly every Sunday they rode, sometimes to somewhere on the Liverpool side of the river, but more often to somewhere on the Wirral, on the other side of the Mersey.

Sometimes Tony's friend Jerry came, or Eileen's current boyfriend, sometimes friends of others in the group, but Anne and Sarah agreed that they enjoyed outings best with just the family and Sarah. Often Anne thought of suggesting that John Redmond might join them, and even hinted to Sarah, although she added, 'Of course he's in a rambling club, isn't he?'

'Rambling club, my foot!' Sarah said. 'Mum and Dad might believe that but I don't. He spends the day with his cronies from that Communist Club.'

'But he can't be a Catholic *and* a Communist!' Anne exclaimed. Sarah only shrugged.

'John thinks rules are for other people,' she said. 'He's always so sure he's right.'

Anne was silent, uncertain what to say, and Sarah grimaced. 'I make him sound awful, don't I?' she said. 'He's all right really and I'm very fond of him, but he has some cracked ideas. Grandad thought it wasn't right that some people have more money than they know what to do with while others are starving.'

'I agree with him,' Anne said. 'I don't think they're cracked ideas.'

'Neither do I,' Sarah said. 'But Grandad was working quietly to get things changed, and our John thinks he can do it in five minutes. That's why he hangs round with those fellows, because he thinks they'll get things done quickly, and no one else seems to care about poor people.'

'Well, I admire him for that,' Anne said staunchly. 'Although I don't think he should get mixed up with Communism.'

'Remember that night we went to the pictures and met John on the way home?' Sarah said. Anne smiled inwardly. Did she! Sarah went on, 'He commented later on your house being big and I said you were a big family. That's because I was expecting him to suggest that you took a few tramps in to fill up the rooms.'

Anne laughed and Sarah smiled with her but said, 'Honestly, Anne, I'm not joking. That's the sort of daft idea he gets. Mick brings him down to earth though. He says John should give up his own bed to a tramp if he feels like that. He shares the room and says he would agree, because he knows John would never do it.'

'He wouldn't be able to fit a tramp in our house anyway,' Anne said. 'We only have three bedrooms and a boxroom and the bathroom, and the four lads share two attic bedrooms. Maureen had to give up her bedroom and move in with me and Eileen when Grandma came to live with us.'

'Did she mind?' asked Sarah.

'She never complained,' Anne said. 'I'd have been moaning like hell if I had to give up my room and have a bed pushed in ours, but she doesn't. We pull her leg because she's so devout but she lives it too in things like this.'

'I thought she was lovely,' Sarah said. 'Really *good* somehow, but not miserable with it.'

'She is,' Anne said. 'I wonder . . .' She stopped. Even to Sarah she was unable to talk about her doubts and instead said, 'Maureen often sees Michael at church.'

'Yes, he's in your parish,' Sarah said and changed the subject. She went to the cinema with Michael about every two weeks but said little about it to Anne or Mabel.

Grandma Houlihan had questioned Julia about the party at the Andersons', and about who was there, and Julia had to tell her that Minnie had sent a message that she was not well enough to come.

'I'm sure she'd have been to see me if she was all right, now that I'm here,' Grandma declared. 'I wouldn't blame her not coming while I was with our Carrie and that skitting family of hers. My poor girl! I'd go to see her myself if I was able.'

'I'll go on Wednesday afternoon when Anne's here to stay with you,' Julia promised, but Grandma was annoyed.

'What's to stop you going today?' she demanded. 'There's no need to wait for Wednesday. I don't need a keeper, just because I can't get about like I used to. God knows I spent many a day on my own while Carrie gadded about.'

Julia knew that it was useless to defend Carrie so only said quietly, 'All right I'll go today, Ma, if you think you'll be all right on your own.'

She set off right after lunch and as soon as Dympna opened

the door to her Julia realised why there was a wedding planned. Her niece was obviously pregnant and as Julia went into the kitchen Minnie said belligerently, 'Come to spy out the land, have you?'

'I've come chiefly because Ma's worried about you,' Julia said quietly. 'But Carrie and I have been too. We all have our troubles and we should be helping each other with them.'

'Well, you can see what's been happening here,' Minnie said less aggressively. 'Still, Dympna's not the first and she won't be the last in this situation.'

'That's true,' Julia agreed. She turned to her niece who was slumped in a chair, picking her nose. 'Are you keeping well?' she asked, trying to hide her distaste.

'Orl righ',' Dympna muttered, and Minnie said triumphantly, 'She's getting married anyhow. A week on Thursday. I'm going to ask Fred Anderson to give her away. Our Brendan will be best man.'

'I'm sure Fred will be pleased to do it,' Julia said. There were numerous questions she would have liked to ask but she felt too intimidated to venture them.

The young man's name had not been mentioned, but with Dympna glowering at her from the armchair and Minnie's aggressive glare from the other side of the kitchen, Julia felt that even such a simple question would seem to show unwelcome curiosity.

Minnie appeared to think that the subject was closed. 'So Ma's had as much as she could take of that Anderson madhouse?' she said. 'I don't know how she's stuck it for so long.'

'She was happy and well looked after at Carrie's,' Julia said indignantly. 'She only came to us because Carrie was bedfast with sciatica.'

'Aye, but she's up now and Ma hasn't gone back, has she?' Minnie sneered.

'Only because I think Carrie and Fred have done enough,' Julia said. 'Me and Pat think it's time we took a turn.'

Minnie sniffed. 'That wasn't what I heard.'

'Then you heard wrong,' Julia said. Her usually quiet voice was loud and her gentle manner transformed by anger. 'I'll go,' she said. 'I can tell Ma that she needn't worry about you. You're just the same as you always were.'

She was still angry when she reached home, but fortunately Carrie had called to see her mother, and when Grandma dozed off Julia was able to tell her about Minnie.

Carrie could give many more details about Dympna's wedding because Minnie had already asked Fred to give the girl away and Fred had not hesitated to ask questions.

'The lad's name is Harold Duffy,' Carrie said. 'He didn't want to marry her but Minnie told Fred that Brendan came home to see him and now the wedding's on. She asked Fred to give her away instead of Brendan so that he could be best man. He's riding shotgun, I think.'

They both laughed but then Julia said seriously, 'It's not much of a start to a marriage, is it?'

'The lad's family are not going to the wedding, and most of our family will be working at the time, but I think that's how Minnie wants it,' Carrie said.

'I didn't see Brendan. Is he living at home?' Julia asked.

'No, Minnie says she doesn't know where he's staying. He just calls to see them.'

Grandma woke and they had no further conversation, but the family were intrigued by the news later.

'How did the quare feller get to know about Dympna?' Pat asked. 'I thought no one knew where he was.'

'Carrie said all along that Minnie knew, and it must be right about gangsters looking for him. She said to Fred: "Brendan's a good son to me. He risked his skin to come and look after us."'

Only Carrie and Julia, and Fred who took time off from his

work, were able to go to the wedding ceremony, but the Fitzgeralds clubbed together and sent Dympna a dinner and tea service as a wedding present, and Julia gave her a tablecloth and napkins.

The Andersons gave her sheets and pillowcases and Carrie an eiderdown.

Pat and Fred each gave the young couple ten pounds and Dympna gave them grudging thanks. The bridegroom was a thickset young man with dark hair growing low on his forehead and a face pitted with acne scars. Carrie whispered, 'As God made them he matched them,' but Julia was quietly weeping.

She could see no prospect of happiness either for Dympna and Harold or for Minnie with whom they planned to live, and thought of Francis, long dead through a freak accident, who might have altered the course of their lives.

Brendan stood close to Harold while the vows were made. They were not having a Nuptial Mass and as soon as the brief ceremony was over Brendan disappeared.

It had been necessary to tell Grandma Houlihan about the wedding and the reason for it. 'I blame Minnie,' she declared. 'She hasn't reared those children properly.'

'Poor Minnie,' Julia said, still with thoughts of Francis in her mind. 'She's had her own share with those two and can't be responsible for them now they're grown up.'

'The time to train a child is from soon after it's born,' Grandma said. 'Mind you, these talking pictures have been the ruination of young people.'

'I didn't see one until 1928, Grandma,' Anne protested. 'Tony took me and Eileen to see *The Singing Fool* at the Hippodrome. Tony was seventeen and Eileen about twelve. I was eight so we were all too old to be influenced by it.'

'The other things then, the silent films,' Grandma said stubbornly.

Julia was signing to Anne not to argue and Grandma went on,

'Poor Miss Hayes. Those talkies took the bread out of her mouth. She lost her job and now she has to teach girls like Eileen to keep herself and her mother.'

'I didn't know Miss Hayes played for the silent pictures,' Anne said.

'She did so, and the man who taught Joe the violin – he was years in the cinema orchestra, God help him,' said Grandma.

'I'm sorry, Gran, I'll have to go,' Anne said, then added mischievously, 'I'm going to the talkies with Sarah.'

She and Sarah were going to the cinema with Phil and Charlie, the young men they had met at the party. 'I don't feel I'm two timing Michael,' Sarah told her, 'because I don't think he cares. I suppose you could call ours a platonic relationship, like those two film stars in the *Picturegoer*.'

'Except for the way you look at each other,' Anne said. 'I'm still sure he's in love with you, Sarah.'

'I wish I was,' she sighed. 'And I wish he wasn't so handsome, then maybe I wouldn't feel like this about him.'

'Our Maureen says he looks like "the noblest Roman of them all". As though he should have a laurel wreath around his head.'

They both laughed and Anne said, giggling, 'At least you don't have Edie's problems.'

Sarah's friend Edie Meadows, who lived a few doors away from her, had told her that the boys she went out with were 'only after one thing'.

She had also told Sarah that as soon as they began to get 'hardfaced' she told them there was nothing doing, and if they still persisted gave them a clout.

'Mind you, a clout from me wouldn't have the same effect,' Sarah told Anne. 'One fellow told Edie she should be in Pudsey Street at the Boxing Stadium.'

One day in June Sarah came in looking very downcast and

worried, but it was only when Mabel decided to go home because she had a boil on her neck that Sarah could tell Anne the reason.

'I don't want Mabel or anyone to know,' she said. 'I feel so ashamed. John's been in the Bridewell all night and he'll be in court later on.'

'Why? What's he done?' Anne gasped.

'He went to an open air meeting and the policeman said he got up on the platform and starting shouting treason.'

'Treason! You can be hanged for that, can't you?' Anne said in horror.

'Not this sort,' Sarah said. 'Mum and Dad had gone to the dance at the Grafton, the first time since Grandad died. When the bobby arrived he told me to fetch them.'

'Were you on your own?' Anne asked.

Sarah nodded. 'Peggy Burns who lives opposite saw the bobby and told Grandma and she came over. Luckily she knew the policeman and he was much nicer with her than he'd been with me. He said John might get off with a fine but most likely he'll go to gaol because he was a ringleader. Oh, Anne, I feel so ashamed.'

Sarah began to cry and Anne said, 'How could he be a ringleader if he was only at the meeting?'

'I don't know, but it'd serve him right if he did go to gaol. He never thinks of anyone but himself,' Sarah said.

Some customers came in and Sarah fled into the storeroom. Anne served them, her mind in a whirl. Sarah had said that John was moody, but she had also said that he'd loved his grandfather dearly and had been influenced by him. Surely Lawrie Ward, so deeply respected, could not have been involved in treason?

A little later Sarah returned, red-eyed but composed, and in the intervals between serving said to Anne, 'I didn't mean that. I'd be heartbroken if our John had to go to gaol, but he's so reckless, Anne.'

176

'But if he takes after your grandad, what did the bobby mean about treason?' Anne asked in a bewildered tone.

'I suppose he's got Grandad's ideas but not his ways,' Sarah said. 'Grandad always told John to fight injustice and try to get fair shares for everyone, but John thinks Grandad's way was too slow.'

'But things *are* getting better gradually,' Anne said.

'Yes, but John's so impatient. He told me once that Grandad's generation and even Dad's were too cowed down. He said we shouldn't ask for equal shares but demand them as our right.'

'He's clever, isn't he?' Anne said admiringly.

'Yes, but I wish he'd keep away from that club in Byrom Street,' Sarah said. 'I think they talk a lot of hot air and egg each other on.' She sighed. 'I don't care what he believes in and talks about if he'd only keep it to himself and stop arguing with Dad and upsetting Mum. And now this!'

'Never mind. It might all blow over,' Anne consoled her.

When Sarah returned from her lunch she told Anne that John was still in court. 'I'm sorry I'm going out with Edie tonight,' she told Anne. 'I'd rather see you and talk about this, but I promised her ages ago I'd go to the pictures with her. Of course, if it's bad news I won't be going out with anyone.'

'Don't cross your bridges before you come to them,' Anne said, mimicking Mabel's voice to cheer her up. She was sorry too that she was not seeing Sarah, as she was burning to know what had happened to John.

Later she picked up her father's newspaper as soon as he laid it down, and searched through it, but could see nothing about the meeting or the court appearances.

The following day Sarah told her that John had been fined five pounds.

Sarah said, 'I got a shock when I got in and John wasn't there, but Mum said he'd gone into work for the afternoon. She said he'd probably gone to the hospital on his way home because two of his fingers were broken and his face was badly bruised, especially his eye.'

'Gosh, it must have been a rough meeting,' Anne exclaimed. 'But thank God he didn't have to go to gaol. Your mum would be upset then, wouldn't she?'

'She's upset now, all because of him and his big ideas,' Sarah said bitterly. 'I went to the pictures with Edie and when I got in there was a terrible row going on. Our John was squaring up to Dad and poor Mum was trying to separate them. She was really upset. I never thought I'd see such a thing in our house.'

'I suppose everyone was just on edge because of the worry.'

'Mick said he'd tried to stop it, but I made John go to bed. Mum broke her heart crying and Dad was as white as a sheet. I could have killed our John. All for blasted politics.'

'It's a pity he doesn't start courting, to keep his mind off them,' Anne said. 'But he doesn't seem interested in girls, does he?'

Sarah glanced at her and Anne felt her face grow red, but Sarah only said, 'It might be a good idea but I'd pity the girl.'

Grandma Houlihan was still with the Fitzgeralds. When Carrie recovered from the sciatica she suggested that Grandma should return to live with her and Fred but Julia and Pat insisted that Grandma should stay with them.

Carrie called round to see her mother and talk to Julia, and when Grandma was having her usual rest the sisters talked in the back kitchen. 'Ma can come back to us, Julia,' Carrie said. 'I don't think you're really well yet and I'm fine.'

'I'm grand now too,' Julia said. 'And Ma's settled well. The children get on well with her too.' She laughed. 'They watch their tongues so they don't offend her.'

'But I don't want your family put out,' Carrie said. 'Ours are used to her little ways.'

'Yes, because she was with you so long,' Julia said. 'But she's

178

my mother too, Carrie, and we're glad to take our turn. As long as Ma's willing to stay she's welcome. You'll be busy with Theresa's wedding soon, anyway.'

'I hope they're doing the right thing,' Carrie said. 'It was supposed to be a two-year engagement, and to tell you the truth I thought that would give Theresa time to be really sure. It's just that they want one of those new houses and Jim has got savings. Fred's delighted and talking of buying furniture for them, but I'd rather they waited a while.'

'You've no need to worry about Theresa changing her mind,' Julia declared. 'She's been out with so many lads she's bound to know her own mind about Jim. There'd be more to worry about if he was the only lad she'd ever known.'

'I'm glad you think so,' Carrie said. 'Fred said something that worried me about hoping she'd be content with one lad when she was used to playing the field.'

'He didn't mean it. It was only one of his little jokes and he wouldn't expect you to worry about it. No, you've only to see Theresa and Jim together to know they're well suited.'

'But Jim's so quiet and she's so lively,' said Carrie.

'That's why they suit so well. It's not like you to worry like this, Carrie. I don't think you're properly over the illness yet.'

'Maybe not. But I can always talk over worries with you, Julie, that I couldn't discuss with anyone else. Sorry to be such a misery. Have you seen Bridie lately?'

'Yes, I was there the other day and she's *huge*,' said Julia.

'Like a barn door,' Carrie agreed. 'And she reckons she's still got six weeks to go. I told her that I was like that with the twins.'

'But the twins are on Fred's side of the family,' Julia said. 'He told me he had twin brothers although they died young, and his cousin had twin boys.'

'Yes, Bridie's will be a big baby, I suppose, unless she's carrying a lot of water,' Carrie said.

The following week a note came to say that Bridie had given birth to twins, a boy and a girl, and mother and babies were well. Julia dashed to her house immediately with a basket filled with treats for Bridie and baby clothes.

When she returned home she told the girls that both babies were healthy and well formed. 'And they're a good size, about four and a half pounds each the midwife said. Bridie's so happy we nearly had to tie her to the bed to stop her floating off.'

'I thought they weren't due for another month,' Anne said incautiously, but her mother was too excited to notice. 'And Jack,' she said, 'you wouldn't think he'd been a father twice before.'

'But he hasn't had twins before or a little girl,' Maureen said. 'Who are they like?'

'It's hard to tell, but the little girl is fair and the boy dark. Good lungs on them anyway. Danny and Teddy are thrilled to bits.'

Maureen, Anne and Eileen went to see Bridie and the babies on Sunday and found Bridie's two little stepsons sitting on her bed.

'Teddy and Dan are helping me to choose names,' she explained when the babies had been admired.

'I like Veronica,' Danny declared. But Teddy said, '*I* don't. I like Hazel.'

'Hazelnut,' Danny scoffed.

'What do you like, Bridie?' Maureen asked. 'You and Jack.'

'We thought of Patrick for the boy and Patricia for the girl, then they could be Pat and Tricia, but I'm having second thoughts. I'd like the boys to choose. They both like Michael for the boy and so does Jack so that's settled.'

'Why don't you pick a name beginning with M for your sister?' Maureen said to the boys.

'Mary,' shouted Teddy.

'Too many Marys,' Danny said firmly. He thought for a moment. 'I know – Martha.'

'Ugh, no. I hate Martha,' Teddy said. They showed signs of coming to blows and Bridie said quickly, 'I think she looks like a Monica.'

The boys knelt up and peered at the sleeping baby while the girls watched with amusement. 'Yes, Monica,' Danny and Teddy said with satisfaction. 'Michael and Monica.'

The girls had brought fruit for Bridie and sweets for the little boys, and Maureen had brought a parcel of clothes for the babies. She and her mother had each knitted a shawl and Maureen had made matinee coats and bootees. Eileen and Anne had bought tiny nightgowns and embroidered them with feather stitching. Bridie was delighted with the gifts.

'I'm so glad of them because I only prepared for one baby. And they're all beautiful. You're all very handy. I can do anything with a needle bar sew as my ma used to say. I feel very close to her, girls, now that I'm a mother myself.'

Maureen kissed her impulsively and when they had left said to Anne and Eileen, 'God bless Bridie. I hope she's always as happy as she is now.'

'She deserves to be,' Eileen said. And Anne added, 'Wasn't she tactful with the little boys? That's one story with a happy ending.'

'Ending! It's only the beginning,' Eileen exclaimed, and Anne laughed and agreed.

Chapter Fifteen

Sarah told Anne that John would be twenty-one in September and his parents had suggested a party but he had refused. 'I think he's mean,' Sarah declared, 'I'd love to have a party.' And Anne secretly agreed with her.

They both enjoyed the impromptu parties which were held at the Fitzgerald house on Sunday nights. Friends and relations were often invited to tea on Sundays and afterwards they would all gather in the parlour for a sing-song with Eileen at the piano.

Carrie and Fred were usually playing cards in the kitchen with Julia and Pat and would come in later, Pat to sing Irish ballads and Fred to sing Just A-Wearying For You and Mighty Like a Rose.

Stephen had been given an accordion for his birthday and Carrie surprised the younger people by playing it expertly.

'Unsuspected depths in you, Aunt Carrie,' Stephen joked, and Pat said heartily, 'Ah, sure there's a lot we old ones can do that would surprise you.'

'Hey, not so much of the old ones,' Carrie protested. Sarah was nearly always there and Anne felt a double pleasure in the parties because she knew her friend enjoyed them so much.

The two girls now had a new interest. Classes in Irish dancing were being held in the parish hall of Anne's church because of the *caelidhes* being held at various places in Liverpool.

ELIZABETH MURPHY

Anne and Sarah proved apt pupils, light-footed and quick to learn the intricate steps of the dances. They still went often to the cinema, sometimes with each other, sometimes as a foursome with two young men, and sometimes Sarah with Michael or Anne with a young man who had asked for a date.

Now everything except Sarah's cinema visits with Michael was swept aside by the new interest. They went nearly every evening to the *caelidhes* which were held at halls and clubs throughout the city.

Grandma Houlihan showed a surprising interest in the dances Anne talked about. 'God be with the days of my youth,' she sighed. 'We danced those same dances at the crossroads in Ireland: The Haymaker's Jig, The Four Hand Reel and The Stack of Barley. We used to gather there from the villages and farms all around, and I was the fleetest footed of them all.'

'I hope I've inherited that from you, Grandma,' Anne said.

'Happy days,' she sighed. 'I din't know then the long hard road before me when I married Jeremiah Houlihan, the good man.'

'Grandma had a lot of trouble in her young days,' Anne's mother said.

'I did so. We lived on the farm with his brother Eamonn and sure it was nothing but hard back-breaking work for all of us from morning to night, and little to show for it. Poor stony ground it was.'

She looked round the warm comfortable kitchen. 'Sure I never thought then that I'd end my days in such comfort.'

'It's better that way than the other way round,' Julia said. 'Hardship is easier to bear when you're young.'

'But if I'd had a tenth of this comfort then maybe I wouldn't have lost my children one after another,' Grandma said mournfully.

'Never mind, Ma, it's all in the past,' Julia said. 'Will I make you another cup of cocoa?'

Anne took the opportunity to escape. These old tales were interesting, she felt, but they were ancient history. She felt quite sure that a full and happy life lay before her, if she was careful in her choice of husband.

She was still interested in John Redmond but Sarah said he was very quiet now, and still not showing any interest in girls. 'I think he's still going to the club in Byrom Street,' she said when they had seen John as they waited in the queue outside the Paramount in London Road.

They were with two young men they had met at a *caelidhe* so Anne was glad that John passed without noticing them. There was an item on the cinema newsreel about a revolution in Spain led by General Franco and Sarah said to Anne the following day, 'Our John is all excited about that business in Spain. He never goes to meetings now but I'm sure he's still involved.'

There had also been an item on the news about a man throwing a loaded revolver in front of the King, and Mabel had been at a cinema and seen the Pathé News. She could talk of nothing else the next day.

'I'm really terrified for him,' she told customers. 'It's ridiculous leaving the Coronation until May when you think of what Gypsy Rose Lee said: "He would be a King but would never be crowned".'

Anne looked at Sarah and rolled her eyes heavenwards. 'I wish I could get hold of Gypsy Rose Lee,' she whispered. '*She* wouldn't make it to May, never mind the King! When I think of what she's put us through with Mabel.'

Sarah chuckled and Mabel looked over at them. 'It's all right laughing. I know you girls think I'm soft in the head but I believe in these predictions. Some people *can* see into the future.'

'I wish I could,' Anne said. 'I'd like to know who I'll marry, wouldn't you, Sarah?'

'It's all very well for you girls,' said a customer who worked in a nearby shop, 'saying *who* you'll marry and not *if* you'll marry. Women of my age didn't have no choice. The lads we would've married were killed on the Western Front.'

'Were you engaged, Beattie?' Sarah asked.

'No, but two lads I'd been out with were killed on the Somme and my own brother too, and later on all the lads round our way seemed to get killed or badly wounded. The lad from next-door to us is still in a Military Hospital after all these years.'

'These two will marry,' Mabel said. 'Spoiled for choice they are with all the lads they go out with.'

Anne hoped that John might change his mind about the party but Sarah said he was adamant. 'Mum thinks it's because he couldn't bear to have a party without Grandad there, but I think it's more than that.'

'I wonder why?' Anne said.

Her question was answered late in October. Sarah told her that John had told his mother he was going to Paris for the weekend, but later had admitted he was making his way to Spain to fight with the International Brigade.

'I knew he was still involved with that crowd,' she said. 'That's why he wouldn't let Mum and Dad give a party for him, because he knew he was deceiving them. It all has to be secret until he's abroad, Anne, so don't tell anyone, will you?'

She promised, but could not resist asking questions about all that had happened.

'There's nothing much to tell,' Sarah said. 'I was surprised at how calmly Mum and Dad took it. Mick says he had an idea and he thinks Dad did, and you know I said John was still full of barmy ideas.'

'Was it a shock to your mum?' Anne asked, and Sarah nodded. 'She said he must do what he believed was right, though, and Grandma was calm about it too. John told me she said he hadn't been right all year and maybe this would get it out of his system.

He laughed and said she'd cut him down to size. I must say he seems very happy, Anne.'

Before long a postcard arrived from John who was in Paris, and Anne felt that there was now another bond between herself and Sarah. They both watched eagerly for letters from their brothers who were abroad.

Joe wrote regularly to his mother and father, and to each of his brothers and sisters in turn. Anne had just received a letter from him in which he told her about flying fishes and other strange sights.

'The moon has risen and it looks enormous. Very romantic! How are your romances going? Are you and Sarah still playing havoc with the affections of all the young men in Liverpool? Sarah's brother sounds rather an idealist, but no worse for that,' he wrote, and Anne took the letter to show her friend.

'I do miss our Joe,' she said. 'I always felt I could say anything to him or Maureen and they'd understand.'

'But you've still got Maureen to talk to anyway,' Sarah said, and Anne nodded and changed the subject. Maureen was as gentle and loving as ever, and as willing to give advice, but to Anne it seemed that certain subjects were taboo. She no longer felt as close to her sister as she once had.

She thought about her family that night when she was having a rare evening at home. She had washed her hair and was putting it into Dinkie curlers and her mind wandered back to when she was a child. Then she had thought all her family were the same, part of a united loving whole.

Now that she was older she realised that they were all individuals, each different from the other in spite of the surface harmony. Children of the same parents and with the same background yet totally different in many ways.

Eileen and Maureen – who would believe that they were sisters? Anne wondered. Maureen so quiet and reserved, so devout and with moral scruples which made her unable to speak ill of anyone. Hear no evil, see no evil, speak no evil, that was Maureen, thought Anne. Yet she was always ready to join in family fun and enjoyed life in her own quiet way, mostly in activities connected with the church.

Eileen's way was completely different. A big boisterous girl, her favourite expression was: 'I don't give a damn.' She played netball and hockey, swam and skated, and was never without an escort for anything she wanted to do.

She had learned to drive on a two-ton lorry which one of her boyfriends drove for a haulage firm and was pressing her father to allow her to buy a motorcycle. But she could be sensitive, too, and was miserable because of the unkindness of another girl in her office.

Tony seemed to have outgrown his moody fits since his twenty-first birthday, Anne thought, and was always having a good time, with money in his pocket, a job he liked and plenty of friends. Yet even Tony . . . Somehow there was always a hint of sadness about him when he was sitting quietly at home.

Anne caught sight of herself in the mirror and laughed aloud at her solemn expression. Good job they don't know how I'm picking them apart, she thought. I'd never live it down. Yet later she thought again about her family.

Was everyone more complex than they seemed? Was it possible ever to know everything about a person? She and Sarah were such close friends, but she had thoughts that Sarah knew nothing about, and probably the same applied to Sarah. I suppose it's only when you are married that you really know everything about someone else, she thought.

On 1 December Dr Blunt, the Bishop of Bradford, spoke of the King's need to be aware of his responsibilities. None of the stories about the King and Mrs Simpson that Joe had told them had appeared in the British newspapers, but suddenly the flood-gates were opened and every paper carried the story. Mabel was inconsolable.

At first all her anger was directed against Mrs Simpson. 'She should be run out of the country,' she declared. 'The scheming creature! *Two* divorces. The King should be protected from women like that.'

'But what can they do if he wants to marry her?' Anne asked. She was strongly tempted to remind Mabel of the way she had almost called Joe a liar, but felt too sorry for her to pursue it.

'She's just a gold digger,' Mabel declared. 'You see those sort of harpies on the pictures and men haven't got a chance against them. But *someone* should do something.'

Within a few days her anger had turned from Mrs Simpson against Stanley Baldwin and the Government who were insisting that the King must choose between Mrs Simpson and the throne.

'My newspaper says he could have a morganatic marriage,' she said. 'She could be his wife but not Queen. They say other Kings have done it.'

'But who'd be Queen?' Sarah asked.

'There doesn't have to be one,' Mabel snapped. 'I'm disgusted with them all going on about morals. Hypocrites! What about Edward VII and all his women? No better than prostitutes some of them, but you didn't hear no moaning over them.'

Both girls sympathised with Mabel in her distress, but were less interested in these events because other things occupied their minds. Sarah told Anne that another letter had arrived from John and he was now in Lyons. 'Mum's very worried about him, but he seems happy.'

'I suppose he's doing what he thinks is right,' Anne suggested. Sarah had brought in a photograph of John taken before he left for Spain, wearing an open-necked shirt and shorts, with a ruck-sack on his back.

He looked happy and carefree, and Anne also thought that he looked very romantic. She hoped that Sarah would say more about the letter but instead she spoke about her sister Kate who was sulking because she had not been chosen to appear in *Puss In Boots*.

Many of the customers agreed with Mabel and there was universal condemnation of Mrs Simpson but great affection for the King, especially when it was realised that he would be forced to give up his throne.

On 10 December a woman brought a special edition news-paper into the shop. 'Them lot in London have won,' she said dramatically. 'The King's going to make a speech on the wire-less tomorrow. He's abdicating.'

Mabel snatched the paper from her. 'It can't be true!' she cried. Everyone began to talk at once. 'That Yankee faggot,' one woman said. 'She must've bewitched him.' And another declared, 'It's that lot in London. It suits them to get him out because he was going to do something about the miners. God forgive them.' Mabel was in tears and so were many of the customers.

For the next week Mabel could talk of nothing but the Abdication speech by Edward VIII and spoke bitterly of the new King and Queen, but gradually she warmed to them.

'At least she's a good respectable woman, even if she hasn't got Royal blood,' she said. 'And the little Princesses are lovely. I wonder if it's true that Princess Margaret Rose is deaf and dumb?'

Because they were fond of Mabel, Anne and Sarah humoured her and listened patiently to her constant references to the Royal family, but their interests lay elsewhere.

A week before Christmas Michael asked Sarah if he could see her that evening. She was about to refuse but he said quietly, 'I'd like to explain something, Sarah. Perhaps we could go to a café and talk?' She agreed, and later when she told Anne they both tried to guess what he would say but neither could guess the truth.

The following morning Sarah told Anne that Michael felt he had a vocation for the priesthood. 'A priest!' Anne gasped.

'Yes. He said he had almost decided he had a vocation, but then he met me and was attracted to me and thought it was a sign that he was not called to be a priest. All this year he's been pulled two ways and couldn't decide.'

'So what decided him?' asked Anne.

'When I told him I had a date and he didn't feel jealous. Then he thought he wasn't being fair to me. He's been to the parish priest for advice and soon he'll be going to the Seminary at Upholland.'

'I can just see him as a priest somehow,' Anne said thoughtfully.

'Yes, we always felt there was something different about him, didn't we?' Sarah said.

'Are you upset, Sar?' asked Anne, but she shook her head. 'No. I told Michael I'm glad to know that there's nothing wrong with me to make him so cool.'

Mabel thought it was a waste for such a handsome man to become a priest but Sarah said quietly, 'It's not the outside that matters if he feels like a priest inside, Mabel,' and the older woman said no more.

Although all the family missed Joe they enjoyed Christmas. Their mother seemed better in health, and he had written that he was determined that this would be his last Christmas at sea.

Grandma Houlihan was still with them, but now she spent most of her time in bed. She came down for Christmas dinner then returned to her room. The family found it easier to carry trays to her and to stay to talk or read to her than to have to be constantly watchful while she was downstairs, in case anything they said or did offended her rigid standards.

On Boxing Day a lady from the church came to sit with her while the rest of the family went to a party at Carrie's house. As usual friends were also welcome and Anne invited Sarah. She arrived wearing a tiny gold watch which she said had arrived on Christmas Eve from her rich aunt in America.

'I wish I had a rich aunt,' Eileen said, examining the watch. 'This is exquisite.'

'I don't like her though,' Sarah said. 'I suppose I'm a hypocrite taking the watch, but I couldn't resist it.'

'That's not being a hypocrite. It's being practical,' Eileen said with a grin before moving away.

'I think your family are lovely, every one of them,' Sarah whispered to Anne, and she felt a glow of pride.

Bridie and Jack had arrived with their family, and the twins were passed round and admired. They were placid babies and made no protest, but Teddy and Danny followed them, watching anxiously over the babies.

'You've got good minders there, Bridie,' Fred said, and she said fondly, 'Yes. I don't know what I'd do without the lads to help me.'

Minnie and Dympna were absent but Carrie told Julia that Dympna was having a difficult pregnancy. 'I went to ask them to come tonight and felt really sorry for Minnie *and* for Dympna. They both looked terrible.'

'I know. I feel so sorry for them too,' Julia said. 'Minnie came to see Ma at Christmas and she broke her heart crying. Ma told me afterwards that Dympna's husband is always out drinking and he comes home and threatens Minnie and her if they say a word to him. It's a thousand pities she ever married him.'

'Poor Minnie,' Carrie said. 'She's got a wicked tongue, but she hasn't had much luck in life, has she?'

Carrie was called away and Tony came with his girlfriend to sit with his mother. Helen was a tiny girl with a pretty face and a warm personality, and all the Fitzgeralds liked her. Anne thought she had never seen Tony so happy. Helen had been to tea with the Fitzgerald family, and Tony had been invited to her home.

Anne had decided that as soon as Christmas was over she would try again to see Kathleen O'Neill, and on the next Wednesday went to wait near the coal merchant's office. Mrs O'Neill and Cormac were not there and Anne was delighted to see Kathleen leaving the office with another girl.

She sped across the road to Kathleen. 'Hallo,' she said breathlessly. 'How are you?' Kathleen seemed pleased to see her and introduced her to the other girl as a friend from school. 'Ella works with me,' she explained. 'And she lives in the next street so we walk home together.'

'No sense in her mother coming out in all weathers to meet Kath when I pass her door,' Ella said robustly. She was a well-built girl with bright dark eyes and plump rosy cheeks, and Anne thought she would be just the right person to overrule Mrs O'Neill.

'How are your mother and Cormac?' Anne asked.

'Fine. He had a bad chest and was in bed for three weeks but he's better now,' Kathleen said. 'Are your family okay?'

'Yes, thanks. Mum wasn't well but she's better now. We've got my Grandma Houlihan living with us,' Anne said. She hesitated. If Kathleen had made a friend she was unwilling to intrude, but felt that she should say more.

'We never *did* have that night out, did we, Kathleen?' she said with a smile, and Ella said cheerfully, 'I'm tired trying to get her to go out more, but we did go to the flicks one night, didn't we, Kath?'

'Yes, but Mother worries so much when I'm out,' Kathleen said. 'I don't like to upset her.'

'If you went out more she'd get used to it then she wouldn't worry,' Ella said briskly. Anne said goodbye to the two girls thinking that if anyone could help Kathleen it would be Ella with her no-nonsense approach. She felt the weight of responsibility for Kathleen roll away, and walked away with a light heart.

Chapter Sixteen

The winter was milder than the previous year's, and after Christmas Anne and Sarah were out nearly every evening and at weekends. They were still as popular with the young men at the *caelidhes* and still as determined not to start courting seriously with anyone.

None of the young men Anne went out with interested her as much as John Redmond, although she said nothing to Sarah.

Theresa's wedding took place on the second Saturday in January, but neither Minnie nor Dympna attended.

'I suppose you can't blame them,' Julia said to her mother. 'They're bound to feel the difference in the circumstances, God help them. Poor Dympna's marriage and the way it's going, and everything set fair for Theresa. I thought she made a beautiful bride.'

'She did so,' said Grandma Houlihan, who had attended the Nuptial Mass in a wheelchair. 'She looked like a little girl with Carmel and Eileen as bridesmaids. The size of them!'

'It's a pity you weren't able to stay for the wedding breakfast, Ma,' Julia said, ignoring the remark about Eileen. 'Sure there was no stint of anything.'

Pat had come in and said heartily, 'Aye, trust Fred. He really pushed the boat out. Must have cost him a fortune.'

'Well for him that he has it,' Grandma said. 'A lovely Mass and a grand sermon from Father Ryan. I hope the girl realises that was more important than all the food and drink there was all the fuss about.'

'Dympna must be near her time,' Julia said. 'It seems she's not sure when she's due.' She was only trying to change the subject but the following morning word was brought that Dympna's baby had been stillborn and she was very ill.

Julia went down to Minnie's house and found Carrie already there. She was trying to comfort Minnie who was crying bitterly and said quickly to Julia, 'Dympna's been taken to hospital. She's in good hands.' But Minnie refused to be comforted.

'What time's the visiting?' asked Julia.

Minnie wailed even louder and Carrie said, 'Should we make you a cup of tea?'

Minnie wiped her eyes and stood up. 'I'll do it myself,' she said. 'I don't like other people in my kitchen.'

She went into the back kitchen and Carrie whispered, 'We could go anytime to see Dympna. She's on an urgent note.'

'Jesus, Mary and Joseph watch over her,' Julia exclaimed, crossing herself. 'She's very bad then?'

Carrie nodded, and under cover of the clink of crockery whispered hurriedly, 'Brendan came home and had the husband beaten up. It brought Dympna on.'

Minnie came in with the tray of teacups and Julia asked if they could go with her to the hospital. 'No, they wouldn't let you in,' Minnie said.

'But, surely, one of your sisters?' Julia said. '*Someone* should be with you.'

'I'd rather be by myself,' Minnie said. She seemed anxious to hurry them away, and only when Julia put her arms round her and wept did she say gruffly, 'Our Brendan will meet me there.'

Carrie came back with Julia to see her mother and on the way told Julia what she had learned. 'It seems the husband had come home in drink at New Year and hit Dympna, and Minnie when she tried to interfere. Brendan must have got word and a couple of fellows set about Harold Duffy and battered him. He came home covered in blood and Dympna went into labour.'

'Good God, it could have been the death of the girl,' Julia gasped, and Carrie said grimly, 'It might be yet.'

'Oh, Carrie, let's hope not. Please God, she'll be all right. She's young and strong,' said Julia. 'I wish Minnie'd let us help her.'

'She couldn't get rid of us quickly enough, could she?' Carrie said. 'I keep saying I'll have no more to do with her, but she gets a cob on if we don't go yet doesn't seem to want us when we do. She doesn't know what she wants.'

'Ah, well, I suppose she can't help her nature,' Julia said gently. 'Bad as he is, it's a good thing she has Brendan. He does try to be a good son to her.'

'By getting his brother-in-law knocked about?' Carrie said ironically, but they had reached Julia's house and carefully edited what they told their mother.

Later when Julia told Pat he said shrewdly, 'The quare feller must be near enough to get home pretty quickly if he was going to the hospital with Minnie. I wonder how she gets word to him?'

'God knows. We'd never find out from her. She's as deep as a drawn well.'

Dympna slowly recovered, but by the time she left the hospital her husband had disappeared. With Dympna unable to work and her husband gone, the family thought she might be worried about money and Carrie tried tactfully to tell Minnie and Dympna that Fred and Pat would look after them.

Before Minnie could speak Dympna said rudely, 'We don't want your charity. Tell them to stick it where the monkey stuck the nuts.'

Carrie's eyes widened in shock. *'Well!'* was all she could say.

'Dympna, that's not nice,' Minnie said, then turned to Carrie.

197

'She's right, though. We don't want your charity.'

'Charity! I've never heard it called charity – families helping each other,' Carrie said angrily. 'You've changed your tune anyway, Minnie.' She stood up. 'I won't bother you again. If you need us, you know where to find us.' She hurried out but as she went through the front door heard Dympna say loudly, 'Good riddance.'

Tears of mortification filled Carrie's eyes but by the time she reached Julia's house anger was uppermost. Fortunately Grandma Houlihan was in bed and she was able to pour out the whole story to Julia.

'The impudent faggot!' she exclaimed. 'And such a low expression. Sure the dregs of the gutters don't talk like that.'

'I'm finished with them,' Carrie declared. 'I mean it. I'll tell Fred I want nothing more to do with Minnie, but I won't tell him or anyone the expression Dympna used to me. I'd be ashamed.'

'And neither will I,' Julia said. 'The girl must have mixed in low company. I never heard the expression and I don't know what it means but it *sounds* low.'

Carrie was able to keep to her resolve not to see Minnie or Dympna again, but Minnie visited Julia's house to see her mother. 'I bid her good morning and she goes right up to Ma's bedroom,' Julia related. 'God knows what she's saying to Ma, bending over her whispering when I take in a cup of tea, but Ma's twice as cantankerous when she's been.'

'But she drinks the tea?' Carrie said.

'No, she leaves it there to go cold,' said Julia. 'The first time I asked would I pour her a fresh cup, but now I pour it away when she's gone and say nothing.'

'I asked you because I had a spell like that with her one time. When you were ill it was. I just took up the tea whenever she came and handed a cup to Ma so that she drank it, but I said nothing to the quare one and quite suddenly she started drinking the tea again. I don't know what bee she had in her bonnet,' said Carrie.

'I don't like anyone to leave my house without bite or sup, but I'll just keep taking up the tea and say nothing,' said Julia.

'And you say Ma's awkward after Minnie's gone?'

'Yes, she picks on one or another of the family, and it really vexes me. It was Eileen last time. Ma was downstairs when Eileen said something about that creature in the office that makes her life a misery and Ma practically said it was Eileen's own fault. She said the others in the office got on all right with the woman.'

'That sounds like one of Minnie's bullets made for Ma to fire,' Carrie said grimly. 'How would Ma know anything about the office?'

'Ah, never mind. Tell me about Theresa's house,' Julia said. 'Eileen tells me it's grand.'

The family all worried about Eileen's unhappiness. She worked in the office of Benson's Engineering, where Tony was a tool-maker, and for the first few years was happy there. Now she had a superior who did all she could to make life difficult for Eileen, constantly finding fault with her work and humiliating her before the rest of the staff.

After Grandma Houlihan had gone to bed after criticising Eileen, Tony told the family the reason for the woman's treatment of his sister.

'That Ruby can't do the work,' he said. 'We're always finding mistakes in the paperwork. Our Eileen can run rings round her and some of the lads have said so. Ruby's jealous of her.'

'If she's so thick why was she promoted?' Terry said.

'Ah, there's a reason for that,' Tony said. 'She's Bill Haddon's girlfriend on the sly and can wrap him round her little finger.'

'But, Tony, he's married. His wife comes in the shop,' Anne said. 'They live in Queen's Road.'

'Yes, and don't you repeat what I've said to anyone, Anne,' Tony warned her. 'I didn't know you knew his wife. It's common knowledge in the works but he and Ruby manage to keep it quiet outside. I wouldn't want his wife to find out through me.'

'So Eileen has no chance no matter how hard she works?' Stephen said. 'The only hope is for her to find another job.'

'Or for this to come out and Ruby get the push,' Terry said.

'Why just Ruby? Why not the fellow as well?' Anne said indignantly.

Terry laughed. 'Is this Sarah's influence?' he asked. 'Dom told me you were both arguing about the Spanish Civil War.'

'How did he know?' Anne asked.

'He knows a fellow who goes to the *caelidhes*. Sarah's brother is fighting for the International Brigade, isn't he?'

'Yes, and they were saying at the dance that the Church is on Franco's side and John should be fighting for Franco. Sarah told him in a letter but she doesn't know whether he'll ever get it.'

The Redmond family had received several letters from John, written when he arrived in Spain and later when he was moving to the fighting area. On the back of the last one he had scribbled a note that trucks had arrived to take them to defend the road to Madrid.

Since then there had been reports on cinema newsreels and in newspapers that there had been heavy fighting in Spain and many casualties, and no more letters had arrived.

'That note was written on the first of February,' Sarah said. 'That was weeks ago.'

'No news is good news,' Anne said, as much to cheer herself as her friend.

'My dad went to the club in Byrom Street to ask for news,' Sarah said a few days later. 'They told him John was in the fighting in the Jarama Valley, but his name wasn't among the casualties. They said letters might be held up.'

'So you can stop worrying,' Anne said, and Sarah rather doubtfully agreed. Anne told herself that it was ridiculous to be so concerned about someone she had met so briefly, but John Redmond was constantly in her mind.

Meanwhile the two girls continued to enjoy the dances and to make dates with many young men. Mabel had had numerous colds during the winter and a succession of boils and Mrs Dyson decided that she was rundown and was working too hard.

She engaged a young school leaver to help with odd jobs in the shop and Rosie listened open-mouthed to Anne and Sarah talking about their boyfriends.

'Don't you be copying these two, Rosie,' Mabel said sourly, 'They'll be getting themselves a bad name.'

'Oh, Mabel, they're all harmless,' Anne protested, and Sarah added that most of the young men were related or she and Anne knew their families.

'Mabel's always the wrong side out these days, isn't she?' Sarah said, but a letter had arrived from John and she was too happy to care about Mabel's moods.

He told them that he had been wounded in the foot and was now in hospital, and that he had received letters from home.

'He said if anyone says this is a Holy War by Franco, tell them that he has bombed towns and villages, and innocent men, women and children have been killed by bombs dropped without warning,' Sarah said. 'He said there are Muslim Moors fighting on Franco's side too.'

'So we can give anyone an answer if they start about that.'

Mabel's health improved but not because of Rosie. She was a stupid girl who seemed unable to remember the simplest instruction, but she listened to every conversation and was always ready to air her views.

'Youse three are always talking,' she said pertly when Mabel reprimanded her.

'Yes, but we work as we talk,' Mabel said. 'You don't see Sarah or Anne standing round with their mouths open. They get on with the work.'

Rosie was unconcerned and continued to listen in to conversations even between Mabel and customers, and either said something to the customer or tried to gossip about her when she left. She was impervious to snubs. Billy the bakehouse boy had always joked with the girls when he brought through the trays of hot pies and took away the empties, but they were all usually too busy for more than a quick comment. Now Rosie stood in his way and talked until the pie tray was nearly empty and Mr Dyson in the bakehouse roaring for Billy. She continually went into the bakehouse on one pretext or another until one day Mr Dyson appeared at the door into the shop.

'Keep that girl in the shop, will you, Mabel?' he said. 'She's getting in Billy's road while he's at the oven.'

Anne told her family that she was fed up. 'I can't speak to Sarah without Rosie standing there listening with her mouth open or else chipping in, and Mabel's always in a bad temper. She was a bit touchy before but we knew she wasn't well and made allowances. This is different. She just can't stand Rosie.'

Sarah warned Anne to keep the sharp cake knife away from Mabel one day when another row involving Rosie broke out. She had been told to fill up a half-empty cake tray from another one and a customer complained that she was licking her fingers as she handled the cakes. Mabel scolded her, Rosie answered back, and Sarah told Anne that she thought Mabel was at breaking point.

Rosie went for her dinner and Mabel said to Sarah, 'I've had enough. I don't like to throw Mrs Dyson's kindness back in her face but I'll have to tell her that girl will have to go.'

Fortunately before she did so Rosie returned and told them that her sister had 'spoken' for her in the bag warehouse. 'I don't like it here,' she said frankly. 'Youse are all too grumpy. Our Essie says they have a gear laugh in the baggy.'

Whether it was Rosie's departure or the imminent Coronation the girls were unsure, but Mabel was suddenly herself again. It had been decided to hold the Coronation of George VI on 12 May, the day fixed for the Coronation of Edward VIII who was now known as the Duke of Windsor and rarely mentioned by Mabel.

'It would be a waste to have a different day when the preparations were so well ahead,' she said to Anne, and all her interest now was in dressing the shop window. Mrs Dyson had allowed her some money for it, and Mabel had a striking display which was mentioned in the local newspaper.

Mabel painted her front door red, white and blue, and draped her house with bunting. Photographs of the King and Queen and of the two young Princesses were displayed in the front window, and when someone said to her, 'Gypsy Rose Lee was right after all,' she only said, 'Yes, but it all turned out for the best in the end.'

Anne and Sarah were pleased to see Mabel her own pleasant self again. As the summer approached they spent much of their time cycling but most Sundays went to North Wales on the pillion seats of motor cycles owned by two brothers whom they met at a *caelidhe*.

'I'm glad to be out of the house,' Anne confessed to Sarah. 'My grandma never stops moaning and picking faults. My poor mum can do nothing right for her. I don't know how she stands it.'

In spite of these words Anne was unprepared to come home one day and hear that her mother had collapsed. Mrs Bennet the cleaning woman had found her in the back kitchen and had helped her on to the sofa. In spite of Julia's pleas for her to tell nobody, Mrs Bennet had gone to Carrie's house and she had dashed up to take over.

Mrs Bennet had come back in the evening and the family had thanked her profusely. 'She didn't want me to say nothing, but she put the heart sideways in me, the colour of her, and the ould one carrying on ringing a bell and calling. I run down for Mrs Anderson and I was afraid to come back for fear of what I'd find,' Mrs Bennet said.

'Thank God you came in, Mrs Bennet, and got Auntie Carrie. Mum takes notice of her,' Maureen said.

'She must have been feeling bad and keeping quiet about it,' Pat said. 'For fear she'd upset her mother, I suppose.'

'Aye, she was too soft altogether and the old lady played on her,' Mrs Bennet said. 'Mrs Anderson had her shifted down there in no time, statues an'all. She'll know how to handle her.' She went up to see Julia but she was deeply asleep. A black bottle stood on the floor by the bed and Maureen put it inside a cupboard without comment.

Julia recovered quickly and three weeks later was downstairs again. 'I feel ashamed,' she told Carrie. 'The years you looked after Ma and I did a thing like that after less than two years.'

'Don't be daft,' Carrie said. 'You took her when I was sick and I've taken her while you're sick. Ma doesn't mind. She likes the change.' She laughed heartily. 'We'll just have to be careful not to be sick at the same time.'

In spite of her many activities Anne always found time to visit the Misses Dolan. They had suddenly become very frail and she was worried about them, but they told her one day that the parish priest had persuaded them to let two rooms to a widow with a small girl.

'He was very persuasive,' Miss Louisa said. 'He told us that it would be a Christian act to take in the widow and child, but I suspect he told her that it was her Christian duty to live with two old ladies and look after them.'

The widow, Margaret, was a plump cheerful girl who seemed to accept her state philosophically. 'What can't be cured must be endured,' she told Anne. 'Me husband was always away on long voyages from when we was married so I can't believe he isn't just at sea.'

She had not disturbed the Dolans' parlour which was full of memories of their family but had cleared out two upstairs rooms as a bedroom and living room for herself and her daughter Molly.

The little girl had just started school, and her mother went cleaning on three mornings a week. Molly soon became a firm favourite with the Misses Dolan and every time Anne saw them she was told of Molly's quaint sayings and beauty and intelligence.

Anne was pleased to see the pleasure the child gave to her old friends, and pleased too to see how Margaret watched over them and helped them unobtrusively. A few months after Margaret came, Miss Louisa told Anne that she and her sister had inherited sums of money from two relatives who had died.

'I'm afraid we have now outlived all our family,' she told Anne with a sad smile. 'We have discussed it and as we have no one left to inherit from us feel justified in using the money for ourselves.'

'Of course. That's a good idea.'

'We have to face the fact that we are both becoming a little infirm,' Miss Louisa said. 'Margaret helps us but she is out on three mornings a week. This money will enable us to pay her a small sum to compensate for her income from cleaning and she will stay here with us instead.'

'That's a splendid idea,' Anne said enthusiastically. 'I'm sure Margaret will be delighted with that arrangement.'

'I know you offered to help us, Anne,' Miss Ellen said. 'Don't be hurt, dear, because we declined. You are at work and then your dear mother needs help. We have asked Margaret and she has agreed.'

Later Anne saw Margaret and told her how relieved she was that the sisters would be cared for. 'They're so independent even though they're frail. I don't know how they've managed for so long.'

'I know you and your family have been good to them,' Margaret said, 'but they need someone with them all the time, to look after them and cook meals and such. I thought they might object to Molly but she's quite a favourite with them.'

'She's brought them a lot of pleasure,' Anne said.

Later she told her mother how pleased she was. 'I've been worried about them but I didn't know what could be done,' she said. 'This is perfect.'

Anne was feeling very happy at events in her family. Her mother seemed so much better and Grandma Houlihan had settled back with the Anderson family. Joe was due to return home in August, and Eileen had found another job, working as a pools clerk.

Helen Daly and Tony had told the family that they wished to become engaged and everyone was delighted.

'Ah, the darling girl. I couldn't wish for a nicer wife for you, Tony, or a better daughter-in-law for me,' Julia said. 'If all my children do as well I'll be happy.'

'We'll have a party,' Pat exclaimed. 'I tell you what. How about announcing it when our Joe comes home? Make it a joint celebration.'

Tony felt Helen's hand tighten on his and saw the loving glance she gave him, and he was able to say without hesitation, 'Yes, that's a great idea, Dad. Isn't it, Helen?' The days when he would feel jealous of Joe had gone, never to return.

Chapter Seventeen

Anne was excited about Joe's homecoming but felt that she had to tone down her behaviour in the shop. The Redmonds had not received any more letters from John, but a few days before Joe arrived Sarah came into the shop flushed and breathless with joy.

'We've had three letters at once,' she said. 'John's coming home because his foot won't heal.'

'Oh, dear me,' Mabel said sympathetically, but Sarah went on, 'Dad says they haven't got the medical supplies there. It'll soon heal when he comes home.'

Anne felt too excited to speak. Surely now she would meet him again and show him that she was not just his sister's young friend? I'll find a way to tell him I'll be eighteen in January, she vowed, and meanwhile could show her own joy about Joe.

Preparations were going ahead for his return and Mrs Bennet was as excited as the family. Tony shared a bedroom with Joe and while he was at sea Tony's belongings had gradually filled the room. Now he declared that he was afraid to step on Joe's half of the floor.

'I've cleared all my stuff out of his chest of drawers and his half of the wardrobe, but that's not enough for Mrs Bennet. She left me a note saying I'd rumpled the cover on Joe's bed and made footmarks where she'd polished round it,' Tony said. 'I don't know how I'm supposed to get to the window.'

'Be glad she's taking such an interest, Tony,' Maureen said. 'If she didn't do it Mum would be scouring and polishing and tiring herself out.'

'I don't see the need for it at all,' Pat said. 'Joe's not going to notice or care whether the curtains are washed.' But Julia said firmly, '*I'd* notice, and I'd be uneasy if the house wasn't spotless to welcome him home.' Anne was quite happy to forgo the dances and spend the weekend preparing for Joe, especially as she knew the same orgy of cleaning was taking place at Sarah's home, ready for John's return.

Maureen, Eileen and Anne took it in turns to do the weekend baking. They each had a speciality. Maureen made delicious fruit cakes, Eileen had a light hand with scones, and Anne's forte was pastry. On the Sunday before Joe's return it was Eileen's turn to bake, but it was decided that instead Maureen would make a fruit cake, Anne some apple and some rhubarb pies, and Eileen would make scones on the day of Joe's return.

'I'm *dying* to see him again,' Anne said to Sarah. 'You must meet him this time, Sarah. You'll really like him.'

'Who is he like?' she asked.

'To look at?' Anne said. 'Like me, I suppose, or Maureen.'

'Like a flamenco dancer?' Sarah teased her. Flamenco dancers had been shown in a film in a local cinema and Anne had been teased at the dances and called 'senorita'. Sarah had said she could fall for the male dancer.

Anne laughed. 'Yes, he does look like that, but without the curling lip and the high-heeled shoes!'

There was a joyful reunion when Joe arrived home. 'So much has happened since you went away,' his mother said, and during the following days he met Helen, and Theresa's husband, and heard of the misfortunes of the Connolly family.

There was no opportunity for him to meet Sarah but she was invited to the party on Saturday night, and her parents also.

Joe had met Mrs Bennet and thanked her for the help she gave his mother and for her defence of his share of the bedroom which Tony had told him about. Julia invited Mrs Bennet and her daughter to the party too.

'God bless us, you'll need elastic walls,' she said. 'Are Mrs Anderson and her family coming?'

'Oh, yes, all the Andersons,' Julia said. 'My mother won't be able to come because she's bedfast at present, but Joe's been to see her a few times, and he'll go on Saturday before the party.'

Tony and Helen had been for the engagement ring, a half hoop of diamonds, but Helen would not wear it until the engagement was announced at the party.

Maureen had made and iced a cake with the words 'Best wishes to Helen and Tony on their engagement' written on it, and had hidden it in a hatbox in her bedroom. She took Joe up to see it, and a little later Anne went to her bedroom for a magazine.

She went up quickly, as she did everything, and as she bounded up the stairs and rushed past the door of Maureen's room had a fleeting glimpse of Maureen and Joe sitting on the edge of her bed with Joe's arms around his sister and her head on his shoulder.

She clattered about in her bedroom for a few minutes then dashed downstairs again without a glance at Maureen's room, but she wondered. Was Maureen telling Joe her worries about their mother or was it something else? But in the bustle of preparation for the party she forgot about the incident. Sarah's parents had been invited in addition to Sarah, and Anne took them to her mother when they arrived. Mrs Redmond was unlike Sarah in appearance, with dark curly hair and brown eyes and dimples in her cheeks when she smiled. Her father looked more like John as Anne remembered him, with a firm handshake and a deep pleasant voice.

Julia greeted both of them very warmly. 'I'm delighted to meet you,' she said. 'We're all very fond of Sarah.'

Later, after they had met Helen and Tony and other members of the family, Julia drew Mrs Redmond to sit beside her on the sofa. 'I'm so pleased that Anne and Sarah are friends,' she said. 'Especially with them together all day.'

'And so am I,' Mrs Redmond assured her. 'These adolescent years, a good friend is very important, I think.'

'Indeed and that's true. While they are neither a child nor a woman they need a good influence. Anne thinks the world of Sarah.'

'And she's very fond of Anne. We all are. She's a lovely girl. A real charmer,' said Mrs Redmond. 'They enjoy every minute, those two, don't they?' Julia agreed and then asked about John and when he was expected home.

Soon they were both claimed by other guests but Julia told Anne later how much she liked Sarah's mother. 'A lovely warmhearted woman,' she said. 'I can see why Sarah's such a nice girl. And her father's a real gentleman too.' It was the start of a warm friendship between the two women.

The party went with a swing, with the older guests gathering in the roomy kitchen and the young people in the parlour. Anne had proudly introduced Joe to Sarah, and Terry had put his arms round both girls. 'The Queens of the *caelidhes*,' he told Joe. 'They've been out with half the boys in Liverpool.' And there was much joking and teasing among the group.

Maureen joined in, and Anne thought she looked happier than she had seen her for a long time. A little later all the older people began to crowd into the parlour and Eileen and Stephen served everyone with glasses of punch.

Pat Fitzgerald held up his glass. 'Welcome, everyone,' he said. 'This party is for two reasons. One is to welcome home our son Joe. Step forward, Joe.' He stepped forward from the crowd, looking embarrassed, and Mrs Bennet shouted: 'Welcome home.' Everyone echoed her and drank the toast and Joe stepped back thankfully.

'The other reason,' Pat said, 'is to announce the engagement of Helen and Tony and welcome her into our family. Raise your glasses to Helen and Tony.'

Maureen had slipped away and now she wheeled in a tea trolley with the cake on it. There were cries of admiration and Helen said, 'Oh, Maureen, it looks too nice to cut.'

'Come on, girl, the sooner it's cut the sooner it's eaten,' Fred Anderson called. He had already joked because Helen was so tiny, she only reached Tony's shoulder, and Anne had said she would make sure he was out of the country when she was married.

'But he's very good,' Maureen said. She turned to Sarah. 'You know Grandma Houlihan lived with us for two years and was very difficult? She'd lived with Fred and Aunt Carrie for ten years before that, but they willingly took her back when Mum was ill and they're very kind to her.'

Joe put his arm round her shoulders and squeezed them. 'Still seeing the best in everyone, Mo?' he said fondly.

There were several family gatherings during the next two weeks, sometimes at the Fitzgerald house and sometimes at the Andersons'. Shaun was now a commercial traveller for a firm of wine shippers and often away from home but Joe saw him once and was invited to dinner at Theresa's new home in West Derby. Eileen was also invited.

'I'm trying myself out on you as a hostess,' Theresa said. 'We can only fit four in the dining room so we'll have to have people in relays.'

'She's been dying to use all her wedding presents,' Jim said, smiling at her, and afterwards Joe said to Eileen that he thought it was a truly happy marriage that would last.

'I think so too,' Eileen said. 'And I think Tony and Helen will be the same. It's very chancy, though, isn't it, Joe? One mistake and you're stuck for life.'

'Yes, so we'd better be careful, hadn't we?' he said, smiling at her.

The family organised several outings during the following weeks, to the theatre or the cinema and several times to a *caelidhe*.

Terry and the Anderson twins had started to attend the *caelidhes*, although not always the same ones as Anne and Sarah. They had been learning the steps of the dances, and made up in enthusiasm what they lacked in skill.

Pat and Julia were in the party for the visits to the theatre and the cinema, but otherwise the group was of young people including Sarah and Dom and Desmond.

Joe had told Anne that he thought Sarah was a very nice girl, but there was little opportunity for him and Sarah to talk to each other even at the *caelidhes*. As soon as a dance was announced she was claimed by Terry or one of the Andersons, and between dances seemed always to be hedged in by other people.

When Joe had been home for ten days Sarah came into the shop with the news that her brother was in England and would be arriving at Lime Street Station on the following day.

'Do you think Mrs Dyson would let me have the day off, Mabel?' she asked. 'All the rest of the family are going to be there to meet him.'

'I'm sure she will,' Mabel said, and disappeared into the bakehouse to ask.

She came back to tell Sarah that she could have the day off. 'You don't mind, you and Anne?' Sarah asked.

'Of course not. We'll manage fine, won't we, Anne?' Mabel said. 'And all the better without that Rosie.'

Anne was about to say 'I wish I could come with you' but thought better of it. The next day she thought often of the

Redmond family and wondered whether John had arrived and how he was.

When Sarah returned to the shop she told them that John had arrived on crutches. 'There were about eight of them,' she said. 'John's foot was bandaged and the bandages were filthy, but Dad soon dressed it properly.'

Her father was a member of the St John Ambulance Brigade and Mabel said approvingly, 'Yes, your dad would know what to do. Between him and your grandma your brother'll soon be all right.'

The following evening the girls had arranged to go to the cinema together, and Anne called for Sarah. She came to the door and took Anne through to the kitchen where John was lying on the sofa. He attempted to rise to his feet but Anne said quickly, 'Don't get up.'

'You're honoured, Anne,' his young brother Mick said with a grin. 'He's been lying there like the Sultan of Morocco while everyone else has been in and out.'

Sarah's father was at work but her mother greeted Anne warmly. 'Of course you've met John before, haven't you, love? He's a lot thinner, isn't he?'

Anne smiled and agreed and Mick said mischievously, 'Don't tell Anne why, Mum.'

John coloured. 'Big mouth,' he said to Mick, and then to Anne he murmured, 'I had dysentery.'

'How is your foot?' she asked, and he said gratefully that it was much better. 'We just didn't have the medical supplies in Spain.'

'Anne's brother is home too after a long time at sea,' Mrs Redmond said to John. 'We were at a lovely party at Anne's house to welcome him home and for the engagement of her other brother.'

'So you've got two brothers?' he said, smiling at her.

'I've got four – five really. My eldest brother died when he was six,' Anne said. 'And two sisters.'

Before they could say more Sarah came back into the kitchen wearing her coat. 'We won't be late, Mum,' she said, and when Anne stood up John held out his hand to her. 'Nice to see you again,' he said, and she smiled and blushed before turning to say goodbye to Sarah's mother.

'Goodbye, love. Enjoy the picture,' Mrs Redmond said. 'Remember me to your mother.'

The Fitzgeralds had hoped that this time Joe would be able to leave the sea, but a job that he had been promised had gone to someone else. He tried elsewhere without success and eventually signed on again for another trip.

On the Sunday before he was due to go aboard the family decided to cycle to Thurstaton on the Wirral. Tony had dropped out of the group and spent his Sundays with Helen, so Joe was able to use his cycle. They called for Sarah who had just discovered a puncture in her tyre.

Mick was mending it in the backyard, and Anne was disappointed to find that John was still in bed. Mrs Redmond invited them in for lemonade while they waited, then excused herself to finish her baking. Joe, Stephen and Terry went through to help Mick while the girls sat in the parlour, but eventually they grew suspicious.

'They can't *still* be mending it,' Sarah said, and they went through. Joe was standing leaning against the sideboard in the kitchen, talking to Sarah's mother, and the other boys had finished the repair and were all in the shed looking at Mick's model aeroplanes.

'I might have known,' Sarah cried indignantly, and Eileen and Anne raged at their brothers. 'It'll be dark before we even set out,' Eileen said, but Terry flung himself on his knees before Sarah. 'Mea culpa, mea culpa,' he groaned, pretending to weep as he clasped her round her knees.

'Get up, you fool,' the girls said in unison, but they had to laugh at his antics and their indignation vanished. It was a lovely sunny day and they set off in high spirits.

They sang as they rode to the Pier Head, then as they crossed the Mersey on the *Royal Daffodil* and rode through the country lanes. There were few motor cars although there were many groups of cyclists or hikers, and Terry and Stephen shouted cheerful greetings to them.

'I wish I wasn't going back,' Joe said as he rode beside Anne and Sarah in a quiet lane. 'I suppose you do this every Sunday?'

'Yes, whenever the weather's fine, and sometimes when it isn't,' Anne laughed. Sarah said shyly, 'Perhaps this will be the last time you have to go to sea.'

'Yes. I was really banking on that job, but now I've put my name down at a few places so something might come up by the time I'm home again,' Joe said.

A group of cyclists approached and he had to fall back behind the girls. At Thurstaton they left their bicycles under a tree and climbed to the summit of the hill, but before Joe could help Sarah, Terry had taken her hand.

When they came down to eat their lunch under the tree again he lay beside Sarah talking about the *caelidhes* and Joe had no opportunity to speak to her again. On the journey home Terry rode beside Anne and Sarah, pretending to serenade them with his hand on his heart.

They returned home in time to prepare for the *caelidhe* and met again at eight-thirty. 'We must be mad,' Stephen said. 'I'm as stiff as a board after cycling and sunburned as well.'

'The dancing won't cure the sunburn,' Eileen said. 'But it should help the stiffness.'

It was the custom at the dances for people to stand on the platform and sing between the dances, accompanied by the pianist, and soon the MC announced that a popular singer,

James Duffy, would sing: Believe Me If All Those Endearing Young Charms.

The dancers sat in silence enjoying the song, and when the singer reached the line 'But the heart that has truly loved never forgets', Terry leaned forward, placing his hand on his heart, and looking soulfully into Sarah's eyes.

The rest of the group smiled but Anne kicked his ankle. 'Stop it. You'll embarrass her,' she hissed. When the song was finished Terry rubbed his ankle.

'Are you trying to cripple me?' he said to his sister. 'It was only a bit of fun. I won't be able to dance now.'

'You can't anyway,' she retorted before she was claimed for the dance and Terry held out his hand to Sarah. 'I could dance with you, alannah, if I had two broken legs,' he said.

'She'll think you have,' Anne teased over her shoulder. Her partner was a man known as Thomaseen Rafferty who spoke with a thick Irish brogue although he was born and brought up in Liverpool.

'Indeed and your brother is terrible smitten with the young gurl that's wit yez,' he said.

'Oh, no, it's only a joke,' Anne said. 'He's always fooling about.'

'Ah, sure it looks like a right case to me,' Thomaseen said, and Anne looked over to where Terry and Sarah stood together waiting for the sets to be formed. They were both laughing and Anne suddenly thought: I wonder? Wouldn't it be lovely if Sarah and Terry were courting, and me and John?

Anne often saw him when she was at Sarah's house. His foot healed quickly but he never asked her to go out with him.

Roote's aircraft factory had opened in Speke on the outskirts of Liverpool making Blenheims and Beaufort planes and Joe had written to them and to several other firms, telling them that he would be away for nine months, but asking to be put on a waiting list for when he returned.

Pat Fitzgerald called Joe into the parlour one night to say to him, 'Listen, Joe. I've just been keeping going with the business, sort of keeping my head above water, but things are beginning to pick up. I can take you on for labouring until you find something better.'

Joe hesitated, feeling sorely tempted, but then he thought of the young man who had hanged himself. 'No thanks, Dad. If you've got a job it should go to someone like Jimmy Getty. I often think about him. At least I've got a berth at sea and haven't a family depending on me. But I don't think you've really got a job for me, have you?'

His father shrugged. 'Well, no, I haven't, lad, to tell you the God's truth, but I could carry you for a few months until you got fixed up, son.'

'And what if I didn't?' Joe said. 'Thanks all the same, Dad, but I'll take my chance. Something might come of all the applications I've sent in.'

Later Pat told Julia about the conversation with Joe. 'I respect the lad for refusing me,' he said. 'It's true I'd only be making the job for him, and at least he has a berth and lucky to have it.'

'Do you think he'll ever get a job ashore, though, Pat?' she said. 'He seems to feel it more than ever this time, having to go away from the family. I suppose it's because he's had a bit longer at home, and God knows we'll miss him too.'

'He'll get a job, girl, I'm sure of it,' Pat said heartily. 'All them letters he's sent off, and the months will soon pass.'

It was true that Joe felt more reluctant than ever to leave his home. He felt that he was just settling back into the family routine, becoming able to take part again in the verbal sparring between his brothers and sisters and understand the family jokes.

217

There was another reason too why he was sorry to go. He had felt instantly attracted to Anne's shy little friend Sarah Redmond and wanted to know her better, but the opportunity never arose. Terry always seemed to be before him, and while Joe hesitated, unsure about his brother's feelings, the chance with Sarah passed.

Terry was forever declaring his devotion to her, flinging himself on his knees at her feet or serenading her with his hand on his heart, and Joe wondered how much of this was Terry's fooling about and how much he really felt for Sarah?

If Terry really cared for her, Joe felt that he could not interfere, but it was impossible to find out. He even asked Terry on one occasion, but unfortunately it was at the *caelidhe* and his brother had just been talking to Thomaseen Rafferty and began to imitate his thick brogue.

'Am I fooling, you ask me, or do oi mean it? Amn't I destroyed – I mean desthroyed – wid love for the gurl? Sure me Irish blood leaps when I see the colleen.'

'Shut up, Terry, he'll hear you,' Anne hissed at him, and in the general laughter Joe's question went unanswered. Sarah's shyness meant that her only response to Terry's antics was to blush, and that told Joe nothing.

It was time for him to go back to sea before he could learn any more. Sometimes in the months that followed he wondered why he had not been more forceful and found out the true position, but decided ruefully that though he could hold his own on board ship, at home he reverted to the shy and diffident young man he had been before his first voyage.

It will change when I'm working ashore, he told himself. He often thought of Sarah's shy smile and gentle manner, and thought too of the applications he had sent. Surely one of them must bear fruit, and this would truly be his last trip?

Anne missed Joe, as did all the family, but now she had another interest. She looked forward to seeing John when she visited the Redmond home, either to call for Sarah or when she was invited for Sunday tea.

He was always friendly, but then so were all the rest of the family who always made her feel very welcome so Anne was careful not to show her special interest in John. She treasured the remarks he made to her, though, and carefully stored up memories of his smile and deep voice.

He was now able to get about on crutches and sometimes Anne met him when she was returning from work. She walked now as the bakehouse boy had borrowed her bicycle for an errand and damaged the frame, and she took a short cut through Grant Gardens at the end of Everton Road.

Several times Anne met John there and they sat on one of the seats with his crutches propped beside them, unaware of time passing as they talked. He told her stories of Spain and of his hopes and plans for the future.

Anne had never taken much interest in politics, but like John had been familiar since childhood with the misery and destitution in the poorer parts of the city. She could sympathise with his dreams of a better world for everyone.

Chapter Eighteen

Anne said nothing at home about the meetings, or to Sarah, because she quickly realised from her conversations that John had not talked about them at home. Why? she wondered. Perhaps because he didn't think they were important?

Meanwhile she enjoyed their talks and felt that they were getting to know each other better. John could still surprise her sometimes. In October 1937 Oswald Mosley, leader of the British Union of Fascists, was speaking at a meeting held on waste ground in Queens Drive, Liverpool, when he was hit on the head by a stone and taken to hospital.

'It served him right,' Anne declared when she met John a few days later. 'They've got a cheek, strutting round in blackshirts and jackboots like an army.' She knew that John detested Fascism and expected him to agree with her, but instead he said forcefully, 'I don't agree with stone throwing. It's going down to their level for one thing, and for another everyone should be able to get up and have their say without being threatened.'

'But I thought you were dead against him?' Anne said. 'You said it was the Fascists like Herr Hitler and Signor Mussolini who interfered in the Civil War in Spain and did that awful bombing.'

'Yes, but I still think Mosley or anyone else should have their say,' John explained. 'Anyway, the more they talk, the more people will see what they are.'

'Even though they cause trouble?' Anne said.

'Yes. As a famous man said: "I don't agree with what he says but I'll fight to the death to preserve his right to say it."' Anne gazed at him admiringly. How clever he was, she thought, quite different from the fellows she met at the dances.

There was another difference between them unfortunately. Her dancing partners asked to take her out and John never did. He seemed to be quite content to meet her by chance, or to see her occasionally at his home.

Their meetings were less frequent now because it was dark when Anne returned from work and Grant Gardens were closed. John had discarded his crutches and was limping about trying to strengthen his foot by walking, he told Anne. He had applied for many jobs but without success.

She still looked hopefully for him as she walked home but weeks went by without her seeing him. Anne was hurt. She was not free to stroll about looking for him but if he wanted to see her, he knew her homeward route and was free to wait at some point for her.

When Sarah asked her to come to tea she dressed carefully, sure that she would see John and he would explain. Always optimistic, she felt cheerful and happy as she walked to the Redmonds' house expecting to discover the reason why she had not seen John, and perhaps even be established as his girlfriend before she returned home. He had made it plain to her that he liked her, she thought, by the way he looked at her.

It was a shock to find that John was not there when she arrived and that no one seemed to think that his absence needed an explanation. It was a cold day and Anne was wearing a scarlet hood and scarf combined, knitted for her by Maureen.

'That colour suits you, Anne,' Mrs Redmond said. 'It looks lovely and warm too. What a good idea to have a hood and scarf combined.'

'My sister works in a wool shop and she knitted it for me,'

Anne said. 'They do a lot of knitting when they're not busy, mostly baby clothes to sell.'

John's grandmother was there, a thin spare old lady with a very straight back and white hair drawn into a neat bun on the nape of her neck.

'Grandma did lovely knitting until her hands got stiff with the arthritis, didn't you, Mam?' Mrs Redmond said.

'Aye, but good or bad I think I kept half of Liverpool supplied,' the old lady said dryly.

'My dad was always giving away the scarves and gloves Grandma made him,' Mrs Redmond said, laughing.

'To poor people, Mrs Ward?' Anne asked and Sarah's grandmother nodded.

'Aye, and if it wasn't scarves it would be his overcoat. He had a bad chest and I'd get a good thick coat from Paddy's Market and alter it to fit him, and the next thing he'd come home without it. "There was this poor fella, Sal," he'd say.'

They all smiled and Anne said earnestly, 'But he was very well respected for his kindness though, wasn't he? I remember everyone in the shop was crying when we heard about – about his death.'

'Indeed he was, Anne,' Mrs Redmond said. 'And that was a consolation to all of us, wasn't it, Mam?'

And her mother smiled at Anne. 'It was,' she agreed.

There was a sound in the lobby and Anne looked eagerly at the door, but it was Mick who came in. 'Brr, it's cold out,' he said. 'Getting foggy too.'

'I've lit the parlour fire,' Mrs Redmond said to Sarah, and she said to Anne, 'We've got two new records – Bert Ambrose and his Orchestra and Paul Robeson singing Just A-Wearying For You.' They went into the parlour where there was a cabinet gramophone, but before they went Sarah's grandmother asked her daughter, 'What time do you expect John?'

'God knows, Mam. When he gets talking with that crowd he

forgets the time,' Mrs Redmond said. 'We won't wait tea for him anyway.'

Anne looked thoughtful as she sat down by the fire while Sarah wound the gramophone. Was it just chance that Mrs Ward said that, she wondered, or had she noticed that I looked at the door and decided to let me know he was out?

Sarah had often told her how observant her grandmother was, and how wise and kind too, and Anne felt that even if Mrs Ward had realised her feelings for John, she would tell no one else.

When they were called into the kitchen where tea was laid, John had still not arrived. They sat down and Mick said cheerfully, 'Gosh I'm starving. If our John doesn't hurry up there'll be nothing left for him.'

'Food will be the last thought on his mind,' Mrs Redmond said. She turned to Anne. 'When he gets talking with his friends he forgets everything else. Food means nothing to him.'

Neither do I, thought Anne. She could feel herself blushing and avoided looking at Mrs Ward but suddenly pride came to her aid and she said brightly, 'I don't know anything that would keep my brothers from food. Mum says they must have hollow legs, the amount they eat.'

'They show for it anyway,' Mrs Redmond said. 'Fine big lads all of them, and your mother so small and thin.'

'But very strong,' Anne said, and Mrs Redmond said easily, 'Indeed she must be. She has a home and a family to be proud of.'

'You notice your father gets no credit at all?' Sarah's father said, smiling at Anne as he passed her the bread and butter.

'Have some more beef, Anne,' said Mick. 'Come on, you can't let your family down by picking like a bird.'

'It depends which bird you mean,' she said, laughing at him. How nice they all were, she thought, and how she would love to be part of the family, but it seemed it was not to be. John seemed to have as little interest in girls as before he went to Spain, in spite of their happy meetings. They had meant so much to her but evidently nothing to him.

Sarah had asked several times why Anne was not using her bike for work now that it was repaired and she had made various excuses. Now she was determined to start using it again.

When she reached home she asked Terry to oil her bike and pump up the tyres for her. 'I'm going to work on it tomorrow morning.'

'I can't see why you haven't used it for weeks now,' he said. 'You can get there in half the time.'

Anne shrugged. 'I just got used to walking, I suppose. But I've had enough.' And enough of hanging about hoping to see someone who can't even be bothered to see me at his own home, she thought.

She put thoughts of John firmly out of her mind and there was plenty to distract her. Christmas was fast approaching and the shop was busier than ever. Mrs Dyson's sister came to the shop occasionally but not to help. She had strong opinions about everything and never hesitated to air them.

'You're sitting on a gold mine here if you only shaped your-selves,' she told Mrs Dyson. 'Those bakehouse girls go home far too early.'

'But they start at seven,' Mrs Dyson said.

'Start them at half-past six or let them work an extra hour later and you'd have that much more to sell,' Miss Meers said. 'You could stay open an hour later and all the stuff would go.'

She marched off into the bakehouse and Mrs Dyson said to Mabel, 'Don't take no notice of her. We won't make any alterations. Albert and me are satisfied and it's got nothing to do with her.'

'You wouldn't think you were sisters,' Mabel said forthrightly.

'She's never been no different,' Mrs Dyson said. 'She loves a fight. I'd better go. Albert wouldn't be past landing her one if she annoys him.'

She dashed into the bakehouse from where raised voices could be heard and a few minutes later Miss Meers emerged into the shop. 'You just can't help some people,' she said. 'I told you, Nelly, you'd live to rue the day you married that fellow.'

'Well, I haven't,' Mrs Dyson shouted after her as she swept out, then they all looked at each other and began to laugh.

Mr Dyson came to the door of the shop. 'Has she gone?' he demanded, looking at their smiling faces in amazement.

'Yes, and I gave her a flea in her ear,' Mrs Dyson said proudly.

'Bloody battleaxe! Don't you let her in my bakehouse no more,' he said, turning back, but they knew she would return.

There were special Christmas dances as well as the usual *caelidhes*, and Anne and Sarah were never without partners. They were frequently asked for dates, too, and Anne accepted, consoled by the thought that though John might not want her, plenty of other people did.

She had managed to bury thoughts of him and was astounded to be reminded of him on a visit to Grandma Houlihan. She and Eileen had spent a pleasant hour in Bridie's happy home then gone to see Aunt Carrie and their grandma.

Bridie had warned them that Minnie had come into circulation again, and had been to see her and told her that her little girl looked sickly.

'She doesn't. She's lovely and a picture of health,' Anne said indignantly.

'But she *is* small, isn't she?' Bridie said with a worried frown.

'She's dainty,' Eileen said. 'You didn't want a big boiling piece like Dympna, did you?'

Bridie laughed. 'No, no. I think Monica's just right, but you know Minnie. She puts these ideas in your head.'

'Don't let her,' Eileen said. 'Faggot! I liked it better when she had the huff.'

When they reached Carrie's, Grandma was sitting beside the fire with Minnie beside her. 'Oh, you're honoured today, Ma,' said Minnie. 'Two of them.' She turned to the girls. 'Ma tells me you haven't been to see her this long while.'

'We've been here since *you* were last here, Aunt Minnie,' Anne said.

Minnie's eyes narrowed. 'I told you, Ma,' she said triumphantly.

'What did you tell her?' Anne demanded.

'Minnie was after telling me you were mixing with the wrong people, child, and sorry I am to hear it,' Grandma Houlihan said. 'And that you were grown very disrespectful.'

'I don't know what you're talking about,' Anne said angrily to Minnie. 'You don't even know who I mix with.'

'Oh, yes, I do. We saw you, me and Dympna, talking to that fellow that's been in Spain fighting on the side of the Anti-Christ. We saw you outside Ariel Gray's, quite hardfaced talking to him, and you hadn't just met him either. We saw you come out of the shop under the dwellings.'

'So you were spying for a while?' said Eileen, but Anne said, 'I don't care who saw us and how long they were there. I can meet my friend's brother and talk to him any time I like.'

'You should be ashamed, a fellow like that,' Minnie said.

'He's a better man than your son'll ever be,' Anne declared. 'And as for your talk of the Anti-Christ . . . Franco had Muslim Moors on his side as well as foreigners dropping bombs from aeroplanes on innocent people.'

'You know all about it, don't you?' Minnie sneered, and Grandma wailed, 'Jesus, Mary, and Joseph, protect us! You've grown a terrible bold girl, Anne. Your poor mother, and with the Hand of God on her too.'

'What do you mean?' Anne and Eileen demanded together, everything else forgotten. Just then Carrie stormed in.

'Out,' she said to Minnie. '*Out!* And take your dirty tongue with you. Don't show your face in my house again.'

Minnie stood up with a satisfied smile. 'I won't see you again, Ma, until you're in your coffin,' she said. 'Seeing that I won't be allowed to see you here, and you can't get out. It's a pity Julia couldn't wait to dump you back here.'

Grandma Houlihan burst into loud wails and Carrie grabbed Minnie's shoulder and hustled her to the door.

'Grandma, what did you mean about Mum?' Eileen said, leaning over her grandmother and staring into her face, but Grandma covered her face with her hands and wept even more loudly.

They heard the slam of the front door and Carrie came back. Immediately the girls begged her to tell them what their grandmother had meant by 'the Hand of God' on their mother.

'It meant nothing, girls,' she said. 'That bitch has been haunting us for the last few days, dripping her poison into Ma's ear, and she believes everything Minnie tells her. I heard her going on about Sarah's brother and I'd have warned you if I'd known you were coming.'

'I'm glad she was here when we came,' Anne said. 'So I could face her with it. But why did Grandma say that, Aunt Carrie?'

'Because Minnie put it in her head. If Ma hadn't said it she'd have found a way to say it herself but it means nothing. You've heard her: "Such and such a one looks pale. I think the Hand of God is on her and she's not long for this world." Don't let it worry you, girls. That's what she wants.'

'It's true,' Eileen said. 'It's the sort of thing she says. We've just come from Bridie's and she's been trying to upset her too. Why didn't she stay out of friends? It was much better.'

'She missed causing trouble,' Carrie said shrewdly. 'And I had to let her come to see Ma, but she's gone too far this time, she didn't pick up on what you said about Brendan though, I notice, Anne.'

'It's true. John Redmond is a better man than Brendan, but who isn't?'

Both girls looked anxiously at their mother when they returned home, but she had been cooking and was flushed with the heat of the fire, and bright-eyed with happiness because a letter had arrived from Joe, so they were reassured.

Julia's birthday fell on 28 November and Anne went to town alone to buy her mother's present on the previous Wednesday. As she walked home up Brunswick Road she realised that Kathleen O'Neill was walking ahead of her and quickened her pace to catch up with her.

'Kathleen!' she said. 'Aren't you working?' She was dismayed to see how pale and ill Kathleen looked, with dark shadows beneath her eyes and even her hair dull and lifeless.

'Hello, Anne,' she said, her voice as lifeless as her hair. 'Mr Skelly gave me the afternoon off. He told me to get some fresh air and some roses in my cheeks.'

'Where have you been?' Anne asked.

'Just walking round,' said Kathleen. 'I don't want to go home until I'm due out of the office.'

'It's too cold to be walking round,' Anne said. 'You're more likely to get a red nose than roses in your cheeks.' Kathleen laughed and Anne said impulsively, 'Come home with me for a cup of tea.'

As Kathleen seemed about to refuse Anne added, 'There's nobody in. Mum's gone to see my grandma and she won't be back for ages.' She linked her arm through Kathleen's and they walked along, Kathleen silent but Anne chattering about the present she had bought her mother and the prospect of Christmas shopping.

The fire had been banked down but Anne quickly had it burning brightly, and Kathleen sitting close to it with a cup of tea and a piece of fruit cake beside her.

Anne talked about her job and her family until they had finished their tea, then said jokingly to Kathleen, '*Now* you've got roses in your cheeks. Mr Skelly would be pleased. It was a fire you needed, not fresh air.'

Kathleen smiled but said nothing and Anne said more seriously, 'Why were you pale, Kath? Haven't you been well?'

'I've been worried,' she said. She sat looking into the fire for a moment then suddenly covered her face with her hands. 'Oh, Anne, I don't know what to do,' she wept. Anne slipped to her knees beside her and put her arm around Kathleen's shoulders.

'What's up, Kath?' she said gently. 'What are you worried about?'

'Mammy says I mustn't be friends with Ella. She says I have to choose between them,' Kathleen said with a sob.

'But I thought Ella was a very nice girl.'

'She is. She is. But Mammy says we mustn't make friends with ordinary people. She says we're different. A Royal line,' Kathleen said. She took out a dainty little handkerchief and wiped her eyes.

'Oh, that,' said Anne. 'Does Ella know?'

'No, I haven't told her. I don't know what to do, Anne. When I'm in the office it all seems so simple and I want to be friends with her and go to the pictures and all that . . . It's just – when I go home it all seems different.'

'Have you been going round with Ella?' Anne asked.

'Yes. It started when Cormac was ill, and she walked home with me every night. I went to the pictures with her twice. The first time Ella just took it for granted. She came for me and Mammy didn't have a chance to say anything.'

'But there was no harm in just going to the pictures.'

'That's what Ella said, and I *did* have a lovely time, but when I got home Mammy was upset. I said I wouldn't go again but then in the office they were talking about Fred Astaire and Ginger Rogers and the new waltz, so I went to see them in *Swing Time* with Ella.'

'And what happened?' Anne prompted her.

'Nothing that time because Cormac's chest was terrible that night, but last night I told Mammy Ella had asked me to go to the Forum when *Shall We Dance* comes on there at Christmas. Mammy said I loved Ella more than her and Cormac and I had to choose but I was breaking her heart, and Cormac shouted at me as well.'

'But that's daft,' Anne said, but Kathleen quickly added, 'You don't understand. Mammy just lives for us and says we shouldn't want anyone but each other. It seems right when I'm at home, but when I'm in the office it seems all wrong. I'm like two people, Anne. I don't know my own mind and sometimes I think I'm going crazy.'

It was growing dark, but Anne remained with her arms round Kathleen. She felt that it was easier for Kathleen to confide in her in the dim room lit only by firelight.

'Doesn't Cormac ever want to go out?' she asked.

'No, but he has a terrible temper. He gets in awful rages. Once he said he hated Mammy and she was upset.'

'But, Kathleen, it's only normal for children to grow up and grow away from their mothers,' said Anne. 'Our Tony's engaged and Eileen's courting and my cousin Theresa's married.'

'Yes, but we're different,' Kathleen said stubbornly. She hesitated then said, 'Mammy said Cormac and I couldn't marry anyone but each other. It was what happened in ancient times in Ireland in Royal families, if there was no one else with Royal blood.'

'That can't be right!' Anne exclaimed.

'It is,' Kathleen insisted. 'Mammy has all these books about the High Kings of Ireland and their courts. If a brother and sister married their child was doubly Royal when it came to the throne. It might have happened in England too in ancient times, or in Wales.'

Anne stood up and lit the gas, feeling that the conversation was getting out of hand. No wonder Kathleen's confused, she thought. Her mother must be absolutely barmy.

Aloud she said, 'Your mother doesn't mind your going to work, Kath?'

'She doesn't like it, but we need my wages. Mammy lost one of her cleaning jobs.'

'Couldn't Cormac go to work? He might enjoy it,' Anne said.

But Kathleen said vehemently, 'Oh, no. He's not strong enough.' She looked at the clock on the mantelpiece. 'I'd better go. I want to meet Mammy at the usual time.'

'You'd better rinse your face,' Anne said, and took her up to the bathroom. While she waited on the landing she thought about Kathleen's situation and considered what she could do.

'Is it just Ella?' she said when Kathleen came out. 'I mean, has your mother just taken a dislike to her? Would she let you come out with me?'

'No-o,' Kathleen said evasively, 'it's just – just with us being different, you see. Mammy only wants what's best for me and Cormac.'

Like marrying each other, Anne thought. Ye gods!

She offered to walk down with Kathleen who refused to let her. Anne hugged her impulsively as they parted at the door. 'Try to make your mum see that you need a bit of fun, Kath. Tell her it doesn't mean you care any less for your home.'

'I will,' she promised. 'But, Anne, don't tell anyone what we've talked about, will you?'

'No, I won't,' promised Anne. 'But I'll worry about you. Try to get out with Ella.'

She turned back into the house when Kathleen left, thinking how fortunate she was to be born into the Fitzgerald family. Her mother was surprised when she arrived an hour later to find a pile of ironing done, the table laid and her slippers warming in the hearth.

'God bless you, child, you've worked hard and on your half day off too,' she said as Anne brought her a cup of tea.

'Just to show I appreciate you,' said Anne, flinging her arms round her mother who was much smaller than she was.

Julia looked up at her, smiling. 'Appreciate, is it? Sure I'm the one that's lucky to come home to a peaceful house and everything done for me. Your poor Aunt Carrie's having her own share with Grandma.'

'Why, what's she doing?' Anne said.

'I don't know what's wrong with her at all. She does nothing but argue. My poor ma. I think she's going strange in the head.'

She's not the only one, Anne thought, wishing she could tell her mother about Mrs O'Neill, but she had given her promise to Kathleen to say nothing.

Chapter Nineteen

Although Anne had made up her mind to forget her dreams about John Redmond, she still listened eagerly when Sarah talked about his efforts to find a job, now that his foot was completely healed.

'Who were the friends he was with when I was at your house?' Anne asked carefully, avoiding looking at her. 'Were they from that club?'

'No. Just a crowd who talk hot air like himself,' Sarah said scornfully.

'You think he's daft, don't you?' Anne said, laughing.

'In some ways,' Sarah conceded. 'But I've got to admit he works for what he believes in. Collecting for Spanish Food Relief in all weathers, and for the Goodfellow Fund.'

Anne felt a glow of pride at Sarah's words. But only because he's a friend, she told herself hastily.

Sarah seemed equally pleased to hear good news about Joe. Three replies had been received to the applications he had sent, and had been opened by his father as Joe had asked. One said it was pointless to put him on a waiting list, but letters from a grain merchant's and from Littlewood's Pools promised to file his application and interview him when he returned home.

'I feel almost guilty that so many good things are happening to us, when such a lot of people are having a bad time,' Sarah said. 'We're very lucky, aren't we, Anne?'

Anne often thought of Sarah's words during the following months. They *were* lucky, she felt. Everything seemed to be going right in both families. Her father's order book was better filled than it had been for years, her mother's health seemed good, Eileen was happy in her work as a pools clerk, and Tony and Helen were happily planning their wedding.

All the family were enjoying life, and even Maureen seemed to have forgotten whatever it was that troubled her and to be quietly happy again.

Best of all, Joe was sure of being able to stay home after his trip. Even if nothing came of the interviews, he could work for his father.

When Pat had told them of his new orders he said to his wife, 'You'll have your lad home again, Julia, however it goes with these letters he's had. Now I can fix him up without him thinking he's taking the bread from someone else's mouth.'

'Thanks be to God,' was all that Julia said, but Anne knew how much the news meant to her and to all the family.

The news was all good in the Redmond family too. Mr Redmond had been looking after the woodyard where he worked while his employer was on a cruise to restore his health, and Sarah told Anne that her father had been given fifty pounds as a mark of appreciation when his employer returned.

Sarah's brother Mick was the star pupil at his College and great things were predicted for him, and John was now fully recovered and walking without a limp.

'He still can't find a job,' Sarah said to Anne. 'But at least he's home and safe.'

'"God's in His Heaven, All's right with the world",' Anne said gaily, and Mabel was shocked.

'That's blasphemy, Anne!'

'No, it isn't, Mabel, it's poetry,' she said.

'I never heard it,' Mabel said doubtfully.

'But you get all your quotations from the Bible, don't you,

Mabel?' Sarah said mischievously. Mabel often quoted lines of poetry to make her point, and whether they came from Tennyson, Keats, Wordsworth or Rupert Brooke, she always prefaced them with 'As it says in the Bible'.

At first the girls had tried to correct her, but Mabel ignored their efforts and they accepted it as one of her little quirks. 'Shelley was elevated to the Bible this morning,' one of them would whisper to the other, but they were fond of Mabel and would never hurt her.

Anne had been to tea again at the Redmond house and this time John was at home. He greeted her pleasantly, seemingly unaware of the length of time since they had last met, and her pride made her take her cue from him. Mrs Redmond talked about Bridie's babies, whom she had seen the previous day, and asked Anne about her grandmother.

As usual after tea Anne and Sarah went into the parlour to play records, and soon they were joined by Mick and John, but the conversation was still general. Anne stole a glance at John occasionally, and several times caught him looking intently at her, but each time he looked away quickly.

Sarah's young sister Kate came in and offered to do her step dancing to one of the records. She was a pretty girl with fair curly hair and brown eyes, very self-possessed and a good dancer. Anne thought she was vain and cheeky, quite unlike shy Sarah.

After she had been applauded and had gone out again, Mick announced that he would now demonstrate his Fred Astaire number. He swooped about, holding an imaginary partner, and John said to Anne, 'You must think my family are cracked.'

'You haven't met my brothers,' she laughed. 'They're mad, aren't they, Sarah? Especially Terry. And even our Eileen learned to drive on a two-ton milk lorry.'

'Your sister can drive?' Mick said, dropping down beside Anne. 'I'm trying to persuade Dad to buy a car. Your brother's bought one, hasn't he?'

'Yes. Our Tony. He's engaged and they're saving up to get married, but Helen and him thought it'd be better to buy one now because they'll have a lot of expenses after they're married and won't have Helen's wages.'

Mick asked many questions about Tony's car, none of which Anne could answer. 'I only know it has four wheels and it goes,' she said, laughing.

'That's all you need to know,' said John. 'Mick gets all his information off the back of cigarette cards.'

Sarah had changed the record and was winding the gramophone, and Mick asked Anne to dance. She was surprised by how well he danced, but suspected that Mick did most things well.

'I don't dance, I'm afraid,' John said when the record finished and Anne sat down. 'I've just never thought about it.'

'Too busy putting the world to rights,' said his brother.

Sarah had pulled out another record. 'Harry Roy,' she exclaimed. 'Come on, Anne. This is a quickstep.' The two girls danced together, then sat talking about the *caelidhes* and the characters they met there.

They were all surprised when Mrs Redmond appeared with a supper tray. 'Gosh, hasn't the time gone quickly?' Sarah said, and Mick added, 'And not a word about world affairs for once.'

'That's good,' Mrs Redmond said. 'This is the time you should be enjoying yourselves, not bothering your heads about such things.' She looked at John as she spoke and he looked back at her and smiled. I wish he'd smile at me like that, Anne thought.

As the weather improved and the days lengthened Anne saw John several times, but usually she was on her bicycle and he was on foot. They exchanged brief greetings but one day he was walking slowly past the end of Magdalen Street as she cycled up. Suddenly bold, she stopped by the kerb and spoke to him, and they were still there half an hour later when Eileen walked through from the tram.

Anne introduced John and when Eileen moved away, Anne said goodbye to him and walked up the road with her sister, wheeling her bicycle.

'He's a nice-looking fellow, isn't he?' said Eileen. 'Was he the one who was fighting in Spain?'

'Yes, he was wounded in the foot but it's healed now.'

'I'd love to do something like that,' said Eileen. 'Fellows have all the fun.'

'You don't do so badly,' Anne laughed, and Eileen had to agree.

After that meeting with John, Anne often met him strolling along near her home and always stopped to talk to him. The conversation usually turned to matters that were never mentioned in Anne's home. Her father was only interested in his family and his business and although he took the *Evening Express*, only read local news.

Tony's interests had been wider at one time, but now his mind was full of plans for his marriage with Helen, and his new car.

Like most young men of their age, Stephen and Terry were absorbed in sport, particularly football and Everton Football Club.

John was unlike anyone Anne knew with his views on everything that happened in the world. On Palestine and Ireland and Hitler's plans for Germany. He seemed to assume that she was as interested in these questions as he was, and she began to read newspapers thoroughly and listen to news broadcasts on the wireless.

Although Anne had always read voraciously it had been novels and poetry, or volumes of letters and diaries which were her particular favourites. An Irish relative had told her that Ireland was now to be known as Eire but she knew nothing of the reasons for this, or of what was happening in Germany.

She and Sarah had been indignant and sad to see a picture of Emperor Haile Selassie of Abyssinia on the Pathé News Gazette at the cinema after Mussolini had invaded his country. A tiny dignified man wearing a cloak and headdress, they had thought him both tragic and romantic but had known nothing about the background of the struggle.

Now John recalled that struggle and told her that the Italians had invaded Abyssinia and taken Addis Ababa with modern weapons, including poison gas, in spite of a declaration by the League of Nations. 'I'd call the League a toothless tiger, wouldn't you?' he said.

Anne had to admit that she had never called the League a tiger, toothless or otherwise, and had known nothing of it until recently.

'I never knew there was so much going on in the world,' she said to John one day.

'Very few people do, Anne, and there's not much information available to ordinary people. That's why the statesmen can get away with so much,' he said.

Anne did not allow her new interest in world affairs to interfere with her enjoyment of life, however, and although John never asked her out many other young men did. She and Sarah tried to arrange their dates for the same evenings, so that for the rest of the week they were free to go out together. Anne never seemed to have a free moment.

'Slow down, child, slow down,' her mother begged as Anne raced around. 'Sure you'll wear yourself out.'

Tony was teaching Maureen to drive and Anne asked if he would teach her too. 'Where would you find the time?' he asked and she had to admit it was impossible.

'You'll learn quickly when you *do* have the time,' Helen said. 'You won't be like me.' Helen had been trying to learn for some time, but she found it very hard although Tony was endlessly patient with her.

'It's that kangaroo juice he puts in the engine,' Terry teased her after she had started from outside the house in a series of jumps.

'Ignore him, love. All you need is confidence, and that will come,' Tony said protectively. Maureen showed an unexpected aptitude for driving and learned very quickly but Helen was not jealous. All the family were very fond of tiny Helen, who was a gentle loving girl. Tony thought she was very like his mother in appearance and character.

Julia had been free of pain for many months, but still she had grown weaker. Mrs Bennet came to clean four times a week now, and another woman came for the washing, and Julia often wondered how she would have managed without them.

In the spring of 1938 the old doctor who had attended her died suddenly and a young man took over the practice. Maureen asked him to call to see her mother, and the doctor examined her carefully. 'You say you have been free of pain for nearly two years?' he said, when he had finished.

'That's so, doctor, but you know I have the strange feeling that it's still there, biding its time. I can't seem to get back my strength,' she said.

The doctor looked carefully at her fingernails and neck, then said abruptly, 'I want to admit you to the Royal. They can take an X-ray photograph of you. It would help me to know what is wrong and how to treat you.'

Julia said nothing for a moment then she said quietly, 'Thank you, doctor, for the offer, but I don't think I'll go in hospital if you don't mind.'

'It would only be for investigation,' he said.

'I know, doctor, but you see I'm all this time without pain and I think I'll let sleeping dogs lie. I'm grand apart from the weakness.'

The doctor shrugged. 'I think you'd be wise to go,' he said. 'But if that's how you feel. Promise me that you'll let me know if the pain returns. I trained at the Royal and I'll be able to get you a bed immediately.'

He left after giving instructions that she was to rest as much as possible and drink plenty of milk. Mrs Bennet showed him out and returned with a pint glass full of milk. 'I think a glass of Guinness would do you more good,' she said. 'But you'd better do as he tells you. He seems to have more idea than the ould feller.'

The wool shop now closed on Wednesday afternoons so often Maureen drove her mother and her Aunt Carrie to visit Theresa, whose baby was due in June, while Anne stayed with Grandma Houlihan. The old lady was becoming more confused, and often failed to recognise Anne but she allowed her to make a meal for her.

She talked at length, often about people who had died before Anne was born, but she pretended to remember them. At other times Grandma sat silent but apparently happy with her Rosary beads slipping through her fingers.

Anne had hoped to wait outside the coal merchant's office to see Kathleen, but Wednesday was the only day she was home early enough, and now there was never an opportunity. She was relieved when she and Sarah met Kathleen and Ella in a cinema queue one evening. It was for a Bing Crosby film and Ella said jokingly, 'We had to come. Kath's got a pash on Bing.'

Kathleen blushed and said, 'And you've got one on Ronald Colman.'

'Sarah's mad about Hugh Williams but mine is Leslie Howard,' Anne laughed. She pretended to swoon and the four girls laughed and joked together until the queue moved into the cinema.

Anne was secretly delighted to see Kathleen behaving so normally, and felt that she could stop worrying about her. Maureen had told her that the O'Neills' neighbour had been in the wool shop and had told her that she was sure they were all mad. 'She said the scenes in the house are terrible,' Maureen said. 'Crashes and bangs and all of them screaming and crying.' But Anne decided that the woman must be exaggerating.

Theresa's son was born on 28 June 1937 and christened James Frederick, and Carrie said that Fred's feet had not touched the ground since the child's birth.

The baby's christening was held at Carrie's house so that

Grandma Houlihan was able to hold the baby. She seemed to think that it was her own child and showed signs of distress when Carrie took the baby from her. 'He's not dead, is he?' she whimpered. 'God help me, I can never rear a lad.' But fortunately the baby began to cry loudly, and Grandma seemed happy again.

It was clear that she was very close to death, and Julia began to worry because Minnie had not been informed.

'She *is* Ma's daughter, after all, Carrie, and she has a right to know,' Julia said. 'And for all we know Ma might realise that she hasn't been to see her.'

'I doubt it,' said Carrie, 'but I suppose you're right, Julie. She does have a right to know. But when I think of the trouble she's caused!'

'I know,' Julia said gently, 'but maybe she can't help her bitter nature, and God knows, Carrie, she's her own worst enemy. Always falling out with people, and her children are no comfort to her.'

It was decided that Julia should go to see Minnie and escort her to Carrie's house if she wished to come. Minnie wept when she heard the news and willingly accompanied Julia to see their mother.

Carrie greeted her coolly but Fred said heartily, 'That's right, that's right. No sense in bearing grudges at a time like this.' No one replied and Julia took Minnie up to the dying woman.

Minnie fell on her knees beside the bed, holding her mother's hands and murmuring, 'Oh, Ma, it's me, Minnie.' Her mother looked at her vacantly for a moment, then she said in a weak voice, 'My poor girl. God help you. You won't – won't —' Her voice died away and she slipped into sleep again.

Minnie wept bitterly. 'She's the only one in the world who ever cared about me,' she said, but when Julia protested, Minnie sneered, 'It's all right. You don't have to lie to me. I know the score.'

Julia ushered her out of the bedroom, afraid the sound of conflict might reach her mother. Carrie offered Minnie a cup of tea, but she refused it. 'I've done what I came for,' she declared, marching out of the house.

Grandma lay for a few days drifting in and out of sleep, unaware of everything about her, until one afternoon when Julia and Carrie were sitting with her. She spoke rationally to them and asked about their families, but during the night she died in her sleep.

'Don't grieve for her,' the priest said to the family. 'She would only have grown more confused. Now she's had a peaceful end and she's gone to her reward.'

'I wish I'd liked her better,' Anne said. But Eileen replied reasonably, 'None of us was keen on her, Anne, but we hid it for Mum's sake and Grandma never realised it. There's nothing to regret. You can't *make* yourself like someone.'

Minnie and Dympna were in church for the Requiem Mass, but sat apart from the family. Julia thought that Minnie showed genuine grief, and at the end of the Mass, she spoke to her and Dympna. Fred joined them and urged them to come to the cemetery in the funeral cars.

Minnie refused, saying that Brendan had provided a car for them, and later she and Dympna appeared at the graveside, again standing apart from the family. As the mourners left, Fred said quietly to Pat, 'Did you notice those plainclothes coppers?'

'Two big fellows in macs?' Pat said. 'I wondered who they were?'

'They were coppers all right,' Fred said. 'Probably watching for the quare fellow. I wonder what he's been up to now?'

'God knows,' said Pat. 'But he'll need to be slippery all right, with coppers *and* criminals after him.' They said nothing to the family and no one else had noticed the men.

Julia's soft heart had been touched by Minnie's grief, and she was prepared to be friendly with her, but Carrie was adamant. 'I want nothing more to do with her,' she said. 'I tolerated her while Ma was alive to keep the peace for Ma's sake, except for the past few months, but no more. You do what you like, Julia, but I've had enough of her.'

'But it's a terrible thing to be out of friends with your own flesh and blood,' Julia mourned. 'And it's a sin too, Carrie. Didn't Our Lord say that he would forgive us as we forgave others?'

'I don't think it's a sin to be at odds with Minnie,' Carrie declared. 'Not when I think of the trouble she's caused, and she'd cause more if she got the chance.'

'But she'll miss Ma. She said only Ma ever cared about her.'

'And whose fault is that?' said Carrie. 'The number of times we've made it up with her after falling out because of her trouble making, and in no time she's been at it again. Carrying tales and making nasty remarks. No, I'm sorry, Julia, I want no more to do with her, sister or not.'

She looked flushed and angry, and Julia said no more. She knew that despite her fury, Carrie would be the first to offer help to Minnie if she needed it.

Now that she was not restricted by nursing her mother, Carrie was free to travel to West Derby as often as she wished to see her grandchild. Sometimes Julia accompanied her, and as they travelled home one day Carrie said thoughtfully, 'You know I never wished Ma dead, Julie, but I've got to admit her death came at the right time for me. I'm able to see James every day, either at our house or Theresa's, and these first months are precious, aren't they?'

'They are indeed,' Julia agreed. 'And you did your duty to Ma, and more. You and Fred have nothing to reproach yourselves with. You deserve the joy of your grandchild.'

Anne still met John Redmond occasionally, and tried to keep up with world affairs so that she could hold her own when talking to him. He puzzled her. She felt it was not just chance that they met so often near her home, yet he only talked about what was happening in other parts of the world, never of people they knew or of his feelings towards her. Perhaps I've tried to be too clever, she thought, reading up world affairs, and he thinks that's all I want to talk about.

Often as they talked he kept his gaze on her face, looking into her eyes, and as she stood with her hands on the handlebars of her bicycle his hand often covered hers as though by accident. At times Anne felt sure that he was attracted to her, but if so why did he never ask to meet her, and why did he conceal these chance meetings from his family?

It was obvious that Sarah knew nothing of them, and Anne was too proud to tell her. If he's ashamed to tell his family, I'm not going to, she thought. Sarah told her that John had secured a job in an hotel but had been sacked after a few days.

'It was the same when he got that job on a building site and was sacked after a few days, although they said there was nothing wrong with his work. He thinks he's on some sort of blacklist because he was in the International Brigade.'

Anne shrugged. 'Perhaps he is,' she said with assumed indifference. She was hurt that John had said nothing to her about it, and decided that she would avoid him in future. He can find someone else to lecture about Sudetenland Germans and Czechoslovakia and all that, she thought angrily. I'll stick to fellows who talk about ordinary things.

She began to take a different route so that she approached her home from the other end of Magdalen Street and avoided a meeting with John. It was a miserable time for Anne as she was unable to attend dances or the cinema during the period of mourning for her grandmother.

'I feel a hypocrite,' she told Sarah. 'I can't really grieve for my grandma. She was always saying she'd be glad to go to her reward so she's got what she wanted, and I was never very fond of her. I hate this black dress too.'

Her dress had been made by a local dressmaker who had made it with a deep frill of black satin round the neck.

'I feel like Dog Toby in it,' Anne complained.

'Why don't you take the frill off and have a plain round neckline?' Sarah said. 'My aunt in America sent us a photo of herself in a black dress after Grandad died and it was very plain. It looked chic.'

'Oh, Sarah, it probably cost the earth. And then your aunt is beautiful, isn't she?' Anne said. 'My dress fits where it touches.'

'Why don't you ask your mum if you can take the frill off and I'll ask mine to alter your dress if it's all right?' Sarah suggested.

Most of the family were present when Anne asked her mother if she could have her dress altered, and after she had gone to see the Misses Dolan Tony said, 'I think it's a shame Anne can't go out and enjoy herself. I know it was very upsetting for you, Mum, when Grandma died, but we can't expect a kid like Anne to live like a hermit for six months.'

'I don't see the point of it myself, either,' Eileen said. 'If it was one of us it'd be different. The last thing you'd want to do would be enjoy yourself, but everyone says it was a happy release for Grandma.'

'God between us and all harm!' Julia exclaimed, crossing herself. 'Don't even say such a thing, child.'

'When we were young it was deep mourning for a year and half mourning for six months,' Pat said. 'I don't know when this six months idea came in but it's little enough to show respect for the one that's gone.'

'Sure I knew people that were never out of black with the deaths coming the way they did,' Julia said.

Pat sat smoking in silence for a few minutes and no one else spoke but suddenly he said, 'How much of it was real, Julia, when you come to think of it, and how much for fear of what people would say? We carried on the traditions but young ones want to question everything, and maybe they're right.'

''Twill do Anne no harm to leave off the dances for a few

247

months out of respect for her grandma,' Julia said. 'There's nothing wrong with the old ways.'

She agreed that Anne should have her dress altered by Mrs Redmond though and Anne was delighted with the result. Mrs Redmond called to see Julia one afternoon as she sometimes did now and Julia told her of the conversation about mourning.

'My dad didn't believe in mourning. Well, public mourning,' Mrs Redmond said. 'He said you could grieve without having to prove it to the neighbours by wearing black.'

'But it's a matter of showing respect to the dead,' Julia said, and Mrs Redmond agreed rather doubtfully.

'That's what people are brought up to believe.'

'Our young ones don't seem to think we should be in mourning for my mother because she was glad to go,' said Julia.

'My dad didn't welcome death and we were broken-hearted,' Mrs Redmond said. Her eyes filled with tears and she hastily wiped them away. 'I went out to work waiting on and some of the women were such comics I couldn't help but laugh at them. I felt guilty and then I thought of what my dad would have said. He was such a loving man. He'd only have wanted us to be happy.'

'I'm sure he would, the good man, Lord rest him,' said Julia and Mrs Redmond went on, 'I came home one night and Sarah told me my mother had told her she should start going out and enjoying herself, and I was relieved. I wanted to suggest it to Sarah but I didn't know how Mam would feel about it. She said it would help Sarah to get over the loss, and it did.'

Julia was half convinced that she should tell the young people to go to the cinema and dances again but she consulted Pat. 'Let them leave it another two weeks to make the two months,' he advised. 'And don't be upset because they want to, girl. They mean no disrespect to your ma.'

'You're right, Pat,' she agreed. 'Life is short and they're only young once.'

Chapter Twenty

Anne and Sarah began to attend modern dances and were an immediate success with the young men who went there. They still visited the cinema and the *caelidhes* so before long Anne's life was as hectic as ever.

Sarah told her that John was so discouraged by his failure to find work that he had decided to try elsewhere in the country. 'He thinks the blacklist will only be for Liverpool, but he says he won't go until after Christmas.'

Anne felt a stab of pain, although she told herself that she was not interested in John Redmond any more, yet eagerly accepted an invitation to Sunday tea from Sarah.

She feared John might not be at home but he was, and was very excited because he had been promised a job. 'I hated the thought of leaving Liverpool,' he said, looking intently at her.

Anne blushed and said quickly, 'And what's the job?'

'It's labouring. Stan Johnson, the chap my father works for, has a finger in all sorts of pies, including housing. Dad told him I'd lost that labouring job and he said if that was what I wanted to do, he had a job repairing houses he owns.'

Anne hid her doubts and congratulated him, but later she said to Sarah, 'It seems a bit of a waste for John to do labouring, doesn't it? I mean, after he stayed on at the College to sixteen then worked in offices. Do you think he'll like labouring?'

'He says he will,' Sarah said, and laughed. 'You know John. He's been going on about the dignity of labour.'

Anne smiled. 'He practises what he preaches though, doesn't he?' she said, and Sarah agreed.

At teatime Anne was seated next to Sarah's grandmother who talked to her about her family at first then said, 'It's good news about John's job, isn't it?' Anne nodded and Mrs Ward went on quietly, 'He's been a troubled lad this last year or two, but he'll sort himself out soon.'

'How do you mean?' Anne asked.

'He takes things very much to heart like his grandad did,' the old lady said. 'Both worrying about the troubles of the world and how to cure them, but John's been talking to his dad about this Spanish business and other things and he'll work things out soon.'

'He knows so much about everything,' Anne said. 'Things that are happening in foreign countries.'

'Too much,' Mrs Ward said. She smiled at Anne. 'His heart's in the right place but he's a bit mixed up so we'll have to give him time.'

Anne felt a rush of affection for the wise old lady whom she felt was offering comfort and advice to her. After tea Sarah and Anne and John went into the parlour to play records and John sat down beside Anne and began to talk about his job.

She felt that they were really making progress but Sarah's friend Edie Meadows, who lived nearby, came in. She was a big, boisterous girl with a loud voice and dominated the conversation.

'I've just come for the skirt your mum's fixed for me,' she said. 'Oh eh kid, I had a smashing time last night. I went on a chara to Blackpool with the girls from work, and we never stopped singing. We had a real good time but of course me dad had to spoil it when I got home. Carrying on and saying I was up to no good, out till that time. I hate him.'

Anne looked at her in amazement, not sure that she had heard aright, but Edie rattled on, 'I'm beginning to think me Aunt Mary's right to hate fellers.' She looked at Anne. 'I've had a fight with my feller, haven't I, Sar? I don't care if I never see him again.'

'You don't mean that, Edie,' she said, but Edie said defiantly, 'Yes, I do. Is that the time? I'd better go. I'm supposed to be meeting a feller for the pictures at eight o'clock.'

'So you don't hate all fellows?' John laughed.

'They're all right to take me to the pictures,' she said. 'Ta, ra then.'

'Poor Edie,' Sarah said when she had gone. 'She's really upset about falling out with Bert. They've been going out on and off for years.'

'I couldn't believe my ears when she said she hated her father,' Anne said.

Sarah shrugged. 'I don't like him either, but her mum's nice, isn't she, John?'

'Yes. She's been Mum's friend since they were kids,' he said. The conversation was general for a while then John excused himself, saying he had to find out more details about the job from his father.

Anne was disappointed. She had felt that they were getting on so well until Edie appeared. Why does he blow so hot and cold, she thought, even within the space of a few hours? When she was leaving, John reappeared and he and Sarah accompanied her to the corner of Magdalen Street.

When Anne left them she thought of the first time she had stood on that corner saying goodnight to John. I had such high hopes then but all this time and we're no further on, she thought. Why don't I just forget him?

Yet although she was annoyed with herself for doing so, she was now coming home again every night by the route where she had so often met him. It was several weeks before she realised that now that he was working he would not be free to walk about the neighbourhood.

Sarah told her that her father and John had been discussing the possibility of war with Germany, but they had hastily changed the subject when her mother came in.

'But they don't think *we'd* fight with Germany, do they?'

'I don't think so. Dad was saying that Herr Hitler had done wonders for Germany. Pulled them up by their boot strings, was what he said, but then they were talking about the Treaty of Versailles and about war reparations being hard on Germany.'

'You hear some interesting conversations in your house, don't you?' Anne said. 'I never hear anything like that at home.'

'Do you really want to?' Sarah said with a grimace. 'I think you have great talks in your house when all the family are in. I really enjoy them and they're not worrying like this war talk.'

'I think it's just talk,' said Anne. 'I know Hitler is always falling out with foreign countries but it's got nothing to do with us, has it?'

Sarah came to tea on Sunday and when all the younger members of the family were in the parlour afterwards, Anne spoke about the talk of war. She implied that they had heard it in the shop and Tony said reassuringly, 'Don't worry about it. There's always talk like this, Anne, but it's usually politicians just trying it on for some advantage. What they call diplomacy, and some people call sabre rattling.'

Anne happily dismissed the gloomy thoughts from her mind, which was filled as usual with thoughts of young men, dancing and cycling. But in August Sarah came into the shop one Monday morning looking worried.

'I went to Dovecote yesterday to see Maisie,' she said. 'When the tram passed Springfield Park, you know, by Alder Hey Hospital, I could see trenches dug all over the park. A woman on the tram said we'd be at war by Christmas.'

'How would she know?' Anne said scornfully. 'The trenches might have been dug for anything, water pipes or sewers or something.'

'But Maisie told me there were gas masks in some depots ready to be given out. Even ones for babies.'

'You always hear tales like that. I don't know who starts them,' Mabel said. 'Don't be such a worrier, Sarah.'

But suddenly in September everyone was talking about war. A customer asked Sarah if her brother had been near Guernica in Spain when bombs were dropped on it from aeroplanes. 'Hundreds of people were killed,' the woman said. 'That's what'll happen to us.'

'Don't be daft,' Mabel said. 'It's different with these foreign countries. Stands to reason nobody'd dare to bomb us, because we'd do the same to them and they know it.'

Everyone began to listen carefully to the news bulletins on the wireless and to buy newspapers as soon as they were printed, yet people found it hard to believe that war could really happen. Except Mabel. She had completely changed her views and now declared that she was sure war was imminent.

The Foreign Office issued a warning to Hitler on 28 September of the consequences if he attacked Czechoslovakia, and the following day the Fleet was mobilised.

'And our Joe still at sea,' Anne said fearfully to Sarah. 'Mum says she wouldn't mind if only he was home and we could all be killed together.'

Everyone was frightened and worried, but on 29 September the Prime Minister flew to Munich and returned waving a document which he said meant: 'Peace in our time.'

'God bless Mr Chamberlain,' Anne said. 'I didn't realise how worried I was until I stopped worrying. I'm really going to enjoy life now.'

Mabel had told everyone that she was sure that war was about to start, and at first she seemed disgruntled that she had been proved wrong, but soon was as ecstatic as everyone else about the news.

Services of Thanksgiving were held in all churches and very well attended, and in cinemas when Mr Chamberlain was shown on Pathé News holding up the document, audiences stood and cheered. He was Anne's hero, too.

Sarah told Anne that her parents were annoyed with Mick, who was now sixteen years old and appeared older. He had gained five distinctions in his Matriculation examinations and it had been decided that he would stay on at the College until he was eighteen to take Higher School Certificate.

During the war scare he had tried to enlist in the Royal Air Force, giving his age as eighteen, but had been refused. 'The trouble is they'll send for him when he is eighteen, and we were hoping he'd win a scholarship to go on to University. They'll be annoyed at the College too,' Sarah said.

'What does Mick say?' asked Anne.

Sarah shrugged. 'You know Mick,' she said. 'He doesn't care if it snows.'

Another result of the scare was that Edie Meadows and her boyfriend made up their quarrel and became engaged, to the delight of Edie's mother.

'I don't mind Mrs Meadows being pleased, and I can understand it because it makes things a lot easier with Mr Meadows, but she's sort of sympathising with Mum because I'm not engaged!' Sarah said. 'I've told her I've no intention of settling down with anyone yet. I'm having too good a time.'

'Same here,' Anne said, but neither girl was being entirely truthful. Anne felt that she would be willing to abandon the good times to settle down with John, although pride prevented her from admitting it.

Sarah's interest in her friend's brother was far more vague. Joe Fitzgerald was so much older and moved in a different circle, and on the few occasions that Sarah had seen him he had shown no interest in her, but she liked him and knew that he enjoyed reading and poetry as much as she did.

They were both amazed to find that because of the war scare young men who had been quite content to go out with them on their terms suddenly wanted to start serious courting.

'I don't know what's wrong with fellows lately,' Anne complained. 'They know we've always gone out with more than one of them and they've always accepted it. I don't care if they go out with a different girl every day of the week as well as me, but suddenly they want to be the one and only.'

'I know,' Sarah said. 'I can't understand it.' She had a row with a young man named Nick Owens when they were all at the *caelidhe* one evening and he told her that he wanted her to be his girl and not go out with anyone else.

They were a large group including the Anderson cousins and were all amused to see quiet, timid Sarah so furious. 'He's got a cheek,' she raged. 'Why should I settle down with him out of all the fellows I've been out with? I told him I'd just as soon have Bob Doyle or Jimmie Rafferty, but I'm not settling down with anyone.'

'Never mind, alannah,' Terry said in a mock brogue. 'I'll be your steady feller.'

'She's not that hard up,' Anne retorted amid laughter, but soon she had the same experience with another young man.

'What's got into them?' she said to Maureen. 'I know I went to the ice rink and the pictures with Bill O'Hagan but he knew I went out with other fellows as well. Now he's talking as though he owns me.'

'They probably feel they should sort out their lives because of the risk of war,' Maureen said. 'But don't be hustled into anything unless you really want to, Anne.'

'I won't,' she said, 'and neither will Sarah. We like these

255

fellows but we don't want to marry them.'

'Then don't. Wait until you're really sure,' Maureen said, and Anne hugged her affectionately.

'I suppose the war worry took people different ways,' she said. 'Me and Sarah just feel that life is twice as sweet. Sarah says it's like being in the condemned cell and being let out. The grass is greener and the flowers more beautiful just because we nearly lost them.'

Maureen laughed. 'Very dramatic and poetical,' she teased. Anne giggled. 'I suppose we are,' she admitted, but it was true that life felt sweet to them.

She had not seen Kathleen O'Neill again, but she met Ella one day and heard news of Kathleen. 'I was glad to see her at the pictures with you,' Anne said. 'I feel guilty because a teacher in school asked me to stay friends with her after we left, but somehow I never seem to have time.'

'It's hard for her though,' said Ella. 'Her mother's so queer. It's a battle every time Kathleen wants to go out with me, with that brother of hers as well as her mother.'

'But she still goes out with you?'

'Yes, but not often, though. We only go to the pictures but there's a scene to face every time when she goes home. I tell her to stick it out and they'll get used to it. She'd have no life at all otherwise, Anne, and she's such a nice girl. Her family are so queer.'

Anne wondered if Ella knew just how queer they were but only said, 'I think it would be better all round if Cormac tried to get a job. Kathleen says he isn't strong enough, but he seems strong enough to me.'

'She told me it wouldn't be right for him to work, her mother said. Have you ever been in the house?' Ella asked. Anne shook her head.

'I've only been in once. You should see it! Material draped

all round the walls and swords and things hanging on them. A couple of chairs like thrones. Queerest place *I've* ever been in,' said Ella. 'I was only there a minute but I was glad to get out.'

'It's a shame,' said Anne. 'Because Kathleen's quite different when she gets away from them, isn't she?'

'She is,' Ella agreed. 'I've been trying to get her to look for a living- in job, a hotel receptionist maybe, but she won't leave her mother. I'll stick at it, though. I'll get her out of their clutches somehow.'

'I hope you do then I won't feel so bad about her, but tell me if I can help, Ella,' Anne said.

She felt happier about Kathleen now that she knew that she had a champion in Ella, but she had little time to dwell on the O'Neills. The shop had suddenly become very busy as Christmas approached, and although the cycling was finished Anne and Sarah continued to spend every spare moment enjoying themselves.

The usual family gathering at the Andersons' was held over until late January as Theresa had invited her parents and brothers and sister to her house for Boxing Day, and Pat said he thought it was a good idea.

'Spreads things out a bit, so we haven't got all the jollifications within a couple of days.'

'The only drawback is the weather gets worse and the nights darker after Christmas,' Carrie said. Everyone began to tell her that the shortest day had been passed and Fred sat down beside Anne. 'That reminds me, girl, be careful. Don't come home on your own late at night.'

'Why, Uncle Fred?'

'A young girl got attacked last week, my mate in the police told me. A respectable girl. She was nearly home and someone jumped out at her and battered her with a piece of wood. They found splinters in her. She could have been killed, only someone disturbed him.'

'Where was it?' Anne asked.

'Not far from here, near Boaler Street, so just be careful, young Anne. If he's done it once he can do it again.'

'I will,' she promised, and promptly forgot about it until Sarah said during the week, 'That girl Ella that you know, Anne. Is her name Eleanor Hopkins?'

'Yes. Why?'

'Peggy who lives next door to my grandma told us she's in hospital. She was attacked coming home from a dance and nearly killed.'

'Ella was?' Anne gasped. Cormac, she thought, or even Mrs O'Neill, remembering Kathleen's doll, but then the next moment told herself she was crazy. Anyone could have attacked Ella. Why should it be the O'Neills just because Ella had tried to befriend Kathleen?

Nevertheless she felt uneasy and was almost glad to hear that a second girl had been attacked in a different part of Liverpool. She would have been less relieved had she known that the second girl had been attacked by an ex-boyfriend, who had been arrested.

She enquired at the hospital about Ella and was told that only family visiting was allowed, so she left some fruit there and without analysing her feeling of relief, pushed the incident to the back of her mind.

It was easier to do this because Joe was due home and all the family were happily preparing. Julia seemed to take on a new lease of life and now that the weather was improving she often walked to Carrie's house or to see Bridie and her family.

Joe had letters ready to post to Littlewood's and the grain merchant's as soon as his ship docked, and within days was called to Littlewood's Pools for an interview. There was great jubilation in the family when he returned home to tell them that he was to start in the Despatch Department in two weeks' time, in the huge new office in Edge Lane where Eileen worked.

'The beauty of it is, it's permanent,' he said. 'And the prospects are good because Littlewood's are growing all the time. They're good employers, too.'

All the family were delighted to have him home again, but none more than Maureen. On Joe's previous leave he had noticed how quiet and unhappy she seemed, and persuaded her to tell him the reason. Eventually she told him that she had fallen in love with a man who was already married and her conscience was greatly troubled.

Joe had comforted her, and told her that no one could help falling in love, and if she was not breaking up his marriage she was doing no harm. There was no opportunity for further discussion. Privacy was hard to achieve, especially while all the family wanted to spend as much time as possible with him.

Before he'd left he'd managed to say to her quietly, 'Don't worry so much, Mo, and don't let religious scruples worry you either. You're doing no harm. We'll have a longer talk when I'm home again.' Maureen had been comforted as much by Joe's loving concern for her as by his words.

She had looked forward to long satisfying talks with him, when she could tell all about her feelings and all the worries she had kept to herself for so long, but it was not easy for Joe to spend time alone with her.

His mother clung to him and wanted to tell him all about her mother's death as well as telling him how happy she was to welcome Helen into the family.

His father had recently had electricity installed and wanted to show Joe the fittings and switches in each room. He even took him down to the cellars to see the lights and the point for a plug there.

'You know we always used candles down here when we were using the workbench, Joe. The feller that did the wiring told me it was dangerous, especially with all the wood about.'

259

'I suppose he's right, Dad,' Joe said. 'Although I've never thought about it if I was doing a job down here.'

'He said it was a good dry cellar,' said Pat. 'Sandstone foundations. Said we were lucky being high on the hill like the new cathedral on St James's Mount. I had lights put in the coal cellar and wash house too while he was at it. Cost me another two quid but it was worth it.'

'Handy for filling the coal buckets,' Joe said. 'And there wasn't much light in the wash house. Good idea, Dad.'

Neither of them realised then just how handy the cellar lights would be before long.

Chapter Twenty-One

Anne claimed Joe to talk to him about the books she had read and all that had happened to her since he went away, and Terry and Stephen wanted to talk to him about football and their latest craze, greyhound racing.

Even Tony was anxious for Joe to spend some time with him and Helen, and to show off his new car. Maureen, always self-effacing, would never have demanded time with him but Joe took matters into his own hands.

'Are you going to Benediction, Mo?' he asked. 'If so I'll walk down with you, and then we might do a bit of visiting afterwards or even just go for a walk.'

'It's a grand night for a walk, and it would do you good, Joe, after being cooped up on that ship,' his mother said. 'Let the visiting wait.'

Joe tucked Maureen's arm under his as they left the house. 'Now, Mo, how are things with you? I hope you've stopped worrying.'

'I did in a way, Joe,' she said. 'I felt much happier after talking to you, although nothing's really changed.'

'Tell me about this chap,' he said. 'What's his name?'

'Chris. Chris Murray,' Maureen told him. 'You'd like him, Joe. He works in Lipton's, near to our shop, but I only really met him when he came in to order baby clothes.'

'For his own baby?' Joe asked.

'Well, yes,' Maureen said, then suddenly burst out, 'He was tricked into marriage, Joe. His wife's a horrible woman. Horrible!'

'What happened?' asked Joe.

'He was at a party. He had a few drinks and fell asleep and when he woke up he was in bed and Beryl was lying beside him. She said he'd – he'd misbehaved. He'd have remembered, wouldn't he, Joe?'

'I'd have thought so,' he said, and Maureen went on, 'He didn't remember anything after falling asleep but they got married right away and Beryl just lay around like an invalid until the baby was born six months later.'

'*Six* months later?'

'Yes. She said it was premature but she hadn't made any provision for it, and wouldn't look at the baby. That's why Chris came in for the baby clothes.'

'And when did you realise how you felt about him? Does he know by the way?'

'Yes, and he feels the same way. I thought he looked so lost and unhappy that I just wanted to comfort him at first, and Chris says he just thought I was kind. Neither of us wanted to admit even to ourselves how we really felt,' Maureen said. 'He was a married man.'

She and Joe had walked through to West Derby Road and were approaching St Michael's Church. He said, 'Do you want to go to Benediction, Mo, or would you rather walk and talk? I would.'

'So would I,' she agreed. 'Sometimes I wish I hadn't been born a Catholic, Joe. It would make things so much easier.'

'I think you're worrying too much about the religious aspect of it,' he said. 'I don't think you've done anything wrong. You can't help your feelings.'

'Beryl wouldn't look after the baby so her sister took it temporarily, but then Beryl really *was* ill with poliomyelitis so the little boy stayed with her sister. Chris has to pay a woman to sit with Beryl during the day and he looks after her after work,' Maureen said.

'And when do you see him?'

'In my lunch hour. We take a tram to the Pier Head. I go inside and Chris goes on the top deck and we meet on a quiet corner near the end of the Landing Stage,' Maureen said. Joe had slipped his arm round her waist and she suddenly turned her head into his shoulder.

'Oh, Joe,' she said, 'it all sounds so furtive and nasty, but it isn't, honestly. We never meant this to happen but we can't help ourselves. I love him, Joe.'

She was weeping now and he guided her to a low wall in a secluded corner where they sat down. 'I know, love,' he said gently. 'Don't cry, Mo.'

She wiped her eyes and sat up. 'I'm just another worry now for my poor Chris and God knows he's got enough. His wife hates him, I'm sure she does. She does everything she can to make life difficult for him.'

'Couldn't he leave her if she feels like that? Pay someone to look after her full-time?' Joe said. But Maureen said sorrowfully, 'She wants him there even though she never speaks civilly to him. And how could he leave her, Joe? She's his wife and a sick woman and he promised "In sickness and in health".' She tried to smile. 'Don't worry about me, Joe. It's not all misery. When Chris and I are together we have some lovely happy times.'

'But it's not much of a life for you, Mo,' he said gently. 'I mean, you're never going to meet anyone else unless you make the break, and this is all a bit hopeless, isn't it?'

'I don't *want* anyone else,' Maureen said. 'Anyway, I'm not likely to meet anyone now. I'll be thirty-one this year.'

'How old is the child?' he asked, and Maureen's head jerked round to look at him in amazement. 'Didn't I tell you?' she said.

'The little boy died. That's when this really started. Oh, we'd felt like this for years but we wouldn't acknowledge it, and then we started meeting casually and standing talking for ages, but it was only when I met him and he was so upset about the baby and – and other things. I put my arms round him and suddenly, well – it all poured out.'

'How did he die?' asked Joe.

'Of diphtheria, but he'd never been strong. Chris's sister-in-law really loved the baby and when he died she was so upset she told Chris that little Tommy had never had a chance. She said Beryl took things before he was born because she didn't want a baby and that's why he was sickly.'

'Good God!' Joe said. 'And did he face her with it? His wife, I mean?'

'Yes, but she denied it, and then she said she didn't know why he was making such a fuss because it wasn't his child anyway. Chris said she laughed and he had to rush out of the house or he'd have killed her . . . He had to go back in the end because there was no one else to put her to bed, but he hated touching her.'

Joe said nothing and Maureen said anxiously, 'I suppose you think he's weak, Joe, but what can he do? She said when he went back that she was only teasing about the baby not being his! But said too that he'd married her in church and he'd promised to look after her always.'

'I can see his difficulty,' Joe said carefully. 'But I'm concerned about you, love. You deserve to be happy, Mo.'

'I *am* happy, Joe, most of the time. Especially now that I can talk to you about Chris. It's been so hard keeping it all to myself.'

'Does no one else know?' Joe asked.

'No. Mum guessed there was something and in the end I told her that I was in love with a married man. I thought she'd be shocked but she wasn't, although she said she thought I should try to forget him because it would only mean unhappiness for me.'

'And that's all Mum wants,' Joe said fondly. 'For us all to be happy.'

'I'm glad she knows. She always turns the conversation away when Aunt Minnie starts about marriage and me being an old maid.'

'I wouldn't expect *her* to be cheering for marriage,' Joe said. 'Not after Dympna's experience.'

'She's like a lot of other people,' Maureen said wryly. 'She thinks that any husband is better than none.'

They stood up and Maureen glanced at her watch. 'We'd better get back or they'll be sending out a search party,' she said. 'Thanks, Joe, for listening to me. It's helped a lot.'

They strolled home, talking now of family matters, but as they neared Magdalen Street Maureen said suddenly, 'There's a lot more about Chris and me, and – and other things I haven't had time to tell you, Joe. Don't worry about me, will you, because of what I've said tonight?'

'I'm sure there is a lot more,' he said, giving her arm a comforting squeeze. 'Thing is, Mo, we're going to have plenty of time to talk now I'm home for good.'

'Yes, thank God,' she said happily. 'I've missed you so much, Joe. We all have.'

Joe settled back happily into family life, enjoying the warmth of his welcome. He had lost touch with his friends but had the company of his brothers and sisters to compensate.

Terry and Stephen attended Victor's Dancing Academy in Prescot Road and urged him to try it, but he put them off. He went very willingly to watch Everton Football Club, and to the Parish Club where they played billiards and practised with dumbbells and a punchball, and to greyhound racing.

Anne had talked so much about the gramophone at the Redmond house that Pat had bought a cabinet gramophone for the parlour, stipulating that the family must buy the records. Now to the recordings of jazz, dance bands and romantic ballads Joe added his choice of light classical music and operatic arias.

Coming back to the family after being away for so long except for short periods, Joe saw them with new eyes. Tony had always been serious, always very much the elder brother, checking Terry and Stephen, protective towards the girls, but now he seemed more relaxed.

For the first time Joe realised that Tony had really been lacking in confidence. Now Helen, loving and admiring him, had given him the confidence he needed to be happy. Terry and Stephen were not complex characters, but Eileen, always simply considered a tomboy, was sensitive and vulnerable.

It was only now that she was happy with the girls in Littlewood's Pools that Joe realised how much she had been hurt by the cattiness in her previous job. He was surprised at how grown up Anne suddenly appeared although she was still as light-hearted as ever. Her friend Sarah, although the same age, was so shy that she appeared much younger.

She often visited the Fitzgerald house and Joe enjoyed discussions about books with her and Anne. He was pleased to find that both girls shared his taste in music, although they also liked sentimental ballads and dance music.

Terry still made extravagant gestures of devotion to Sarah but to Joe the situation seemed much as it was when he was last at home. The more he knew Sarah, the more he liked her, but he wondered if she saw him just as Anne's sedate older brother, not part of the flirting casual crowd of her own age group as Terry was.

Anne and Sarah were attending Victor's Academy in addition to the *caelidhes* now. Eileen joined with them but before long she met a young man and started courting so dropped the dances.

'We could do the quickstep and the waltz but we thought we'd join to learn the more complicated dances like the tango and the slow foxtrot,' Anne told Joe. 'And Terry and Stephen seemed to have such a good time there. Why don't you try it, Joe?'

The system at Victor's Dancing Academy was that beginners were taught on the ground floor, then progressed to the ballroom on the first floor when they were proficient. Anne and Sarah, Terry and Stephen had all been promoted to the ballroom and Anne said to Sarah, 'I'm trying to persuade our Joe to come. I'm sure he'd enjoy it but with us all upstairs he'd have to go downstairs on his own, and he's not pushy like our Terry and Stephen.'

'I wonder if our John would go with him?' Sarah said. 'I was talking about some of the funny things that happen there and Mum said it was the sort of place he should be going to.'

Anne tried to hide her eagerness for the idea. She still saw John occasionally but felt that he deliberately kept a barrier between them, although the way he looked at her belied his stilted conversation. Her pride made her speak as formally as he did and always be the one who moved away first.

When Sarah told her that he had been offered and refused a foreman's job, Anne was bitterly angry that he had said nothing about it when they met the previous evening, but now she was unable to resist saying, 'Yes, that would be great,' as coolly as possible.

Anne told Joe that Dominic and Desmond had joined Victor's with Terry and Stephen. 'They got thrown out though,' she said. 'You know what they're like. They played all sorts of tricks while they were learning and then when they came upstairs Victor was doing an exhibition dance, a tango. He takes it very seriously too.'

'And what did they do?' Joe asked, smiling.

'They'd got a tail off a fox fur and pinned it on the back of Victor's coat just before he started the dance. It looked so funny, Joe. Victor holds his neck stiff and keeps a sort of stony expression on his face, sort of supercilious, and this tail was swinging out behind him.'

'I'll bet he was mad,' said Joe.

'Everybody was roaring laughing. They couldn't help it. And when Victor realised what they'd done he was furious. He said he'd had other complaints about them and barred them from the dances. They don't care though. They don't care if it snows, that pair.'

'It's only when they are together, though. Aunt Carrie said Desmond is a real good worker when he's on his own with his dad, and Dominic seems to behave himself at work,' said Joe. 'It's only when they're together they get up to their tricks, but there's no harm in them.'

'It's lucky that Des showed a flair for Uncle Fred's leather-work and Dom didn't then,' Anne observed, and Joe agreed.

'At least Bridie won't have that trouble with her twins,' said Anne. 'Aren't they lovely, Joe, and both so different? Monica's like a little blonde doll.'

'I liked the way the older boys each seem to have adopted one of the twins,' Joe said.

'Yes, Danny with Monica and Teddy with Michael,' Anne laughed. 'It was funny to see it when the babies started to crawl and the boys watched over them. Always paired off the same. Lovely to see them all so happy, isn't it, Joe?'

Joe met John Redmond and arranged to go with him to Victor's Academy and both enjoyed meeting and talking as much as the dancing instruction. Other members of their families were upstairs dancing, and afterwards they all walked home in a group.

Anne found John Redmond beside her, gazing intently at her but only talking about dancing. What's wrong with him? she thought crossly. It's one step forward and one back all the time with him. The way he looked at her made her feel that he was attracted to her, yet always he seemed to draw back.

Always optimistic, Anne felt sure that now that she would see him regularly at the dance, she would soon find out how he really felt about her, but it was not to be. At the next dance an announcement was made that Victor's would close during the summer months for alterations and re-decorating.

Although Joe had been careful not to criticise Chris to Maureen he felt indignant with him. All right, the fellow has his troubles, Joe thought, but why has he involved Maureen in them? If he really loves her he would have kept away from her. He decided to try to see Chris while he was still free during the day before starting work.

It was rare for a man to shop in a grocer's but Joe could think of no other way to see Chris Murray. He only knew that Chris worked on the grocery side of the shop, and wondered how he would know him, but his problem was soon solved.

He walked into Lipton's and stood behind a fat woman who immediately said, 'Ee are, Chris, serve this chap. I know you fellers don't like waiting.'

Joe saw a man with a pale lined face and thinning brown hair who said quietly, 'Yes, sir? Can I help you?' Conscious that the fat woman had seated herself on a stack of biscuit tins and was listening avidly, Joe said 'Er, I want to take some groceries to an old lady. Can you tell me if this is right?'

He had written something on a scrap of paper and folded it over at the bottom. Within the fold he had written, 'I am Maureen's brother. Can I speak to you?' Even before Chris had unfolded the note he had looked at Joe and some colour had come into his pale face.

'Tea and sugar's what you want, lad,' the fat woman said, leaning forward eagerly. 'Maybe some Bovril if you've got the money.' But fortunately another assistant had arrived. 'Can I take your order, Mrs Jones?' he said, and as she turned away Chris leaned over the counter and said quietly, 'I finish at seven o'clock. Can we meet outside?'

Joe agreed and to satisfy the fat woman who was watching

curiously, bought tea and sugar, a jar of Bovril and a tin of cocoa. The fat woman said approvingly, 'That'll be just what she wants, God luv her. You're a good lad.'

Joe left the shop blushing and as soon as he was safely away from it, gave the brown paper parcel to an old woman who shuffled along, her worn shoes held together with a large safety pin. She clutched a black shawl above a patched and shabby skirt, her eyes sunken in her gaunt face, and on an impulse he put half a crown in her hand and hurried away. He was back at seven o'clock, waiting round the corner from the shop.

When Chris came out they turned away down a side street and Chris said immediately, 'I knew you were Maureen's brother as soon as I saw you. You're so like her. I'm glad to meet you.'

'Maureen doesn't know I'm here,' said Joe, 'but she told me all about you. I know you're going through a bad time, but my main concern is Maureen.'

'And so is mine,' Chris said eagerly. 'I'd do anything to save her from pain.'

'Then don't you think you should break this off?' Joe said. 'What future is there for Maureen in this situation? She has too much integrity, she's too scrupulous, to have any happiness with a married man. And I'm not going to stand by and see her hurt.'

'You're absolutely right, I know,' Chris said. 'But we've tried and Maureen can't bear to finish any more than I can. God knows I tried when I realised what was happening to us, although it was like a starving man walking away from food for me. I love her. I never thought it was possible to love anyone as much as I love Maureen.'

In spite of himself Joe was impressed by the earnestness in Chris's voice and said less forcefully, 'I know it's easy for me to talk, I've never been in this situation, but what's going to happen? You say you don't want Mo to be hurt, but she's bound to be if this goes on.'

'What did Maureen say?' Chris asked.

'She was very upset at first,' Joe said. 'She's troubled about the moral aspect of it, and she's worried about you, but she did say you were happy sometimes,' Joe admitted.

'We are,' Chris said. 'When we meet at the Landing Stage and have even half an hour together, it just makes life worth living. It sets us up. Makes us able to face things.'

'I don't know much about your life,' Joe said, feeling that they were becoming too emotional. 'Maureen seems to think your marriage is a bit of a sham and you were tricked into it. Is that true?'

'I might have been,' Chris said. 'It's all rather complicated and I don't really know, but whatever happened in the past I have an obligation to look after Beryl. I made a promise and she needs me. She's an invalid.'

'What is it, the illness?' Joe asked.

'The doctor thinks the condition is partly hysterical, nerves really, but she's not malingering. He went into her family history and said it explained a lot. He wants to take her into the Royal Infirmary for tests.'

'Do you mean she inherited some disease?'

'No, but her mother and father lived in the same house and never spoke to each other for over thirty years.'

'Good God!' Joe exclaimed.

'You can imagine the sort of childhood Beryl and her sister had. They were terrified of their father and even more of their mother. Perhaps she did trick me but, well, I can see why she was frantic and why she's as she is.'

They walked in silence for a few moments then Chris said, 'Maureen thinks I should hate Beryl. I do hate her sometimes, very often in fact, but not all the time. I can see why she's like she is. My trouble is I can always see both sides, and I see she's what life has made her.'

'I can understand that,' Joe said. 'I'm a bit like that myself. Always seeing the other person's point of view.'

They stopped at the corner and Chris said anxiously, 'I'm afraid I've said all the wrong things, seemed to dwell on my side of things. Believe me, none of this was planned. Maureen and I – we thought we were just friends. We slipped into loving each other before we realised what was happening.'

'I know. I realise that.'

'I suppose that's when we should have called a halt, but now I don't know how either of us could bear it.'

'But it must be done,' Joe said firmly. 'I know it'll be hard but it'll be better for Maureen in the long run. I think you should be the one to do it, Chris. You might think I've got a cheek to interfere but someone's got to look after Maureen. She never thinks of herself.'

'I know you're right. I'll do my best,' Chris said wretchedly.

Joe held out his hand, they shook hands and walked away from each other, Joe feeling that he had done what he could to save Maureen from wrecking her life and suffering years of pain but troubled by sympathy and liking for Chris.

In the excitement of his new job and other things that were happening he pushed the thought of Chris to the back of his mind until he realised that Maureen looked red-eyed and unhappy.

At the first opportunity he drew her aside. 'What's up, Mo?' he asked. 'Why are you upset?'

'Chris wants us to break up,' she said, her eyes filling with tears. 'I couldn't bear not seeing him again.'

'But it's the sensible thing to do, Mo,' he said gently.

'Sensible! You've never loved anyone or you couldn't say that,' she exclaimed. Joe was silent for a moment, holding her close, then he asked what Chris had said.

'He'd been avoiding me, I knew he had, then I met him and

he said it was time to finish,' Maureen wept. 'He tried to say it was too much worry for him but I know him too well to believe that. Then he said I was too innocent to realise how hard it was for him just to see me for half an hour and a kiss and cuddle.'

'But, Mo, he's right. There's no point in it. No future for you, only pain.'

'I don't *care*,' she said passionately. 'Don't you understand, Joe? I don't *care* about the future. Half an hour now with Chris means more than anything in the future.'

'I'm only thinking of you,' he said. 'Now you're confused by your feelings, but just think. His wife could live for years.'

Maureen's head jerked back. 'You don't think I wish her dead? Truly I don't. She's gone into hospital and it might mean she'll get better but I don't wish her harm, Joe, even though she doesn't deserve to be happy.'

'And what have you decided, you and Chris?' he asked.

'He admitted in the end that he was suggesting the break for my sake, and I told him how I felt about *that*. We're going to meet tomorrow after he's been to the hospital and take a tram somewhere and talk.' She wiped her eyes. 'I know you think I'm mad, Joe. If it was anyone else I'd think so too. I just can't explain how I feel, but we'll have to pray we'll be guided to do what's best.'

'You have your talk tomorrow night,' he said, giving her a hug. 'Then decide to do whatever makes you happiest. You're not taking anything from his wife that she wants. She only wants a home.'

Maureen looked at him in surprise and he said hastily, 'That's how it sounds to me. And you can tell Chris that's what your brother thinks.' He laughed and Maureen said, 'Oh, Joe, I'm so *glad* you're home.'

She gave him a quick kiss before running upstairs and Joe felt guilty. *I wonder if she'd say that if she knew I was to blame?* he thought. Talk about fools rush in. I'll have to learn to mind my own business.

A couple of days later Maureen whispered to him that she and Chris were going to meet as before and just take every opportunity to be together.

'It'll be the crumbs that fall from the rich man's table,' she said gaily. 'But who cares?'

Chapter Twenty-Two

Anne had saved a copy of the *Daily Sketch* to show Joe the photographs of the Coronation of Pope Pius XII in March. She took it from the cupboard and as usual became engrossed in the other pages of the newspaper.

'That girl would read tissue paper if there was nothing else,' exclaimed Carrie who was visiting Julia.

'Some interesting letters in it, Aunt Carrie,' Anne said, laughing.

'I'll take your word for it. I haven't time to read newspapers,' Carrie laughed.

The letter that had caught Anne's attention was from a girl who said she earned one pound seventeen shillings and sixpence a week. She gave her mother fifteen shillings for her keep, and had more than a pound left to spend on herself.

'Why should I marry and become the slave of a man earning four pounds a week?' she asked. 'I prefer to keep my dignity and freedom.' Anne looked thoughtful. Was that why John drew back from a closer relationship? Did he think he should not start courting on a labourer's wage? Yet he had been offered a foreman's job and refused it. I give up, thought Anne. I'll never understand him.

There were two other letters that she thought might interest John, one on the subject of salary being paid during illness, and

ELIZABETH MURPHY

suggesting a code of employment, and the other about National Health Insurance.

Joe had become friendly with John Redmond, and they still met occasionally even though the dance hall was closed. Joe was interested in John's tales of his time in Spain, but when he spoke angrily about the condition of the poor in Liverpool, Joe said mildly that he thought things were improving.

'Look at the way some of the slums are being cleared and council houses being built in Norris Green and Huyton and other places,' he argued. 'Good houses too. Well-designed. Wide roads and gardens front and back, and bathrooms and indoor toilets. Working hours are being reduced in some trades too.'

John disagreed. 'I'm talking about the very poor,' he said. 'People at the bottom of the heap. Kids who never have a chance from the day they are born. My grandad fought for them all his life, but the things you're talking about, they're only scratching the surface.'

Joe had smiled at his vehemence and John had laughed too. 'I'm on my hobby horse again,' he said ruefully.

Joe was thinking of John as he walked through to Everton Road one day. He cut through Reservoir Street into Cresswell Street where on one side high railings surrounded the playground of Steer Street School. The Pools were working summer hours so although Joe was off it was a school day.

The playground was empty but he could hear the sing-song voices of children reciting tables as he paused by the railings. A boy ran across from the toilets to the drinking fountain in the centre of the playground from which hung an iron cup on a heavy chain.

He was a bullet-headed child whose shaven hair showed that he had recently been sent to the cleansing station as verminous. He wore the police issue of corduroy clothes and heavy clogs, but when he saw Joe watching him he struck a pose, one hand on his hip and the little finger of the other crooked genteelly beside the iron cup.

Joe laughed and the boy grinned back. Then Joe called him to the railings and handed him sixpence. 'A tanner!' the boy said in incredulous delight, 'Ta, Mister.' He thrust the coin among his clothes and started to run away but turned back to say, 'You a Yankee, Mister?'

'No. A Liverpudlian like you,' Joe said, and the boy gave him a thumbs-up signal as he ran back to his classroom.

Joe walked away, smiling. Not much to worry about there, he thought. Maybe the lad was at the bottom of the heap, but his spirit had not been broken. He'll fight his way up or I'm a Dutchman. How quick the kid had been to recognise that his suit had been bought in New York.

Joe talked about the incident at home and was surprised at Anne's interest and her questions about the boy. There was a lot of deep feeling in his little sister, Joe thought, in spite of her gaiety and light-heartedness.

Anne and Sarah were true to their pledge to enjoy every moment of their lives after their fright the previous September. They ignored the talk of war which they heard and concentrated on their pleasures. In August Sarah was invited to a dinner dance by a commercial traveller who came to the shop.

Anne thought often about Sarah and her sophisticated partner on the Saturday night of the dinner dance. She knew that Sarah planned to wear a midnight blue taffeta dress, with silver sandals and her mother's diamanté clips and fur cape. Her own visit to the cinema with an inarticulate young man from the West of Ireland seemed very dull by comparison.

She went to Sarah's house on Sunday to hear details of the evening but found her friend very subdued. She told Anne that the man, Ronald, had sent a taxi to take her to the dance and had bought her a casket of chocolates as they went in, but she had felt uneasy several times during the evening.

'It was the way his hands kept roaming round when we were dancing,' she explained. 'Then when we were sitting down he kept trying to stand on my foot.'

'On your new sandals?' Anne said indignantly.

'I should have been warned, I suppose,' Sarah said. Then, blushing, she told Anne that when they had left Reece's and were walking up Parker Street Ronald had suddenly pushed her into a shop doorway and attacked her. She had brought the casket of chocolates down on his head and run away.

'And he seemed such a gentleman!' Anne exclaimed.

'You wouldn't have thought so if you'd heard him shouting after me as I ran away,' Sarah said. 'And he tried to put his tongue in my mouth and when he pulled me in the doorway he – he unfastened the front of his trousers.'

'The dirty thing!' Anne gasped. 'Wait until I tell Mabel. He'll get no more orders in *our* shop.'

'I think we should stick to the lads we know in future, Anne,' said Sarah. 'It was horrible.'

'Never mind,' Anne consoled her. 'We've got to live and learn. You'll be coming to the *caelidhe* tonight, won't you?'

'I don't think so,' Sarah said. 'Nothing to do with last night. It's just that my throat is sore and I'm aching all over. You don't mind, Anne? You can go with the family, can't you?'

'Yes, of course. Stay off tomorrow if you don't feel any better and I'll tell Mabel.'

'I'll go to bed early with some of Grandma's jollop,' Sarah said. 'I'm sure I'll be all right tomorrow.'

Anne missed Sarah at the *caelidhe*. Part of the fun for them came from commenting on the other dancers and inventing private nicknames for them, such as Big Feet, Sir Galahad, Merrylegs, Dreamboat, and many others.

She hoped to tell Sarah about the *caelidhe* on Monday, but a message came that she was too ill for work. Soon it became clear that Sarah was seriously ill with rheumatic fever and would not be able to work for some time, and another girl, Hetty, was engaged temporarily.

Anne visited Sarah but at first she was too feverish and in too much pain to talk. Gradually the fever subsided and all the skin peeled from her body, but her limbs were very stiff and the doctor insisted that she should stay in bed, lying flat as far as possible.

After Anne's first visit to Sarah, John had walked home with her. She had been shocked and upset to see her friend so ill, and suddenly John realised that she was weeping as she walked along with her face averted.

'Don't cry, Anne,' he said gently, putting his arm around her. 'She'll be all right. The doctor told Mum that Sarah had everything in her favour. She'd always had good food and warm clothes and a comfortable house to live in. My gran's a wonderful nurse, too, and so is Mum.'

'So many young people die, though,' Anne sobbed. 'I hear of them from customers, and girls from school . . .'

'That's mostly TB,' John said gently. 'Believe me, Anne, this is rotten for Sarah now but she *will* get better.' He held her close in his arms and wiped her face gently with his handkerchief, and she became calm.

'I'm sorry,' she said. 'I shouldn't be talking to you like this when you're worried about your sister and I'm only her friend.'

'You're more like a sister to Sarah now,' John said. 'Perhaps —' But he stopped, and Anne was left wondering what it was that he had nearly said.

Sarah soon began to recover, although it was clear that it would be some time before she was completely well again. Hetty, who had taken her place in the shop, told Anne that two of her brothers who were Reservists had been called up.

Several customers had similar tales to tell although there seemed none of the panic of the previous year, only a feeling that war was inevitable and a preoccupation with details. Many of the customers had young children and were worried about the plans for evacuation.

Mr Dyson was stocking up with sacks of flour and sugar and boxes of dried fruit, and the shelves high on the walls of the shop carried forty-eight pound jars of jam and mincemeat.

'We'll be more likely to get killed with them falling on us than anything what the Jerrys throw down,' Hetty said. Anne found it difficult to like Hetty, although she had to admit honestly that it was partly because she was not Sarah.

She was a tough girl with an abrasive manner, and seemed very knowledgeable about the seamy side of life. Anne felt that she considered her a green fool, and Mabel was indignant that Hetty was very ready to accept the 'perks' of the job, such as the cakes and bread given to the staff by Mrs Dyson, and the extra money from Mr Dyson, but was always on the alert for any infringement of her rights.

'We all pull together in this shop,' Mabel told Hetty. 'We don't mind doing a bit extra if it's needed.'

'You're fools then,' she retorted. 'No one's not going to put on *me*.'

Anne had continued to visit the Misses Dolan frequently even after Margaret had moved in to look after them, and been very happy to see her old friends so well cared for and so delighted with Margaret's lively little girl.

'It's a new lease of life for them,' she told her mother, but just before Sarah became ill Miss Louisa suffered a stroke and was confined to bed, and two weeks later Miss Ellen had a heart attack and was also bedridden.

Anne went to offer to help Margaret with the nursing but she said that she could manage. 'Thanks, Anne, but honestly they make it so easy. They'd never ask for anything if I didn't suggest it. Your mother's been very good sitting with them, and the girl across the road takes Molly to school and brings her home.'

Anne's mother told her that she had suggested that Molly came to them while Margaret was busy with nursing, but she and Margaret had decided that the company of the little girl did the old ladies more good than doctor's medicine.

'They count the hours until she comes home from school,' Margaret said. 'Molly likes having an audience for her tales and it passes the hours for them.'

When Miss Louisa had a second more severe stroke at the end of August, and Miss Ellen another heart attack, both old ladies died within a few days of each other. Their friends could only feel that death was merciful in the circumstances, especially with war imminent, and that Molly had made the closing months of their lives very happy.

Anne had wondered what would happen now to Margaret and Molly and if they would be allowed to stay in the house, but Margaret confided that the death of the Misses Dolan had solved a problem for her. 'Not that I wanted them to go,' she said. 'I loved them and was hoping they'd have many more years, but I was worried about Molly. I didn't want her to be evacuated without me, but I'd never have left the old ladies.'

As there were no surviving relatives, Pat arranged the double funeral. They were later surprised to find that the Misses Dolan had left wills, leaving the house and contents, except for some specific bequests, to Margaret 'for her devoted care of us', and a cabinet containing a doll's china tea-set and porcelain figures which she had played with 'to our darling Molly'.

A mahogany bookcase and the books it contained was left to Anne 'with gratitude for our long friendship' and a Sheraton occasional table to 'our good neighbour Mrs Fitzgerald'.

'I'm delighted they left you the house,' Julia told Margaret.

'You deserve it, but I was afraid they weren't the sort of people to make wills and the house would go to the Crown or whatever they do in these cases.'

'But I feel bad about it,' Margaret said. 'After all, I've only been with them a few years.'

'Very important years,' Julia said. 'And wasn't it kind of them to leave the things to Anne and myself and the nice messages?'

'At least they're spared all this war business,' Margaret said with a sigh.

Anne was sad at the death of the Misses Dolan but too much was happening for her to dwell on it. War now seemed inevitable and she said so to John as he walked home with her. 'Just when things are getting better in Liverpool,' she said. 'More jobs and everyone happier.'

'But that's the reason for the jobs,' he said. 'War's been inevitable for a long time, Anne.'

'I know it said in the paper that Germany was prosperous because of all the armaments they make, but we don't make them in Liverpool.'

'Don't we?' John said. 'We've been preparing for war for ages. That Littlewood's Pools building in Edge Lane, and Vernon's new place at Aintree – they were subsidised by the Government and they'll be taken over if there's a war, or rather when there's a war.'

'But Eileen and Joe work in Edge Lane,' Anne said. 'What about them?'

'They'll probably have something else to do.'

'What will you do?' Anne asked.

'I'll join up,' he said. 'I don't believe in war. I don't think it solves anything – it's only twenty-one years since the last lot – and I saw enough in Spain to make me hate it. Still, Hitler will have to be stopped.'

To Anne it all seemed unreal. The weather was beautiful and

side by side with the talk of war and the preparations for it, life went on as usual. The usual scramble for the bathroom in the morning, cycling through the sunny streets to the shop, serving cakes and pies and bread all day, then cycling home and the rush to prepare for a dance or a visit to Sarah.

Mothers of young children seemed to be the people most affected. Bridie had been in tears when Anne called to see her. Danny and Teddy had to be evacuated with their school and Bridie had found lodgings as near as possible to where they were going for herself and Monica and Michael.

'I'm worried about Jack,' she told Anne. 'How can I sit there in safety while he's in danger here and fending for himself too?'

'Jack won't mind that,' Anne consoled her. 'He'll just be glad that the kids are out of danger and you're there to watch over them.'

Margaret had taken a living-in job in the country where she could have Molly with her. 'This evacuation,' she told Julia. 'The mothers'll only be skivvies anywhere they get billeted, so I might as well choose my own place. I'd have taken in lodgers only for the war, but the solicitor advised me just to close the place up for the time being. It might all be over by Christmas anyhow.'

'Please God it will,' Julia said fervently. Pain had her in its grip again, but with the help of the black bottles of medicine she was able to conceal the worst of her suffering from her family. This was easier because everyone was so preoccupied with other matters.

Even Maureen, usually so alert to anything that happened to her mother, was lost in her dreams of Chris, and Pat's mind was filled with worries about his business. Joe watched his mother anxiously but she managed to convince him that she often had these little spells, and there was no need to worry.

On Friday 1 September the customers in the shop talked of nothing but the news that German troops had invaded Poland at five o'clock in the morning.

On Saturday the news was that France and Britain had issued an ultimatum to Germany either to withdraw their troops or face war with France and Britain.

Rain fell heavily all day to add to the misery of people who came in the shop, many of whom had lived through the Great War, and told Anne some of the horrors of that time.

She felt depressed and frightened by the time the shop closed and she was able to go home. Her mother told her that there had been nothing on the wireless all day except music and news bulletins. 'God forgive that man,' she said. 'To invade those poor people in Poland when they're only just getting over the last war.'

She told Anne that Aunt Carrie had been to see her. 'She says Shaun and the twins will have to go, but she's more upset about Theresa and the baby. Theresa's had to get a gas mask for little James but she can't imagine how she'd ever put it on the poor child. He screamed when he was tried in it.'

'Doesn't it seem awful, Mum, gas masks for babies?' Anne exclaimed. 'Whatever's going to happen to us.'

She was sitting on a stool beside her mother's chair and Julia laid her hand against Anne's cheek. 'We are in God's Hands, child,' she said gently. 'We must just trust in Him.'

'Oh, Mum, I wish I could believe like you,' Anne exclaimed.

'You're young yet, pet,' her mother said gently, 'and impatient. Trust in God, Anne. Haven't I always taken my worries to Him and found ease?'

On Sunday morning the sun was shining again and Anne felt happier. The Fitzgerald family went together to early Mass and as they walked home everything seemed normal. More people had attended the early services, but the day seemed as quiet and peaceful as usual with only the sound of church bells and the occasional ship's hooter breaking the silence.

In the kitchen the meat sizzled in the oven and a big pan of potatoes stood on the hob. Anne was chopping mint at the kitchen table and the sound of the Salvation Army band playing as usual on the corner of the street drifted through the open window.

She felt a sense of unreality until all the family except Tony gathered round the wireless set. The ultimatum to the German Government expired at eleven o'clock and at eleven-fifteen Mr Chamberlain was to broadcast to the nation.

His sad tones prepared them for the news as he announced that German troops had not withdrawn from Poland and consequently Britain was now at war with Germany. He concluded his speech by saying, 'God bless you all. I am certain that right will prevail.'

They were all silent as he finished until Julia said softly, 'And God bless that good man. He did all he could to stop this.' There seemed nothing to be done except carry on with the dinner, but in the afternoon Anne went to see Sarah.

She thought of all the changes the news would make in her life as she walked to Egremont Street and wondered how soon her brothers and friends and dancing partners would be called up. She had met John briefly on Friday night and he told her that someone had told him that men who fought with the International Brigade would not be accepted in the Forces.

Anne had been indignant but secretly glad that he would not go away until she understood how he really felt about her.

Sarah was distressed when Anne arrived. 'All men eighteen to forty-one years of age to be called up, Anne,' she said. 'That's practically everyone we know.'

'I know. Our lads say they'll try to join the Irish Guards. Terry and Joe and Stephen anyway. Tony won't be allowed to go because of his job, and Stephen might be reserved too.'

'Mick's too young and Dad's too old,' Sarah said. 'And John —'

'He won't be accepted, will he?' Anne said indignantly. 'Just because he fought in the International Brigade. As though that makes him a traitor!'

She blushed when she realised that Sarah was trying to hide her surprise but her friend only said, 'I wonder will the *caelidhe* be on tonight? Someone said all places of amusement will be closed.'

'I've no idea,' Anne said. 'I can't stay long, Sar. I met our Tony and Helen as I was coming here and they told me not to be long. Helen looked excited. I wonder will they bring the wedding forward?'

'Edie Meadows' wedding is next Saturday,' Sarah said. 'It was planned ages ago and it was going to be a big do, but I don't know what will happen now.'

'They'll probably go ahead with it,' Anne said. 'Unless something happens first.'

The girls glanced at each other then Anne smiled cheerfully. She picked up the string of the cardboard box containing her gas mask and slung it over her shoulder. 'I wonder will brides have to carry these along with their bouquets, or even wear them? I'll suggest it to Helen and Tony,' she said.

She went out laughing, but her smile vanished as soon as she left Sarah. Helen and Tony were in the kitchen with the rest of the family when she reached home, all excitedly planning to bring forward the wedding to the first Saturday in October.

It was decided that Eileen and Anne would be bridesmaids and that the wedding reception would be held at the Fitzgerald house, as Helen's mother was a widow and a semi-invalid, and Helen was an only child.

When Tony had left to take Helen home, Joe, Stephen and Terry decided to walk into town. They all felt restless and unsettled, and met other young men who were walking round the town for the same reason. Joe met a man he had sailed with, and he told him that a ship had already been sunk by a submarine.

'Do you think it's true?' Stephen asked when they left the man, but Joe thought it was unlikely. 'There'll be all sorts of rumours flying around,' he said. 'We won't say anything at home anyway.'

The next day they found that the rumour was only too true. The *SS Athenia* left Liverpool on 2 September, bound for Montreal, carrying nearly fifteen hundred passengers. Many of them were children being sent to safety in Canada and there were also some Americans returning home.

When the captain heard that war had been declared he told the passengers that they were protected by international law, but he blacked out his ship as a precaution. When she was two hundred and fifty miles off the coast of Ireland the *Athenia* was attacked and sunk by a submarine.

Other ships converged to pick up the passengers but many were lost. The first news said over two hundred, but as more ships brought survivors the number dropped to one hundred and twenty, but eighty-five of these were women and children.

The news sent a shock of horror through people who were not yet hardened by the horrors of war, and this was followed by a surge of rage.

'What sort of people kill innocent little children?' people asked each other, and men flocked to join up.

Chapter Twenty-Three

Many mothers felt the tragedy of the *Athenia* more keenly because they were upset at the prospect of their own children being evacuated. For most of the children it was a big adventure, at least when they were setting off with their school friends. Homesickness and disillusionment came later for some of them.

A teacher friend of Eileen's told her that although most of the mothers were genuinely upset, some were pleased to have their children taken off their hands. Within a week the evacuation was complete. Stephen had been told he was needed in the factory which had turned over to war work but Joe and Terry had applied to join the Irish Guards, and Eileen to join the WAAFs.

The Pools had closed down and Eileen and Joe were unemployed but Littlewood's had made arrangements for their staff to sign on for unemployment pay at the Edge Lane office.

'How will all these people ever find jobs?' Eileen said to Joe as they joined the hundreds of people streaming up Edge Lane.

'Easily,' he said. 'A lot will go in the forces like us and there'll be jobs in ordnance factories and other places. Someone said this building will be used by the Censorship people.'

Anne was surprised at how quickly all that seemed so strange became normal. Remembering always to carry her gas mask, stumbling home through the blackout with only a narrow beam of light from her torch to help her, and going to services in churches lit only by candles with a blackout curtain over the door.

The blackout precautions were a constant worry to Julia, and Eileen declared that they were an excuse for petty tyrants to enjoy themselves. Mrs Morton, who had once forbidden Anne to take her daughters on days out, was the Air Raid Warden for the street, and the slightest chink of light brought her screaming and banging on the door.

'She'll give my mum a heart attack one of these nights,' Anne said. 'I never liked her and now I hate her.'

'Little Hitler,' Sarah said. 'Old Ashcroft in our street is the same. Much use he'd be in an air raid anyway.'

The doctor who attended Sarah went into the forces and the elderly man who took his place discharged her as fit for work. Sarah was delighted, but others thought she was still not well enough.

'Silly old fool,' Mabel said to Anne. 'God knows what damage she'll do to herself coming back so soon. We'll have to watch she doesn't do too much.' It was arranged that Hetty would stay on in the shop for a while, and Sarah would work from ten o'clock until three for the first few weeks.

Helen and Tony were married on the first Saturday in October. Minnie did not attend the wedding but everyone else thought that Helen was a beautiful bride. She wore a long full-skirted dress of white organdie and a headdress of artificial lilies of the valley, and carried white roses and carnations.

Anne and Eileen wore blue taffeta dresses and carried pink carnations and stephanotis, and Mrs Redmond had made a suit in darker blue and a white blouse for Julia.

Anne felt her eyes fill with tears as she looked at Helen and Tony kneeling at the altar during their Nuptial Mass: Helen so tiny and ethereal and Tony proud and protective beside her, looking at each other with love.

Will John and I ever be like that? Anne wondered. No doubts

or misunderstandings, a courting couple who can show that we love each other? It seemed unlikely. Whatever the reason for John's shutting her out, it seemed he was not prepared to tell her about it.

Now that Sarah was back at work Anne was not visiting the Redmond house as frequently, and she missed her visits there. The more she saw of the Redmonds the more she liked them, particularly Sarah's grandmother. Mrs Ward's shrewd gaze missed very little and she longed to ask her why John behaved as he did. Why he seemed so determined to treat her as a friend when all her instincts told her that he was in love with her.

The wedding of Helen and Tony was the last time all the Fitzgerald family would be together. Stephen and Tony were both in reserved occupations but Joe and Terry were called up into the Irish Guards and sent to Caterham Barracks and a week later Eileen left for the WAAFs.

The air raids and gas attacks that everyone had feared did not take place but Anne and Sarah agreed that it was the small inconveniences of war that were hardest to bear.

'I'm forever forgetting my gas mask or identity card and having to go back for them,' Anne said. 'And this damn' blackout! I tore my stockings and cut my knee when I fell over that step, and now this.' She had misjudged her nearness to a wall, and crashed into it, scraping her cheek and bruising her face.

'I know. I'm fed up too but I suppose we shouldn't grumble,' Sarah said and Anne agreed that other people had worse troubles. Several families they knew had sons or fathers missing or drowned at sea, and men were being sent to France with the British Expeditionary Force.

Sarah had been able to attend the *caelidhes* again, warned by her mother that she must not do more than two dances, but she found them greatly changed.

Some of the men they knew had gone home to Ireland to

escape being called up for the forces, but many more were serving in the Army, Navy or Air Force or were at sea with the Merchant Marine.

Letters had arrived from Joe and Terry and from Eileen who was desperately homesick, although she made a brave attempt to write cheerfully. Terry seemed to have settled in easily to Army life, but although Joe made no complaints it was clear that he missed the family.

'Terry's all right,' Anne told Sarah, 'but I think our Joe feels being away more because he'd just got used to being at home. Poor Eileen's terribly homesick. We've all written to her and sent her parcels to cheer her up.'

'I'll write to her,' Sarah promised. 'And send her some hand-cream and cigarettes. I'm sure the first few weeks will be the worst for her.'

Desmond and Dominic had joined the Cheshire Regiment and Shaun the Royal Air Force, so the Anderson house seemed very quiet. 'We'd hardly got used to being without Theresa in the house,' Carrie told Julia. 'I don't think Carmel will be at home long either. She wants to join the WRNS.'

Carmel had shed her puppy fat and was now very elegant. Julia smiled. 'She'll certainly suit the uniform,' she said. 'Anne and Maureen have said nothing about wanting to join anything yet. I wish Eileen had waited and they might have gone together like the lads, although God knows, Carrie, I dread the thought of any more going.'

'The girls are doing their bit here and that's just as important as going in the WAAFs or the WRNS. Maureen's doing the Civil Defence driving and Anne helping at Atlantic House. Thank God we haven't been bombed, and Theresa hasn't had to put that gas mask on the baby.'

'A lot of people are bringing their children back home,' said Julia.

Bridie came home bringing Teddy and Danny with her as well as the twins. 'I've never worked so hard in my life,' she told Anne and Julia when she called to see them. 'I got the rooms through the billeting officer, in a big house. The lady who owned it had a cook, a kitchenmaid, and two other maids.'

'How did you get on with them?' Julia asked.

'I didn't get the chance to find out,' said Bridie. 'The four of them left to work in a factory that opened near the village. I think my being there was a put up job between the lady and the billeting officer. I helped her at first but it was a mistake.'

'Why?' said Anne.

'Because she just took it for granted that I was there to wait on her. She expected to live her life as though she still had four maids with me doing their work.'

'What cheek!' Anne exclaimed, and her mother said, 'Did you explain that you couldn't do it, Bridie?'

'I'd have been wasting my breath, Julia. She was so arrogant, so sure that nothing must interfere with her comfort, that she wouldn't have listened.'

'Sarah's brother says the war will level some people down and others up and things will be a lot fairer,' Anne said. She blushed as she spoke but Bridie and Julia noticed nothing.

'If I'd been there much longer she'd have been levelled down all right,' Bridie said with a grin. 'With a left hook.'

The weather was still bitterly cold and snow fell on 28 December. The following day it froze as icy winds swept the country. 'This wind's coming from Finland,' a customer told Anne. 'It's the coldest winter there for fifty years.'

'It can't be any colder than here,' a woman said as the thick snow froze ever harder on the icy roads. 'I put my washing to soak in my dolly tub and it was frozen solid this morning – in my back kitchen! What a start to 1940!'

'I'm wearing as many skins as an onion and I'm still

freezing,' Anne told Sarah. 'It must be terrible for people in the forces who haven't got a warm house to go back to.'

'And poor people who haven't got warm clothes,' Sarah said. 'Mum's routing out all our spare clothes, and John's taking them to families he knows through Grandad. I've got layers on in case they've vanished when I get home!'

'There was something on the wireless about the earthquake in Turkey,' Anne said. 'They said it was like Dante's Inferno. We could do with some of that heat here.'

Later Anne thought over Sarah's words about clothes for people who needed them and felt ashamed that she had not thought of their plight. What would John think of her? When she went home she spoke to her mother about it, and she told Anne not to worry.

'I've given all the outgrown clothes and anything spare to Mrs Bennet. She knows people who'll make good use of them, especially in this weather,' she said, and Anne felt even more ashamed that the thought had not occurred to her.

Maureen, who was now the manageress of the wool shop, had warned them that wool might be in short supply so they had all bought plenty of every colour, including a lot of khaki. Anne and Maureen and their mother had all made balaclava helmets, gloves and scarves to send to Joe and Terry.

They had also sent knitted comforts to Eileen, and Anne had made a balaclava helmet for herself which she wore in bed as well as a pair of her father's socks and a cardigan over her pyjamas. She had always shared a double bed with Eileen and now missed the warmth of her sister's body beside her.

One night when she was ready for bed she called Maureen in to see her preparations. 'If I got married do you think this could be part of my trousseau, Mo?'

Maureen laughed. 'Why?' she teased. 'Have you got someone in mind?' Anne laughed but she blushed too as her mind turned to John.

Day after day the bitter weather continued and sliding and slipping home on the frozen snow through the blackout was a nightmare. Even when there was a full moon in the middle of January, and bright moonlight to light the way home, the cold seemed to intensify. Frost was so thick that it looked like newly fallen snow.

Hetty had left the shop to work in an ordnance factory soon after Sarah returned, and now to add to the misery of the two girls, Mabel went to train as an auxiliary nurse and Mrs Dyson's sister came to take charge of the shop.

The girls had always worked quickly and willingly but nothing satisfied Miss Meers and Mrs Dyson seemed afraid to stand up to her. 'Try not to fall out with her,' she begged the girls. 'Albert's got so much on his plate with worries about supplies. I don't want any rows to make it worse for him.'

Anne and Sarah tried to keep the peace but Miss Meers was a slave driver, and would never allow them to stand still for a moment. She did nothing to help but constantly chivvied the girls and interfered when they were serving customers.

Before long the woman who cleaned the shop had a row with Miss Meers and left, and she refused to replace her. 'The girls can do the cleaning,' she told Mrs Dyson, and Anne and Sarah rarely left the shop before eight o'clock at night.

Anne was concerned about Sarah, who was not fully fit again and looked exhausted. 'She'll be ill again if this goes on,' she told John when she met him as she left the house one morning. Both families advised the girls to complain to Mrs Dyson, and if she did nothing, to leave the shop. They made their complaint but when Mrs Dyson timidly approached Miss Meers she was so abusive that both girls gave in their notice to leave the following week.

'We're sorry to go like this,' they told Mrs Dyson. 'You've been good to us – you and Mr Dyson – but we can't stand it any longer.'

'Albert would soon sort her out if it wasn't for his worries,' Mrs Dyson said. 'I'm sorry to see you go, both of you. You've been good girls and worked hard for us, and I wish you luck.'

The girls wept as they left the shop but soon they were eagerly planning to apply to one of the factories such as the Meccano which was now on war work. 'I don't want to go in any of the women's services after what I've heard from Eileen,' Anne said. 'But we'd be helping the war effort just as much in a factory, wouldn't we?'

They both applied to the factory in Edge Lane; Anne passed the medical examination and Sarah failed it. She went to the Labour Bureau and the clerk there told her that she would be passed fit for clerical work and sent her to the Ministry of Defence Office.

Both girls liked their new jobs, although they missed working together. Anne's job involved shift work, six o'clock until two, two o'clock until ten, and ten o'clock until six in the morning, so she was rarely free to go out with Sarah.

Joe and Terry had finished their training and were due to come on leave when Joe was promoted to Lance Corporal and sent on a course, and Terry came home alone. He looked very smart as he walked down the street in battledress, his boots shining like glass and his shoulders back.

All the family, and especially his mother, were very proud of him. 'I suppose it's the drill, son, that makes you walk so straight and hold your head back?' she said.

'No, Mum, it's the cap,' he said, laughing. 'With the peak covering my eyes like this I have to hold my head back to see where I'm going or I'd break my neck.'

'Mother of God!' Julia exclaimed. 'Could you not get one that was a better fit?'

Terry laughed even more. 'The peak's cut like this deliberately,' he said. 'Wait till you see our Joe.'

Maureen was upset when she heard that his leave was postponed but the rest of the family thought it better for their mother that she still had Joe's leave to look forward to, so Maureen said nothing.

It was easier for her to see Chris now. His wife had been admitted to hospital for observation, and then evacuated to a hospital in Shropshire when war was declared.

Chris was now an auxiliary fireman and he and Maureen could meet only when their duties permitted. For both of them, though, the marriage vow was binding, and although they had been tempted, their relationship was still platonic.

Terry was disappointed to find so many of his friends scattered and his family with so little free time to spend with him. 'I know Tony's got his own house now,' he said to his mother, 'but what's happened to everyone else?'

'Anne is on this shift work now, and Dad and Maureen have their duties with Civil Defence. With Dad's being a builder he's showing fellows how to get people out if a house is demolished.' She crossed herself. 'God between us and all harm, Terry, I hope it'll never be needed, but they have to be prepared.'

'I hope he's not overdoing it, all that after a day's work,' Terry said. 'Although Maureen seems to be kept busy driving after work and I think she looks better than she has for ages.'

'She does, thank God,' his mother said quietly. 'It's a pity that Stephen has met this girl who seems to want his every free minute or he'd be company for you.'

'It sounds as though you don't like Claire, Mum?'

'Well, I haven't the fondness for her I have for Helen,' Julia said diplomatically.

'It must be lonely for you with everyone out so much,' he said, looking at her searchingly. 'How do you feel now?'

'I do very well,' she said cheerfully. 'Carrie is often here, and Bridie, and Sarah often comes to see me. She works ordinary hours so Anne's not often free to go out with her now.'

'I think I'll go down to see her tonight,' Terry said. 'Perhaps we could go to the pictures or something?'

'Yes, do that, son,' said Julia. 'That's a good idea. She's a lovely girl, and good company for all she's so quiet.'

Terry went to the cinema with Sarah, and to the *caelidhe* with her and Anne when his sister was free to go, but he found the dance very changed with so many men away from home.

The Fitzgeralds had never known their neighbours very well, partly because Magdalen Street was wide, with houses set back behind small gardens and with steps to the front door, and partly because their big family made them self-sufficient.

Now he found a young man from a few doors away was home on leave from the Royal Engineers and spent some of his leave with him and some visiting relations, as men on leave were expected to do.

Soon it was time for him to return and it was arranged that Anne and Sarah who were both free would see him off at the station. He walked down to the Redmond house with Anne to collect Sarah and to say goodbye to the Redmonds.

A framed photograph of Sarah, taken on her eighteenth birthday, was on the sideboard. Terry admired it and asked Sarah if she had another copy, and she said casually, 'Yes. I got three.'

Her mother took a folder from the drawer of the dresser and Terry took out one of the photographs. 'Can I have this?' he asked. 'I'd put it up above my bed.'

'In the gallery?' Sarah said sarcastically, but he dropped on one knee and put his hand on his heart.

'Ah, no, alannah, the one and only,' he said soulfully.

Mrs Redmond laughed but Sarah said, 'I believe you but thousands wouldn't!'

And Anne said scornfully, 'Get up, you fool.'

'"He that calls his brother a fool shall be damned",' Terry said, and laughing and teasing they left the house and took a tramcar to Lime Street Station.

At the station he kissed each of the girls in turn, lifting them off their feet and swinging them round, cheered by a couple of other soldiers. 'Don't be greedy, Mick,' one of them shouted, but Terry put an arm round each of the girls and kissed them again.

When the train had gone and they left the station Sarah seemed quiet and thoughtful and Anne thought that she was more upset by Terry's leaving than she had shown while he was there.

She slipped her arm through Sarah's. 'We'll be able to go out a bit while I'm on this carly shift,' she said consolingly. 'It'll be like old times, won't it?' Sarah looked startled but agreed.

Chapter Twenty-Four

Anne enjoyed her work in the factory. It was light and clean, and although the parts she was working on were tiny, Anne was neat and dextrous and found the tasks easy.

A cross-section of women were employed. Some were girls like Anne, former shop workers or clerks, and many had worked in other factories. The woman on Anne's left at the bench, Ruby, had worked in a factory making doll's eyes, and the girl on Anne's right had never worked before.

She was the indulged only child of wealthy parents and had spent her days playing golf or tennis or riding, and her evenings at various social functions. Her name was Penelope but she quickly became Penny in the factory.

'Mummy didn't want me to come here,' she told Anne in what Anne thought of as a 'far back' voice, 'but I didn't want to arse around playing Lady Bountiful. I wanted to do *real* war work. Daddy has gone in the Army and I can handle Mummy so here I am.'

Anne was surprised and fascinated by Penny's earthy language, delivered in the same plummy voice. She could hold her own in the bawdy jokes and the double entendres, many of which meant nothing to Anne, although she laughed when the other girls did.

Anne's quick wit made her popular and one of the women said admiringly, 'You can tell you come from a big family, girl, the way you come out with the wisecracks.'

Everyone talked about boyfriends and husbands, especially those who had both, and Anne was quizzed about her boyfriends. She talked freely about the many young men she and Sarah had been out with, and sometimes had the women in fits of laughter, but she never mentioned John.

Now that they were working different hours it was not so easy for him to contrive to meet her 'accidentally on purpose' as Anne privately called it.

The bitter weather was ending and everyone was feeling more cheerful when Joe was due to come on leave, but shortly before he arrived his mother had a vivid dream in which she saw him lying dead on a battlefield. She clung to Joe when he came home, and he spent most of his leave with her, though he went with Anne one day to see Sarah and her family, and told Sarah that Terry had her photograph pinned up above his bed.

She seemed embarrassed and muttered that her mother had given Terry the photograph, but before she said any more Mrs Redmond began to ask Joe about the war news. 'Nothing seems to be happening in France does it?' she said. 'Do you think it's true that the Germans are starving, Joe?'

'No. I think the Germans are probably being told the same about us,' he said, smiling. 'It does seem to be stalemate though, doesn't it?'

'Perhaps it will all just fizzle out?' Anne said hopefully.

When Anne and Joe left the house he said, 'Aren't they a nice family, Anne?'

'Yes, Terry's a lucky fellow,' she said.

Joe said nothing for a minute then he said in a low voice, 'It's quite settled then, Sarah and Terry? She said her mother gave him that photograph.'

'Well, she did, but it was when we were going to the station to see him off. He asked Sarah for the photo and he was doing his usual stuff, you know, hand on heart. Sarah seemed quiet and upset when we saw him off anyway.'

Joe had several long conversations with Maureen and she told him that the war had brought happiness to her and Chris. 'I know it's wrong, Joe, when it's been a tragedy for so many people, but it's made life easier for us. Chris only has to go to see his wife once a week in that cottage hospital and we're able to meet quite often now.'

'How long will they keep her there?'

'I don't know. I think they've tried to send her out several times but she likes it there so she's managed to discover fresh symptoms and stay on longer. Chris and I just make the most of each day.'

'And you don't let scruples about his being a married man trouble you, I hope?'

'No-o,' Maureen said doubtfully. 'Nothing troubles me while I'm with Chris, but sometimes at night I worry.'

'Don't,' Joe advised her. 'It's a sham of a marriage that should never have taken place, and you're doing no one any harm. Except maybe yourself,' he added. 'I worry about your future, Mo.'

'Don't, Joe,' she said. 'Who knows what's in the future for any of us? It's best to live for the day.'

Joe saw Tony only briefly as he was working long hours. He and Helen were blissfully happy, alone now in the house where they had lived with Helen's mother for the first few weeks of their marriage. With the threat of bombing it seemed sensible for Mrs Daly to go to stay with a widowed friend in Rainford, and she seemed to have settled there very happily.

Julia tried to smile as she said goodbye to Joe but she hugged him fiercely. 'Be careful, son,' she begged him. 'I'll be praying for you.'

'Don't worry, Mum,' he said, kissing her. 'The Army aren't going to waste all this training.'

* * *

Only a short time after Joe left, the 'phoney war' as it was called seemed to be over when Hitler invaded Norway and Denmark. Later in the month Terry arrived home again on a short embarkation leave, full of stories of the Irish Guards leaving for, he thought, Norway.

'You should have seen what they took with them,' he laughed. 'Any amount of cases of champagne for the officers and crates of beer for the other ranks.'

'They'll never be able to fight with that inside them,' his mother said, but Terry only laughed. 'Take more than that to affect our fellows.'

Terry arrived late on Friday night so on Saturday he went to see Sarah with an invitation to tea from his mother. Anne had to leave for work, but Helen and Tony arrived and Stephen's girl-friend Claire.

After tea Sarah and Terry, Stephen and Claire, and Tony and Helen went to the *caelidhe* and all enjoyed it. Helen whispered to Sarah that it had been confirmed that she was pregnant and the baby was due in late November.

'We'll tell Tony's mum after Terry goes back, to cheer her up,' she said. 'But we'll keep the news in the family for now.'

Terry had to go back on Sunday night and before he left for the station hugged his mother and looked fearfully into her drawn face. 'You'll have to eat more, Mum,' he said urgently. 'You're only skin and bone.'

'I'm grand, son,' she said gently. 'God bless you now and guard you always.' A shadow seemed to have fallen over them, perhaps a premonition that they would never see each other again, and they stared at each other as though trying to commit each other's features to memory.

Anne and Sarah saw Terry off at the station, and Anne tact-fully went to the station bookstall while Sarah and Terry said goodbye. Terry was still feeling the sadness of leaving his mother and was more subdued than on their last leavetaking.

Anne came back with cigarettes and chocolate and magazines and said goodbye to Terry, then she said she would wait for Sarah at the entrance and left them together.

'I'll be going abroad soon,' he told Sarah. 'But we'll write often, won't we? You're my girl now, aren't you?' Sarah kissed him and nodded, her eyes filling with tears, more in sympathy with the stricken couples around her than on her own account.

The news bulletins were confusing, giving different versions of what was happening in Norway, and the accounts of a debate on the situation in the Commons only confused people still more.

There had been noisy, angry scenes and in the end a member of Chamberlain's own party stood up and said to him, 'Depart, I say, and let us have done with you. In the name of God, go.'

Anne was angry and upset when she heard the news, and found that many of the women at work agreed with her. 'What a way to treat a man who saved us like Chamberlain did,' Anne said. 'Leo Amery . . . I've never heard of him. What gives him the right to talk like that to a man like Mr Chamberlain?'

'Trying to get himself noticed, I suppose,' said one of the other girls, and an older woman said angrily, 'Churchill in charge! Look at the men who got killed in the Dardanelles because of him.'

Less than a week later Churchill made a speech telling the British people that 'All he could offer was blood, toil, tears and sweat', and strangely this united the country behind him.

'I think we might be safer with him,' Anne said, 'but I still think that fellow shouldn't have spoken like that to Mr Chamberlain.'

Eileen was home on leave when a letter came from Terry to tell them that he was off to France. 'He'll soon be home again,' she comforted her mother. 'The German Army must be too spread out, with going into Belgium and Holland as well as Norway and all the other places.'

'I'm sure you're right, love,' her mother agreed. 'Terry seems in good spirits anyway. You mustn't let this spoil your leave.'

A letter card came from France, but it told them little except that he was well and a letter followed. The news from France was that the French Army was withdrawing into prepared positions to lure the German Army into a trap, but soon everyone realised that the Germans must be sweeping all before them.

'If only we knew what was happening,' women said to each other as news came that Holland had been flooded and then that Rotterdam had been blitzed and the Dutch had surrendered.

'What in God's name is happening to our lads in France?' said Ruby whose son was with the British Expeditionary Force like Terry. But they could only wait and listen for any scrap of news.

Soon it was clear that France was overrun and men began arriving home from the evacuation at Dunkirk. Desmond and Dominic were among them. They had managed to stay together although they had lost all their kit and most of their clothes.

'Did you see anything of Terry?' Carrie asked them anxiously, and they only said that they had not seen him without saying how ridiculous the question was. They had both been asked about other men who were in France and answered patiently, knowing that the distraught women who asked them were only clutching at straws.

Sarah had been surprised at Mrs Fitzgerald's calmness but Anne told her that her mother and Maureen spent every possible moment in church and it seemed to comfort them.

Joe came home on leave and this brought even more comfort to his mother. He told her that he thought Terry was a prisoner of war because he had spoken to men who had returned from his Company. 'Most of them were accounted for,' he said. 'The wounded men were taken off and other fellows saw what happened to the men who were killed. The ones not accounted for were in little pockets that were cut off and taken prisoner and I think that's what happened to Terry.'

'But will the Germans ill treat him?' Julia said anxiously.

'No, Mum, they're not allowed to by the Geneva Convention,' he said gently.

Soon after Joe went back the family were notified that Terry was a prisoner of war, and given the address of the Stalag in which he was held. Anne ran down to tell Sarah before she left for work, and was surprised by how calmly her friend took the news.

All her concern seemed to be for Terry's family, especially his mother, and Anne was even more surprised when Sarah refused to go back to the house with her. 'I have an important document I have to finish,' she said, and insisted on going in to work. 'After all, it's your celebration.'

Sarah's mother and grandmother had followed her so they stood in a group on the step with several neighbours adding their congratulations. 'Come in, Anne,' Mrs Redmond urged, but she said she must get back to her mother.

She was running back home when she turned a corner and met John pushing a handcart full of building materials. He stopped and Anne excitedly thrust the official letter at him.

'Our Terry's alive! He's a prisoner,' she said joyfully.

'Good!' he exclaimed, impulsively flinging his arms round her. 'That's smashing news.' Anne hugged him in return, her face bright with happiness. At last! she thought, looking up at John.

He kissed her and held her close. 'Oh, Anne, I love you. I've wanted to do this for ages,' he murmured.

'And I love you,' she whispered, drawing his head down to her and kissing him. He still held her close, but several people passed and he raised his head and drew away from her. 'This is too public,' he said. 'Can I meet you later and have a talk?'

'Of course,' Anne said immediately, 'I can meet you tonight after work.'

'We could go in the park,' he said. 'I'll meet you where the gates used to be if that's all right with you.' Anne agreed, disappointed that he had not suggested meeting her outside the factory where her friends could see him, but happy to meet him anywhere.

He looked lovingly into her face, but made no attempt to kiss her again. Anne could see, though, that he was trembling as he picked up the handles of the handcart and moved away. She almost skipped home. Some of her joy was because of the news about Terry, but most was because John had at last told her that he loved her.

After all this time of wondering, when her instincts told her that he was in love with her yet he seemed to draw down a shutter between them so often, it seemed almost too good to be true. Her mind was filled with memories of his words and his kisses, and thoughts of their coming meeting.

Her mother was surprised that Sarah was not with her but Anne explained that she had important work to finish. 'She seemed more glad for us than for herself,' she said. 'And not very excited at all.'

'Everyone's different, child,' her mother said. 'Sarah's not one for showing her feelings, that's all.' She looked fondly at Anne's bright eyes and happy face. 'Your joy is plain to see, anyway, pet.'

The day dragged for Anne but at last she was free to hurry to meet John. He was standing by the bushes near to where the gates had once been, and he took her in his arms and kissed her passionately. 'Thank God for the blackout,' he said. 'I don't want us to be seen together, Anne.'

'Why ever not?' she exclaimed in surprise and indignation.

'I'm a bit of an outcast, love,' he said, 'and I don't want you to be involved with all that.' He slipped his arm around her and they walked through the park to sit on a secluded seat there.

'What do you mean – an outcast?' Anne asked in bewilderment.

'Because of my time in Spain. Ever since I started this job for Stan I've had wisecracks about being an Anarchist, Anti-Christ, the lot. And it's not only the fellows I work with either. Other people think that about me too.'

'But you go to church!' Anne exclaimed, then blushed. 'Sarah told me you went to Confession and Holy Communion at Easter.'

'That doesn't mean anything to those fellows,' John said. 'I've told them that I was fighting Franco and he's a Fascist the same as Hitler, but once these fellows get an idea in their heads they just don't listen.'

Anne slipped her hand into his. 'They're probably jealous too because you got the job through your dad, and then you were offered the foreman's job.'

'You're probably right,' he said with a look of surprise. 'You know, Anne, you can get too close to a problem and not see it properly. You're very wise.'

'I'm not often accused of that,' she said, laughing, and John smiled at her. 'I know the sly digs are worse after Stan's been at the job. He has a habit of giving me messages for my dad or asking about the family that doesn't go down well. Mind you, I earned that foreman's job, but I didn't take it because I knew the problems I'd have had with the men.'

'You should disregard them. They're just ignorant,' Anne urged, but John said stubbornly, 'Yes, but the fact remains I'm an outcast. Look at the times I've been refused for the forces. They don't *say* it's that, but I know it is.'

'You'd think they'd be glad to have you because you've got experience in fighting,' Anne said indignantly.

'Exactly, but I'm afraid it's the old class system again, Anne. Fellows from universities who fought in Spain are being given jobs in Intelligence or Censorship where they could do a lot more damage as traitors than a squaddy like I'd be. They're appointed by fellows from the same public school or university or club, I suppose.'

'It's not fair,' Anne said passionately. 'I didn't know you had all this to put up with, John.'

'So now you know why I didn't want you to be known as my girlfriend, Anne. I didn't want this stigma on you too. But you knew how I felt about you, didn't you?'

'I'm not a mind reader,' she flashed, but then she said more gently, 'I'm not worried. I don't see any stigma, as you call it.'

John put his arms round her and kissed her passionately. 'I love you, Anne.'

'And I love you,' she whispered. They kissed again and John held her so close that she could feel the beat of his heart, but then he said stubbornly, 'I wanted you to know, love, but I don't want us to be known as a courting couple, not by our families or anyone, until I get this cleared up.'

'That's ridiculous! You don't think our families think that about you?'

'No, but then other people would know. This must just be between us. Promise me.'

Anne promised, too proud to plead for others to be told, yet at the heart of her joy there was a small core of resentment that John was dictating terms to her.

Now though she stifled that feeling and gave herself up to the joy of being in his arms and hearing how long and how deeply he had loved her.

It was difficult for Anne to hide her feelings but she said nothing, even to Sarah although she knew that her friend was puzzled by the situation. They both avoided mentioning John though Anne longed to talk about him.

She met John frequently now by arrangement but always they spent the time where they were not likely to be seen. Sometimes Anne was annoyed by this unnecessary furtiveness and some-

310

times wondered why John had not explained the situation to her sooner and let *her* decide whether she wished to be involved with him, but she pushed these doubts aside.

Fortunately she was unaware how often in future years she would resent John's making decisions which involved both of them without consulting her.

These were small details now, swallowed up in the joy of knowing that she was loved by the man she had loved silently for so long.

It would have been harder to conceal their happiness at another time, but now everyone was engrossed in weightier matters. Now that France and the Low Countries were overrun the Germans were bombing shipping in the North Sea and threatening to invade England on 18 July.

Churchill had made a speech after the surrender of France in which he said, 'We shall fight them in the fields and in the streets, we shall fight them in the hills, we shall never surrender', and his belligerence was echoed everywhere, not least in the factory where Anne worked.

The news that Hitler was planning to invade Britain was greeted with derision. Queenie, a woman who worked opposite Anne, had her own theory. With a fine disregard for geography she decided that if the Germans came by sea they would land at the Pier Head.

'They'd have to come through Liverpool and they wouldn't get very far, I can tell you. I'd batter any German who came down our street, and all me neighbours say the same.'

Other women joined in saying, some in detail, what they would do to the German soldiers, and one woman, generally considered to be a part-time prostitute, boasted that she could see off any German.

'What would you do, girl, give them VD?' Queenie said, and

there was a general laugh. Anne was unaware what was meant by VD until Penny enlightened her.

John told her that Mick, who had finished his examinations for Higher School Certificate, had been called up for the Royal Air Force. 'He says it's because he volunteered when he was too young and now he's been pestering them, but I've been pestering all three services and got nowhere.'

'It's a pity you can't pull strings,' Anne said. 'A fellow at work said the class system here is as bad as the caste system in India.'

'Yes, and at the moment I'm an Untouchable,' said John. 'Some fellows I knew in Spain see this as a capitalist war and don't want to fight. I don't believe in war myself unless everything else fails but I want to fight now, Anne. England's my country and I want to fight for it.'

'You might get your chance if the Germans come here,' she said.

'"If the mountain won't come to Mahomet, Mahomet must go to the mountain",' said John, laughing heartily. 'I'll just have to keep pestering and hope for the best.'

Chapter Twenty-Five

The eighteenth of July 1940 arrived and passed without any sign of the invasion threatened by Hitler. There were several air raid warnings in late July but little damage.

In August Maureen's friend Mary Mullen was married and a girl who worked with Anne was married on the same day. All the talk of weddings made Anne feel downhearted and impatient with the secrecy that John insisted on.

When would they ever marry? she wondered. When would they even be known as a courting couple? She knew that John truly believed that he was protecting her by keeping their love secret, but she was becoming frustrated and annoyed about the situation.

She went to watch Mary Mullen's wedding on Saturday as Maureen expected her to be interested, but the sight of their happiness made Anne feel even more miserable.

She felt even worse when she saw Stephen's girlfriend in church, flourishing the engagement ring she had persuaded him to give her before he left to organise a factory in Newcastle for his firm.

Anne tried to appear cheerful when she said goodnight to her mother but she was glad to go to bed to try to sort out her thoughts. She tried to decide whether she should swallow her pride and tell John how she felt or whether to just go on and hope for the best.

She slept badly and felt tired and depressed all day on Sunday even though she saw John briefly late in the evening. She was working on the two o'clock to ten o'clock shift at the factory and on the Tuesday morning was up early to do some ironing, then she began to prepare the midday meal for herself and her mother and father, and Aunt Carrie who was visiting them.

She went listlessly to answer a knock on the door and was amazed to see John there and to be swept into his arms. 'They've come, love,' he said jubilantly. 'Two letters. One from the ordnance factory and one from the Army. Both on the same day. Isn't that typical?'

'What – what will you do?' Anne stammered. 'Which —?'

'Oh, the Army. I'm sure they have priority and it's what I want anyway. I'll have to notify the factory,' John said excitedly. 'Oh, Anne, I feel free now, free to ask you to marry me. Will you, Anne, will you marry me, love?'

'Yes, I will,' she said quietly and John held her even closer and kissed her passionately.

'Gosh, I feel so happy,' he said. 'I love you, Anne. I've waited so long for this.'

It's too much, too much, she thought, pressing her face against John's. The change from misery to this singing happiness was almost more than she could bear.

'Can we get engaged then?' he was asking, and she nodded, unable to speak.

'Can we go right away now for the ring?' he said, but there was a sound upstairs and Anne lifted her head.

'Dad's home for his dinner. You'll have to ask him,' she said, looking at him with delight.

Pat Fitzgerald appeared and began to walk down the stairs and John met him halfway down. 'I've got my papers for the Army, Mr Fitz. Can Anne and I get married?' he said eagerly. 'Can we get engaged today?'

'Aye, if you want to, lad,' Pat said, his calmness such a contrast to John's excitement that Anne began to laugh. She felt as though she was floating on air.

They went into the kitchen and John said to Julia, 'I've asked Anne to marry me. Will you give us your blessing, Mrs Fitz?'

'Indeed I will, and gladly,' she said. 'Sure I couldn't wish for a better husband for her.' John bent and kissed her, and Carrie kissed and congratulated Anne, saying, 'You never know the minute!'

'There's nothing sudden about it,' John said. 'I've been getting a lot of flak about fighting in Spain and I didn't want Anne to get any. We've been in love for a long time – well, I have anyway.'

'And so have I,' she said.

'I suppose that's why the other lads got the brush-off then?' Carrie said, laughing, and Julia smiled at them.

'Ah, yes. Anne was a good child but terrible stubborn. If she once got an idea in her head you'd never move it,' she said. 'The blessing of God on you both anyway.'

Anne and John went immediately into town, and chose a three-stone diamond engagement ring, then went to see John's mother and grandmother who were delighted at their news. Anne had to leave for work for two o'clock but she proudly displayed her ring to her friends and they all sincerely wished her happiness.

Anne managed to change to the early shift, six until two o'clock, so she had the rest of the day and evening to spend with John. He was due to report a week later, but he left work immediately and they spent every possible moment together.

John told Anne something of the abuse he had suffered.

'It wasn't just the fellows at work, although they were the worst, but the word had gone round. I was refused for the Rescue Service, you know.'

'But why, John?'

'Because they're fools,' he said. 'Some of them are so thick they thought I was fighting against *England* in Spain.' He laughed ruefully. 'And of course I always had to argue instead and make things worse.'

'Never mind. It's all over now,' she said. She wondered why John had not been more open with her but now she felt that she understood his situation better and they spent a blissful week together before he left.

The air raids were becoming heavier and more frequent. Eileen came on leave on 28 August and it was fortunate that she was with her mother. There was the heaviest raid so far, lasting four hours. Anne was on night shift, Maureen was now driving an ambulance at night, and Pat was using his skill as a builder to rescue people from bombed houses.

Mill Road Hospital was one of the many places hit and Maureen was injured there, fortunately only slightly, and taken to another hospital. Later Sarah and her mother came to see Julia, and she told them that Joe was at Dover and Anne had written to reassure him about them.

'He's worried about us,' she said. 'Lord Haw Haw said nearly everyone in Liverpool was dead and the few left were starving. Not that anyone believes that man.'

'He's a fool,' Mrs Redmond said. 'I believe he said weeks ago that Hitler would be in Buckingham Palace and he'd be in Knowsly Hall. I hope it keeps fine for them.'

'Joe won't hear anything from the BBC News,' Anne said. 'Everyone gets annoyed at work because there's always a lot about the raids on London but when Liverpool gets it they say "the North West".'

'Isn't that a good thing for people far from home, love?' Mrs Fitzgerald said in her gentle voice and Anne smiled and agreed.

Sarah had told Anne that her grandmother's lodger Josh Adamson had died of a heart attack at the start of the raid, but they said nothing of this to Julia nor of the casualty lists which were posted up containing many names of people they knew.

Maureen soon recovered and returned home, and letters came from Terry who seemed less downhearted than they expected. Stephen and Claire had become engaged before he went to Newcastle, but the engagement was short-lived.

All the family felt that Stephen had been hustled into the engagement by Claire, who was a hard, devious girl, and were relieved when it was broken when he returned from Newcastle.

Helen and Tony had been delighted when Helen became pregnant, but she had suffered a miscarriage in June and although always hopeful, had not become pregnant again. 'Perhaps it was all for the best you lost the baby, Helen,' her mother said when Helen went to visit her. 'But I don't think you should stay in Liverpool, with or without a baby.'

Helen pressed her lips together for a moment then said quietly, 'My place is with Tony, Mother,' and left as soon as she could. The feeling of comradeship now in Liverpool, the feeling that everyone was in it together and helping each other, was something that her mother would never understand, she felt, nor her grief for the baby.

The raids were increasing in number and volume. Maureen had returned to the wool shop and told Anne that her customer who knew the O'Neills had said that Kathleen had been injured on her head and shoulder by shrapnel and been taken to hospital in Winwick several miles outside Liverpool.

'What about her mother and Cormac?' Anne asked, but Maureen said she thought Kathleen had been hit returning from work.

Anne felt guilty that she had not attempted to see Kathleen after Ella's injury. I was daft to think that was Cormac's doing, she thought, but it was partly the reason why she had not tried to see her friend.

'Are they sure it was shrapnel?' she asked Maureen who looked surprised. 'Of course. I was nearly hit by some myself one night.' And Anne felt foolish.

In October and November the raids were taking place nearly every night, but in spite of the disturbed nights almost everyone turned up for work next day.

'It's worse than having a teething baby,' Ruby grumbled. 'I'm up and down the stairs and in and out of the bloody shelter like a hen on a hot griddle. I think I'll stop going to the shelter. After all, if it's got your name on it you'll get it anyway.'

After the night of 28 November even Ruby changed her mind. She had gone into a street shelter soon after the raid started at seven o'clock, and incendiaries, heavy bombs and parachute mines had fallen on the city and suburbs.

The street shelter had been hit and Ruby had been dug out to see a crater where her house had been and fires burning fiercely everywhere she looked.

'It was like them pictures of Hell we used to get in Sunday school,' she told the other women when she returned to work two days later. She wore a large dressing over one eye and her hands were daubed with gentian violet, but she insisted that she had been lucky.

'Nineteen people in our street killed and them poor souls in Durning Road School. Three hundred, I got told.'

A parachute mine had fallen on the shelter beneath the school, and various figures were given for the number killed there. In addition to those who usually sheltered there were the passengers from two tramcars, and people from a shelter that had already been hit.

It was the worst raid so far but Maureen who had not yet returned to driving was with her mother in the shelter and Anne, who finished work at ten o'clock, had reached home, dodging from shelter to shelter.

Wardens had yelled at her, she had stumbled over rubble and hosepipes, her path lit by the glare of hundreds of fires, she had been terrified by the throbbing of the engines of the bombers overhead and the crump of bombs, but she had run on. She felt sure that one of those burning houses was her own and fear for her mother drove her on.

'Oh, *Mum*,' she said, stumbling down the cellar steps and falling to her knees beside her mother. 'I thought our house had been hit.'

'We're quite safe, Anne,' Maureen said, looking at her warningly. 'Dad reinforced all this cellar.'

'Indeed you wouldn't find better anywhere,' said Mrs Bennet who had joined them in the cellar with her daughter. 'Even a flush WC in the old washhouse an 'all. He done a good job.'

Julia lay on her bed smiling at them, seeming unconcerned about the tumult outside, with her Rosary beads slipping through her fingers. But she welcomed Pat with tears of relief when he returned home after the eight-hour raid.

'How was it, Dad?' Anne whispered as she took his dust-covered clothes to shake in the yard.

'Awful, girl, awful,' he said. 'But we tunnelled through and got two little kids out alive. Saved by a piano falling and holding up a beam, thank God.'

A few days later before Anne went to work her mother asked her to go for bread. Anne took a tea-towel from the dresser drawer. She paused with it in her hand. How quickly what had seemed strange had become normal, she thought. Taking a cloth to wrap bread because of the shortage of paper, and queuing for things bought so casually before the war, like hairgrips and torch batteries.

Ruby had told of buying a pair of corsets and having to carry them along Church Street unwrapped. 'I tried every way to hide

319

them,' she said. 'In the end I held them against my side under my arm with the suspenders dangling down and some woman said, "Eh, girl them suspenders look as if you should be milking them." And me thinking I was hiding them! I felt ashamed.'

It was strange, too, Anne thought, that everyone got on with their normal lives, in spite of the constant raids and disturbed nights, and had become used to seeing servicemen in so many different uniforms thronging the streets and the cinemas, and in the public houses she was sure, although she had never been in one.

She and Sarah had been to the cinema the previous night and when the air raid warning sounded some people had left but most stayed. She and Sarah had been sitting under the balcony and when the warning was given they moved forward but continued to enjoy the film in which John McCormack sang Believe Me If All Those Endearing Young Charms and The Dawning of the Day.

When the All Clear was given they walked home, recalling the dances and parties at which those songs had been sung and Anne thought Sarah was near to tears. I suppose she's thinking of Terry, she thought, and squeezed Sarah's arm, although Believe Me If All had been Joe's favourite rather than Terry's.

Eileen came home on leave at Christmas and Stephen who had returned to Newcastle also came home. Their mother seemed to rally as she always did for her children but no matter how she tried to conceal it, it was clear to all of them that she was near the end of her strength.

Maureen decided that while Eileen and Stephen were home, the family should decide whether to tell Terry how ill his mother was. Helen and Tony came and Sarah was asked to come to a family conference. The young people gathered in the parlour.

For a few moments there was a general discussion then Tony

turned to Sarah. 'What do you think? Would it be better to warn Terry so it's not too much of a shock to him if anything happens to Mum?'

Everyone waited for her opinion but Sarah said hastily, 'I don't know. I think you all know him better than I do.'

They all looked surprised but Helen said firmly, 'It's not fair to put the decision on Sarah. I think we should vote on it and ask Joe's opinion too.'

'I *have* written to Joe about it,' Maureen said, 'but there hasn't been time for a reply yet.'

Anne thought Helen was right and Maureen said that she had been told when in hospital that patients often had remission in the disease their mother suffered. 'Sometimes months or even years when they're not cured but don't get any worse.'

'And Terry wouldn't believe it if we *did* warn him,' Tony said. 'He'd pretend it wasn't happening and it would still be a shock to him.'

They decided not to warn Terry when they wrote to him, and later Tony said quietly to Sarah, 'I wasn't criticising Terry when I said that, Sar. It's just the way he is.'

'I'm sure you're right,' she said. 'Anyway, we couldn't decide without Joe.'

'That's true,' he agreed, and Anne who had joined them said consolingly to Sarah, 'Maybe the war will be over soon anyway, and Terry will see Mum.'

'Let's hope so,' she said, and told them that her parents were furious because Josh, her grandmother's lodger, had left all his money and possessions to Kate and not even mentioned her grandmother who had looked after him for years.

'What does your grandma say?' Anne asked.

'She said she doesn't want his money but she hopes it won't be the ruination of Kate,' said Sarah. 'It's about a thousand pounds.'

'Whew,' Anne said. 'I wish someone would ruin *me* with that sort of money.' Afterwards she felt that Sarah had deliberately steered the conversation away from Terry, and recalling her remark that they knew him better than she did, Anne felt uneasy without quite knowing why.

Joe came on leave in January, but Anne remembered little of it when he went back. She had been moved to a different room in the factory and was doing more intricate work which involved the use of a micrometer and much greater concentration.

She was on day work now but working very long hours, often increased by overtime, and was very tired.

The work was satisfying but Anne missed the friends she had made and the free and easy atmosphere of the large room, and the jokes and the singing. Her present working environment was very quiet.

She felt downhearted for another reason too. She had been unable to visit Kathleen O'Neill but had heard that she was still in hospital and receiving treatment for the wound on her head.

The day before Joe came home Anne heard the shocking news that Cormac O'Neill had hanged himself and his mother had found his dead body. The shock had been too much for her precarious hold on sanity and she had been removed to Rainhill Asylum in a strait jacket.

It was just one horror in the midst of many taking place daily but it affected Anne deeply. She had always pitied Kathleen and never liked Cormac, who had not tried to protect his sister, but now as she lay awake at night she saw him for what he was: a pitiable victim of his mother's obsession.

How long had Mrs O'Neill been mad? Surely this was something that had been threatening for years? Could nothing have been done? Why had that doctor and priest not forcibly removed Cormac and Kathleen? What had finally driven him to do this dreadful thing?

Anne wept for him and for Kathleen, who must be told the news, and decided that she must definitely find out where Kathleen was and visit her.

Anne managed to discover that Kathleen O'Neill had been moved to a small hospital near St Helens in Lancashire and she travelled there to visit her on Sunday.

She expected to find Kathleen prostrated by the tragedy in her family, but although she spoke sadly of Cormac's wasted life and her mother's collapse, Kathleen seemed remarkably untouched by the tragedy.

She gave Anne potted biographies of all the other patients and told her about her own treatment. 'A tiny fraction deeper and I'd have been dead,' she said. 'I was very lucky, Doctor Boland said.'

'Gosh, and that was shrapnel?' Anne said. 'I've often seen it falling when I've come home through a raid, from that Anti Aircraft gun. So you could have been killed by one of our own guns? Red hot too, isn't it?'

'I don't remember anything about it,' said Kathleen. 'Not until I woke up in hospital.'

They said no more about her family, but Doctor Boland dominated Kathleen's conversation and when Anne left she felt much happier about her friend. When Anne had tentatively broached the subject of where Kathleen was to go when she left hospital, she said, 'Doctor Boland says I've not got to worry about that. I may train as a nurse.'

Anne was never miserable for long, and the visit to Kathleen, added to an apparent halt in her mother's disease and long loving letters from John, soon made her feel happy again.

John was stationed near Cambridge and said in his letters that he liked the men he was with. 'We have good discussions,' he wrote, 'but there are none of the snide comments about "my Russian mates carving up Poland" or "my Commie friends getting more than they bargained for" when Russia invaded

Finland, that I had on the building job.'

Mrs Bennet came every day to look after Julia now and Bridie and Carrie came nearly every day to visit her.

Bridie's husband Jack was now in the Merchant Navy and she and Carrie exchanged news about their families as they sat with Julia who lay quietly letting her Rosary beads slip through her fingers.

Finally Carrie said guiltily, 'Here we are, Julie, going on about all our worries and you never say a word about yours.'

'I'm very lucky,' she said gently. 'Tony and Stephen are still at home and Terry's safe out of it all in Germany, Joe's safe too training the young lads, and so is Eileen. I'm well blessed. I have Maureen and Anne with me still.'

'Maureen's doing a grand job driving that ambulance,' Carrie said. 'And Anne firewatching now on top of that hard job. They're all doing their bit.'

'And you in the WVS and Bridie helping in that canteen,' Julia said with a sigh. 'Sure there's only me that can do nothing but lie here and pray for all of you.'

'And that's the best of all, Julie,' Bridie exclaimed. And Carrie said, 'Yes, it's a comfort to everybody to know they have your prayers.'

Julia smiled at them and Carrie said suddenly, 'I didn't want to upset you, Julie, but I've been dying to tell you. Our Minnie and Dympna have flitted!'

'Flitted!' Julia and Bridie exclaimed in unison.

'Yes. I went to the house and got no answer then the woman next door told me that Brendan came in a posh motor car. He put four big suitcases in the car then Minnie and Dympna got in and he drove off.'

'Perhaps he's taken them for a holiday?' Julia suggested.

'No, the neighbour said she heard a noise and thought Minnie was being burgled so her son got through the window and let her in. I think she just wanted a good nose round. The house was stripped bare except for the furniture, and I suppose Lord Muck will provide that wherever he's taken them. They've scarpered all right, Julie.'

'Surely to God she wouldn't go without a word to her own family!' Julia exclaimed.

'She's always been deep,' Bridie said. 'And for all the way she bullied other people, she's always been under that fellow's thumb and so has Dympna.'

'Perhaps she'll write to us,' Julia said, still unable to believe that her sister would just disappear.

'I wouldn't like to be hanging until she does,' Carrie said grimly, then noticed that Julia looked upset and said quickly, 'No, I think you're right, Julia. I'm sure she'll write and explain why they went off like that.'

'And whatever kind of a rogue the quare fella is, he's a good son to Minnie, isn't he?' Bridie said, and Julia looked happier.

The air raids continued, increasing in number and intensity. Maureen's friend Chris was now a full-time fireman and she worried about him constantly. She was still working in the wool shop by day and driving an ambulance at night.

During a raid in March she heard that a bomb had dropped on a burning building, killing six firemen and injuring others. She was frantic to know more but her own ambulance was involved in an accident and she could do nothing until the end of her duty to learn whether or not Chris was involved.

Fortunately he was safe on that occasion, but Maureen's fears for him increased. Their duties made it difficult for them to meet frequently but they seized every opportunity to be together and their love grew stronger every day.

Chris's wife was now in a different hospital in Shropshire, and seemed content to stay there. He and Maureen decided to live for the day and not worry about what the future would bring for them, good or bad.

All the family thought that in spite of Maureen's arduous lifestyle, she looked better and happier than she had for several years.

Chapter Twenty-Six

John came on leave in April. In contrast to the previous month there were few air raids on Liverpool in April and although the warning sounded several times, no bombs were dropped until the twenty-sixth of the month.

'Perhaps this is the end of it?' Anne said. 'I know Belfast has just been bombed, and London, but maybe Hitler's coming to the end of his resources. This might be the answer to the Day of Prayer.'

John smiled at her. 'We'll hope so anyway,' he said. He had evidently made up his mind not to argue with anyone while on leave, and Sarah told Anne that his family thought that she was a good influence on him.

Anne managed to get a few days off work during his ten-day leave, and as he had few relatives to visit, they were able to spend blissful hours alone.

They went to Chester and wandered round the medieval Rows, then took a rowing boat on the River Dee. Trees were bursting into leaf and birds singing as they wandered along the banks of the river, their arms entwined round each other.

'"Sweet lovers love the Spring",' John murmured, and Anne looked at him with surprise and delight. She had been disappointed that he showed no love of the poetry and books which meant so much to her, only reading about industrial history and dry facts and figures.

'That's the first time I've heard you quote poetry,' she exclaimed, and he laughed.

'We sang it as a song in Junior School,' he admitted, but Anne was still happy that he had thought of it.

Another day they went to take flowers to the grave of John's grandfather, Lawrie Ward. 'I wish you had known him, Anne, and he'd known you,' John said. 'You'd both have got on like a house on fire. He was a lovely man.'

'I feel I do know him,' she said. 'I've heard so many stories about him and all the good he did, and my dad was delighted when he found I was working with Sarah because she was his grand-daughter.'

'I know there were crowds at his funeral,' said John. 'I just couldn't stand it. I went off. I realise now it was very selfish of me. It wasn't fair to my mum or my grandma.'

'I'm sure they understood,' she comforted him.

'Sometimes I think they were *too* understanding,' he said. 'I got away with far too much. Dad wouldn't have let me, but he held back because he didn't want to upset Mum and I took advantage.'

'They're pleased with the way you've turned out now anyway,' Anne said. 'They're all very proud of you.'

'Oh, Anne, I don't deserve you,' he said impulsively, flinging his arms round her and kissing her. 'I wish we were married now.'

'So do I,' she said, drawing his head down and kissing him.

'Do you think we could get married on my next leave in September?' he said. 'We don't need a big fuss, do we? Or if I go abroad before then will you marry me on my embarkation leave?'

'Of course,' she said, and John asked if her parents would object.

'No. Things are different now,' she said. 'Before the war people were engaged for years to have time to get a home together, but nobody waits for that now.'

'When this is over we'll have a nice home, Anne, I promise,' he said, as she slipped her arms round his neck and kissed him again.

'I don't care, John, as long as we're together,' she said, and he kissed her passionately.

Both their families were pleased about their plans to marry in September, but John had to go back before any details were discussed.

He left on Thursday 1 May and there was a comparatively light raid that night, but it was the start of eight days and nights which would never be forgotten in Liverpool.

For Anne it was not only the ordeal of the air raids but even more the terror that her mother would die on the bed in the cellar, with only Anne of all her family with her.

Julia's illness had suddenly become worse and she was in great pain. Maureen as an ambulance driver and Pat as a rescue man were badly needed, but Anne's firewatching at a large store was less essential and it was decided that she would stay with her mother.

'Let them that owns the shop watch over it,' Mrs Bennet said, 'instead of skulking in Southport while the likes of youse risk yer lives for it.'

Many people who were not needed were leaving Liverpool each evening to sleep in the woods at Huyton or at various halls and cinemas on the outskirts of the city, but Julia was too frail to be moved.

On the Friday night Pat carried his wife to the cellar when the raid started, then he and Maureen went on duty. Mrs Bennet and her daughter Jinny arrived a little later.

'I feel safer here than anywhere,' Mrs Bennet said, 'and more comfortable.'

Her words scarcely registered with Anne as she knelt beside the bed where her mother lay, perspiration running down her white face and small moans escaping her as she was fiercely gripped by pain.

Anne felt helpless, only able to wipe her mother's face and grip her hands, praying for some relief for her. Her doctor was busy ministering to the injured and dying victims of the bombers and could not be called to help Julia.

At some stage during the night an ARP man brought some of the neighbours to the shelter. 'They were in a street shelter and it got flattened,' he said. 'Three dead but these were just shocked. Will you look after them?'

Mrs Bennet and Jinny took charge of the two women and two small girls, making tea for them and wrapping them in blankets. While Jinny served the tea Mrs Bennet brought a tall clothes maiden from the wash house and draped a sheet over it to give Anne and her mother some privacy.

The following day Maureen brought out a black bottle of medicine from the cupboard in her mother's room. 'I was saving this until Mum was desperate,' she said. 'But I think she needs it now.'

'What is it?' Anne asked, looking curiously at the tall black ribbed bottle.

'It's some stuff Mum used to get in the market, but this is the last bottle,' said Maureen. 'I think there's opium in it, Anne, and if she took it too often it wouldn't help when she really needed it. I'll give her a dose now, a small dose, and if you have to give her some tonight make sure it's a very small amount.'

'I'll be glad to have something to give her,' Anne said. 'I felt so helpless last night.'

The air raid began at six-thirty and continued until about five o'clock on Sunday morning. The throbbing of the engines of hundreds of bombers overhead, the clatter of the Anti Aircraft guns, the crump as thousands of high explosive bombs, land mines and parachute bombs found their targets and buildings collapsed, were a background to the terror Anne felt that her mother was about to die.

At about two o'clock there was an explosion so close that Anne threw herself across her mother to protect her. The house seemed to be sucked in then out again and the foundations shook, but it was solid and well-built and it stood firm, although there were crashes and roars from immediately overhead.

Julia managed to raise her hand and weakly pat Anne's face. 'Don't be frightened, child. Trust in God,' she whispered through bloodless lips, and Anne wept that even now her mother was trying to comfort her. She had given her a tiny dose of medicine just before the explosion, and now Julia closed her eyes.

Anne watched her anxiously, not sure whether she was asleep or unconscious. Her mother seemed scarcely to breathe as she lay immobile, and Anne felt a tremendous surge of relief when the cellar door opened and Helen came down the steps.

'Helen, what happened?' Anne exclaimed as she came into the light and they saw that her head was bandaged and her right arm strapped across her chest. Her WVS overall was torn and blood-stained but she smiled reassuringly at Anne.

'The rest centre was hit,' she said. 'And I couldn't do any more to help so I came here.'

'Oh, Helen, I'm so glad to see you!' Anne exclaimed. 'I don't know whether Mum's asleep or . . .'

Helen bent over her mother-in-law. 'Don't worry, love,' she said to Anne. 'It's a kind of sleep, and she doesn't feel pain while she's like that. Has she had anything to ease her?'

Anne showed her the black bottle. 'Maureen told me to give her just a small dose, and I did,' she said. 'And, oh Helen, Mum said: "Don't be frightened . . ."' She could say no more and wept bitterly. Helen comforted her and Anne wiped her eyes. 'I'm ashamed carrying on like this after what you've been through,' she began, but suddenly there was another tremendous crash and roar.

The lights went out and Mrs Bennet said, 'Bloody hell. I was just going to make a cup of tea, and now the lecky's gone.' There were candles in readiness and Anne quickly found some and lit them. Her mother's eyes were open and Helen bent over her and reassured her.

One of the children was crying loudly and Mrs Bennet said, 'Ee are, queen, here's a biscuit I just found in me pinny pocket.' She held a candle aloft and saw the other child looking at her with eyes like saucers. 'And here's one in me other pocket, girl. She got one for crying and you can have this one for not crying.'

'Isn't it exciting, just having candles?' Helen said gently to the little girls.

'I wish I'd had time to make that tea,' Mrs Bennet said. 'We could do with a cup, especially you, girl.'

Helen smiled. 'I'm all right,' she said. 'Someone gave me one at the First Aid Post. I wish Tony was here. He's working a double shift though.'

'He'll be all right in Edge Lane,' said Anne. 'It seems to be mostly round here, doesn't it?'

'It's everywhere, Anne,' Helen said. 'The whole city seems to be on fire, and across the river too. The ships and the docks.' Then as she saw their startled eyes in the light of the candles, she added hastily, 'Of course it's hard to tell. It's probably scattered incendiaries.'

'Jeez, I could do with that cup of tea,' Mrs Bennet said, putting her hands over her ears to shut out the tumult above, and Anne decided to go upstairs to see if the gas was still on.

She picked up a candle and ran nimbly up the steps and into the kitchen. There was no need for the candle. The room was lit by a red light from the burning houses behind it as Anne crunched over broken crockery and plaster. The window frame hung drunkenly across the cupboard in the corner with a piece of glass held together by the criss-crossed brown paper hanging down from it like a flag.

She looked for Patrick's photograph and saw it under the sofa. The glass was cracked, but it was otherwise intact and Anne looked at the smiling face of her dead brother. 'Oh, Patrick, pray for us,' she whispered, holding the photograph close. She shivered. Would her mother soon be with Patrick, the child she had never ceased to mourn?

She looked round the disordered kitchen. The dresser drawers fallen out and spilled, the dishes from the shelves above in fragments on the floor, the chairs thrown about as though by a madman, the table upended and even the black kettle from the hob lying among the debris.

Suddenly Anne thought of the kitchen as it had been throughout her childhood, a warm, secure and loving haven. She remembered when she was the only child at home, playing with her dolls on the rag rug before the fire and listening to the purring of the kettle on the hob, her mother singing as she worked in the back kitchen, waiting for the others to come home.

Her father and Maureen! A stab of fear went through Anne as she thought of them out there in that inferno. What was happening to Aunt Carrie and to John's family? Bridie, she knew, had taken the children out to sleep in a church hall in Ormskirk so they would be safe.

What would John and Eileen and Joe think when they heard of this? She must write a note to each of them to tell them the families were safe as soon as they were all accounted for.

She peeped into the hall and drew back in shock. The front door and the vestibule door had been blown off and the heavy mahogany coat stand lay across the foot of the stairs.

Anne went through to the yard. The heavy drone of the bombers still filled the air as they came in wave after wave, but the searchlights which criss-crossed the sky were almost lost against the fierce orange glow as Liverpool burned.

There was an ominous whooshing sound and a loud crash nearby and Anne hastily dashed back to the scullery. She was able to light the gas and make tea in the big brown family teapot. The tea was much appreciated but everyone urged her not to leave the cellar again.

It was the longest night she had ever known. Her mind was divided between fear for her mother and worry about her father and Maureen and Tony, and she was immensely grateful that Helen was with her.

When at last the All Clear sounded her mother was undisturbed by it, and so were the two little girls asleep on a bunk bed. Helen advised the women to leave the children asleep while they checked on their houses, and Jinny Bennet offered to stay with them and bring them home when they woke.

'I hope they've still got a home,' Helen whispered. 'I couldn't believe it when I was walking here, Anne. The damage all the way. London Road, Shaw Street, Westbourne Street. I couldn't even get up Plumpton Street so I came up Fitzclarence but there were fires and damage there too.'

Mrs Bennet had hurried away to check on her house but was soon back. 'My place isn't bad,' she said. 'Bit knocked about like but the end of our street on the other side is flat, God help them. I didn't wait to find out about them. I've come back to get your ma's room straight so she can come upstairs.'

Anne found a bottle of sherry in the cupboard and poured a glassful for each of them. It seemed to revive them and Helen carried a glassful down to the cellar for Jinny then stayed sitting beside Julia at Anne's insistence.

Anne and Mrs Bennet quickly cleared the thick layer of gritty dust which lay over everything in Julia's room and remade her bed. The shutters had been closed so there was little damage.

Just as they finished Tony appeared. His red-rimmed eyes peered from his grimy face anxiously and Anne said swiftly, 'It's all right, Tony. Helen's sitting with Mum and they're safe.'

'Thank God!' he said. 'You'd think there'd be no one left when you look at the city. The end of our place has gone, the canteen and the office part luckily. About twenty injured but no one killed, and the main works aren't damaged.'

Shortly afterwards Maureen arrived, but only to check the family was safe. Her mother was still sleeping and Maureen hastily drank a cup of tea then returned to her ambulance.

She looked exhausted and Anne said anxiously, 'Oh, Maureen, haven't you done enough?'

Maureen turned on her. 'Done enough?' she snarled. 'Do you know what it's like out there? Mill Road has got it again. Most of the hospital wrecked and ambulances on fire. More than a dozen of our drivers killed and more injured, the same for the staff and patients.'

Anne stood in stunned silence as tears filled Maureen's eyes and she dashed them away. 'We've been moving patients to other hospitals. I'll have to go.' She ran down the steps but turned back for a moment to say, 'Uncle Fred's injured but he'll be all right. I saw him lying in a hospital corridor.'

The next moment she was gone and when Anne learnt of the devastation of the city she could understand Maureen's rage at her innocent question.

The whole line of docks seemed to be ablaze and ships in the river, shops, offices, streets of terraced houses and mansions, as well as beautiful and historic buildings like the Walker Art Gallery, the Museum and Central Library, had all suffered as high explosive bombs, land mines and incendiary bombs had rained down upon the city from hundreds of aircraft.

Anne and Mrs Bennet did what they could to clear up the house. The damage seemed to be mostly at the back. The blast which had flung down the doors at the front had strangely left the windows intact, but when Pat arrived home it was decided that it would be better to leave Julia in the bed in the cellar.

'Those bastards'll be back,' he said. 'They use the fires from the night before as markers for their bombs. Blackout is no good while fires are still burning to show them the way, the bloody swines.'

Anne had never heard her father swear before. It seemed to be part of this dreadful time, with the responsibility for her mother like a crushing weight on her. Julia's pain seemed to have left her, and she lay seeming to drift in and out of sleep or unconsciousness, Anne could never be sure which, as she sat beside her, wiping her face, or tried to feed her with beef tea from a feeding cup.

Mrs Bennet had been into town and brought back details of the damage. Anne asked her to check on Egremont Street but before Mrs Bennet returned Sarah appeared on the cellar steps. Anne's mother seemed asleep so Anne left her and went quickly to meet her friend.

'I came to see if you were all safe,' Sarah whispered, and Anne said eagerly, 'Yes, except Uncle Fred's injured, I think. What about all of you?'

'All safe,' Sarah said. 'But Grandma's and Peggy Burns' houses have gone.'

'Gone?' Anne echoed.

'Yes, bombed,' Sarah said. 'A high explosive, I think, Grandma's and Peggy's and about four houses in the street behind. Thank God Grandma and our Kate had gone out to Huyton in the lorries and Peggy had gone to their Meg's shelter. The Major who lodged with Peggy stayed in the house and he was killed and his wife blown through the window, but she's all right.'

'I hope John doesn't hear about the bombing, or our Eileen or Joe before we can tell them we're all safe,' Anne said. 'I've written short notes to all of them. I hope they get through but the Post Office got it last night, didn't it?'

'Yes, but they just work from somewhere else,' Sarah said. The next moment Mrs Bennet arrived and Anne was glad that Sarah had come before her as Mrs Bennet gave a graphic description of the damage in Egremont Street.

Sarah said quietly, 'Yes, but as my mother said, Mrs Bennet, at least we're all alive. That's not true of a lot of people this morning.'

'No, it's not. Seventeen killed in them houses at the top of our street. You should just see the town, Anne. Lewis's and Blackler's burnt out, and Lime Street – you can't hardly move for the hosepipes all over the ground.'

Anne seemed to be scarcely listening and at a sound from her mother dashed back to her side, followed by Sarah and Mrs Bennet.

'It's all right,' Helen whispered. 'She's just settling down. I think she'll sleep naturally now.'

Jinny had taken the little girls home and Sarah and Mrs Bennet left. Soon afterwards Tony took Helen away.

'I think she should be in bed,' he said, and Anne agreed. Helen, who had been so calm during the night, was now cold and shaking with delayed shock, and Anne told her how glad she had been of her company.

When Maureen and her father eventually returned they both fell into an exhausted sleep after seeing Julia resting peacefully, her breathing shallow but regular.

When they woke Maureen told Anne that she was sorry she had snapped at her. 'I was just worked up,' she said. 'A friend of mine, a fireman, had been injured and burned.'

'Oh, Lord, is he bad?' Anne exclaimed.

'He'll live,' Maureen said, 'but his injuries are very painful. Two of his mates were killed, though, at the same incident.'

Anne put a cup of tea down beside her. 'I didn't realise all this was happening,' she said. 'I was so frightened about Mum. I was glad to have that black bottle.' She put her arm round Maureen's neck and kissed her cheek. 'Don't worry about your friend, Mo. At least he's out of it for a while,' she said, unaware of how much Chris meant to Maureen.

There was only a large crater where the wool shop had stood so Maureen was free to stay with her mother and Anne went to work on Monday.

There had been another bad raid on Sunday night but soldiers and gangs of workmen were clearing the roads of the debris from shattered buildings and fire crews from all the surrounding districts had come to help fight the numerous fires.

Anne had to make many detours to reach the factory and felt triumphant when she arrived there, but she found that most of the women had come in.

Some, though, would never come again. Ruby, who had said that she was safe, that lightning never struck twice, had been killed with her daughter and two of her grandsons by a direct hit on their shelter.

Doris, the girl who worked next to Anne, had been killed and her parents injured after they had been taken to a rest centre from their bombed house. Anne wept at the news.

Doris's husband was due home on leave. She had told Anne on Saturday that she had received her last letter before the leave.

'Every leave I tie up all the letters I've had since Stan's last, then start again when he goes back,' she said. Anne remembered envying her because her husband was coming on leave just as John went back.

What had happened to those carefully hoarded letters, she wondered, and who would tell Stan when he arrived? The supervisor put her hand on Anne's shoulder. 'Sad about poor Doris,' she said. 'But – life has to go on. The harder we work, the more our lads will have to throw at the bastards.'

Sarah's grandmother and her friend and neighbour Mrs Burns seemed to accept the loss of their homes calmly, in public at least. Sally Ward moved in to live with her daughter's family, on the opposite side of Egremont Street, and Peggy Burns went to live with her daughter Meg and her husband.

Anne's mother was still free from pain but almost too weak to move. Mrs Ward came every day to help Maureen to make her mother comfortable until the doctor could arrange for nursing help.

He appeared one morning looking haggard and after a quick examination of her mother gave Maureen a prescription for medicine for her.

'This should help her but give it as sparingly as possible at first,' he said. Maureen said that her mother seemed free of pain but he warned her it could return at any moment. 'We don't know why there are these remissions or why it strikes again. You're a sensible girl. Use your own judgement.'

Fred had been helping to rescue a family trapped in a cellar when a collapsing beam held him trapped by his left arm and leg for several hours, but he made a good recovery.

'I'm the most well blessed man in Liverpool,' he joked. 'Four different priests gave me conditional absolution before they got me out. I couldn't tell them they weren't the first.'

Carrie was able to come every day to sit with Julia, and Maureen was able to travel to Whiston Hospital where Chris had been taken. She told Carrie only that she was visiting a friend.

There were still occasional air raids but none with the ferocity of the 'May Blitz' as it was being called and now Julia was back in her own bed in the bright and sunny back parlour.

The doctor and the Sisters of Charity who came to help with the nursing were amazed at her tenacious hold on life, but Julia had told Mrs Ward that she was determined to live until Anne's marriage. 'I won't spoil the child's wedding day,' she whispered, and although her pain had returned she held on.

Sarah's mother also came often to see Julia, and to discuss the wedding. She suggested that the wedding reception should be held at the Redmond house, telling Julia that it would help her mother to get over the loss of her house if she could organise the wedding.

Julia smiled and pressed her hand, recognising the tact and

kindness of the suggestion. Clothes rationing had suddenly been introduced, much to Anne's dismay. 'If only I'd got my clothes for the wedding,' she mourned. 'I'm mad because I had the money for them but I just couldn't get time to shop with the hours we've been working.'

Fortunately the material for her wedding dress had already been bought. Eileen, Sarah and Kate were to be the bridesmaids, and Kate produced a bolt of pale pink taffeta for their dresses telling her mother that it came from a fire damage sale.

Sarah's aunt who lived in America sent food parcels so Mrs Redmond also made the wedding cake and provided much of the food for the wedding breakfast.

Julia's bedroom was now the heart of the house with the family spending every possible moment with her, and although her face was almost fleshless she could always manage a smile to greet them.

For Anne it was a happy time in spite of her mother's illness. Always ready to look on the bright side she expected that the remission would last for a long time, and there was a conspiracy between Maureen and her mother to conceal Julia's suffering from her.

Letters came almost every day from John and although he talked about Hitler's invasion of Russia and other war news, he always remembered to tell Anne that he loved her. Her letters to him gave news of all the preparations for the wedding, but were tender and loving too.

John's brother Mick who was in the RAF was to be best man, and had a week's leave in September before moving to Manchester. Eileen and Joe both obtained a week's leave for the wedding and Stephen came on a week's holiday so all the family except Terry were together. Anne worried that Sarah would be upset, but she assured her that she was perfectly happy, and certainly seemed so.

Chapter Twenty-Seven

The wedding day was typical September weather, with clear blue skies and mild sunshine falling through the church window to shine on Anne and John as they stood at the altar.

Anne looked beautiful in a dress of white organdie with a wreath of orange blossom on her dark hair. She carried a large bouquet of white roses and pink carnations and her bridesmaids Eileen, Sarah and Kate, wore their pink taffeta dresses and carried white and pink chrysanthemums.

It was a Service wedding, with John and Joe in khaki battle-dress and Mick in Air Force uniform. Maureen had borrowed a wheelchair for her mother and wheeled her close to the altar to see Anne and John married, then drove her home until the Nuptial Mass was over.

Later she took Julia to the Redmond house where the wedding reception was taking place. She could only stay a short time, but long enough to hear John thank her for the gift of her daughter. Anne and John came to kiss her and she blessed them. 'I'm so glad to have you as a son, John. I know you'll both be happy. God bless you.'

The effort exhausted her and Pat wrapped her in a blanket and carried her to Maureen's car. Sarah had come to the car with them and Julia asked Pat to go back to the reception. 'Sarah will come with us, won't you, love?' she said in her weak voice, and Sarah gladly agreed.

'Aye, not much fun for you, love, with our Terry away,' Pat said. 'But your turn will come, pet.' She mumbled something and blushed as she hastily climbed into the car.

When Sarah had helped Maureen to put her mother to bed, the sick woman took Sarah's hand. 'I won't be here for your wedding, love,' she whispered. 'Whichever one you marry.'

Sarah's eyes opened wide in surprise and Julia smiled weakly at her. 'I know, love. I saw the way you and Joe – but don't hurt Terry.'

Sarah bent close to her. 'We won't, I promise. We'll wait until he comes home and sort it out,' she said quietly.

'That's good children,' Julia whispered. 'Terry'll be all right, but look after Joe. Don't make a mistake.' She closed her eyes for a moment then said faintly, 'Marriage is for life, love.'

Tears were running down Sarah's face and Julia lifted her hand to touch her cheek, then her hand fell back. 'Be happy. You and Maureen help each other,' she said.

Maureen bent and kissed her. 'Rest now, Mum,' she said gently. She poured out a dose of medicine for her mother and soon she fell asleep.

Like Anne, Maureen had often felt uneasy about Sarah's relationship with Terry and thought that she seemed to regard him more as a brother than a lover. Partly because of her own dilemma, and partly because she was so close to Joe, Maureen had gradually realised that Sarah and he were in love.

'Did you know?' Sarah asked her. 'About me and Joe?'

'I guessed,' she said. 'But I didn't know that Mum had guessed too. I'm sure no one else has and Mum won't have said anything about it, even to Dad. What will you do, Sar?'

'What can we do?' Sarah said. 'Only try to hide how we feel and wait until Terry comes home to sort it out. I couldn't tell him while he's there. My dad guessed too but no one else knows.'

In turn, Maureen confided her hopeless love for Chris. 'That's why Mum said we can help each other,' she said. 'Just to be able to talk to someone means so much. I can talk to Joe but there's no one else. Nine years and two months I've been in love with Chris.'

Later Joe came to see his mother and they were able to tell him that his and Sarah's secret was known to them. Julia was awake and Joe and Maureen tenderly lifted her higher on her pillows. She took Sarah's and Joe's hands in hers. 'God bless you both,' she whispered.

Maureen stayed with her mother but Sarah and Joe walked back to the Redmond house together. Sarah told Joe what his mother had said, and they spoke about Chris and Maureen.

At the reception numerous people said to Sarah, 'Never mind. Your turn next,' and she said to Mick, 'I wish they wouldn't. I'm not jealous of Anne or in any hurry to get married. I feel a hypocrite.'

'You and me both,' he said cheerfully. 'I've only had twelve hours' flying instruction and flown one solo – never even frightened a German – but people keep telling me I've saved Britain. They think I'm a fighter pilot.'

'It's the uniform,' Sarah said. 'And Churchill's speech.'

'I know. I tried to tell them at first, but now I just smile and say nuffin', like Brer Rabbit.'

Anne changed into a wine-coloured suit made by Mrs Redmond to go away.

She and John went first to see her mother, then to a hotel in Chester overnight, and then to spend a week in North Wales. For Anne it was a magical time. The war seemed remote as she and John wandered through woods, scuffling their feet through crisp fallen leaves, or lay in the deep feather bed in the farmhouse bedroom.

He was a gentle lover, and for Anne it was all strange and

wonderful. 'I didn't know it'd be like that,' she said, as she lay in his arms. 'I enjoyed it.'

'Don't sound so surprised,' he teased her, kissing the tip of her nose. 'You're supposed to.'

'Not from what I've heard,' she said, and John asked in surprise, 'Why? What have you heard – and where, for that matter?'

'At work,' she said. 'I didn't understand half some of the women said, but they gave the impression they didn't like it. You remember Penny I told you about? She wasn't married but went with a chap after a big dance, and Ruby said, "What did you think, chuck?" Penny just said, "Frankly, I think it's very overrated."'

John threw back his head and laughed and Anne laughed with him. 'Very overrated,' he kept saying, and soon they were laughing so much that they had to put their heads beneath the blankets to stifle the noise, in case the farmer and his wife wondered at their hilarity.

When they returned to Liverpool Joe, Eileen and Stephen, and John's brother Mick, had already gone back, but at a family gathering John was soon involved in an argument.

Bombers were still going over Germany and he argued that it was indefensible to bomb cities where women and children could be killed. After the recent events in Liverpool few people agreed with him and Kate said pertly, 'Our John's always out of step with everyone else.'

'So was his grandfather,' Sally Ward said. 'And he was usually proved right in the end.'

Anne smiled at her gratefully.

It seemed that although sheer determination had kept Julia alive until the wedding, suddenly she could fight no longer. The tearing pain returned and the doctor prescribed large doses of morphia which he had kept for this time.

For the last few days of her life Julia lay in a drugged sleep, free from pain and still managing a faint smile for Pat as he hung over her, gripping her hand. As quietly and uncomplainingly as she had lived she slipped away in her sleep at two o'clock in the morning of 21 October.

Pat Fitzgerald was devastated. 'What'll we do without her?' he asked pitifully, and repeated it to all those who came to offer sympathy. Sally Ward was better able to comfort him than anyone else, yet it seemed to the family that she did little but simply hold his hand. From her he seemed to draw sufficient strength to get through the days until the simple funeral was over. Tony attended to all the arrangements and Maureen wrote to Terry with the sad news. Joe and Eileen were given short compassionate leave and Stephen came home for the funeral.

The family drew together to help each other, and most of them had additional sources of comfort. Sarah seemed to be closer to Maureen at this time than to Anne, as she and Maureen could speak freely to each other about the love they had to conceal from others. Maureen could see Chris more often now. He was living alone as Beryl was now in a private nursing home in Llandudno, and Maureen was working in the Co-operative Stores.

'I feel closer to Chris, doing the sort of work he used to do,' she said to Sarah. Anne seemed uneasy now with Sarah, anxious not to show her happiness with John too clearly while there seemed no prospect of the end of the war and Terry's return. Sarah too was uneasy about concealing her love for Joe.

Anne was more comfortable with the married women she worked with, many of them with husbands in the Forces and with the same problems and hopes as herself.

John had been moved to Norfolk and promoted to Corporal and he wrote to Anne nearly every day, loving letters which helped to make her grief for her mother more bearable.

All the family found their grief for Julia hard to bear and to see how their father suffered grieved them still more. Only when Helen and Tony told him that Helen expected a baby before Christmas did he seem to come out of his stupor of misery.

Later Helen told Maureen that they had intended to wait until nearer the time to announce their news, but that seemed the right moment. 'We were only being cautious anyway, thinking of waiting to tell people, but everything seems to be going smoothly this time.'

In May Maureen registered for war work and was directed to a clerical job in an office near Sarah's. Her left elbow was still stiff since her injury in the air raid and she failed a medical for heavier work.

Joe wrote nearly every day to Sarah, enclosing the letters in an envelope addressed to Maureen, and now it was easy for her to deliver them.

John was due for leave in June and Maureen suggested that Anne and John should make two rooms in the Fitzgerald house into a flat. Pat had agreed and Anne and John spent a blissful leave fitting it up as their first home. Pat told them to take what they liked and Carrie gave them linen and other items which were now impossible to buy.

In November church bells were rung to celebrate the victory at El Alamein, and everyone felt that at last the war might be near the end, although Churchill told them they were wrong.

'It is not the end, not even the beginning of the end,' he warned. 'It is the end of the beginning.'

'The old misery!' Anne said indignantly to Sarah when they met. 'He's worse than Lord Haw Haw.'

Sarah smiled. 'Yes, but Winnie does tell us the truth, doesn't he, even if we don't like it? I'm not going to worry, though. Anything can happen, can't it? No one really knows for sure.'

Anne was glad that Sarah could be so philosophical about the war. She felt that she was longing more than ever for it to end so that she and John could spend all their time together. She spoke about it to Helen, who said gently, 'It's a shame, Anne. You and Sarah are missing so much. I feel almost ashamed that Tony and I are so lucky. Not just that he's home with me but we had our courting days and you and Sarah missed even those. It doesn't seem fair.'

Later Anne thought about Helen's words and began to feel angry with John. Sarah and Terry had no alternative but she and John could have had months of courtship before he went away if it had not been for his stubbornness.

I should have been consulted because it affected me too, she thought, and wrote a terse letter to him. She read it through the following morning and decided not to send it, but a small niggle of grievance stayed in her mind.

On 15 December Helen's baby, a tiny perfect girl, was born, but her labour was long and difficult and she was very ill for a few days after it. Now that Anne was a married woman Carrie spoke more freely to her, and told Anne that the midwife was to blame.

'She should never have suffered like that,' Carrie said. 'That flaming midwife hates calling the doctor in but Helen needed him long before he came.'

By Christmas Helen was well again and the baby, Moira, was a delight to her proud parents and to all the family, especially her grandfather. In January Joe came home on embarkation leave and was more free to see Sarah because his father was so engrossed in the baby.

Joe was still careful to keep their meetings secret lest some kind friend wrote about them to Terry, but Maureen and Sarah's father made the meetings easier for them. Sarah had a few days' leave while Joe was home and Maureen suggested, while Anne and her father were present, that Joe took Sarah out sometimes.

'Aye, she doesn't have much fun, poor lass,' said Pat, 'with our Terry so far away.' Joe coloured and felt guilty at deceiving the family, but no one seemed to see anything strange in the arrangement.

In March Joe wrote from North Africa where the Irish Guards were engaged in heavy fighting, but he seemed cheerful, and hopeful that the end of the war was coming closer.

Anne was afraid that John would soon be sent abroad but the months went by and he was still in England. When the campaign in North Africa ended in success for the Allies in May everyone expected Joe to come home, but his company went straight to Italy. He wrote that it was not as he had pictured it as the weather was bitterly cold and wet with some snow. To Sarah he wrote that he would take her to Italy some day when the sun was shining.

Late in January news bulletins mentioned the Anzio landing in which they knew the Irish Guards were taking part and in February the dreaded news came that Joe had been wounded. No details were given, except that he was now in hospital in Naples.

Pat had left for work when the news came and Anne and Maureen decided to telephone Tony at the factory. He was calm and decisive. 'Don't start guessing about Joe's injuries,' he said. 'It could be something quite slight and they'd still let us know officially. I don't think we should say anything to Stephen or Eileen or of course Terry until we know more. I'll tell Dad though because he has a right to know.'

'Thank God for Tony,' Anne said. They decided that they should go to work as no more news could be expected yet and Maureen hurried first to see Sarah.

They clung together in the waiting room outside Sarah's office and Maureen told her what Tony had said. 'I can't help thinking though – as long as it's not his eyes, Sar.'

'Or a very bad wound,' Sarah said fearfully.

Two days later the family received a letter from Joe written in a field dressing station before he was taken by boat to Naples.

Sarah told Maureen that she had received one by the same post. He wrote that he was only slightly wounded in the left arm and leg, and was scribbling this note in case some officious nerk notified them.

Suddenly it seemed that all the news was good. The German Army was in retreat in Russia, and the Italian campaign was over. Joe recovered enough to rejoin his battalion and sailed for home on 7 March.

He was given leave almost immediately. Very few of the battalion returned home as their losses had been so heavy, and Joe told the family he was now in a holding battalion. 'Mainly cooks and cripples,' he said cheerfully, and the family hoped that this would mean that he stayed in England, but when he returned to London after his leave the battalion was made up to strength and moved to Howick in Scotland.

'I think they're getting ready for the Second Front,' Sarah told Maureen, 'although Joe didn't say so.'

All the talk now was of the Second Front, and everyone thought that the Army would have to land in France to finish off the war. 'It won't be like Dunkirk this time,' Mr Redmond said to Anne when he saw her worried expression. 'We are well prepared this time, and Hitler is much weaker.' She smiled at him gratefully.

Sarah had told her that John had always argued with his father and defied him, and she wondered why he could ever have behaved like that with this gentle man. Greg Redmond was a quiet diffident type, tall with grey eyes and dark hair like John, and Anne felt liking and respect for him.

She could see that, although never aggressive, he was the strong rock on which his family relied. Much stronger than John for all his carry on, she thought, and then was shocked by her

349

disloyal thought. It's because of that talk with Helen, she mused, and decided that she must tell John about her grievance when he came home.

Mick Redmond had finished a tour of operations and was on leave when John came on leave so the brothers were able to spend some time together for the first time for years.

John told Anne that this was embarkation leave and he would soon be going to France but warned her not to mention it to anyone. 'Careless talk costs lives,' he joked. He had been promoted to sergeant and sometimes spoke very masterfully to Anne, until she reminded him, half in fun and half in earnest, that she was not one of his soldiers.

In spite of these small brushes, they spent a very happy leave, planning all that they would do when peace came, and making love passionately every night.

Kate Redmond was now engaged to a quiet American, Gene Romero, and he had been moved to the South Coast in readiness for the invasion. Soon after John's return from leave he was moved to Eastbourne.

In June the Second Front began and John was in the first wave of troops to cross the Channel. Gene landed a few days later and in July Joe went out with reinforcements.

Just before John left England, the doctor had confirmed that Anne was pregnant and that the baby would be born in January. 'I'm not surprised, are you, love?' John wrote. 'After that wonderful leave. I'm absolutely walking on air.'

Anne was excited and happy about the baby, but she began to worry that John might be killed before the child was born. Maureen scolded her gently. 'This is not like you, Anne,' she said. 'Looking on the black side. You usually expect everything to go well.'

'Because it always has for me,' she said. 'Except for losing Mum I've always been lucky, but it's bound to change sometime.'

'Don't be daft,' Maureen said. 'These are just baby nerves, love. John will be fine, you'll see.'

Anne hugged her sister and smiled again. 'What would I do without you, Mo?' she said. 'It's just that the news is like a see-saw. One night they say everything is going well, and the next that the troops are boxed in somewhere.'

'Don't worry. I'm sure we're near the end now,' Maureen comforted her.

Chapter Twenty-Eight

In August Eileen wrote to Maureen that she had met a marvellous man. 'His name is Robert White, always known as Whitey. He's six foot two, blue eyes and curly hair, and all the girls are mad jealous because we've fallen for each other. I sound like a soppy young kid, don't I? But honestly, Mo, if you saw him even you would fall for him. He's like a film star only nicer. He's just joined the Squadron but he's been flying for two years.'

'Gosh, she *has* got it bad,' Anne said when Maureen showed her the letter.

'Yes, even I would fall for him,' Maureen said. Something in her voice made Anne look searchingly at her, and after a moment she folded the letter and took her sister's hand.

'I'm very selfish,' she said. 'Always wrapped up in my own concerns. I never ask about yours. That friend from the Fire Service you visited, Mo? What happened to him?'

Maureen shrugged. 'He got better – went back to the Fire Service,' she said, but Eileen's innocent remark seemed to have touched some nerve which made her say bitterly, 'He went back to scrimping and saving to keep his horrible wife in comfort in a nursing home. Had to give up his house and live in one room and starve himself.'

Anne squeezed her hand. 'What's his name?'

'Chris. Chris Murray. He used to work in Lipton's near the wool shop.'

Anne was silent for a moment as she realised the implications. So Maureen had known him all that time. Aloud she said quietly, 'And where's his room, Mo?'

'In a tatty house off Prescot Street,' Maureen said bitterly. 'It's damp and miserable but it's cheap.'

'It's a pity Margaret decided to stay in the country,' Anne said. 'He could have had a room next door.' Then she suddenly jumped up. 'Mo, why don't you ask him to stay here? There's plenty of room.'

'But – what would people say?' Maureen said, looking bewildered.

'Who cares?' said Anne. 'There's only Dad who matters and I'm sure he'd agree. He's out a lot anyway at Tony's or Aunt Carrie's. The rest of us'll just be glad you've got company. Ask Dad when he comes in and then fix it up.'

With Anne, to think was to act and when her father appeared a few minutes later she said immediately, 'Dad, Maureen has a friend who's had to give up his house and live in a crummy room. I've suggested he lives here. What do you think?'

'Whatever you like, girls,' said Pat. 'Any tea in the pot?' Anne was reminded of the day that John asked her father's permission for their engagement, and his calm response then.

Although still doubtful of the wisdom of asking Chris to live in the house, Maureen suggested the move to him. She was not really surprised when he refused. 'No, we've got to think of your good name, Maureen,' he said. 'It was kind of Anne to think of it and not condemn us, but – well, we've managed so far being discreet about it, and I don't think we should change things now.'

'I was doubtful myself,' Maureen admitted, 'but I hate to think of you in that awful room. And Anne – she's so impulsive. She asked Dad right away.'

'I'm surprised he agreed so easily,' said Chris.

'I think Mum really made all the decisions,' Maureen said. 'Dad was only concerned about how things affected her, and now he doesn't really care.'

'Don't worry about that room, Mo,' said Chris. 'I've heard of a better one in Hall Road, just as cheap.'

Maureen told Joe about it when she wrote and he wrote back that he agreed with Chris. 'I know people have a different attitude to things now than we had before the war, but you and Chris are still the same sort of people. I think he realises that living in the same house would be very hard for both of you, and might lead to something that would worry your tender conscience no end.

'I'm glad though that Anne knows how things stand. She won't talk about it to anyone but I'm sure she'll find ways of making things easier for you, Mo.'

Anne was disappointed that her plan was dismissed but suggested inviting Chris for meals. Mrs Redmond often gave her food from the parcels she received from her sister in America and the parcels sent by Gene's family, and she produced a tinned ham and a tin of peaches for the meal.

Helen and Tony came bringing two plate tarts made by Helen and all the attention was focussed on Moira, giving Chris time to overcome his nervousness, helped by Helen's tact.

After the meal they went into the parlour where Anne had lit the fire. 'We used to have great parties here before the war,' Tony said. 'When we were all kids the man who used to teach Joe the violin said we were like a nest of singing birds. How about a song now, Dad?'

'No, not me,' said Pat, shaking his head, and Maureen said quickly, 'I'll try to accompany you if you'll sing, Tony, although I'm not as good as Eileen.'

Tony stood up immediately, realising that it would be difficult for his father to sing the Irish songs he sang at parties, usually sad songs of loss and parting.

'I'll try The Drinking Song from *The Student Prince*,' he said. He had a pleasant baritone voice and they all joined in the chorus, even Moira piping up, 'Dwink, dwink'.

Pat was delighted.

'Fred's talking about starting his Easter parties again now there are children in the family once more,' he said. He took Moira on his knee. 'You'll be the star of the show, pet.'

'Let's hope all the family will be home by then,' Maureen said. 'They'll all have tales to tell.'

'Yes. The twins were in the raid on the Lofoten Islands, you know,' Tony said to Chris. 'God, what a pair! Des was telling me about when they were in training for the Commandos. No one better suited for them, believe me. Des said they had to climb sheer cliffs with their faces blacked and a knife between their teeth. "It was the gear," he said. They're mad, both of them.'

It was a pleasant evening but when Anne wrote to Joe about it, telling him that she had asked Helen and Tony to come, he replied immediately, warning her not to rush things. 'I know you mean well, love,' he wrote, 'but Maureen and Chris have managed for so long *because* they have kept it so low key. Maureen's principles give her strength. Don't make it harder for them, Anne.'

At first Anne felt indignant with Joe, but when she thought it over, realised the good sense of his warning. A few nights later she went with Maureen to Benediction, and as she glanced at her sister, deep in prayer, Anne was conscious of how much Maureen's faith meant to her, and how her own well-meant interference might have severed that lifeline for her beloved sister.

Helen asked no questions about Chris, only saying that it had been a lovely evening and Moira was still talking about the tinned peaches and jelly.

To Maureen Anne said ruefully, 'I think that was a case of "fools rush in". Sorry, Mo.'

'Nothing to be sorry for,' she said. 'Chris and I appreciated it and we enjoyed the evening, but I think it'd be better if we didn't do it again. But I'm glad you know about us, love. I didn't like deceiving you. And don't be hurt, Anne. I said that Joe knew, but – well, Sarah knows too. Mum knew about us and mentioned it to Sarah when we came back here after your wedding.'

Anne was silent for a moment, thinking, then she said, 'Joe came back here too, didn't he? Do you mean Mum spoke about it to you and Joe and Sarah heard her?'

'No. It was – oh, God, Anne, I can't tell you,' she said. 'Oh, if only this damn' war was over!' She began to cry and Anne put her arms round her. 'Don't, Mo,' she said gently. 'I won't ask any more questions, and I'm not hurt that Sarah knows, honestly.'

The next day all this was swept from their minds when a letter arrived from Eileen, saying that she was to be married by special licence.

Eileen wrote first to her father asking for his blessing. 'I hope you won't be hurt, Dad. I know you were proud to give Anne away, and I'd love to be with you and all the family, but we only have two days' leave. I'll bring Whitey to meet you just as soon as I can and I know you'll love him.'

Pat was bewildered, unable to understand why Eileen could not wait to be married from home, but by the next post Maureen and Anne received ecstatic letters from her and tried to reconcile their father to the idea of the wedding.

'She's very much in love with him, Dad,' Anne said. 'And it's quite usual for people in the Services to get married on the station. Especially in the Air Force.'

'But a lad we've never even met?' he said.

'Yes, Dad, but Eileen must know what she's doing. She's

been out with enough lads to know he's the right one for her,' Maureen said.

Pat shook his head and blew out his lips. 'I don't know. Everything's different. Your mum wouldn't have liked it.'

'She would, Dad,' Anne said. 'If it meant Eileen was happy. *I* know. The three of us could go to seven o'clock Mass on Friday morning then it would be like being at Nuptial Mass for her.'

'Aye, and I'll send her a few quid to get some nice things,' Pat said, brightening. The girls knew that the 'few quid' would be a generous sum, and even if she was unable to buy nice things, it would show Eileen that her father approved of the marriage, though he was unable to express his feelings in the letter sent with it.

When Carrie was told she said she was not surprised. 'Eileen was never one for fuss, was she?' she said. 'Not very romantic. I'll have to find something nice for a wedding present.'

'Not romantic!' Anne said to Maureen. 'Aunt Carrie didn't see our letters!'

Theresa was excited by the news and told Maureen that she had sent Eileen two tablets of scented soap and a box of dusting powder with a swansdown puff. 'Not a wedding present,' she said. 'I'll get her something when she comes home for that.'

Anne had convinced herself that no harm would come to John, and now moved through her days in a happy dream. She had left work and spent her time preparing for her baby, and reading and re-reading John's letters.

She went often to see his family. Mrs Redmond worked part-time in Mill Road Hospital, but John's grandmother was always there and delighted to see Anne. She told her many tales of the days during the Great War when John was a baby and he and his mother had lived with her and Lawrie, as they sat together, Sally holding a skein of white wool while Anne wound it into a ball.

After the long drawn-out years of waiting suddenly the war

was going well on all fronts and the end was in sight. Joe wrote of the scenes when Brussels was liberated, of the joy of the population and their wonderful welcome to the troops.

Joe was in the spearhead but John also wrote of amazing scenes he witnessed as his company moved through the countryside. 'Some of the fellows talk of coming back here in peacetime, but it will be England for us, Anne, once I'm safely home.'

She might have resented his calm assumption that she would prefer to holiday in England at another time, but now it seemed nothing would affect her serenity.

Anne was shaken awake by the dreadful news that Eileen's husband had been killed when his aircraft crashed in flames returning from a bombing raid.

She wrote that she would prefer not to come home, but Tony and Maureen got a few days' leave and travelled to Kent to see her. It was a long and tiring journey across country and out to the remote airfield, and a wasted one it seemed.

Eileen was dry-eyed and controlled, standing stiffly within Maureen's arms as she held her and wept, and reiterating her intention to stay at her job. Her lip trembled briefly as Tony hugged her and Maureen kissed her again before they left, but she quickly recovered and told them unsmilingly to give her love to her father and the family.

Eileen's commanding officer took them to a room and gave them tea, and tried to explain to them that it was better for her to remain. 'She's with girls who understand,' she said. 'Some of them have had the same experience, and here she's in a familiar place doing familiar work and I think feeling closer to Whitey.'

Maureen and Tony appreciated her kindness although they could not agree with her. They were sure that it would be better for Eileen to be back among her loving family who could help her to bear her loss.

The commanding officer had given them more details of the crash and assured them that Whitey would have died quickly, although his body was badly burned. His parents emigrated to Canada before the war, she said, and he had been buried in the graveyard of the nearest small village.

They also saw the Catholic padre attached to the station and he took them to see Whitey's grave. They had bought flowers in the village and they laid them on the new grave.

'She could have had his body taken back to Liverpool and buried at home,' Maureen said. 'Then she would have been able to visit his grave.' Tony said nothing. He wondered if Eileen would ever again come back to live in Liverpool.

The padre told them that they must not think that theirs was a wasted journey. 'Eileen is stunned now, poor child,' he said. 'Later she will remember how you came to her and it will comfort her. Try to realise that this is the best solution for her, to stay here. She's like a wounded animal that knows instinctively how it can be cured.'

He drove them to the station and they returned, sad for their sister and still not convinced that it was better for her not to come home. It was a relief to both of them to reach home and find Helen and Anne waiting for them in Magdalen Street, with a hot meal prepared and a warm welcome from them and Moira.

'Fred's been to take Dad out for a drink,' they explained. 'He wasn't sure what time you'd come.'

'We'll have to convince him it's the usual thing for girls to stay there in cases like this,' Tony said. 'Although I haven't been able to convince myself.'

'Well, you can't do more than you've done, love, you and Maureen,' Helen said gently. 'Perhaps the priest was right, and instinct is telling Eileen what to do.'

It seemed in keeping with their mood when bitter fighting broke out in the Ardennes, and hopes of peace were dashed again.

Stephen came home for Christmas, but it was a quiet, sad time for the family. Their only joy came from Moira, who was just old enough to appreciate Christmas, and from the visits of Bridie's children and Theresa's two little ones.

On 19 January Anne's son was born. After Helen's experience the family had insisted that Anne was booked into a hospital and she entered Mill Road a day before the birth.

It was an easy birth and Gerald John, as he was christened, was a large healthy baby with a happy disposition. He was fair and blue-eyed with a strong resemblance to Mick Redmond.

'God help you, Anne,' Mrs Redmond said. 'If he gets up to half the tricks that Mick did.' But she was smiling as she hung over the cot, gazing with delight at the baby.

She told Anne that she could understand how she felt as John had been born when his father was in France during the First World War. 'Please God you won't have to wait so long for John to come home,' she said. 'I'm sure we're on the last lap now.'

It seemed that she was right as the Allies crossed the Rhine and swept through Germany. On 29 April Mussolini and his mistress were shot and their bodies hung upside down in Milan. People in Britain were shocked but relieved to hear it, and two days later Hitler killed himself and Eva Braun whom he had married the previous day.

'The coward!' Anne said indignantly to Sarah who had come to see her, but Sarah thought the world was well rid of him.

'That's true,' Anne agreed, 'but I think he should have been made to suffer for the way others suffered through him. People like our Eileen, and those poor people in places he overran.'

She felt this even more strongly when the news began to come to England of the concentration camps that were discovered when the troops swept through Germany.

Sarah and Maureen were now close friends and spent a lot of time together, and now that Anne was at home, the friendship between her and Sarah was resumed as strongly as ever.

Sarah and Maureen were godmothers to Gerald John, and Mick, who was on leave, was his godfather. There were no other babies in the Redmond family and to Sarah Gerry was a constant delight and source of amazement. She spent as much time as possible with him and Anne.

Suddenly, it seemed, the war was over at last, and Churchill announced on the wireless that 8 May would be Victory in Europe Day. He reminded people that the Japanese had not yet been defeated, but only people like Peggy Burns, whose son was a Japanese prisoner of war, dwelt on that fact.

Anne was wildly excited at the prospect of peace and of John coming home. 'He'll see Gerry while he's still a baby anyway, although he's missed his first few months,' she said. 'Not like when he was a baby and his father was in France until he was about three.'

She glanced at Sarah and said impulsively, 'Here I am going on, and it's even more exciting for you, isn't it, Sar? It must have been terrible for you all these years, but what a day it'll be when Terry comes home, won't it?'

Sarah nodded, but she looked self-conscious and guilty. She was just about to speak, to tell Anne how she really felt, when Gerry gave a loud cry and the moment passed.

Many prisoners of war were now arriving in Liverpool and the girls in Sarah's office made a large Welcome Home banner. The truckloads of returned prisoners drove past the office and the girls draped the banner between two windows and hung from the window ringing a handbell so that the men would look up and see the banner and hear them cheering.

'Wouldn't it be lovely if Terry was one of them?' a colleague said, but Sarah said quietly that she had received a letter from him and knew when he would arrive.

The family were surprised to hear that he had written to his father asking if he could bring a friend to stay. The friend, Frank, had no home to return to as his only relative, his father, had been killed and his home destroyed by a landmine during the 'May Blitz'.

Eileen had been demobilised and had returned home but was very sad and subdued, still grieving for Whitey. Stephen arrived home on holiday, and Tony and Helen came with their young daughter on the day that Terry was due. Anne and Maureen were already at home.

Only Joe was absent, still in Germany. Sarah said she would go to the Fitzgerald house in the evening of Terry's first day at home, and his father was pleased. 'Sarah's a kind thoughtful girl,' he told Maureen and Anne. 'She knows we're anxious to see him, and doesn't expect him to go rushing off to see her the minute he arrives.'

Terry had asked the family to wait at home for him and they all rushed into the hall when he rang the bell with Pat pushed forward to open the door. Terry hugged his father and Frank followed him in, then without waiting for introductions, advanced on the family.

'Hi, folks,' he said breezily. 'I'm Frank.' He gripped Helen's hand. 'You must be our Maureen.'

'No – no,' she stammered, taken aback, then recovered. 'I'm Helen, Tony's wife,' she said. 'And this is – this is Tony.' Tony and Stephen had stood back to let their sisters greet Terry, but they were looking at him and waiting eagerly to greet him, oblivious of Frank.

Helen touched Tony's arm and looked pleadingly at him so he turned and shook hands with Frank then turned back immediately to Terry.

Maureen was torn between her longing to hug Terry and gaze her fill on the young brother who had been lost to them for so long and pity for Frank who had no family to welcome him home.

When eventually they were all in the parlour she said quietly to Frank, 'I'm so sorry about your father. It must be a sad home-coming for you.'

To her amazement he guffawed. 'I'm glad to get away from the camp,' he said. 'But me and the old fellow never got on. Ted knows that, don't you, Ted?'

Terry looked over and grinned. 'I've heard you say it often enough,' he said.

'Yes, the old man battered me when I was a kid,' Frank said, and laughed again. 'We went a few rounds when I was big enough to stand up to him.'

Maureen hid her feelings and plied him with tea and food from the trolley which Helen had wheeled in. Frank went on, 'I cleared off to Canada as soon as I could. God's own country. I'd never have come back to Liverpool only the firm sent me here to fix something up on the docks twelve months before this lot started, so I was just unlucky.'

All the family grew more and more irritated as Frank interrupted every conversation they tried to have with Terry, saying, 'You're not telling that right, Ted,' or 'I could tell them more about that, Ted'.

'I've never heard Terence abbreviated to Ted before,' Anne whispered to Eileen, but she seemed indifferent. It seemed that nothing mattered to her now.

Pat was sitting with his arm about Terry's shoulders as though he wanted to reassure himself that his son had really returned, but even his low-voiced conversation with Terry was interrupted by Frank.

Finally Anne said firmly, 'Why don't you show Terry the good job you made of the cellar, Dad? It was a really safe spot for us during the raids, Terry.'

He and his father stood up and Frank rose to follow them but Tony said quickly, 'Tell us about the prison camp, Frank. Terry couldn't say much in his letters.'

Frank sat down again and launched into a tale of how he had outwitted the guards at every turn and been the mainstay of the prisoners. 'Ted would've been lost without me,' he boasted. 'He was too soft, y'see. Didn't know his way round at all. I suppose you'd all spoiled him, kept him wrapped in cotton wool.'

'Don't be ridiculous,' Anne flared. 'Our Terry was never wrapped in cotton wool, as you call it, and he wasn't soft either. He wasn't a hard knock, just a normal decent lad.' Tony signalled her not to annoy Frank in case he used it as an excuse to follow Terry, but he only seemed amused.

He gave another loud guffaw and said condescendingly, 'Shows how much you know, young Anne. Terry knew nothing. He'd have been a mark for all the wise guys without me to look out for him.'

Anne's face was red and she felt ready to burst with anger but she picked up the baby and escaped to the bathroom.

'Your Uncle Terry's got an odd friend, Gerry,' she told the baby. 'The cheek of him, calling me young Anne when I'm a wife and mother!' But the baby just gave her his toothless grin.

Terry and his father had returned when she went downstairs and the meal was ready. It was a special meal and everyone had contributed to it, either with points, coupons or hoarded treats. Mrs Redmond had sent sugar and tinned meat and jam from the food parcels sent from America by her sister, and the girls were proud of the meal that they had been able to provide.

'Gosh, this is the gear,' Terry said, but Frank seemed unimpressed. Throughout the meal he told them of his success at bartering with the guards, or stealing from the farmers when they were sent to work on farms. 'We'd be a lot thinner than this if it wasn't for me, wouldn't we, Ted?' he said.

As soon as the meal was over Tony said he would go for Sarah. 'No point in her staying away to be tactful and give us time with Terry now this fellow's here,' he said to Helen.

He set off after arranging with the girls that Terry would be sent off to meet them, alone, and Frank prevented from accompanying him.

Tony called at the Redmond house and as Sarah was ready they left almost immediately. 'I'm afraid this fellow he's brought home with him, Frank, hasn't left Terry alone for a minute,' Tony said ruefully. 'He's so thick-skinned, I don't know how Terry can stand him.'

'How is he?' Sarah asked.

'He looks better than we expected – Frank says that's all due to him – and he's quite tanned. They've been working on farms, it seems.' They walked in silence for a moment then Tony said quietly, 'You may find Terry changed, Sar. Older, of course, and more grown up is the only way I can describe it.' He squeezed her arm affectionately. 'Of course you're not the quiet little girl you were, are you?'

Sarah smiled and as they drew near the house, Terry approached them. Tony released her arm, clapping Terry on the shoulder as he passed him, and Terry and Sarah moved self-consciously towards each other.

Chapter Twenty-Nine

Terry took off his cap and bent to kiss Sarah, and she hugged him, but their embrace was brief. They drew away and he crooked his arm for her to slip her hand through it. They walked along, both silent for a moment then both speaking at once.

They laughed and Terry said gallantly, 'After you, Sarah.'

'I was only going to ask if you saw many changes – if everything seems very strange to you?'

'It does really,' he admitted. 'I didn't expect everything to be the same but the house seems smaller and shabbier. And Dad – he looks so old. And Mum . . .'

'I know, Terry,' Sarah said gently. 'It must be hard for you, but she was suffering so much pain. It was better for her.'

'I know. Maureen told me. *She* hasn't changed much, and neither have you, Sar. Our Eileen is the one who's changed most, I think. Anne seems the same although she's married and got a kid, too.'

'Yes, he's a lovely child. But poor Eileen, she's had a bad time,' Sarah said. 'What was it like in the camp?'

'Could've been worse,' he said cheerfully. 'We went out to work on a farm, and some of the Jerrys were okay. It was just the years going past. We got browned off sometimes, but Frank and I managed to stick together. He's at home now. We'd better get back in case he's a bit shy with the family.'

They walked back quickly and Maureen opened the door to them. She managed to detain Sarah and to whisper, 'Well?'

'All right,' Sarah whispered, but only shook her head as Maureen asked, 'Have you talked?'

'He was worried about Frank,' Sarah said, and Maureen grimaced expressively.

Sarah was a favourite with Moira and the child ran to her as soon as she sat down on the sofa with Terry beside her. Sarah lifted her on to her knee and Terry leaned over and touched one of Moira's ringlets. 'That's a nice sausage,' he said.

'Ith's not a thauthage, ith's my *hair*,' she said indignantly, and as all the family laughed Helen firmly lifted the child from Sarah's knee and took her into the kitchen, promising to let her help to make sandwiches.

Frank was introduced to Sarah and again monopolised the conversation, making comments on letters that she had sent to Terry and telling about his clever deals with the guards and other prisoners.

Anne watched with amazement. Her first impression of Terry was that he had scarcely changed at all, although she was sure that she would see a difference in him as time passed. For the moment he had slotted back into the family as though he had never been away, but Anne was astounded at the behaviour of Terry and Sarah.

She had been surprised when they appeared so soon after Tony, and now they were sitting there, joining in the general conversation, and not even holding hands! She knew that Sarah was shy, but surely on an occasion like this she should have been unable to resist hugging and kissing Terry, no matter who was with them?

And Terry too, Anne thought. He seemed to be treating Sarah as though she was another sister rather than the girl he loved and had been separated from for so many years. Gosh, if it was me and John, she mused. For a start we wouldn't have followed Tony in for hours while we walked round catching up on the time we'd lost, and when we came in we'd have been sitting there with our arms round each other, taking no notice of anyone else.

Suddenly Anne realised that Frank was saying loudly to Sarah, 'What do you think about Canada then?' Terry had turned away from her and was making signals to him.

Tony said hastily, 'What do you think of Liverpool, Frank? Do you see many changes?'

'Yeah, what a mess. Even from the bit we saw coming here it all looks shabby and dirty and the people are a miserable-looking bunch,' he said. 'The Jerrys look more cheerful and they've *lost* the war.'

'That's not true,' Helen said angrily. 'The people are not miserable, even though many lost relatives and their homes in the bombing. They're just shabby and tired and not very well fed and the city's been knocked about.'

She was flushed and breathless with anger and Tony put his arm round her shoulders. 'We'll soon get things right now the war's over,' he said, and Terry said soothingly, 'It's just that we remember Liverpool as such a lively place.'

Fortunately, at that moment Maureen wheeled in the tea trolley bearing plates of cakes and sandwiches and the teapot and teacups.

'I've put yours and Sarah's in Dad's den,' Maureen said quietly to Terry, and he and Sarah went into the little room behind the parlour.

Gerry had fallen asleep on Anne's knee and she carried him into the kitchen to put him on the sofa to sleep. Helen followed her with a blanket, and as they arranged it round the sleeping baby, Anne said quietly, 'What do you make of Terry and Sarah? Not very loving, are they, Helen?'

'Sarah's very reserved,' said Helen. 'And they must feel strange meeting again after all this time. It's over five years, Anne.'

'But Terry doesn't seem to feel strange with us, does he? – or with Sarah really. Just not very loverlike.'

'Everyone's different,' Helen said gently, and Anne laughed. 'They sure are!' she said. 'It's ten weeks yet to John's leave and already I'm more excited than Sarah is now with Terry here.'

They settled the baby comfortably and wedged a chair in front of the sofa in case he woke and rolled off, then went back to the parlour. Anne sat down beside her father. 'Happy now, Dad?' she asked. 'We'll soon have all the lads home.'

'Aye, Terry looks well, doesn't he?' Pat said. 'A bit thinner in the face maybe. Another wedding soon, eh?' He turned to Maureen who was sitting nearby. 'Sarah's a good little girl. We'll have to see she has a good send-off, the years she's waited.'

Maureen blushed but only said quietly, 'Let's wait and see, Dad.' Frank jumped to his feet and dashed off to the den before anyone could stop him, but he returned a few minutes later.

'I wanted to know what they'd arranged,' he said. 'But they're still talking. I think Terry and I should go first to Canada and Sarah can follow us and get married there. Terry thinks he should marry her here, and the three of us go out together.'

For a moment everyone was silent with shock then Pat said, 'Canada? You're talking of our Terry going to Canada?'

'Yes, Mr Fitz,' Frank said breezily. 'God's own country. We'll do well there.'

Before anyone else could speak Terry and Sarah reappeared. His arm was around Sarah's shoulders and they were both smiling broadly. 'Wedding bells?' Helen asked, and they both said in unison, 'No.'

'It was all a mistake but we couldn't do anything about it until the war was over,' Terry explained. 'Sarah's just sorted us out.' He laughed and looked at her. 'She's not the timid little girl she used to be.'

'Terry nobly offered to marry me, but I know he has other plans

370

and so have I,' Sarah said, smiling at him. 'It was just unfortunate that he was taken prisoner before we sorted ourselves out.'

'So we'll be able to go to Canada by ourselves then, Terry?' Frank said jubilantly.

'So you'll still go to Canada, Terry?' Pat said, looking bemused.

'Big mouth,' Terry said to Frank, and Maureen stood up.

'Right. That's settled. How about a drink for everyone, Dad? You're not usually slow in that department.'

But Pat only sat shaking his head looking bewildered, and Tony said, 'I'll see to it.'

Terry went to sit beside his father and talk quietly to him, and Anne looked at Sarah's glowing face. That's how she should have looked when Terry came home, she thought.

She went into the kitchen to check on the sleeping baby and Sarah followed her. 'Oh, Sarah, I don't know what to say!' Anne exclaimed. 'You're sure you're not upset?'

'Do I *look* upset?' she said, laughing. 'I'm so glad to have it all sorted out, Anne. I was afraid Terry would come home full of plans for a wedding, but thank God he didn't. Although he said he wanted to marry me because I'd waited so long, until I told him how the land lay, then he admitted he was trying to fit me in with his plans.'

'To go to Canada?' Anne said. 'And with that twerp Frank! I can't believe it.' She looked doubtfully at Sarah.

'You certainly *look* happy enough, both of you.'

'Oh I am, I am,' Sarah said, grabbing Anne round the waist and waltzing her round the kitchen. 'It's such a weight off my mind.' She stood still then with her arms round Anne and said quietly, 'Joe and I have been in love for years but we couldn't say anything while Terry was still a prisoner. We thought the war would never end.'

'You and Joe?' Anne gasped. She plumped down on to a chair. 'God, I can't take all this in. You and Joe! Does Terry know?'

Sarah nodded, her eyes sparkling. 'He thinks we're well matched.'

'You are. You are, Sar, the more I think about it,' said Anne. 'How long —?'

'Ages,' she said. 'You see, it was half a joke with Terry that I was his girl. You remember how he picked up my photo in our house on the way to the station?'

'Vaguely,' Anne said. 'I know he was always acting soft pretending to be smitten with you before the war, but then I thought you got serious.'

'Not really. It was just circumstances. Misunderstandings really with me and Joe. Then I thought I'd see how things went with Terry, because we weren't engaged or anything. But he was taken prisoner and what could we do even when Joe and I admitted how we felt about each other? I couldn't write and tell Terry, could I?'

'Oh, Sarah, what a rotten war you've had,' Anne exclaimed, flinging her arms round her impulsively. 'So what happens now?'

'I'll write to Joe and tell him,' she said happily. 'We'll be able to see each other openly now. We have been courting, y'know, Anne, but keeping it quiet for Terry's sake.'

'Well, you certainly kept it quiet from me,' Anne said. 'Did Maureen know?'

Sarah nodded and Anne said ruefully, 'I must be thick.'

'No, you're not,' Sarah said. 'We were just very careful, but your mum guessed.'

'Mum!' Anne exclaimed.

'Yes. It was such a shock, Anne, because Joe and I thought no one suspected.'

'Mum loved us all so much,' Anne said, her eyes filling with tears. 'That's why she always understood everything about us.'

'I know,' Sarah said. 'She was lovely.' She gave a sudden sob and for a moment the two girls clung together, thinking of Julia, then they drew apart and dried their eyes.

'That's how Maureen knows,' Sarah said, 'because she was here.'

Anne was silent for a moment then she said thoughtfully, 'So this is what Mo was talking about. She told me about her and Chris and said you'd known since my wedding day, but she got upset when I began to ask questions. Said something about the war going on too long.'

'Your Mum said Maureen and I could help each other,' Sarah said. 'I suppose she meant we were both keeping quiet about being in love but we could talk to each other.'

'All these mysteries,' Anne said, smiling. 'I must seem very dull. My life's just an open book.'

'Not to me,' Sarah said. 'I used to wonder why you and John weren't courting when I could see how you felt about each other.'

'Oh, John had this idea that because he was blacklisted, he didn't want me to be linked with him,' Anne said lightly. 'Not until he was accepted for the Forces, anyway.'

'Typical!' Sarah said. 'Another of his barmy ideas.' She stopped and put her hand over her mouth but Anne only laughed.

'Don't worry. I'll cure him,' she said. She took a napkin from the fireguard and picked up the baby, and Sarah smiled at her and went back to the parlour.

'I mean it,' Anne said to the baby, 'I'll cure your dad's barmy ideas, and he'd better not try his sergeant talk here either.' The baby chuckled as Anne laid him down and took off his wet napkin, and she bent over him, whispering, 'Only a few more weeks, Gerry,' and kissing him.

Sarah said goodnight to the family and Terry went with her to escort her home and see the Redmonds, but he told his father that he would soon be back.

Maureen came to the door with them and Sarah said quietly, 'We didn't say anything about Joe to your dad, Mo. We thought it might be too much all at once.'

'Yes, he's a bit overthrown with this Canada idea,' she said. 'He'll be pleased we'll still have you in the family, Sarah, when we *do* tell him.'

As Terry and Sarah walked along he said, laughing, 'It's like the old melodramas where the girls says: "Let me be a sister to you" as she turns the fellow down, isn't it? Except I'm very glad you'll be my sister. I'm very fond of you, Sar.'

'And I am of you,' she said, stretching up to kiss his cheek. 'No hard feelings, Terry?'

'None,' he said, suddenly lifting her up and swinging her round. 'Oh, Sarah, it's great to be home.'

'Hey, be careful. The lights are on now. People can see us,' she said, laughing as he set her down, then her smile faded.

'You won't be going to Canada right away, will you?' she asked. 'You'll be able to spend some time with your dad and the family?'

'I'd like to,' Terry said, 'but Frank is keen to go. He has contacts there and thinks we should strike while the iron is hot.'

'Then you'll have to spend as much time as you possibly can with your dad,' Sarah said firmly, and he sketched a mock salute. 'Yes, ma'am,' he said, laughing. 'By heck, you've changed, Sarah. You couldn't say boo to a goose when I went away.'

They were both laughing when they reached the Redmond house, and Sarah's family greeted Terry warmly. He was introduced to Gene Romero, Kate's American fiancé, and Sarah's father asked about the prisoner of war camp and the conditions there.

Kate and Gene went out and shortly afterwards Terry stood up. 'I'd better get back to my dad,' he said, and Sarah handed him his greatcoat and cap.

'Yes, Frank will be even more like a hen on a griddle,' she said, laughing, then accompanied him to the door after he had said goodbye to her family.

'You're not going back with Terry?' her mother said when Sarah returned.

'Who's Frank?' her father said at the same moment.

Sarah quickly explained the situation, and only her mother was surprised. Her father knew already about her love for Joe, and her grandmother had guessed, but Cathy Redmond's concern was for the Fitzgerald family.

'I can see you're happy, love, and so is Terry, but what about his dad and the rest of the family? Will they mind?'

'No, Mum,' Sarah said. 'I think really so much is happening with everyone that it doesn't seem as important as I thought it would be.'

'And this has gone on since Dunkirk?' Cathy said. 'It must have been very hard for you and Joe, but you behaved very honourably.'

'So did Terry,' Sarah said. 'He was insisting he wanted to marry me because he thought I'd waited so long, until he realised that I didn't want to marry him. The idea was that either Terry and Frank would go to Canada and I would follow them and get married there – that was Frank's favourite – or we'd get married here and all go to Canada together.'

'You mean they wanted you to live in Canada?' Cathy exclaimed, horrified.

'Yes. I don't know what Frank would have done if I'd said I'd marry Terry and we'd stay here. He'd probably have bumped me off.' Sarah laughed. 'He's made up about me and Joe.'

Cathy looked from her mother to her husband. 'Did you know about this?' she asked.

Her mother said calmly, 'I didn't know but I guessed. I had more chances to see them together than you did, but I didn't say anything in case I was wrong. I'm very glad I was right.'

'So am I,' Cathy said. 'I think Terry's a nice lad, Sarah, but I think the world of Joe. I'll be made up to have him as a son-in-law.'

'Yes, and I'm sure you and Joe will be very happy together, Sarah,' her father said, smiling at her.

When Terry and Sarah had left for the Redmonds', the Fitzgeralds felt free to voice their amazement.

'What a shock!' Helen said. 'I couldn't believe my ears, and yet they both look very happy, don't they?'

'I'm worried about that little girl,' Pat said, with a frown, and Maureen sat down beside him. 'Don't be, Dad,' she said gently. 'Sarah and Joe have been in love for a long time, but they couldn't do anything about it until Terry came home and they saw how the land lay.'

'*Our* Joe?' Pat said, looking bewildered, and Frank laughed loudly. 'Oh, aye,' he said. 'While the cat's away the mouse can play, eh?'

Everyone looked outraged but before anyone else could speak Eileen said sharply, 'Don't talk rubbish. Anyway, this has got nothing to do with you. It's family business. Why don't you go and unpack your kitbag or something?'

To everyone's amazement Frank stood up and muttered, 'Sorry,' then went meekly away to the room he was sharing with Terry.

'Good God, I don't know whether I'm coming or going,' Pat said. 'Our Joe.'

'I think Joe and Sarah are well matched,' Anne said. 'And this means Sarah'll still be in the family.'

'And you don't have to worry about her or about Terry,' Helen said. 'They'll both be doing what they want, with no hard feelings.'

There was a knock at the door and Carrie and Fred came in and were told the news. 'You never know the minute when you've got kids,' Fred said. 'Especially now, Pat.'

'Yes, with the war,' Carrie said. 'Everything's upside down and life's different for everybody.'

'That's a good thing, I think,' Tony said. '*We* were all comfortable before the war, but some people had a hell of a life. A fellow I know said he never wore new clothes or had a clean bed and enough to eat until he went in the Army. We don't want to go back to those conditions.'

'But our Terry going off to Canada?' Pat said to Carrie. 'I can't get over it.'

'Aye, it's hard when he's been away for so long,' she said. 'But it's the way things are now, Pat.'

'The young ones have seen a bit of the world and they don't want to live all their lives in the same parish like us,' Fred said. 'I tell you what though, Pat, I'll bet you'll see as much of your Terry as we'll see of Shaun. It'll only be the odd visit now he's settled in Sheffield with his wife's family all round him.'

When Terry returned Frank came downstairs and was introduced to Fred and Carrie, and soon Helen and Tony said that they must take Moira home to bed. Before they left Moira kissed her grandfather and Helen whispered to him, 'Don't be downhearted. Terry hasn't gone yet and you've still got your other children here.'

'And you, girl,' Pat said. 'Tony did us all a good turn when he married you.' He looked more cheerful, and later in a quiet moment Maureen told him that her mother had guessed how Joe and Sarah felt and given them her blessing.

'Well, if Mum was pleased about it, it must be all right,' Pat said, satisfied. 'I don't think the lads will fall out over it, will they?'

'No, of course they won't, Dad,' Maureen assured him.

Sarah had written immediately to Joe, and he was given compassionate leave to see his brother. Terry went alone to the station to meet him and they greeted each other awkwardly, then Terry clapped Joe on the shoulder.

'Good to see you, Joe,' he said.

Joe gripped his arm. 'Good to see *you*, kid,' he said. 'Was it bad?'

'No. Some of the Jerrys were swines, some were all right, same as our lads. Frank and I managed to stick together all through, so we were all right. You got one at Anzio, Mo said.'

'Wasn't much,' said Joe. 'Got me off the beach and to hospital in Naples. Bloody shambles it was. We walked ashore, no opposition, then sat there for seventy-two hours while the Germans got in position before we got the order to attack.'

'I heard about it,' Terry said. 'I met a Mick in the transit camp who was captured there. He reckoned he was lucky. Said the 1st Battalion was wiped out. Said you could have walked into Rome in a couple of days.'

'Maybe that was why we were held up,' Joe said grimly. 'Or there was some bonehead among the command.' They were passing a public house and by common consent turned into it. It was empty but the landlord produced two glasses of beer and seemed disposed to talk.

Joe jerked his head towards a seat in the corner and they carried their glasses there and at last spoke about what was on both their minds.

'I'm sorry about this,' said Joe. 'Sarah and I – we never meant it to happen. I fell for her as soon as I saw her, but I thought she was your girl. Then I thought it might just be fooling with you. I should have done something but as usual I hung back and dithered and the next thing was Dunkirk.'

'Yeah, well, you might have been right,' Terry said. 'I've been thinking about it. I suppose it *was* larking about at first, then I got that photo off her, and the fellows were saying they were going to cut me out with her when they went home on leave. I was just a soft kid, I suppose. I liked the idea of having a girlfriend to write to.'

'This Canada business. It's not because of —?' Joe started.

'No. We've talked about it for years, Frank and I,' Terry said. He grinned. 'Mostly Frank. The idea was that I'd see how Sarah felt about it, and we'd get married and go out there right away. Frank thought we should go first and Sarah should follow and we'd marry there, but I wanted to do what she wanted as she'd waited so long for me.' He grinned again. 'Or so I thought.'

'She did,' Joe protested. 'I don't know what we'd have done if you were keen to get married, but Sarah would do nothing until she'd seen you. She couldn't write and tell you while you were stuck in that Stalag.'

'And I couldn't go into all the Canada business on a letter card,' Terry said. 'Frank blurted something out about it before I had a chance to talk to Sarah, so she knew about it before we talked.'

'I tried to keep quiet about how I felt, but in the end I had to tell Sarah and she said she felt the same way, but we were worried about you. We still kept it from other people though, kid,' Joe said.

'I could see that,' said Terry, and Joe added hastily, 'Only Mo knew, and Mum. She guessed, and when I was home for Anne's wedding she said – she said . . .' He picked up his glass and gulped some beer, then went on, 'She gave us her blessing, but she said "Don't hurt Terry" and we promised.'

'You kept your promise,' Terry said. He blinked rapidly and blew his nose. 'I can't believe it somehow. I keep thinking she hasn't really gone and I'll see her in a minute.'

'It was better for her in the end,' Joe said sadly.

As they left the public house Terry said quietly, 'I'm not so keen on Canada now that I've come home and seen Dad and the family, but I can't let Frank down. It was different when we were in the Stalag and making our plans.'

'You could give it a go,' Joe suggested. 'Then if you don't like it you can always come home again. You can please yourself, can't you?'

'You're right, Joe,' Terry said, grinning at him. 'I'm footloose and fancy free.' They were nearing the house and Joe stopped and held out his hand. 'No hard feelings, kid?'

'None,' Terry said, gripping his hand. 'It was just this bloody war, but it worked out all right in the end. I tell you what, though, Joe. She's a smashing girl. You'd better make her happy – or else!' He gave Joe a mock punch and they walked on and into the house, smiling.

Chapter Thirty

All the family found Frank irritating, but only Eileen made no secret of her feelings and there were many sharp exchanges between them. Maureen and Terry tried to act as peacemakers but Anne told Maureen that she thought Frank was good for Eileen.

'She's just been drifting through her demob leave,' she said. 'Taking no interest in anything. And we've all been afraid to ask what she intended to do. Now she seems to have woken up, and she's talking about going back to Littlewood's. I think it's the best thing she could do.'

'Yes, she does seem more like herself,' Maureen agreed. 'I suppose she got used to being outspoken because of being in the Services.'

Terry and Frank pushed ahead with their preparations for Canada and thanks to Frank's contacts and his persistence were ready to leave within weeks. Terry told his father that he would try life in Canada and return if he didn't like it, which made them all feel more reconciled to losing him again so quickly.

The pain of parting with Terry was offset for the family by their relief at being free of Frank's loud voice and braying laugh. 'Canada's welcome to that fellow,' Pat said to Fred. 'I've told our Terry the money's here for his fare home any time he wants it.'

Business was booming for Pat now that Liverpool was being

rebuilt, and his only worry was obtaining materials.

Anne was counting the hours to John's demobilisation and constantly showed his photograph to the baby and taught him to say 'Dada' clearly. She hoped that Eileen would not be upset by John's homecoming, but fortunately she was due to return to work a few days after his return in September.

John had asked Anne to wait for him at home, and she was sitting on the hearthrug playing with the baby when his taxi arrived.

'Gerry, Gerry, your dada's home,' she cried, rushing to open the door and fling herself into his arms. John held her close and kissed her, then still holding her closed the door of their flat behind him and leaned against it. 'Home at last,' he said with a happy sigh.

The baby had rolled over and was trying to crawl towards them, shouting, 'Dada, Dada!' They rushed towards him and John picked him up, beaming with pride and delight. 'Yes, I'm your dad, son,' he said. 'Home for good. We'll never be parted again.'

He cuddled and kissed Gerry, then slipped his arm round Anne. 'He knew me right away, you see,' he said proudly. She smiled and said nothing of her efforts to coach Gerry.

Later they went into the kitchen to see the family who were all at home by this time. John could talk of nothing but the baby. 'He's so *clever*,' he boasted. 'Only eight months old and he says "Dada" quite clearly, and he was trying to stand up by my knee.' Fortunately they all believed that Gerry was wonderful and agreed with John.

Back in their own rooms they bathed the baby together and John gave him his final bottle. He seemed disappointed that Gerry fell deeply asleep. 'I wanted to keep him up, seeing it's my first night home,' he said. For a moment Anne felt hurt. She'd thought that John would be as anxious as she was to be alone together after their long separation but quickly stifled the thought.

Gerry always slept deeply throughout the night and Anne and John went early to bed. They made love passionately then lay in each other's arms, talking and planning for their future before making love again.

'I've got the best wife and the best son in the world,' John said. 'Oh, Anne, I'm bloody lucky.'

'So am I,' she said, snuggling close into his arms. Please God, let us always be so happy, she prayed silently.

They spent some of John's gratuity on a blissful holiday in the farmhouse where they had spent their honeymoon, with days made even happier by Gerry's delight in all he saw, and nights of tender lovemaking in the farmhouse bedroom with the baby asleep beside them in a cot.

They returned for the wedding of John's sister Kate to her American fiancé in the American Army camp chapel. Maureen looked after Gerry and they enjoyed the wedding and the reception afterwards in the Officers' Mess.

They heard that Gene's father was having a house built for the couple, and his family were to furnish it.

'Trust Kate to fall on her feet,' Sally Ward said to Anne. 'Peggy Burns says some GI brides think they're going to a ranch like on the pictures, and land in a shack miles from anywhere.'

'Gene's family seem quite wealthy, don't they?' John said. 'And Kate's kept in touch with Aunt Mary too. She said in her letter to Mum that she and Sam live *only* about seven hundred miles from Gene's family, so they'll be able to visit.'

Later, as John and Anne walked home, he said, 'That house that Kate and Gene are having built – it's going to be huge and full of gadgets too.'

Anne squeezed his arm and smiled at him tenderly. 'Yes, but it's in America,' she said. 'I wouldn't swop our two rooms for it, would you?'

She expected John to respond as tenderly but he said with

enthusiasm, 'No. I don't want to leave England. Not now we've got a Labour Government and can get all the things done that need to be done.'

'I felt a bit sorry for Mr Churchill though,' Anne said. 'Being pushed out like that.'

'Yes, but we don't want it to be like after the last war,' John said. 'Men used for the fighting, then thrown on the scrapheap afterwards. Fellows have had a chance to weigh things up during the war, and we're not going back to the way things were before.'

'Your dad said it was the Forces vote, the postal vote, that put Labour in,' Anne said.

'All my grandad fought for will come now,' he said. 'Work for all, better housing, a good education for *all* children, enough food and good medical care for everyone.'

'I hope we hear about *our* house soon,' Anne said. 'The Irish Guards are due back in England in January, and Sarah and Joe can have our rooms if they get married then.'

Christmas 1945 was a happy one for the Redmond and Fitzgerald families, and for most people. At last the country was at peace, and although food and clothes were still rationed it was possible to obtain small items 'off the ration'.

The Redmonds were inundated with parcels from America, from Gene's family and his relatives, and from Cathy's sister Mary and her husband Sam, and they shared them generously with relatives and friends.

Mary and Sam also sent a parcel to John, containing food, nylon stockings for Anne, a thick pullover for John, and toys and clothes for the baby.

Anne was particularly pleased with the toys, squeaking rubber animals and toy cars which were unobtainable in Britain.

Stephen had returned to work in Liverpool, and on Christmas morning he, Eileen, Maureen and their father all crowded into

Anne and John's bedroom to see Gerry open his gifts from Father Christmas.

John beamed proudly as Gerry seized his toys, chuckling with delight, and Stephen exclaimed, 'What a smashing kid!' Later John and Anne took the baby with them to Mass, where they met John's family, and afterwards went back to the Redmond house. John carried Gerry and proudly accepted admiring remarks about the baby from friends they met.

'He thinks he's all his own work,' Sally Ward said to Anne. 'You've done a good job with that child, girl, bringing him up on your own so far.'

'He's never been any trouble,' Anne said, but she smiled gratefully at Sally.

John's mother had warned Anne that John might be jealous of her closeness to the baby without realising it, but Anne reflected ruefully that she was the one who might have cause for jealousy.

John had almost monopolised the baby since his return home, and constantly interrupted Anne when she was speaking, to draw attention to Gerry's efforts to speak or stand. He was still on demo-bilisation leave but was due to start work in the New Year in the offices of the timber company, where his father was now a partner.

Anne hoped that he would be less obsessed with the baby when he was forced to leave him in her care during the day and had the added interest of work.

They spent some time on Christmas morning with John's family, as Gerry was the first baby in the family for many years, then returned for Christmas dinner prepared by Maureen and Eileen.

Anne had shared the food from the parcel with Maureen and with Helen, and not without some opposition from John had reserved some of the toys for Moira. The two children played together happily on Christmas Day, and Helen confided to Anne that she longed for a brother or sister for Moira.

Anne expected that Sarah and Joe would marry when he came home on disembarkation leave in January, but Sarah decided that she would wait until he was home for good in May.

She told Anne during Joe's leave that she regretted her decision. 'I just didn't want us to be parted again after we were married,' she said. 'But I'm sorry now.'

'Never mind, the time will soon pass,' Anne consoled her. 'And the weather will be better in May.' Joe was stationed at Chelsea Barracks so he was able to spend several weekends at home before he was finally demobilised.

Kate Redmond had sailed for America and Mick had been demobilised but was now living near Birmingham with another pilot. They were using their gratuities to set up a factory to make plastics.

With the younger generation gone from the house in Egremont Street, John's parents and grandmother planned to move to a smaller, more modern house near Breckfield Park. It had three bedrooms, a bathroom and toilet upstairs, and large gardens front and rear, and was a bright sunny house.

Joe was demobilised in May, and he and Sarah were married the following week. It was a simple ceremony with Anne as matron of honour. She felt near to tears as she watched the shining happiness of Sarah and her brother.

They seemed to be in a dream world from which everyone else was excluded and Anne prayed fervently that they would always be as happy, yet was unable to resist feeling a stab of envy.

The reception was held in Egremont Street, the last festivity there before the family moved to their new house, and later Sarah and Joe left for their honeymoon in Anglesey.

Newly built corporation houses had been requisitioned at the start of the war, for internees and for other groups, but now they had been returned to the Corporation. In April Anne and John were notified that they had been allocated a Corporation house instead of the prefabricated one they expected.

They were given the keys and went to see it, and found that it was not a requisitioned house but one which had become vacant on another part of the estate. It was the end of a small terrace of houses, on the corner of a wide road with gardens front and rear and along the side of the house.

Anne and John were delighted with it. It faced west and had a small kitchen, a living room and parlour, and upstairs three bedrooms, toilet and bathroom. 'It's as nice as your mum's new house,' Anne exclaimed, but John shrugged.

'My dad's buying that house,' he said. 'This is only rented. But we will buy one day, Anne, I promise.'

'I don't care either way,' she said. 'I'm just delighted with this.'

The next-door neighbour knocked on the door and invited them in for a cup of tea. 'The lad that lived there used to grow lovely spuds and vegetables,' she told them, 'but he got called up and drowned at sea, and his mam just lost heart. She'd had a big family but he was the last. The others are all scattered. In fact, she's gone now to a daughter in Southampton.' Mrs Rooney was a fat, smiling woman with grey hair.

'She was nice and friendly, wasn't she?' Anne said when they left.

'*Too* friendly,' John growled. 'She might turn out a bit of a pest.'

'Look on the bright side, for goodness' sake,' she said. 'She might have been like those neighbours your mum told us about when she was first married. Really nasty.'

John looked offended and they waited in silence for the tramcar, but were both too excited about the house to stay out of friends for long.

With help from his father and Anne's brothers, John quickly redecorated the house, and then the women of both families moved in to clean it and hang curtains.

In the second week of June, while Sarah and Joe were still on their honeymoon, Anne and John moved into the house and left their rooms in the Fitzgerald house free for the newlyweds.

Surplus furniture from the Redmond house was moved into the rooms, and on the day they returned Maureen lit a fire and scattered vases of flowers about the rooms to welcome Sarah and Joe home.

All new furniture was labelled Utility and made to a standard design, and to ensure fair distribution as it was so scarce couples were allocated dockets to use when they bought it.

Anne and John were able to buy a Utility dining table and chairs, and a wardrobe, all well made and in light wood, but they had insufficient dockets for any other furniture. From their old rooms they brought their bed, a chest of drawers, a small cupboard to serve as a sideboard, and a plain wooden kitchen table and two wooden kitchen chairs.

John's mother gave them two armchairs from the seven-piece suite in her parlour, and Anne and John felt that their house was well furnished. It was true that nothing matched, and the sitting room was still bare, but Gerry could use it as a playroom until they were able to furnish it.

There were fitted cupboards and shelves in the alcove beside the living-room fire, and John's father brought wood and fitted cupboards in the bedrooms and kitchen.

The sun shone and Anne was so happy that she sang all day as she worked in the house. Mrs Rooney, the next-door neighbour, told her, 'I can hear you singing. You're made up with your house, aren't you?'

'Oh, I am,' Anne exclaimed. 'I love it. Everything's so easy, and the clothes dry in no time in the garden and smell so sweet. The air's so lovely and fresh.'

'It was even better when we come here in 1934,' Mrs Rooney

said. 'There wasn't nothing where them houses are over the main road, only all fields and woods.'

'Is that when you came here – 1934?'

'Yes, we had rooms in a court behind Field Street before and I couldn't keep them clean. We was persecuted with fleas and bugs and cockroaches. I thought I was in Heaven when I come here. And we had the hot water and the boiler.' She laughed. 'I couldn't stop washing at first. The clothes were wore out.'

'We had two rooms in my dad's house,' Anne told her. 'We were very comfortable there, but this! The days aren't long enough to enjoy it.'

'They're not long enough for your feller anyway,' Mrs Rooney said with a smile. 'I seen him out digging the other night with his bike lamp beside him. He's going at the garden like someone demented, isn't he?'

'John never does things by halves,' Anne laughed. She could understand and approve of his absorption in the garden but was becoming resentful of his obsession with Gerry. She tried to make allowances, telling herself that John had missed the early months of the baby's life, but she often felt hurt and angry at the way he shut her out.

Although Anne was so happy, she missed the daily contact with her family and looked forward eagerly to John's return from work. Invariably, though, he went straight to the playpen or cot and picked up the child, and only after hugging and kissing him for several minutes could he spare time to greet her.

When she tried to tell him about the small happenings of her day, she was conscious that all his attention was focussed on his son and he was not listening to her.

Every night John insisted on bathing the baby and putting him to bed, and waved Anne away impatiently when she came to say goodnight to Gerry. She ignored him and kissed and cuddled the baby, and Gerry, who was an affectionate child, clung to her saying, 'Night night, Mama.'

It was a battle of wills every night as John looked pointedly at his watch and opened the book from which he read stories to Gerry until he fell asleep, but Anne was determined not to be intimidated into staying downstairs.

When Gerry was asleep John came downstairs, then either went straight out to work in the garden or went to one of the meetings connected with the various causes he was becoming involved with.

Anne told herself that it was only a small flaw in her happiness, and John would be more sensible about the baby when he had been home a bit longer. All her new neighbours admired Gerry and told her he looked a picture of health.

'He'll break some hearts when he's older,' Mrs Rooney predicted, and Anne agreed with her. Gerry was now nearly two years old, tall and sturdy, with bright blue eyes and fair curly hair, and a happy affectionate disposition.

Anne loved him so much that it was not easy for her to check him when he was naughty, but for the child's sake she was firm with him and tried to train him to be well-behaved and polite. She could do this while she was alone with him but when John was at home in the evenings or at weekends, he allowed the child to do whatever he wished.

If Anne protested he said impatiently, 'Leave him alone. He's only a baby.' Gerry quickly realised the situation and would look defiantly at his mother as he did the things she forbade, like swinging on the curtains and climbing, or snatching food, knowing John would only laugh at his antics.

Anne often lay awake at night worrying that Gerry was being spoiled or that she was too strict with him and wrong to resent John's absorption in the baby. I'm not jealous, she told herself, it's just that it seems unnatural. But other times she thought that she should be glad that John loved Gerry so much.

She would have liked to talk over her worries but was too loyal to confide in anyone and just hoped that time would alter the situation.

Their house lay near to the tram terminus and Anne often travelled back to Everton. There were very few shops on the estate, and she had been advised not to register with them but to leave her ration books where she had previously shopped. There she could be sure of obtaining various items 'off the ration', and under the counter cigarettes for John.

Bread rationing had been introduced in July, and the estate shop sometimes sold out, but Anne could always obtain her ration at the bakery in Everton, and sometimes an additional barmcake or a few rolls too.

Anne always visited her relatives on these trips, and in November Sarah told her that she was expecting a baby, due in late May. 'I wish Helen could start with another,' she said. 'I don't like talking to her about mine because I know she's longing so much for another one herself.'

'It's a shame she hasn't started another yet,' Anne agreed. 'Helen and Tony are such perfect parents.' She smiled at Sarah. 'Don't let it spoil your pleasure, though, Sar.'

'It won't,' Sarah said. 'Nothing will. Oh, Anne, I'm so excited. I hope it'll be exactly like Joe.'

'What does he say?'

'He hopes it'll be exactly like me,' Sarah admitted, laughing. 'It probably won't be like either of us. Gerry's not like either of you, is he?'

'No. He's more like your Mick than anyone else. I hope he'll be as clever.'

'Mick was a terrible handful, though,' Sarah said, smiling at the child who sat happily playing with pegs and an old box. 'Gerry's a good little boy.'

'No thanks to John,' Anne said sharply, then added quickly,

'I suppose he's bound to spoil Gerry a bit. He missed all his early months.' And Sarah agreed.

Anne was always warmly welcomed when she went to see her Aunt Carrie and Uncle Fred, and Fred announced that it was time he started the Easter parties again now that there was another generation growing up.

Bridie's twins were now ten years old, while Theresa had twin girls in addition to her two boys, and Shaun had a son. 'Not many from our family,' Anne said ruefully. 'Only Gerry and Moira, and Sarah's baby to come.'

'Plenty of time for more,' Fred said cheerfully. 'Why, you young ones are only just starting.'

'No sign of Eileen courting again?' Carrie said.

Anne shook her head. 'She just doesn't seem interested,' she said. 'She hasn't got over losing Whitey yet.'

'She often goes to our Theresa's,' Carrie said. 'Theresa says the trouble is Whitey was killed before she found out any of his faults, so now no one else measures up to him. Theresa tries to tell her all men have *some* faults.'

'Except me,' Fred said with a grin.

'Oh, *you*,' Carrie said. 'I wouldn't know where to start with yours.'

'I don't get so many dishes thrown at me these days though,' he said to Anne. 'I don't know whether she's learning to appreciate me or whether your aunt's worried about her aim now.'

'I can't spare the dishes,' Carrie retorted, but she rubbed Fred's balding head affectionately.

No one mentioned Maureen, but Sarah had told Anne that Chris and Maureen had met Bridie and Jack in a queue for a film, and Carrie and Fred on another occasion, but everyone had simply accepted him as a friend of Maureen's. His wife had refused to come back to Liverpool and was still in the nursing home, with Chris paying exorbitant fees for her.

'I'm sure there's nothing much wrong with her,' Sarah said. 'I believe someone told Chris she was seen on the front at Llandudno. I think he should call her bluff, but of course I can't say that to Maureen.'

'I suppose you can't,' Anne said. 'But I think Chris should do something, if only for Maureen's sake. Still, it's not our business, I suppose.'

'Maureen seems happy enough, anyway,' Sarah said.

Anne sometimes took the tram to Breckfield Park to see John's mother and grandmother and enjoyed these visits during the week far more than when John was with her at the weekend.

They were often invited for Sunday tea and always warmly welcomed by John's parents and grandmother. Sometimes all went smoothly, but on other occasions an argument between John and his father seemed to arise quite suddenly.

Anne could see that John was usually at fault. He seemed unable to take even the mildest disagreement with his point of view and immediately flew into a rage, several times flinging out of the house.

The first time this happened Anne was upset and ashamed and could only whisper, 'I'm sorry.'

Cathy hugged her. 'We're the ones who should be sorry, love,' she said gently. And Sally added, 'Yes. We're the ones who had the rearing of him.'

'I'm afraid I caused this,' Greg said. 'But I couldn't let that pass. There are good employers and Stan's one of them. John's got nothing to complain of.'

'Just forget about it, Greg,' Cathy said. 'Let's have our tea. I'm sure we're all ready for it.'

She kept a high chair in the house for Gerry and while she settled him into it, Sally pressed Anne's hand. 'Don't worry, girl,' she said. 'We're used to his moods. Let him walk them off until his stomach brings him home, and we'll forget him and enjoy our tea.'

John had the grace to look ashamed when he returned, and to apologise for his behaviour. His mother only said calmly, 'All right. Sit down and have your tea. I'll make a fresh pot.'

No one said anything more about the incident, and Cathy continued with her stories of the women she had worked with before the war. She told them well and there was much laughter, in which John and Anne joined, but Anne was unable to look at John or to speak to him.

There was extra warmth in the way Cathy and Sally hugged Anne as she left, and John's father gripped her hand and kissed her as he said goodbye. Gerry had fallen asleep and John was carrying him so Anne could avoid taking his arm.

She turned her head and looked out of the window of the tram, answering in monosyllables when he spoke to her. When they reached home she was still angry and when John had taken Gerry to bed and returned downstairs, he said impatiently, 'What are you sulking about now?'

'Sulking!' she said angrily. 'You've got a damned cheek! After the way you humiliated me and made a show of yourself in your mother's.'

'My parents accepted my apology,' he said. 'No cause for sulks from you.'

'Maybe that's the trouble,' she retorted. 'You've got away with too much. But I'm not standing for your tantrums!'

'That's enough,' John said in a loud hectoring voice. 'I don't want to hear any more.'

'Oh, don't you?' Anne began, but he interrupted her.

'That's enough, I said,' he shouted even more loudly. 'I won't hear another word.'

He turned and stormed upstairs and Anne called after him, 'Bully! You're not still in the Army, y'know.' But he ignored her and went into the bedroom, slamming the door.

Anne was trembling but busied herself putting away the homemade loaf and the cake that John's mother had given her, and putting out milk bottles. There was no sound from upstairs but she made a cup of tea for herself, the tears running down her face as she drank it.

It was the first time she could ever remember being spoken to so roughly. Childhood quarrels with her brothers and sisters had been mild affairs, soon over, and the older ones like Tony and Maureen had always been there, loving and protective, to look after her.

She had never before quarrelled like this with John either, but as she sipped her tea she thought bitterly, that that was only because she had never responded when he spoke rudely and overbearingly to her. I've been too soft, she told herself, just feeling hurt and too proud to say anything, but all that's going to change.

She wept afresh as she thought of all her grievances, and of the cutting remarks she could have made to John if he had stayed to hear them. I'd have told him he behaved like an ignorant lout, she thought, and a bad example to Gerry.

Gerry! She stood up and began to walk about the kitchen. That's something else that's going to change, she thought grimly. He's not going to have such a free hand with Gerry. I'll tell him I don't want the child to grow up like him.

Anne was reluctant to go to bed, to lie beside John, but there was no alternative. They had only one bed and not even a sofa. She thought briefly of sleeping in an armchair, but suddenly rebelled. Why should she be driven from her comfortable bed because her husband was unable to control his temper?

When she went up to Gerry in his cot and John in bed, both were sound asleep. Anne undressed quietly and slipped into bed, lying as far as possible from John and with her back turned to him.

For some time she lay awake thinking tearfully of the loving family she had left to marry him and brooding over every cross word or thoughtless act of John's since she had known him. I've been too meek, she decided, too anxious not to start a row. In future I'll tackle him right away when anything annoys me.

She was almost asleep when she suddenly thought, First catch your hare, as Mrs Beeton would say. John would probably have rushed away or refused to discuss the matter before she could sort things out with him. I'll do it though, one way or another, she vowed as she slipped into sleep.

Chapter Thirty-One

Anne woke several times during the night and lay awake thinking bitterly of John's behaviour, and consequently fell deeply asleep at about six o'clock and slept through the sound of the alarm at seven.

She woke to find John standing beside her, fully dressed and holding a cup of tea for her. He bent and kissed her. 'I'm sorry, Anne,' he said quietly. 'You were right. I shouldn't have behaved like that at my mum's.'

Anne sat up and he kissed her again. She slipped her arms round his neck. 'I'm sorry I yelled at you,' she said.

'Never mind. All forgotten now, eh?' he said, and Anne nodded. He stroked her cheek. 'I felt a worm when I saw your poor little tear-stained face, but you're happy now, aren't you?'

She smiled and he hugged her then went to the cot to kiss Gerry. 'I've given him a rusk,' he said before dashing off to work. Gerry had sucked the rusk until it was soft and was now rubbing it over his face and head, crooning happily.

Anne stayed in bed, sipping her tea and feeling pleased that the quarrel was over, but wishing that she had been able to talk things over with John. He seems to think the subject's closed now, and if I tackle him about the way he spoke to me, it might start another row, she thought, forgetting her brave plans of the previous night.

John's remark about her 'poor little tear-stained face' rankled with her too. Sometimes he's so damn' patronising, she mused, but then thrust these thoughts away and sprang out of bed, eager to begin the day.

She enjoyed Mondays. Her washing was always finished by midday and then she took Gerry to the Clinic to be weighed. She had made many friends among the young mothers who attended the Clinic, one in particular, Ina Baxter, whose daughter was born on the same day as Gerry.

The Catholic church was less than ten minutes' walk away and Anne had joined the Women's Confraternity there. The members met every Monday night for Benediction followed by a social evening in the church hall.

Anne was shy with strangers and glad to go with Mrs Rooney for her first visit, but soon she made friends among the younger women who eagerly discussed their children and all that affected them.

By the time John came home from work Anne had decided to forget the quarrel, and he made no reference to it. He took Gerry to bed while Anne cleared away the meal and washed up before preparing for the Confraternity meeting.

Many of the men on the estate had swopped cuttings as plants were separated in the autumn, and some more experienced gardeners had been giving advice to new gardeners. John suggested that this should be done on a more organised basis and that a gardening club should be formed.

There was general agreement, and as John had suggested the formation of the club, he was elected chairman.

That came later, but on this Monday night he had called a meeting in his house of anyone who was interested. He expected at most half a dozen men, and none had arrived when Anne left for church.

When she came home she was astounded to find the house

packed with men, all of whom seemed to be arguing at the tops of their voices about the Nuremberg trials of war criminals.

They all fell silent, looking sheepish when she appeared. 'Er, hello love,' John said. 'Er – there's more interest than we expected in the gardening club.'

'The gardening club?' she said, dimples appearing in her cheeks as she laughed heartily, and the men laughed too.

'I know it didn't sound like it,' John admitted. 'I put the wireless on for the news and there was something on about the trials.'

One of the older men said, 'Right then, lads. Thanks for the use of your house, Mrs. In mine next time, eh, John? A fortnight tonight?'

He agreed and the men began to move away, but Anne whispered to John, 'What about Gerry? We can't both be out.'

He clapped his hands. 'Just a minute, fellas,' he said. 'Tuesday suit you, Stan?' The older man agreed and John shouted, 'Tuesday suit everybody?'

'Yes. The missus is out on Mondays,' another man said, and the men trooped away, saying goodnight to Anne.

'Should I have offered them tea?' she said anxiously when the last man had gone. 'There were so many and we're right on the end of the ration.'

'No, they didn't expect it,' he said. He was rubbing his hands and looking delighted. 'Twenty-three, Anne. Twenty-three turned up. And yet if I hadn't suggested a club, they'd just have muddled along.'

'How did they all fit?' she said.

'All right. Con Rooney went next-door and brought a few chairs in. That's what they were taking out.'

'I didn't notice, I was so bewildered,' she said. 'What did you do?'

'Only elected a chairman and secretary and committee,' John said. 'I'm chairman, Stan's secretary and Con Rooney and two fellows from Brook Road committee members.'

'*Another* committee!' she exclaimed.

As soon as they arrived in the parish John had enrolled in the Catholic Young Men's Society and in the St Vincent de Paul Society, who raised funds for and visited the sick and poor of the parish. Within a very short time he had been elected to serve on the committee of both organisations.

'If I'm asked I can't refuse,' he said smugly, but Anne bit back the comment she was about to make. She hated to be out of friends with anyone, particularly with John, and preferred to shut out of her mind anything that worried her.

She saw Mrs Rooney the following day and they laughed together about the numbers in Anne's house the previous evening. 'I couldn't make out what was different when I got in from the Confraternity,' Mrs Rooney said. 'Until our Con come walking in with the chairs.'

'You should have heard the noise when I got in,' Anne said. 'It was like an Irish Parliament, everyone talking at once.'

'You wouldn't think they'd get that excited about gardening, would you?' Mrs Rooney said.

'It wasn't *gardening*,' Anne said. 'They were going on about the trials – the war criminals.'

'What would you do with them?' Mrs Rooney exclaimed. 'Fellas! Sweet God. You'd think they'd all be glad to forget about the war.'

'I know I am,' Anne said. 'I'm just glad it's all over.'

'It wasn't like this after the first war,' Mrs Rooney said. 'My fella never talked about it. None of them did. I think it was that bad they couldn't bear to talk about it. I never heard nothing about it until this lot started and the lads wanted to join up. Eddie was trying to talk them out of it and he told them a bit about the trenches.'

'They still joined though?' Anne said.

'Yes. You'll find that out with your own kids, girl. Nobody never takes no notice. They've got to find it out for themselves. Eddie told them, "I'll fight a German that comes to my door, to protect me own. But I'd never go to another country to fight to save the nobs' investments." He was a clever man, my Eddie,' Mrs Rooney said with a sigh.

Anne looked sympathetic. She knew that Mrs Rooney's husband had died in 1942. The two sons now at home had been away in the Army, two older sons were working in the Midlands, and her only daughter, once a stewardess on the Transatlantic run, was now married and living in America.

Their father had died too suddenly for them to see him before his death, but the four sons had come home for the funeral.

'I see your Con's on the committee,' Anne said, to change the subject. 'And John's the chairman. That's three committees he's on, the SVP, the CYMS, and now this.'

'He won't have time to do no gardening,' Mrs Rooney chuckled.

'I'd hate to be on a committee,' Anne said. 'But John enjoys it. I'm happy to be an Injun but I think he was born to be a Chief.' They both laughed and Mrs Rooney said comfortably, 'Well, I suppose we need Chiefs *and* Injuns. It's a good job people like John take these jobs on.'

Although the weather became cold and wet Anne was still very happy in her new house. She felt that she and John were settling easily into the community, and she liked her neighbours. A few of them were the original tenants who had been re-housed there after the slum clearance in the early thirties, but the majority were younger people who had moved into the houses immediately before or during the war.

With her talent for friendship Anne soon knew and became friends with most of her neighbours. 'It's because of Gerry,' she said to John. 'He breaks the ice because people stop me to ask

401

how old he is or something like that, and he shouts hallo to everyone.' They both looked fondly at the child, and he jumped up and down in his playpen shouting, 'Hello, hello, hello.'

The women of the parish took turns at cleaning the church, and Anne was on the rota and made friends among the church congregation too.

Anne was sorry to miss the Christmas Day services in their own parish, but the arrangements for Christmas had been made long before. She and John would take Gerry to Mass with her family and spend Christmas morning with them, then go to John's family for Christmas dinner and for the rest of the day.

Gerry was well behaved during the Mass, then pleased all the family with the delight he showed at presents from his grandfather, Maureen, Eileen, Stephen, and Sarah and Joe. He kissed each of them and Pat said, 'He's not like Theresa's lads. They'd do anything before they'd give you a kiss. Think it makes them look like sissies, I suppose.'

'Bridie's lads were the same,' Maureen said. 'And probably Gerry'll change when he's older. Not too much though, I hope,' she added, hugging the child.

'I don't like taking him away,' Anne whispered to Sarah, 'but we've promised to go to your mum's and it's only fair to go to each family in turn for Christmas dinner.'

'Never mind. Next year, please God, you'll be able to stay here and I'll take my baby to Mum's or vice versa,' Sarah said. 'It's lucky we're related to both families, isn't it?'

'Yes, and I warn you, you'll have everyone coming in the bedroom on Christmas Day to see your baby with its stocking,' Anne said, laughing. 'That's if you're still here in these rooms.'

'We will be,' Sarah said. 'We're happy here and we won't be able to afford a house until Joe qualifies.'

Joe was now training as a teacher. There was an acute shortage due to retirement of older men and the demands of the 1944

Education Act. A shortened course had been devised for teacher training which Joe was taking, and the 'dilutees' as they were known were usually excellent teachers. Joe decided that it was what he had always wanted to do, without realising it.

'Your baby'll have a warm welcome here, anyway,' Anne told Sarah. 'Everyone's dying for it.' She gave her an affectionate hug.

Tony and Helen arrived with Moira but only for a brief visit as Helen's mother was due to spend Christmas Day with them. Gerry and Moira greeted one another with cries of delight and Tony said quietly to Anne, 'She'd love a little brother or sister.'

'Plenty of time yet,' Anne said cheerfully. 'Uncle Fred reckons we'll all have full quivers as he calls it.'

'Let's hope he's right,' Tony said, looking happier.

Anne and John arrived at his mother's house for dinner at two o'clock and found a magnificent turkey in the centre of the table.

'Isn't it a beauty?' Cathy Redmond said. 'It was a gift from Greg's boss, Stan Johnson.'

'His boss!' John exclaimed. 'I thought Dad was a partner.'

'My senior partner then,' Greg said with a hint of impatience. 'A very generous gift anyway.'

'It certainly is,' said Anne. 'I don't know how you got it in the oven.'

Sally Ward laughed. 'That reminds me of the year we had a big goose for Christmas. You and Mary were only young, Cathy, but your dad brought in this big goose. He stood in front of it on Christmas Day, with the knife in his hand. "I don't know whether to carve it or fight it," he said.'

As always when his grandfather's name was mentioned, John's expression softened. 'Trust Grandad,' he said fondly. 'He had a joke for everything.'

After dinner they sat round a blazing fire and Anne said anxiously to Sally, 'I hope you haven't left yourselves short of coal with sending that to us?'

The weather was bitter and coal in short supply, but John's grandmother had sent two hundredweight of coal to them by a man who was passing near their house on a wagon.

'Not at all, girl,' Sally said. 'We're well stocked. When my house went the coal house roof fell in but the coal was safe underneath. The lads who cleared up were very good. They shifted nearly all the coal to Cathy's backyard.'

'They couldn't put it in our coalplace because it was full,' John's mother said with a smile. 'I was well trained by you, wasn't I, Mam?'

'Aye, well, I learnt in a hard school,' Sally said. 'When Lawrie was out of work and my poor father was lying ill, we hadn't got two ha'pennies to knock together and I was out of my mind sometimes trying to find money for coal for cooking and drying washing, apart from the warmth. As soon as we got on our feet I swore that I'd never see the back of my coalplace again.'

'And we never did,' Cathy said. 'Winter and summer the coalplace was always full.'

'But are you sure you've got plenty here in this house?' Anne said.

'Plenty, girl,' Sally told her. 'We left some for Bridie, but we could still fill this coalshed, couldn't we, Cath? And we don't have to rely on it for cooking now, with the gas stove.'

'Bridie's made up with your house,' Anne said. 'They were very cramped in that two-bedroom house now the children are growing up.'

'It was lucky we both had the same landlord,' Cathy agreed. 'Houses are so short ours would have been snatched up only the landlord agreed to let Bridie have Egremont Street and leave hers empty for him. He said he'd have been lynched otherwise, with so many people after a house.'

They all laughed and Anne said, 'I'll see Bridie tomorrow. You know we're all going to Fred and Carrie's. Carmel and Shaun and his wife are home for Christmas and Theresa will bring her tribe.'

'How are the twins settling down?' Cathy asked.

'Des seems all right. He's back working for Uncle Fred and he's clever with the leather, but Dom has a new job every couple of weeks. They're as mad as ever in some ways.'

'Won't be easy for them to settle down after being in the Commandos,' Greg said, and John said immediately, 'You could say that about anyone who's been in the forces.'

'No doubt,' his father said, seeming intent on lighting his pipe.

'You should see Carmel,' Anne said quickly. 'She was always so fat and her skin was bad but now! She's working on that fashion magazine in London and looks like someone out of *Vogue*, doesn't she, John?'

'Very sophisticated,' he agreed.

'I saw her when she was in the WRNS,' Cathy said. 'She suited the uniform.'

'Yes. That's when the ugly duckling became a swan,' Anne said, laughing.

Mick was home for Christmas and as Christmas Day 1946 was on Wednesday, arranged to stay until the following Sunday. All the family had been invited to Carrie's house on Boxing Day and Cathy arranged a small party of old friends for Mick on Saturday night.

'Are you sure we won't be too much of a crowd tomorrow?' Cathy said now to Anne, but she assured her that there was nothing her uncle and aunt liked better than a crowd.

They spent a happy day, with Gerry the focus of attention but still behaving well. 'I'm proud of him,' John said, as they sat on the tram on their way home, Gerry asleep on his knee, on Christmas Night.

'Yes, even when he was tired he was good,' Anne said, looking fondly at the sleeping child. 'Sarah says she hopes her baby will be as good.'

'It'll be spoiled if they stay there.'

'Why? Gerry wasn't,' Anne said, but for once John failed to respond to the challenge.

Anne had collected several Christmas cards which had been sent to the Fitzgerald house for them. 'People who don't know you've moved or don't know your new address,' Maureen said as she handed them to Anne.

She forgot about them until she reached home late on Christmas Night. The first one she took out had a name on the back, Mrs A. Kilmartin, and an address in Wiltshire. There was a card inside signed Kathleen and Arthur and a letter.

Anne glanced at the card looking puzzled and began to read the letter. 'Oh, John, it's Kathleen O'Neill. Remember her?'

'Vaguely,' he said, losing interest, but she was rapidly reading the letter.

'John, I feel awful,' she exclaimed. 'I wish I'd kept in touch. She had a nervous breakdown. She says that when I last saw her in Winwick Hospital she was on the borderline mentally, although they were treating her for physical injuries.' Anne began to read aloud.

'"Cormac's suicide and my mother's collapse pushed me over the edge mentally, I see now, although at the time I tied it in to something else. I had a sort of fixation on one of the doctors and when he left to marry and work in Leeds I completely collapsed . . .

'"It was a long dark night, Anne, a legacy of my childhood, and for a long time I couldn't bear to think of my past. I was moved from one hospital to another and finally to a hospital nine miles from here where I had wonderful treatment and was helped to confront my past. I remembered all the tensions, but also your

406

friendship and what it meant to me."

'Oh, John, I feel ashamed,' Anne said. 'I should have kept in touch.'

'So she's cured. Is that why she's written now?'

'Hang on. She says, "Arthur was a conscientious objector during the war and was sent to work on a farm near here. He visited the hospital and that's how we met. When I was cured we married and live here as he is still working on the farm. His parents are teachers in Newcastle who have been very kind to me.

"'I'm writing this more in hope than expectation that you will receive it, Anne. I hear that there is little left of Everton as I remember it, but perhaps there will be someone left who knows you and can forward this to you. I would so like to see you again, Anne, and for you to meet my wonderful husband."

'Oh, dear. I should have gone to see her again but it was such a bad time, the bombing and Mum so ill, and then someone said she'd been moved from Winwick.'

'She doesn't seem to blame you at all,' he said. 'Will you write to her?'

'Of course. Right away,' Anne said.

'*Right* away?' he said meaningfully, and Anne blushed.

'Not *right* away,' she said. She put the letter and cards away and they quickly locked up the house and went to bed.

They had decided that they needed some time before they had another baby, while they settled into the new house and saved a little money, but as Catholics the only method of birth control they could use was the rhythm method. This meant abstaining from intercourse except during a certain safe period each month and the safe period had occurred over Christmas time this month.

John was a tender and passionate lover and in his arms Anne could forget all her doubts. Love for him overwhelmed her and she felt that she could never be thankful enough that he was her loving husband and the father of her child.

The Boxing Day party was a big success. Fred went about rubbing his hands and exclaiming, 'The more the merrier' as more and more people arrived for it.

Bridie and Jack arrived early with Bridie's two tall stepsons and her twin boy and girl. Monica and Michael were ten years old now, and Michael was a tall, thin boy very like his stepbrother, Teddy. Monica was small and dainty, with flaxen hair and pale blue eyes.

'Looks as though butter wouldn't melt in her mouth, doesn't she?' Bridie said to Anne. 'But if there's any mischief going, milady's the one who's started it. She wraps the lads round her little finger.'

'No wonder you needed a bigger house, Bridie,' Anne said. 'The way the lads have grown.'

'I'm made up with your mother-in-law's house,' Bridie said. 'Mind you, I wouldn't have got it if I hadn't been leaving mine for someone else on his waiting list. People'd kill for a house the way things are. She's a lovely woman,' Bridie declared and looked over to where Sarah sat with Joe as usual close beside her, her hand clasped in his.

'She's a lovely girl too,' Bridie said. 'They haven't got a brass farthing while Joe's training but it doesn't worry them. They're in a world of their own.'

Anne looked at Sarah and Joe, then rather wistfully to where John stood deep in discussion with Tony and Shaun. Nothing would draw Joe away from Sarah, she thought, but then gave herself a mental shake. Tony and Shaun were not staying close to their wives either. It was Joe and Sarah who were exceptional, not herself and John.

She smiled tenderly as her mind went back to only a few hours earlier when she had been lying in John's arms, and to their tender lovemaking. As though her thought had reached him, he turned and looked at her and mouthed, 'All right?' Anne nodded happily and he turned back to Tony and Shaun.

Bridie had gone to talk to John's mother and grandmother and Jack to talk to Greg Redmond and Pat Fitzgerald. Theresa had taken Bridie's place beside Anne who told her how well she looked.

'I'm glad you think so,' Theresa said cheerfully. 'I've just found out I'm expecting again.'

'Congratulations!' Anne exclaimed. 'What would you like this time?'

'I don't mind,' Theresa said, 'but I hope it's not twins. Anyone tells you, Anne, that twins are less trouble than two babies, don't believe them. They're hard work, trust me. I thought you might have started again. Gerry'll be two next month, won't he?'

'We thought we'd get settled first,' Anne said. 'But now – I don't mind.'

'No. As long as the fellers pull their weight it's all right. I make sure Jim does his share, I'll tell you.'

Later Eileen played the piano and several people sang. Fred came to where Anne and her father stood together. 'Just like old times, isn't it?' he said happily.

'Yes, it's a great party, Uncle Fred,' Anne said, squeezing her father's hand, and as Fred moved on Pat smiled sadly at his daughter.

'Ah, well, Fred's right, I suppose, girl. Life goes on. I look round and see all these young ones coming along and growing up and it's how it should be.'

'"The hungry generations tread us down,"' Anne quoted and Pat said anxiously, 'No. There's none of them hungry, girl, thank God. You're all doing well.'

'We are, Dad,' she agreed. 'We've got a lot to be thankful for. We're all happy.'

'You always were, girl, and I hope you always will be. Happy Annie,' Pat said, giving her a hug and a kiss.

Chapter Thirty-Two

The party at the Redmonds' house on Saturday was on a much smaller scale as they had few relatives. The guests were mostly old friends and neighbours from the years in Everton.

Anne and John went to the house near Breckfield Park in early afternoon and Anne helped to make sandwiches and slice fruit cake while John took Gerry upstairs and coaxed him to sleep.

'I miss my big kitchen for a sitdown meal,' Cathy said to Anne, 'but if we lay everything out people can help themselves.'

'There's plenty of food anyway,' Anne said. 'And some real treats that haven't been in the shops for years.'

'Yes. Those parcels from America were a godsend,' Cathy agreed.

Peggy Burns, who had been Sally's next-door neighbour until their houses were bombed, was the first to arrive, closely followed by another old neighbour, Josie Meadows.

'God Almighty, Sally!' Peggy exclaimed. 'I never seen such a spread.'

'We got parcels from America from Mary and Sam,' Cathy said. 'And parcels from our Kate and Gene and his family too. I told them they shouldn't now the war's over but they said they knew we still had rationing.'

'Too true it is,' Peggy said. 'I believe we're going to get less bacon and more sugar in the New Year. Mr Strachey's going to announce it.'

'It's the bread units that get me down,' Josie said.

She turned to Anne. 'My married daughter's living with me,' she said, 'and her lads are terrors for jam butties. I'm sure they've got hollow legs.'

'Is that Edie – the married daughter?' Anne asked. Sally had told her that Josie's husband had deserted her for another woman and the married daughter, Edie, had tracked him down and thrown an aspidistra at the woman.

Josie shook her head and pretended to whistle. 'Oh, no,' she said. 'Our *Edith* has got a posh house in Bebington over the water. They don't have no jam butties there. It's jam in cut-glass dishes to match the accent, and bread like wafers. Proper Lady Muck she is now.'

Anne smiled, thinking of the aspidistra, and Josie went on, 'No. It's our poor Sophie that lives with me. Lost her husband two weeks before the war ended – left with two little lads, but she's all right with me.'

'I'm sure she is,' Anne said. 'You've been a friend of Mrs Redmond's for a long time, haven't you?'

'Cathy? Yes, since we were young girls. She fell on her feet when she married Greg Redmond, but she deserves every bit of luck she's had. She's been a true friend to me, Cathy has, and never no different, no matter how she got on. Did you ever meet the other one, Mary?'

'No. She's been in America since before I met Sarah. I think she came home just before I started at the shop.'

'Well, you haven't missed nothing,' Josie said. 'She was another one like our Edie with her big ideas. Her and Cathy was like chalk and cheese, and she wasn't fit to tie Cathy's shoe laces for all she thought so much of herself.'

'I think she's lovely,' Anne said, looking over to where her mother-in-law stood, flushed and smiling, pouring tea from a huge teapot. 'She made me very welcome, and so did Mrs Ward. They all did. I think I'm very lucky.'

'Aye, Sally Ward has a heart of gold,' Josie said. 'She was the one to turn to in trouble, and Lawrie her husband. Did you know him?'

'No, I didn't,' Anne said regretfully. 'I wish I had known him because John idolised him and we can't talk about him, not really.'

'Everyone thought the world of Lawrie,' said Josie. 'My old ma used to say God broke the mould after he made Lawrie. It was a saying the old ones had. My old ma didn't have a good word for many people but she did for him.'

Anne looked over at John wishing that he was with her to hear these words but he was with Mick and a group of school friends with whom Mick had kept in touch.

Gerry had woken and Anne brought him downstairs. Cathy and Sally were still urging people to eat more, and when it was clear that everyone had eaten enough they all moved into the sitting room. Gerry was fully awake now and running about, with John beaming proudly at him.

'He's the image of your Mick,' Peggy announced. 'I hope he's better behaved, Cathy.'

'I was a model child,' Mick protested and everyone began to talk of his exploits when he was a child.

'You had your mam and dad's hearts scalded,' Peggy declared. 'I never thought she'd live to see you grow up. I thought she'd be wore out.'

'Say something, Mum. I'm being slandered,' he cried.

'Slandered!' Cathy said, laughing. 'You're being flattered. Peggy hasn't said the half of it.'

There was general laughter, and Mick wound up the gramophone and put some dance music on. There was no room to dance but the music made a pleasant background to the conversation.

The new neighbours of the Redmond family mingled happily with old friends from Everton, and Greg and Mick poured beer for the men and sherry for the ladies.

Everyone was in harmony and Anne was enjoying herself. John was with a group of young men in the corner of the room when suddenly voices were raised. John had recently joined the Peace Pledge Union and now was saying fiercely, 'Do you know what happened when those atomic bombs were dropped? The devastation? The thousands and thousands of people who were just wiped out? And it'll go on and on. People will be dying for years to come from the effects.'

Some of the other young men were disagreeing with him but John raised his voice again. 'It was an offence against civilisation. A disgrace to humanity.'

Suddenly he was interrupted. Peggy Burns had been sitting in a low chair. Now she seemed to leap up to confront John.

'They was Japs, wasn't they?' she screamed at him. 'I wish they'd all been killed, every last one of them. Wiped off the face of the earth. What about my Michael? A fine big lad – and he was four and a half stone after they'd finished with him. Four and a half stone!'

John knew about Peggy's son who had returned broken in mind and body from a Japanese prison camp but he said stubbornly, 'Two wrongs don't make a right.'

'Japs! You're worrying about Japs being killed?' Peggy accused. 'Easy to see you wasn't there. He'll never get over it, my poor lad, and all the others what was killed by them. If I got me hands on them I wouldn't leave one alive so don't you talk soft, John Redmond. You was always a fool.'

She burst into tears and there was a stunned silence until Cathy put her arm round Peggy and drew her out of the room. John looked round at all the shocked faces then followed his mother and Peggy. Mick picked up a record.

414

'Here you are, Billy,' he said to one of the young men. 'Change the record.' There was uncertain laughter until Billy read from the label, 'I'm Painting the Clouds with Sunshine' and there were cries of 'Good choice'.

Everyone began to talk and pretend that nothing had happened but Anne sat shrinking into a chair, feeling bitterly ashamed. She felt that she should have gone to John but she was too upset and too sorry for Peggy to follow him.

The next moment she heard the slam of the front door and peeping through the curtain beside her saw him walking down the path. She shrank even further into the chair, keeping her head down and hoping that no one would speak to her. Fortunately she was shielded by a girl who sat on the arm of the chair, talking to someone who sat at her feet.

Suddenly she was aware of Mick who had slipped into the space by the window, close to her. 'Hello, Anne,' he said. 'John gone walkabout?' She tried to smile.

'I haven't heard it called that before.'

'Oh, he's an old hand at it,' Mick said easily. 'He saved many a punch-up with me by doing his disappearing act and it stopped Dad from murdering him many a time.'

'I thought it was a recent thing,' she said.

'Oh, no. Ever since he was a kid,' Mick said airily. 'A bit frustrating when you want to have something out with him, and hard on the shoe leather, but better for all concerned in the end.'

Anne immediately felt more cheerful. Mick seemed to understand, she thought, and his casual attitude made John's behaviour seem less important.

'Very fond of my grandad, our John,' Mick was saying quietly. 'They both wanted to set the world to rights, but John never heard the fable of the tortoise and the hare. Grandad was content to work quietly, helping people in his own neighbourhood, and when he tackled bigger issues he did it in such a reasonable way he got things done.'

'John's so impatient and he gets so worked up about things,' Anne said. 'Yet he says himself things are so much better for ordinary people now.' She felt no disloyalty in saying this to Mick, who was obviously fond of John.

'That's true. A lot of the things Grandad hoped for have happened now, but John will always find fresh causes. Always riding out on a white horse in the cause of right,' Mick said, smiling. 'But sometimes he's like Don Quixote tilting at windmills.'

Anne laughed aloud and he squeezed her shoulder. 'So don't worry,' he said. 'One adult cannot take responsibility for another. Everyone must be responsible for how they behave, no one else.'

He grinned at her and stood up. 'Where's the offspring?'

'Creating chaos in the kitchen, no doubt,' Anne said, laughing, and stood up. 'I'd better see what he's doing and tell him to stop.'

She went into the kitchen, feeling more lighthearted than she would have believed possible a short time before. Gerry was sitting on Peggy Burns' knee and she was feeding him with jelly. 'By God, this fellow's got a long drop, Anne,' she said. 'This is his third dish.'

'He never knows when he's had enough,' Anne agreed, relieved that Peggy was so friendly. She showed no trace of tears and nothing was said about the incident, but later Anne took advantage of a quiet moment to say softly to her, 'I'm so sorry John upset you, Mrs Burns. I'm sure he didn't mean to.'

No matter how much she agreed with Mick, she felt that she must apologise to Peggy Burns for John.

'Don't you worry, girl,' said Peggy. 'I shouldn't have flew off the handle like that, but it's just with our Michael, y'know.'

'How is he?' Anne asked sympathetically.

'He's still in hospital, but he's got shifted down to Walton so we can visit him now,' Peggy said. 'I think he's putting a bit of weight on, only he gets these nightmares.'

Sally Ward had come to the table and she put her hand on

Peggy's shoulder. 'He'll get over them, Peg. Don't worry. It'll take time but he's on the mend now.'

'Mend now,' Gerry repeated, and while they were all exclaiming about his cleverness John appeared in the doorway. He walked over to Peggy. 'I'm sorry, Mrs Burns,' he said. 'I didn't think of them as Japanese. I just thought – you know – people.'

'Aye, well, I suppose I'm a bit on edge like with Michael or I wouldn't have flew at you like that. Eh, this lad of yours can't half eat.'

Gerry held out his arms to John and Anne said quickly, 'Mind, John. He's all sticky.'

He picked the child up and held him at arm's length while Anne brought a wet flannel and wiped him.

'You don't want jelly all over your suit,' said Sally.

'No, it's the only one I've got,' he said, smiling at Anne, but she busied herself with Gerry. Everyone's making it easy for John, she thought grimly, but I'm going to have this out with him if I have to lock the doors to keep him in while I do it.

Gerry suddenly yawned and closed his eyes, and Anne was glad to make his sleepiness an excuse to leave without going back into the sitting room.

They said goodbye to Mick who was leaving the following day and he kissed Anne warmly. 'Don't forget what I said,' he whispered. 'You're only responsible for yourself. Let John paddle his own canoe.'

'I will,' Anne said quietly. She grinned. 'And tilt at his own windmills.'

Peggy Burns kissed her too. 'John's a good lad, for all his queer ideas,' she said. 'He's always been a good son to his mam, and he'll make you a good husband, girl.'

'Thanks, Mrs Burns,' Anne said, hugging her.

Later, as they walked to the tram, she said to John, 'I like Mrs Burns.'

'So do I,' he said. 'I was sorry I upset her. She's had a hard life, and she was bombed out on the same night as Grandma.'

'She had a lot of trouble even before that, your mum told me,' said Anne. She braced herself for a discussion of John's behaviour, but before she could speak he suddenly chuckled. 'Peggy'd have made a good spy though,' he said. 'She always gets information before anyone else. Did you hear her about the bacon ration?'

'Yes, and the sugar ration going up.'

'I'll bet Mr Strachey'll announce it soon, but God knows how Peggy found out. I'm sure the Minister of Food doesn't correspond with her,' said John.

'Stranger things have happened,' Anne said, laughing.

The chance of discussion had passed, but Anne hoped the row with Peggy had given John the necessary jolt, and thankfully abandoned her plans for a showdown.

John attended committee meetings several evenings a week, but the weather was too bad for gardening so he spent more time with Anne. They held a family gathering for Gerry's second birthday in January and John was the perfect host, and even seemed to be trying to be less indulgent with Gerry.

He was still a happy, sunny-natured child, but was growing daily more mischievous as he grew taller and stronger. He could open doors by standing on a stool, and easily open cupboard doors and scatter the contents over the floor.

'This is only natural at this age,' Anne told John. 'We'll just have to be one step ahead of him.' But this was harder than they expected. John fixed wedges across the doors, but Gerry soon learned how to move them, and although matches and many other things were put out of his reach, he managed to climb on to the kitchen table and reach them.

When he had climbed for a box of matches and started a small fire in a cupboard full of newspapers, Anne smacked him and John made no protest. 'He's got to learn for his own sake,' she said, and was surprised when John agreed with her.

Gerry was still John's darling, though, and he bathed him and put him to bed every night, and kept him with him as much as possible.

Anne felt excluded sometimes but accepted the situation and told herself that at least John was not frustrating her efforts to bring Gerry up the right way now.

John was interested in everything that was happening in the world, and discussed events eagerly with Anne. The *Liverpool Echo* was delivered every evening and she tried to find time to glance through it before John came home, and to listen to news bulletins.

She took a weekly magazine, too, and the advice to young married women given in it was always to discuss a husband's interests with him. Anne thought it was good advice, but she sometimes wished that John was not interested in so much. The husbands in the magazine seemed only to be interested in 'business'.

John was very excited when the coal industry was nationalised in January 1947. 'No more greedy owners drawing fortunes from the mines, while men are being paid starvation wages and often losing their lives to make those fortunes,' he told Anne exultantly. 'Miners will get a living wage now, and there'll be money spent to make the pits safe.'

Gerry was in bed and Anne sat at one side of the fire knitting while John sat opposite her, reading a newspaper. Her eyes were heavy with tiredness. It was impossible to relax for a moment while Gerry was awake, and that day he had not slept at all.

She tried to concentrate on what John was saying and make sensible replies, but she felt too tired and sleepy. 'Coal is a resource anyway,' John was saying, 'it belongs to the nation and should be used for the benefit of everyone.'

He began to read aloud from the newspaper but the next thing Anne knew he was putting a cup of tea beside her.

'Oh, John, I must have fallen asleep,' she said remorsefully. 'I'm sorry, love. I suppose it's the warmth of the fire, and then Gerry's been a little fiend today. Into one thing after another.'

John crouched down beside her and put his arms about her. 'And then you have to listen to me going on,' he said. 'That's really what sent you to sleep.'

'It wasn't,' she protested. 'Honestly, John, I *am* interested, but I'm just so tired.'

'I know, love,' he said. 'Gerry's one body's work, as Grandma would say. I'm just so thrilled about all that's happening now – all the things we hoped for coming true at last. Makes me think about Grandad.'

Anne smiled and kissed him then John said suddenly, 'Your tea! Typical. I bring you a cup of tea and talk until it goes cold. I'll get you a fresh one.'

He went out whistling and Anne looked lovingly after him. She felt so happy these days that she was almost afraid that it was all too good to last. The tiffs with John rarely happened now, and they had not had one where he had gone 'walkabout' since Christmas.

It had probably been just a settling down time as they adjusted to each other after the war, Anne thought optimistically, and everything would be perfect from now on.

In May Sarah's baby was born and brought joy to all the family. She had booked into the Maternity Hospital so only Joe was allowed to visit, but he brought enthusiastic reports of how wonderful the baby was and how well Sarah looked.

She was discharged after ten days and everyone was delighted with the baby. He was small but perfect, with dark hair and eyes, like a tiny miniature of Joe.

'You got your wish, Sarah,' Anne said when she saw the baby. 'He's the image of Joe.'

'Yes, and of your brother who died,' Sarah said, 'and of you and Maureen. I hope he grows up like you.'

Anne kissed her impulsively. 'With parents like you and Joe he's bound to be happy anyway.'

'We've decided to add Patrick to his name,' Sarah said. 'You don't think it'll be too much of a mouthful? David Joseph Patrick Fitzgerald?'

'No, I think it's nice,' Anne said. 'I'll bet Dad's pleased.'

'Yes, he was,' said Sarah. 'He brought the photograph of Patrick and held it by David and the likeness was uncanny except that David can't smile yet.' She drew back the shawl in which the baby was wrapped, and smiled at him lovingly.

The next moment they heard voices, and Sarah's mother and grandmother came into the room. 'We were at the shops and couldn't resist coming for another look,' Cathy Redmond said. Anne had been holding the baby. She handed him to Cathy, and Sally Ward produced a lollipop for Gerry. 'What do you think of your little cousin?' she said, but he was more interested in the lollipop.

'I've just been telling Anne about adding Patrick to his name,' Sarah said. 'She likes the idea, don't you, Anne?'

'Yes. You know Patrick was only six when he died, about eleven years before I was born, but he always seemed very real to me. His photograph on the dresser was one of the earliest things I remember, and Dad always mentioned him in the family prayers.'

'I think we'll start family prayers when David's old enough,' Sarah remarked.

'Ours at home stopped when everyone was scattered with the war,' Anne said. She laughed. 'No point in us starting them. John's rushing off to meetings so often, or he's late home.'

'He doesn't work late, does he?' Cathy said.

'No, he gets involved listening to speakers at the Pier Head, or the Catholic Evidence Guild on the bombed site of Lewis's.'

'John listening! That doesn't sound like him,' Sally said dryly, and Anne laughed.

'He does get involved sometimes,' she admitted. 'He was in an argument last week with one of the hecklers, but the Evidence Guild man told him to leave it to them. He said they can discuss reasonably without losing their tempers. John told me he hadn't lost his temper, he was just trying to convince the man.'

'I can imagine! Like a tank rolling over him,' Sally said. They all laughed but Anne was glad when Cathy changed the subject by saying that Peggy Burns had told her that Lewis's was to be rebuilt. Lord Woolton would announce it. 'If Peggy says so it's true,' Sally said. 'I don't know where she gets her information but she's always right.'

Joe came in carrying a pile of books and papers which he put down and went to kiss Sarah. 'I found I could do this at home,' he explained. 'How do you feel, love?'

'Fine,' she said. 'And David's been as good as gold.'

Joe greeted Sarah's mother and grandmother, and Anne. 'What do you think of his extra name?' he asked as Cathy handed the baby to him. They all agreed that they liked it, and Cathy said, 'Mick says the initials should look good on a briefcase.'

'Trust Mick,' Sarah said. 'How are you getting on with the telephone, Grandma?'

Mick had arranged for the telephone to be installed to keep him in touch with the family, but Sally was nervous about using it.

'I'm getting used to it,' she said now. 'And it *is* useful. He'll be able to tell us what time he'll be home at the weekend.'

The baby's baptism was to take place on the following Sunday and Anne and John were to be his godparents. Mick was coming home for it, and Maureen had made a christening cake and helped Sarah to organise a small family party after the baptism.

On Saturday Mick arrived home and came up to visit Anne and John. He brought a large coloured ball and some toy cars for Gerry, a bottle of perfume for Anne and a box of one hundred cigarettes for John.

'I went over to Paris a few weeks ago,' he explained casually.

'Your business must be doing well,' Anne said.

'It's booming, Anne. We can't believe it, the way the money's rolling in. Neil, y'know, my partner, has bought a pre-war Daimler. Smashing car but it guzzles up the petrol ration. I've got my name down for a new car but there's none to be had yet.'

'You think plastics is the thing to be in then?' asked John.

'Well, that's what we've found,' Mick said cheerfully. 'We took a chance and it's paid off. As Neil says, nobody ever made a fortune working for someone else.'

Maureen had invited Chris Murray to the baptism, the first time that he had attended a family party, and Anne felt that she should explain about him to Mick.

'He's married but his wife's been an invalid for years,' she said. 'Maureen and him have been friends for ages but . . .'

'Platonic friends,' Mick interrupted. 'We used to hear a lot about platonic friendship before the war, didn't we?'

'I'm not quite sure what it means,' Anne confessed.

'Just friendship between a man and a woman,' Mick said airily. 'Good idea really. If they're not free to marry they can still have a companion for going to the pictures or dancing or whatever. Do you get out together much?'

'Not often,' Anne admitted. 'A friend of mine, a girl I meet in the Clinic, sits with Gerry sometimes while we go to the pictures, and I do the same for her.'

'We're quite happy to stay in, aren't we, Anne?' John said. 'With the garden and things to do in the house and so forth.' She smiled and agreed, too proud to remind him while Mick was there how often she stayed in alone while he was out at meetings.

Later when Mick had gone John said thoughtfully, 'I don't think he thinks much of me as a husband. That crack about us going out.'

'I don't think it was a crack,' Anne said. 'He was only asking.'

'Hmm. He gave me an earful when he was at home at Christmas, y'know. When I went down on my own on the Sunday morning to see him off, after I had a bit of a row with Peggy Burns on the Saturday night.'

'You never told me!' Anne exclaimed.

John shrugged. 'Well, he was going on about you chiefly. Said I'd upset you and I wasn't being fair to you when I went for a walk after a row to think things over. Going walkabout, he called it! Be a man and stand your ground, he said. Supposed to be a joke but I think he meant it.'

He looked so indignant that Anne burst out laughing. 'He's a case, isn't he? But I like your Mick. I can imagine him getting up to some of the tricks I've heard about, but I think it might have been that he was curious about things and more advanced than people realised.'

'He's clever all right,' John said. 'He could run rings round everybody at the College, but d'you know they discovered he has a photographic memory? He can look at a page of writing and remember everything on it.'

'Gosh, I hope Gerry inherits that from him,' Anne exclaimed. She was smiling as they cleared up and prepared for bed. So *that* was why John had stopped going walkabout, she thought, chuckling to herself as she thought of Mick lecturing him.

The christening was a happy occasion and Joe's family in particular were pleased at the choice of names. Patrick's photograph had been cleaned up and re-framed after being damaged in the bombing and Maureen had put it in a prominent position near the christening cake.

'We've got the name Patrick in three generations now, Dad,'

she said to her father who was sitting in his armchair with the baby on his knee.

They had all been out into the big backyard while Mick took photographs with a German camera he had acquired. He took a family group, then Sarah and Joe with the baby, then one with Anne and John with them, and finally one of Anne and John as godparents with the baby.

Anne held the baby and John slipped his arm round her and smiled down at her. During the rest of the day he stayed close to Anne, helping her to food and including her in every conversation he had. He's trying to show Mick what a good husband he is, she thought, inwardly amused.

Gerry had hurled himself at Moira as soon as he saw her, and now the two children played together, watched over by Helen and Tony. Moira was nearly old enough to start school but Helen's hopes of another baby were still unfulfilled.

Suddenly, as the children played, Gerry slipped and banged his head. He began to roar and instantly John snatched him up and said angrily to Moira, 'Be more careful. He's only a baby.' Moira had her mother's gentle nature and shrank back at his fury while Tony, as angry as John, jumped to his feet.

Before anything else could be said or done, John's grandmother appeared and gave Moira a piece of chocolate and one to Gerry, who instantly ceased his roaring. John mumbled, 'Sorry,' looking shamefaced, and carried Gerry to Anne.

Sally said quietly, 'That soon shut Gerry up, didn't it? He's like his father, all noise.'

Helen smiled and Sally said to Moira, 'That's a pretty dress, love. Did Mummy make it?'

Moira looked at her mother and Helen said, 'No, I bought it. I'm afraid I'm hopeless at sewing.'

'It's very pretty and well made anyway,' Sally said.

Tony had still looked angry, even after John's apology, but

Helen laid her hand on his and now he smiled at Sally. 'Do you miss Everton, Mrs Ward?' he asked.

'I miss it as it was,' she said. 'But it's all so changed now and so many people gone from it. We're very happy in the new house.'

'Anne said it's a lovely bright house,' Helen said, and Sally agreed.

Someone came to claim her and when she moved away Tony said, 'She was very quick and very tactful, wasn't she? I nearly punched John then.'

'I was annoyed myself,' Helen said. 'But I think he's just hotheaded. He doesn't stop to think.'

'He'd better learn to curb his tongue,' Tony said, but he had always been good friends with John and added tolerantly, 'He's just crazy about Gerry, that's all.'

Anne was fortunately unaware of the incident. She had taken plates through to the scullery, and although she heard Gerry's cries, by the time she returned to the kitchen John was carrying him towards her. Gerry's roars had stopped and he was eating a piece of chocolate.

'What happened?' she asked.

'He banged his head and Grandma gave him chocolate,' John said, and Anne sat Gerry on her knee and resumed her conversation with Maureen.

After a few minutes John took Gerry into the yard. Anne looked at Joe, who was sitting cradling his baby in his arms and gazing adoringly into its face. Is he going to be like John is with Gerry? she wondered. She was just wondering whether she should warn Joe not to shut Sarah out when he lifted his head and looked at Sarah and she looked back at him, such love in their eyes that it seemed almost as though they touched.

I'll save my breath, Anne thought, feeling a pang of envy, quickly dismissed. John and I are happy too, she told herself. Circumstances were just different for us with Gerry, that's all.

Chapter Thirty-Three

Anne had replied to the letter from Kathleen O'Neill, or Kilmartin as she was now, and since then they had exchanged several letters and snapshots. Kathleen sent a snapshot of herself and her husband and her nine-month-old son at the gate of a pretty cottage.

Anne was pleased to see that Kathleen looked well and happy. Her husband was a tall, thin man wearing glasses and a pleasant expression, and the baby was a bonny little boy.

'I didn't expect Arthur to look like that,' Anne said to John. 'He doesn't look like a farmworker, does he?'

'He looks like a man of principle, the type who would be a conscientious objector,' John said. 'He seems to like the farm work, though, according to that letter.'

'I'd like to see her,' Anne said, 'but it's too far to travel while we've both got young children. I'm glad she's happy at last, though.'

Anne had sent a snapshot of herself and John with Gerry, and news of their families and old schoolfriends. She was surprised when Kathleen wrote: 'So your dream came true too, Anne. I remember you "carried a torch" for John Redmond even in the days when I knew you.' And I thought no one knew how I felt about him, Anne thought ruefully.

She still went to Everton at least once a week to shop and to visit her family, and Sarah came often to visit her. David was a good baby, and slept in Gerry's outgrown pram while the girls sat in the back garden.

John had laid out the garden with a grass plot surrounded by a narrow border near the house, and the rest of the space given over to vegetables. Gerry played on the grass as they talked and Anne said one day, 'I think I'll have to give up gardening until Gerry's older.'

'But I thought you liked it,' Sarah said.

'I do. At first I sort of looked after the flowers and John the veg, but he's more or less taken over the front garden now.'

'It does look lovely, the front garden.'

'Yes. Much better than when I was doing it,' Anne said cheerfully. 'You see, if I was working in it, people would stop to talk and I'd leave the weeding to chat to them. If anyone stops to talk to John he just says "How do" and goes on with what he's doing. And the garden's a sort of showpiece for him being the chairman of the gardening club.'

'How's the club going?' Sarah asked.

'Oh, thriving. They've got the use of a room in the parish hall now there's so many of them. John's gardening before he goes to work very often, because he's out at night, and I get up at the same time and get my washing done.'

'But couldn't you have this part of the back garden for yourself?' said Sarah.

'I do,' Anne said, laughing. 'That's why I say I'll have to give up. Gerry pulls the plants up to see what's at the other end. All these pleasures in store for you, Sarah!' But she only smiled.

Stan Johnson had introduced a five-day week for his employees, and Anne and John took advantage of the Friday night finish to spend a weekend in a boarding house in Llandudno.

The weather was perfect, and Gerry was delighted with the sand and the amusements. Anne and John enjoyed the weekend, but when they were on the train returning home, he suggested that they could have enjoyed it at home just as much.

'We could have taken Gerry to the shore at New Brighton or Crosby, and still slept in our own bed.'

'But I'd still have to plan and cook the meals,' she objected. 'And clean up at home.'

'Yes, but I could help with all that,' he said airily. And Anne thought, Yes, if you weren't out in the garden or talking to a fellow who'd called to see you – but she said nothing.

In July Theresa's baby was born, a daughter whom she named Ciara after her mother. 'But I thought Aunt Carrie's name was Caroline,' Anne said when Theresa told her. Theresa laughed. 'Could you imagine Grandma Houlihan picking a name like Caroline?' she said. 'Mum's name is Ciara Majella, after St Gerard Majella would you believe? My baby's going to get the proper name though – Ciara.'

'I know Mum's name was Julia, but what about Aunt Minnie's? Do you know?' asked Anne.

Theresa laughed again. 'Wait for it,' she said. 'Mary Magdalen! Talk about inappropriate!'

'Moaning Minnie suited her better,' Anne said.

A party was to be held at Fred and Carrie's house after Ciara's christening and Anne looked forward to it with mixed feelings. What would happen with John this time? she wondered.

Two of the committee men from the gardening club had been round to see his vegetables one night and come in for a cup of tea and a sandwich afterwards. The talk had soon turned to the Dominion status of India and Pakistan, and the appointment of Viscount Mountbatten as Governor-General of India, and Mr Jinnah as Governor-General of Pakistan.

John had argued that an Indian should have been appointed Governor-General and the argument had become heated. Even when one of the men had tried to change the subject by talking about the ending of the British mandate in Palestine, John took the opposite view to the others.

Anne, sitting quietly knitting, felt irritated by it all. Why was John always out of step? she thought. And anyway, wasn't there enough nearer home for them to be worrying about? She hoped that he would avoid these topics at the christening and was relieved that Mick would be home for the weekend. He'll keep John in check, she thought.

In the event all went well and it was one of the most successful of Fred's parties.

Anne and John were still avoiding another pregnancy for Anne by keeping to the 'safe period' and one had occurred shortly after their weekend away.

Three of the nights had been wasted because John went as a delegate to a weekend conference at Cambridge, which meant that he was away from home on the Friday and Saturday nights and so exhausted on Sunday night that he fell asleep as soon as he was in bed.

On the Monday Anne went to the Clinic with her friend Ena who had a baby of three months old. Anne only took Gerry there now for the free orange juice and vitamin tablets which were available for toddlers and today found a different nurse there, a big buxom woman.

A woman Anne knew slightly was there with her seventh child, and when he was being weighed said to the nurse, 'Some people are being real nasty about us having another one. They talk as if me husband was a sexual maniac, but it's just he gets a result every time.'

'Don't let that worry you,' the nurse boomed. 'Anyone else says that tell them that well-trodden ground never bears grass.'

There was laughter from the waiting women and Ena whispered to Anne, 'It must be true. See Tricia there. She told me they never miss a night and she's only got two kids. Hannah who's with her said if it was up to her husband, they'd never do it.'

Anne felt shocked at the public discussion but smiled vaguely and Ena went on, 'Fancy a woman starting it. I'm only too glad if Harry just goes asleep.' Fortunately Ena was called before Anne needed to reply. She thought it was a private matter between husband and wife, and would never have discussed the lovelife of herself and John.

Nevertheless, she wondered what Ena would say if she knew that she and John kept their lovemaking to a week or so in the safe period each month, and John had been away for most of the recent period.

It's not as if he's like Hannah's husband, Anne thought. We daren't kiss and cuddle in bed for the rest of the month because one thing leads to another and we can't stop. We can only manage by going to bed separately and saying goodnight downstairs.

His committees must be very important to him, she thought resentfully, but was ashamed of the thought when she reached home. John was at home and had brought in her washing and folded it, and made the preparations for the meal.

'I had a nose bleed while Stan was in the office,' he explained, 'and he told me to go home. I was all right in no time but I didn't argue.'

He produced a bag of her favourite sweets, buttered brazils. 'I swopped some cigs for sweet coupons,' he said. 'I got a penny bar of Cadbury's for Gerry too but I've hidden it till you think he should have it.'

It was a warm sunny day and they sat in the garden, sipping glasses of lemonade. Anne leaned back in her chair and stretched luxuriously. 'Gosh, this is the life,' she said. 'Our "lines have fallen in pleasant places", John, haven't they?'

'A quotation for everything, haven't you?' he said, smiling affectionately at her.

'I'm made up I've found the Public Library in the village,' she said. 'It's a lovely walk up there, and it's really well stocked.'

Gerry had fallen asleep, and Anne and John lay back in their chairs with closed eyes, enjoying the peace and the sunlight falling on their upturned faces.

'How did it go at the Clinic?' he asked idly.

'Very well,' said Anne. An innate delicacy prevented her from telling him of the nurse's comments, but she repeated some of the gossip. 'Hannah's eldest boy should have left school in July, but he's had to stay on until he's fifteen.'

'But surely she's glad he's having an extra year?' John exclaimed. '*You* think it's right the school leaving age is raised, don't you?'

'Yes. I know this is one of the things you were fighting for before the war, John, but it's a bit hard on people like Hannah. She said she was counting on the lad's wages, but still she'll keep the five bob Family Allowance for him.'

'But the eldest doesn't get it,' John said.

'No, but if Bernie had started work, the next child would have been counted as eldest and she'd have lost five bob.'

'You can't suit some people,' John exclaimed. 'I thought everyone'd be pleased for their kids to have the extra year's schooling.'

'All the women are made up about the Family Allowance anyway,' Anne said soothingly. 'Ena told me that Hannah always had a struggle because her husband never earned much, but she got twenty-five shillings Family Allowance the week it came in, and rigged all the kids out in new pumps.'

'You'll have to tell Mum that story,' John said, smiling. 'She used to campaign for Family Allowances. Supporting Eleanor Rathbone, carrying banners and delivering leaflets and that sort of thing. She was only a young girl at the time so it's taken a long time.'

'Yes, but they got there in the end,' Anne said. 'Sometimes I think you're a bit impatient, John, expecting things to change overnight. I know a lot of things are still scarce, but things are getting better, and at least we don't have to worry about people being killed and the horrible blackout's over.'

'Maybe I *am* too impatient,' he admitted, 'but this is the opportunity to get things done, and people are so dozy and there's so much red tape.'

Gerry woke and John picked him up and sat down again with the child on his knee. 'Another thing too, Anne,' he said. 'There's always something else to watch. The atom bomb. English scientists discovered it but then they went in with America and now the Americans have taken complete control.'

'But does it matter?' she said. 'The war's over now.'

'This war,' John said grimly. 'The Americans have got the money for bigger, more powerful bombs, then someone else will have them. It only means a moment's madness, someone's finger on a button, and we'll be annihilated.'

Anne felt as though a dark cloud had come over the sun. 'No one would be so mad, surely?' she said.

'We can't take the risk,' he said. 'Would anyone have believed before the First World War that Passchendaele could happen? The Somme? Ypres? Thousands of lives thrown away for a few hundred yards of ground. And the last war . . . bombing cities, annihilating them and everyone there, including women and children. We didn't know what was being done in our name until it was too late, but this time we do know.'

'But what can we do?'

'Band together. Protest so loudly and forcefully that they'll have to listen. Unity is strength, my grandad always said, and I believe it. We'll demand that the tests of the atomic bombs are stopped and they are all destroyed. That's what the Peace Pledge Union is demanding. Tony's joined, y'know.'

'*Our* Tony?' Anne exclaimed.

'Yes, well, he's got a child too,' John said. He lifted Gerry on to his knee and smoothed back the curls from the child's face. 'We've got to fight for a safe world for them.'

Anne sat silent, her mind in turmoil. She thought of items heard on the wireless or read in the newspaper, disregarded by her as odd happenings at the other side of the world. The picture of a mushroom-shaped cloud at Hiroshima, the reports of the devastation and of people dying from the effects years later.

Suddenly they all came together in her mind and she looked with anguish at Gerry. Why did we have a child? The world's not fit for children.

John looked at her face and drew her into his arms. 'Don't worry, love,' he said gently. 'We won't let it happen.'

They slipped their arms round each other's waist and followed Gerry into the house. John eagerly told Anne of all the protests that had been made and the numerous names that had been collected on petitions, and she privately decided that in future instead of resenting the time he spent with the Peace Pledge Union, she would encourage him.

She managed to put all these dark thoughts out of her mind at the Confraternity meeting that evening and came home as cheerful as ever.

Nothing had been heard of the Connolly family since their flight in 1940, but the following evening Carrie and Fred arrived at the Fitzgerald house in great excitement, carrying a newspaper. Pat, Stephen, Eileen and Maureen were all in, and Stephen called Joe and Sarah into the kitchen.

'Take a look at this,' he said. 'It must be them,' pointing to the newspaper spread on the kitchen table.

There were large black headlines, GANGLAND SLAYING, and underneath the account said that the mutilated body of Buster Leyland, thought to be a member of the Brookland's gang, was

434

thrown from a moving car onto the steps of the White Peacock Club at 3 a.m.

The face had been razor slashed and the head almost severed from the body. Police feared this was another gangland killing which would lead to further violence.

There was a small photograph on the page and Carrie said, 'It's him all right, Brendan, isn't it?' And the family agreed.

Although the face was fatter and wore a pencil moustache the photograph was indisputably of Brendan. Stephen read aloud, 'He was known to the police for several years, under different names, but they were never able to charge him.

'A police spokesman said, "He was as slippery as an eel, and so vicious that witnesses were afraid to give evidence against him."'

'Good God!' Pat said. 'Are you sure it's him? He was a bad lot all right, but this!'

'Read the rest,' Carrie said.

Stephen read aloud: 'When our reporter arrived at the luxurious flat where he lived with his mother and sister, two hefty thugs wearing knuckle dusters barred his way. When the police arrived an hour later the thugs had vanished and so had Leyland's mother and sister. The flat showed signs of a hasty flight.'

Maureen crossed herself. 'Lord rest him! Minnie and Dympna were still with him then. At least he was always a good son.'

'Used them for cover more likely,' Fred growled.

'"The neighbours were shocked to hear of the double life led by the man they knew as Mr Collins,"' Stephen read. '"They were obviously wealthy but they lived very quiet lives," said Miss Penelope Morgan. "They used a chauffeur-driven car, and went abroad for holidays. They kept themselves to themselves and Mr Collins never said more than good morning or good evening."'

'Sounds as though she'd have liked to know him better,'

Eileen commented. 'Maybe she had a lucky escape!'

'I don't think so,' Stephen said quietly to her, pointing to the next paragraph. She leaned forward and read, 'Leyland/Collins also owned a smaller flat in Mayfair where he entertained his men friends who were usually younger than himself. He was never known to have a woman friend.'

She looked at Stephen, then glanced to where Maureen was making tea and the others were discussing Minnie.

'Couldn't put it much more plainly, could they?' she said quietly. 'It's a wonder the police couldn't get him for that if they knew about it.' Stephen shrugged.

'Minnie won't come back here,' Carrie was saying positively. 'She probably thinks we know nothing about this.'

'And the gang'll probably look after her and Dympna,' Fred said. 'She'll have been whisked away abroad somewhere. Ten to one Minnie'll have made sure she's got some hold over them.'

'I can't believe I'm talking about my own sister and nephew,' Carrie said. 'My poor ma must be turning in her grave. I wonder if anyone else will have heard about them.'

'I don't think so,' Eileen said. 'They didn't have many friends here, and her house – most of that street, in fact – was wiped out with that landmine.'

Anne and John heard about it the following evening. Anne's friend Ena had been unable to babysit for them since the birth of her own baby, who was delicate and very cross. Eileen had volunteered to take her place, and now she came straight from work every Wednesday so that Anne and John could visit the cinema. On this Wednesday she brought a copy of the newspaper to show them, and they discussed it during their meal.

'I can't believe it!' Anne exclaimed. 'You read about these things, but Brendan! And Minnie and Dympna! People we know.'

'I'm not surprised,' Eileen said. 'Not about that last bit either. Brendan never had a girlfriend when he was here, did he? I always thought he was as queer as a nine-bob note – as well as being a bad hat.'

'Is that what it means?' Anne said, re-reading the final paragraph.

'Yes, but they have to be careful how they put it,' Eileen said. 'I said to Stephen it's a wonder the police didn't get him for that. Like Al Capone and the income tax evasion. Get him for something and put him out of circulation.'

'He's out of circulation now, poor beggar,' John said. 'It shouldn't be a criminal offence though, being like he is. He couldn't help being born like that.'

'It should be if he was corrupting young boys,' Eileen said indignantly. 'And there's such a thing as free will. He might have leanings that way, but he doesn't have to give in to them.'

John was about to reply but Anne suddenly exclaimed, 'We're going to miss the start of the programme. Will you be all right, Eil? I've left a drink of orange juice for Gerry in case he wakes up, and there's a piece of pie and some fruit cake for your supper.'

Anne discussed the affair with John as they walked to the cinema, but as they stood in the queue she suddenly giggled. 'I'm just thinking, John, how we've changed since the war. Imagine fellows and girls talking like we've been talking with Eileen, before the war!'

He smiled. 'Our mums and dads would have been shocked, wouldn't they?'

'Mum wouldn't have known what we were talking about,' Anne said. 'Neither would I, for that matter. That factory certainly educated me!'

John laughed and squeezed her hand. 'Remember our honeymoon,' he said in a low voice. 'Remember telling me Penny thought it was very overrated.' They laughed together and sat close during the film.

When they left the cinema the air was warm and still, and a

full moon hung in the sky. 'A bomber's moon,' he said.

'No, a harvest moon,' Anne corrected him. 'That's how I think of it now.' They walked home slowly, their arms around each other, and Anne resting her head against John's shoulder.

He kissed her gently. 'I love you, Mrs Redmond,' he whispered.

Anne pressed her lips against his. 'And I love you.'

They were almost sorry to reach the house, but Eileen reported that Gerry had been very good. 'He didn't cry but I heard a noise and went up,' she said. 'He was sitting up in his cot singing Twinkle Twinkle, Little Star. I was going to get him the orange juice when he suddenly fell back as though he'd been poleaxed.'

'I know,' Anne said, laughing. 'He always falls asleep like that. He was singing Twinkle Twinkle in church on Sunday. Every time the choir started a hymn Gerry struck up at the top of his voice.'

She looked flushed and happy, and Eileen stared at her quizzically. 'You enjoyed the picture then?'

'Yes. It was good. *Weekend in Havana.* I like Alice Faye,' Anne said innocently.

'And I like Carmen Miranda,' John said. 'Don't you think she looks like Anne, Eileen?'

She laughed. 'I just wondered how much you'd seen of it, that's all,' she teased. 'I like the paper in Gerry's bedroom, John.'

'I suppose it's not really suitable for a child's room,' he said, 'but it's great to get *any* paper with a pattern on it.'

'We're going for the lino on Saturday,' Anne said. 'I've left the dockets at Cohen's and they'll send the single bed when one comes in. He's getting far too big for his cot.'

John took Eileen to get the tram to Everton and when he returned Anne was in bed. He soon followed her and took her in his arms. 'Shall we celebrate Gerry's room being got ready?'

he whispered. 'We don't really want an empty cot, do we?'

Anne snuggled closer to him. 'No, we don't want too big a gap between them.'

'As long as Gerry's nose isn't pushed out,' John said, and Anne drew back a little.

'I don't see why it should be,' she said, more sharply than she intended, and John hastily drew her close again. They made love with tenderness and passion, but after John had fallen asleep Anne lay awake.

She had longed for another baby since she had held Sarah's in her arms, but if another baby was born to them, she hoped that John would not see it as a threat to Gerry.

She thought it would be good for Gerry to have a brother or sister as a companion, and that it would relieve Gerry of John's obsessive love which might in time become a burden to him. Yet she knew she would love the baby for its own sake rather than what it would mean to Gerry, and hoped that John would feel the same.

I'm sure he will when he sees it, she thought and as she drifted off to sleep she smiled, thinking that quite literally she was counting her chickens before they were hatched.

Chapter Thirty-Four

Anne sang as she cleaned windows and polished furniture the following day. She was happy not only because of her hopes for another baby but also because Eileen had seemed like her old, pleasant self.

Since returning from war service she had been prickly and sour, quick to take offence, and always ready with a sharp comment. The family had borne with her, partly because of her past suffering, and partly because just occasionally she was again the pleasant, helpful girl they had always known.

It was during one such spell that she had offered to babysit for Anne and John, but Anne found it a mixed blessing. She had to be always alert to fend off trouble between Eileen and John, but still there would be sharp exchanges between them at times

Perhaps she's got over all that now, Anne thought optimistically. She was really nice last night. Her hopes were dashed on the following Wednesday.

Anne had queued for liver to make Eileen's favourite meal of liver and onions, with mashed potatoes and home grown sprouts. Eileen had scarcely touched the meal, and had refused plate tart made with precious bottled blackcurrants.

Anne was disappointed but said nothing, hoping that given time her sister would come out of her mood. She recalled an old friend of her mother's who lived with a cantankerous aunt, who

441

used to say, 'I let her soak and she comes round.'

Eileen showed no sign of 'coming round'. After the meal Gerry was running about and fell against the corner of the table. John rushed to pick him up and comfort him and Anne tried to wipe away his tears, but Gerry still roared, more with shock than pain.

There was a small graze on his forehead and John said excitedly, 'He's bleeding, Anne. Get the First Aid box.'

Eileen lay back in her chair, smoking and watching sardonically. 'The more you fuss, the louder he howls,' she said. 'Ridiculous. It's only a little bump, for God's sake.'

'It's swelling and it's bleeding,' John said angrily. 'He's not crying for nothing.'

'You're not doing him any favours, making a namby pamby of him,' Eileen said. 'He'll be at school in a couple of years. God help him if he behaves like that.'

Anne had returned with the First Aid box and a wet cloth, and as John sat down with Gerry and she bent over them, she made urgent signals to John to stay silent. He scowled but concentrated on Gerry, and within minutes the child was playing happily with his toys.

Anne talked about a letter from Kathleen, then John took Gerry to bed while Anne and Eileen washed up. Anne and John prepared to go out to the cinema and Anne said as she always did, 'You'll be all right then, Eil? I've left a drink for Gerry and some rissoles for supper.'

'Yes. If you can trust me with your precious son,' Eileen sneered.

Anne laughed, pretending that Eileen was joking, but as they walked down the road, John said, 'I'm not so sure about leaving Gerry with her. He wouldn't get much sympathy if he hurt himself.'

'Oh, John, you know she idolises him,' Anne protested. 'I

suppose we did make rather a fuss about that fall. He soon got over it.'

'That's because he's a brave little lad,' said John.

'I got a shock when Eileen said that about Gerry and school,' Anne said. 'I always think of school as in the remote future for him.'

'I don't know why she brought school up anyway. He's not three until January,' John said. 'She takes all the good out of the night out.'

Anne squeezed his arm. 'Let's just enjoy it,' she said. 'She'll probably be all right when we get home.'

They enjoyed the film and the walk home, but Eileen was still as grumpy. She had not eaten the rissoles. 'You on hunger strike?' John joked, but she said unsmilingly, 'No. But I please myself when I eat.'

She said the wireless programme had been rubbish and the news broadcasts had annoyed her. 'All about India and Pakistan having Dominion status, and British troops leaving Palestine. Some Committee proposing partition into Arab and Jewish States. Let them do what they like, I say, as long as our soldiers are out of it.'

'The Arabs might need some protection,' John said. 'They've been on that land for twenty centuries, as Bevan said, and they were good friends to Britain during the war.'

'Oh, but John,' Anne said, 'those awful concentration camps the Jews were taken to. I couldn't get it out of my mind after the pictures of them were on at the Gaumont.' She glanced at Eileen and saw a half smile on her face. We're playing into her hands, Anne thought. She wants us to argue.

Before John could speak she said quickly, 'Didn't you want a word with Con?'

'Oh, yes, about tomorrow night,' he said, going through into the back garden and calling Con.

'Out again tomorrow night, is he?' Eileen said, but Anne only said calmly, 'Yes. A Peace Pledge meeting. How are things at work?'

Eileen shrugged. 'Usual bitching and back biting,' she said. 'I think at least half of my section are slow-witted.'

'You'll have to make the bright half work harder then, won't you?' Anne said with a smile. She was determined to keep things light, but that changed when she asked Eileen about the family.

'Sarah and Joe drooling over the child,' she said waspishly. 'Maureen drooling over that drip Chris Murray. Stephen drooling over his latest little tart. Dad either in the pub or at Fred's every night. I feel like doing myself in sometimes.'

Suddenly, overwhelmingly, Anne longed for her mother. She dashed into the kitchen and bent over the sink, gripping the edges until her knuckles were white. Hot tears spilled from her eyes and dripped into the sink as she cried soundlessly, Oh, Mum, Mum, come back. She tried to compose herself and hide her distress.

A noise at the door alerted her that John was coming through the kitchen and she hastily filled a glass with water and drank it, then splashed cold water on her face before following him into the living room.

Eileen stood. 'What took you so long?' she said, but John just smiled. 'We get carried away once we start. Sorry.' He brought Eileen's coat and Anne went to the door with them to see them off.

The Fitzgeralds always kissed on meeting or parting but when Anne kissed her sister tonight, Eileen suddenly hugged her. 'Sorry, kid,' she whispered. 'I didn't mean to upset you. I'm the wrong side out today.'

Anne kissed her again. 'It'll all be better tomorrow, Eil,' she comforted her. John had strolled on to the gate and Anne was relieved to see Eileen link arms with him when she caught him up.

'Did she catch the tram all right?' Anne asked when he returned. He only nodded and remarked on the smell of night-scented stock in a garden they had passed. Clearly there had been no unpleasantness.

Anne's mind was still full of memories of her mother and she was glad to go to bed and be able to weep freely for her. John had assumed that she was asleep but a slight sound made him lean over her.

'What's the matter, love?' he asked with concern. 'What's upset you?'

She turned into his arms. 'Oh, John, I miss Mum,' she wept. 'The house – the family. We're falling apart without her. We need her so much.'

John held her in his arms, stroking back her hair and making soothing noises, but Anne still wept.

'You're worried about Eileen,' he said. 'She's had a bad time, but she'll get over it.'

'No, it's all of us,' she murmured. 'We were so happy. She was the heart of the house, I see that now. Oh, why did she have to go?'

'Because she was ill and in pain. I don't know how she hung on for our wedding. Don't wish her back to that, love,' he said, but his arms and his kisses comforted her more than any reasonable explanation.

Even to John, Anne was unable to repeat Eileen's comments on the family. She decided to go to see Sarah the following day and see how true they were.

She was delighted to find Mrs Bennet sitting in Sarah's rooms drinking tea, and Mrs Bennet was equally pleased to see Anne.

She only came in twice a week now, to 'straighten them up like', she said, and called in to Sarah for tea before she went.

'Mrs Bennet doesn't think much of Stephen's latest,' Sarah said with a smile.

'I'm just saying, that girl comes from a low crowd. Her grand-mother was a fishwife and a moneylender and she used to make the poor people that owed her take her bad fish. We used to shout outside her house, "We don't want yer stinking fish, we don't want yer blarney, we don't want yer stinking fish, dirty old Mrs M'Garney."' She laughed heartily at the memory.

'Doesn't sound a very nice family,' Anne said. 'What's the girl like?'

'We don't care for her,' Sarah said. 'But Stephen's not serious.'

'He's just a bad picker,' Mrs Bennet said. 'But don't worry. He'll meet a nice girl and settle down, you'll see.' She was putting on her coat and went to Gerry who was bending over the baby's cot and stroking David's face.

'You'll have to ask yer mam for one of them,' she said cheer-fully, taking out a penny. 'Ee are, lad. Don't spend it all in the one shop.' Gerry thanked her and she said, 'Ta ra then, girls. I'm made up you like the house, Anne.'

'She's a nice woman, isn't she?' Sarah said. 'But I'm glad she's gone. We don't have much time for a talk now, do we?'

'No, we don't,' Anne agreed. 'But I was glad to see her. She was always so good to Mum.'

'She still worries about the family,' Sarah said. 'She often calls to see them to see if they want anything special doing in the house, but more to keep an eye on them.'

'She's like one of the family really, with all we went through together,' Anne said.

Sarah hesitated then said quietly, 'Do you know she's not speaking to Eileen?'

'No, I didn't. Eileen never said anything.'

'There was some sort of a row, and Maureen was crying, and Mrs Bennet told Eileen she had a tongue like a viper. But what really did it, she said Eileen was getting like her Aunt Minnie.'

'Oh, lor!' Anne said. 'That *would* put the cat among the

pigeons. The reason I came today, Sar, was really because of things Eileen said last night that worried me.'

'Why, what did she say?'

'Nasty things about Stephen's girl, and about Chris Murray. She called him a drip. And she said Dad was out every night at the pub or at Fred's,' Anne said. 'Are things bad here, Sar?'

'Only when Eileen makes them bad,' Sarah said. 'You heard what we said about Stephen's girl, but he's not a fool, and Chris Murray – it's just that she's taken a dislike to him. She doesn't like the situation.'

'But why? Nothing's changed, has it?' said Anne.

'No, but I think Eileen thinks he's not being fair to Maureen, but what can he do? You know Joe went to see him once to ask him to stop seeing Mo, so she might meet someone else, but Maureen was so upset that Joe was sorry he interfered. He says you can't tell anyone else how to live their life.'

'I like him,' Anne said. 'I think he should be firmer with his wife, but then it's not my business. As long as Maureen's happy.'

'I think she is, in her own quiet way,' Sarah said. 'I've known other couples like them, y'know, Anne. A woman who lived in Egremont Street was courting for about twenty years and they seemed happy together. It was only after she died of consumption that Mum told me that they couldn't marry because his wife had been in a lunatic asylum since just after they were married.'

'I suppose they think that half a loaf is better than no bread,' Anne said thoughtfully. 'I don't think I could do it, Sarah.'

'Nor me,' she agreed. 'But Mo told me once that once she was crying and your mum said to her, "You've chosen a hard road, child, but never forget, God fits the back to the burden."'

Anne's eyes filled with tears. 'Oh, Sarah, I can just hear her. If only she was here, everyone would be happy.'

Sarah's eyes filled too but she brushed the tears away. 'I mustn't cry while I'm breast feeding David,' she said. 'You'd ·

be surprised, Anne, how it affects him. Anyway, you're doing your bit by having Eileen for tea on Wednesdays.'

'But that's for our own convenience.'

'Yes, but it's a godsend for us. Chris comes here for his tea on Wednesdays. He's working in a pork butcher's now, and Wednesday's his half day,' Sarah said. She began to laugh. 'It was funny last night. Bridie called up, then Tony, then Carrie and Fred, and of course Chris was here. Like the gathering of the clans.'

'Just because Eileen was out?' Anne said in dismay. 'I didn't realise it was as bad as that, Sarah.'

'It isn't, honestly,' she said hastily. 'It was probably just coincidence. Eileen's all right sometimes. It's just that we never know what mood she'll be in, and she's great at speaking her mind.'

'When I think how she used to be,' Anne said sadly. 'Always so lively, her and Theresa. The things they got up to, and the dates and the laughs they had!'

'You know she's not speaking to Theresa now?' Sarah said. 'That's probably why Carrie came last night while she was out. She's annoyed about it.'

'I didn't know,' Anne said, and Sarah looked dismayed.

'I shouldn't be telling you all this if the family said nothing. I'm sorry.'

'I want to know. I don't see Maureen and the lads so much except at weekends. What happened?'

'Eileen had a row with Jim. I don't know what it was about, but Theresa was furious,' Sarah said. 'I'll tell you something else then I'm not going to say any more about Eileen, Anne, because I think I'm giving the wrong impression and she's not bad all the time. Only in fairness to Jim I've got to say that she picked a row with Joe one night.'

'With Joe?' Anne exclaimed. 'What about?'

'I don't know. He went in the kitchen and she said something to him. He was as white as a sheet with temper when he came back but he wouldn't say what she'd said. Just that she'd never say it again.'

'So she's not speaking to Joe?' Anne said.

'Oh, yes, they made it up. But we're all right. We can keep out of the way in here.'

Anne glanced at the clock. 'I'll have to go soon,' she said, 'but I'm glad I came so I know how things are here. I can't help thinking poor Eileen, though. She's her own worst enemy.'

'Yes, and it's the tragedy that made her like this. It takes everyone differently,' Sarah said. 'She'll get over it in time, I suppose.'

Anne felt sad as she travelled home, but her spirits rose as she stepped off the tramcar. The sun was shining and all the little gardens were bright with flowers. She was greeted by several people she knew, and Gerry ran ahead of her shouting jubilantly, 'Home, home.'

The house looked bright and welcoming with vases of fresh flowers Anne had cut that morning, and as she looked out over the sunny back garden while she filled the kettle she thought that surely this weather must make Eileen feel better.

The previous day had been dull and it was a well-known fact that the number of suicides rose in bad weather. She decided to say nothing to John about her talk about Eileen, and only said that she had been to see Sarah.

'I told her about the way Gerry roared when he fell,' she said, 'and she said your Mick was the same. You could hear him in the next street.'

'That's true,' John said. 'Grandma used to say: "Nothing wrong with his lungs." I saw Dad today and he said he'll come on Saturday to help me lay the lino in Gerry's room.'

On Saturday they went to the local chandler's to choose the linoleum for Gerry's room, and John carried it home on his shoulder. His father came later to help him. Gerry loved his grandfather and willingly sang songs for him: Twinkle, Twinkle, Little Star, Little Boy Blue, and then an Irish air, Eileen Aroon.

'I taught him to sing that for Eileen when she comes to babysit,' Anne said, laughing.

'Perhaps he'll be musical like your family,' Greg Redmond said.

'We all like singing. The first thing I ever remember is hearing Mum. She was too shy to sing in company but she was always singing round the house. We often had parties too, either in our house or Aunt Carrie's, and nearly everyone sang or played.'

'Eileen's a good pianist, isn't she?' John said. 'And your Joe can play the violin. We must send Gerry for lessons as soon as he's old enough.'

'If he shows any interest,' Anne said. 'Terry and I went for lessons too but we were never any good and we soon gave up. We just weren't interested.'

'The voice is an instrument that you always carry with you,' John's father said, lifting Gerry to ride on his foot.

Anne smiled. 'Someone once said we were like a nest of singing birds.'

'Did they?' said Greg Redmond. 'Do you know who said that first, Anne? The great Doctor Johnson.'

'Doctor Samuel Johnson?' she asked.

'Yes. Boswell recorded it in his *Life of Doctor Johnson*. When Samuel Johnson was at Pembroke College, Oxford, someone remarked on the number of poets there and Johnson said, "Sir, we are a nest of singing birds."'

Anne was intrigued, both at the explanation and at the fact that Greg Redmond knew of it. She had never realised that he was a book lover, but then he was so quiet and self-effacing that she had not learnt to know him as she had John's mother and grandmother.

John had been out for his toolbox and as he sat beside his father showing him various tools, Anne studied them. At first glance they were very alike. Both had thin faces, with grey eyes and a deep cleft in the chin, and dark hair falling across their forehead, yet there was a difference.

There was nothing weak about Greg's face, but John looked – what? Anne searched for the right word. Tougher – aggressive – belligerent? He looks as though he's always ready for a fight, she thought, then smiled as she remembered Mick's words about John tilting at windmills.

John selected his tools and went upstairs, and his father gave Gerry a final ride on his foot before following John.

He turned and smiled at Anne before he went and she thought, Heavens, that smile! He must have been a charmer when he was young. A memory stirred. Had it been Sarah or her grandmother who had hinted that Mary in America had also been in love with Greg, but he had always loved only Cathy, his wife?

How strange to think of passions like that all those years ago, Anne thought, then glanced at Gerry and wondered whether he would one day think the same about herself and John.

Gerry grinned at her, and she thought regretfully that he had not inherited his grandfather's smile, but then neither had John in spite of his resemblance to his father.

Sarah's smile came closest to it, although she was brown-haired and blue-eyed like her grandmother. What a strange thing heredity was, Anne mused as she rapidly peeled potatoes, and how interesting. How frightening too, as her thoughts turned to Brendan Connolly.

No one in Liverpool had connected the gang member Leyland/Collins with Brendan. Fred had made cautious inquiries about the killing from his policeman friend without disclosing his belief that Brendan was the victim, but the policeman only said, 'Good thing, in my opinion. Let them all kill each other off and save everyone a lot of trouble.'

Several weeks later another mutilated body was found in the Thames and identified as a member of a rival gang. Interest in Brendan's killing was briefly revived but it was now November 1947 and the wedding of Princess Elizabeth and Prince Philip of Greece was the topic that filled the newspapers.

Nothing more had been heard of Minnie and Dympna either and it was clear that they were not going to return to Liverpool.

Eileen continued to babysit for Anne and John every Wednesday, and although she never appeared very happy, she seemed to avoid controversy. Just occasionally she responded to Anne's loving efforts to cheer her and to Gerry's boisterous affection.

Helen had been distressed by the rift in the family, and had gone to see Theresa to try to reconcile her and Eileen.

'If she was sick we'd all be trying to get her better,' Helen pleaded. 'This is a sort of sickness too.'

'Yes, but look at all the other girls who lost their husbands in the war,' Theresa said. 'They don't carry on like that.'

'But you, more than anyone, should understand, Theresa,' Helen said. 'You know Eileen best. You know she wouldn't let herself get involved, then when she met Whitey she let all her defences down.'

'That's true,' Theresa admitted. 'She really did go overboard. All the more because she'd kept her feelings under control so much before.'

'And then for him to die like that, and so soon,' Helen said. 'You can see what a deep psychological shock it was to her. I wonder that they kept her in the Air Force.'

'Eileen puts up a good front,' Theresa said. 'They probably thought she was all right. She did try, y'know, Helen, when she came home. Had a few dates and all that.'

'I know. I thought she was very brave.'

'Of course she ditched them right away. No one came up to

452

Whitey,' said Theresa. 'I'm sorry we've fallen out with her, Helen, but she did say some awful things to Jim.'

'But he's a good fellow,' Helen said. 'I'm sure if you explained to him, Tess, he'd be willing to make friends. It's upsetting your mum and dad, and your Uncle Pat too.'

'I know,' Theresa said. 'My dad's worried about Christmas. It'd be very awkward.' She thought for a moment then said with sudden decision, 'I'll talk to Jim about it.'

'And you'll make it up with Eileen?' Helen said.

'Yes, I'm sure I can talk Jim round. I'll leave the gang with him, maybe just take Ciara to break the ice, and call in when I know Eileen'll be in.'

Helen bent over Ciara. 'She's a lovely baby, isn't she?' she said wistfully.

Theresa picked up the child. 'No sign yet for you?' she said sympathetically.

Helen sighed. 'No. The doctor said it was because things were bungled so much when Moira was born.' She shrugged. 'I wish I had Maureen's faith. She's making a novena for us and she's sure that something will happen soon.'

'Perhaps she'll be right,' Theresa said. 'Perhaps now with the National Health Service you'll be able to have something done. I wouldn't give up hope, Helen.'

'No, I won't,' she said. 'And anyway, we're lucky. We've got Moira.'

Theresa gave her a hug. 'You're a good sort, Helen,' she said. 'Tony's a lucky man.' Helen smiled and blushed.

Theresa came to see the Fitzgeralds a week later, dropping in without warning with her baby. There was a tense moment when Eileen stood up as though to flee, but as though there had never been a rift Theresa said cheerfully, 'Hallo, Eil. Like to hold a wet baby?' and handed Ciara to her.

Eileen took her. 'She's a good weight anyhow,' she said. 'And a wet nappy's not stopping her from sleeping.'

Theresa laughed. 'She sleeps all right during the day,' she said. 'And screams all night.'

Pat was delighted to see Theresa. He stood up and took her coat and pushed forward his chair for her.

'Sit here, girl. Warm yourself,' he said. 'Have you been to see your mam and dad?'

'Yes, I'm doing the rounds while I'm off the leash,' she said cheerfully. 'I've left Jim to referee the fights among the other kids, and I'm making the most of my freedom.'

Maureen was worried about the baby's wet napkin and when Sarah came through asked if she had a spare. 'There's one in my bag,' Theresa said. 'No dusting powder though.'

'I'll take her through and change her,' Sarah said, smiling at Eileen as she took the baby from her. Theresa jumped up. 'Here, have your chair back, Uncle Pat,' she said. She sat down on the sofa beside Eileen and unselfconsciously slipped her arm round her cousin's waist.

She began to talk about some of their exploits before the war and before long everyone was helpless with laughter, including Eileen. Maureen quickly produced a meal, and afterwards Eileen walked with Theresa to the tram stop.

The family always dated Eileen's recovery from that day, although she still had occasional black moods. They had a happy Christmas and Fred's party on Boxing Day was a great success. Eileen and Jim were wary with each other at first, but by the end of the evening they were the best of friends again. John was on his best behaviour, too, and avoided any controversy, much to Anne's relief.

Chapter Thirty-Five

As Anne and John were now hoping to have another child, it was not necessary for them to observe the 'safe period'. They made love so frequently and so passionately that Anne was surprised and disappointed that she failed to become pregnant immediately.

A few weeks after Gerry's third birthday in January, however, the doctor confirmed that she was pregnant and she was booked into the local hospital. The baby was due in September, and everyone was pleased at the news, especially John's mother and grandmother.

Since Anne and John had moved to the new house, Cathy Redmond and her mother had spent an afternoon with Anne about once a week, but just after Christmas John's grandmother slipped on an icy pavement and broke a bone in her foot.

As they were unable to visit her Anne went instead to the Redmond house once a week, and a pattern developed. She stayed for the evening meal and John came home from work with his father for it. Soon after the meal, Greg Redmond, who now had a car, drove Anne and John and Gerry home in time for the child's bedtime.

Anne enjoyed these afternoons, sitting round the fire and talking. John's mother and grandmother both had a fund of stories, Sally Ward of her childhood and early married life before the turn of the century, and Cathy of the days when John and his brother and sisters were young.

Sometimes Anne told them stories of her own childhood, and some of the exploits of her cousins, the Anderson twins, or Cathy talked about her days as a waitress with a firm of caterers. Often Anne was sorry to hear Greg Redmond's key in the door when he and John returned from work.

In March Sarah had a bad bout of bronchitis and her mother went every day to look after her and baby David until Joe, who was now teaching, returned home soon after four o'clock.

Anne still went to the Redmond house and spent the afternoon with Sally. She grew even closer to the old lady whom she had always admired.

Anne had an easy pregnancy and felt well and happy. Her neighbour Mrs Rooney had been pleased to hear about the news.

'It'll be nice to have a young baby about,' she said. 'When are you due, girl?'

'The tenth of September, they said at the clinic,' Anne said. 'It's our wedding anniversary on the eighteenth. It'd be nice if it came then, wouldn't it?'

'It'll come when it's ready and not before,' Mrs Rooney said. 'It'll be company for Gerry anyway. I'm always sorry for only children.'

'Yes, they can be very lonely,' Anne said. She suddenly thought of Helen and Tony and added hastily, 'Sometimes it can't be helped, of course.'

'You was one of a big family, wasn't you?' Mrs Rooney said. 'How many of yis was there?'

'Seven. Well, eight really,' Anne said. 'My eldest brother Patrick died when he was six. We were never short of company to go out anywhere and we had a good time at home too. That's why I'd like a big family myself.'

'Aye, you wouldn't need no friends,' Mrs Rooney said.

Anne looked surprised. 'I didn't mean that. We always had

friends, all of us. Sarah who comes here with little David was my best friend.' She laughed. 'Then I married *her* brother and she married mine.'

'She looks a nice girl,' Mrs Rooney said.

'She is. We all used to go out cycling together, my brothers and sisters and Sarah and friends of the others sometimes. Sarah and I went out dancing or to the pictures nearly every night, but sometimes, especially on Sunday nights, we'd all stay in and our friends'd come round.'

'Your mam didn't mind a houseful then?'

'No. Sometimes we'd have a sing-song, and sometimes just talk and I enjoyed that just as much. The things we discussed!' She smiled reminiscently. 'Anything and everything. Sarah used to enjoy the discussions.'

'What about John?' Mrs Rooney asked.

'Oh, I didn't know him then.'

Mrs Rooney laughed. 'Good job. No one would've been able to get a word in edgeways.' Before Anne could decide whether or not to be affronted, Mrs Rooney added, 'He's like our Con. Talk the hind leg off a donkey, the pair of them.'

Anne continued to go to the Women's Confraternity every Monday, to Benediction followed by a social evening, and to the cinema with John on Wednesdays. Occasionally Eileen had a date, or an outing had been arranged from the office for Wednesday, and on these occasions Maureen came instead to babysit.

Sometimes one of Maureen's friends came with her to keep her company, either Annie Keegan or Mona Dunne, and Anne was pleased to see that her sister was not devoting all her time to Chris.

Anne was happy too that Eileen was taking up the threads of her life again and coming out of the dark depression which had engulfed her.

Anne and John had many visitors, either friends made locally or family and friends who took the tram out from Liverpool to visit them. 'People like coming here,' Maureen told her. 'It's such a happy house.'

The summer months passed pleasantly for Anne, but some humid days at the end of August made her long for the baby to be born. She began to feel large and unwieldy. The Berlin airlift had started to take food to the British and French zones and film of the wide aircraft used was shown on the cinema news-- reels.

'I look like them,' Anne whispered to John one night, but he told her that she looked fine. 'It won't be long now, love,' he comforted her. 'Perhaps it'll be born on my birthday.'

His birthday was 22 September and Anne exclaimed in dismay, 'I hope not. I was hoping for it to come on our wedding anniversary but now I don't care if it comes tomorrow.'

Anne's family were unaware how often she was alone during the evening because of John's various commitments, but his family knew and worried about her.

Greg Redmond offered to pay for the telephone to be installed, but John brusquely refused.

'Mick paid for ours and it's been very useful,' Greg protested. 'Grandma enjoys a chat with Anne and she could have it without either of them leaving the house.' But John was adamant.

'Thanks all the same, Dad,' he said, 'I'll apply for one and pay for it myself.'

'You should have told him we were worried about Anne,' Cathy said, and Greg said grimly, 'Yes, and I can imagine his reaction to *that*.'

On 1 September 1948 Anne turned out the bedrooms then cleaned through the rooms downstairs. She felt well and energetic but was tired when she finished, with a niggling pain in her back, so she went early to bed.

The following morning the pain had gone. John was going straight from work to a meeting but told her that he would be home by ten o'clock. Shortly before six in the evening Anne went to Mrs Rooney. 'I've had a show,' she said. 'When that happened with Gerry, it was eight hours before he was born, but now I'm getting regular pains.'

'How often?' Mrs Rooney asked, and when Anne told her fifteen minutes, said immediately, 'You'd better get to the hospital, girl.'

Con was at the same meeting as John, but Mrs Rooney sent her other son, Barty, to the public telephone to call an ambulance. She came back with Anne and helped her to get Gerry ready for bed. Anne's case was already packed, and when Barty returned he was accompanied by a neighbour, a young widow whose husband had died in a Japanese prison camp.

'Barty says your husband's not home from work yet,' she said. 'Would you like me to come to the hospital with you?'

'That's a good idea, Milly,' Mrs Rooney said before Anne could speak. 'I'll stay here with Gerry until John gets in from work, but you can see her in and bring her clothes home.'

'But what about your children?' Anne said, then suddenly clutched the fireguard as pain hit her.

'My eldest is twelve,' Milly said when the spasm had passed. 'Old enough to look after the others. I think that's the ambulance now.'

'God, I hope so,' Mrs Rooney muttered, and the next moment the ambulancemen were in the house.'I'm coming with her,' Milly said to them. 'Her husband's working till ten.'

'Never mind, you'll have a nice little baby to show him when he comes,' the older man said soothingly.

'Don't worry now, girl. I'll fetch Gerry in and put him to bed when you've gone,' Mrs Rooney said. 'You'll soon have it all over.'

Only ten minutes after Anne reached the labour ward, her daughter was born, a small baby with a fluff of dark hair and neat features.

Anne was delighted with her but felt tearful and found that she was trembling. She knew that she was upset that John had not been there when she needed him, but as she shed a few tears she told herself that she was weeping because she was touched by the kindness of her neighbours.

The labour ward sister appeared beside her. 'What's this? Tears! Your baby's quite perfect, you know.'

'I know,' Anne said. 'It's just – I can't stop trembling. It was so quick, and the panic to get here.'

The next moment the sister was replaced by a young doctor who gave Anne an injection and she drifted off to sleep and woke in the post-natal ward. The ward sister looked into the cot.

'Look at that determined little mouth,' she said. 'This one will know her own mind and do what she wants to do.'

Anne watched the clock anxiously, longing yet dreading to see John, and still uncertain how to greet him or even how she really felt about being left alone. The baby could have been born while he was at work, she thought one minute, but the next was angry again that he had gone to the meeting when he should have been with her.

There was a sudden panic about a baby who was sick just before visiting, and John was beside Anne's bed before she realised and bending to kiss her.

'I'm sorry, love,' he whispered. 'You must hate me.'

'No. I was all right,' Anne stammered, and he said again, 'I'm so sorry, Anne. I thought it would be another couple of weeks.'

'Mrs Rooney was smashing, *and* Barty, and Milly from across the road. Was Gerry all right?'

'Yes, fast asleep when I got home. I tell you, Anne, I felt about an inch high when Mrs Rooney told me. I came up here, you know, but the porter couldn't tell me anything.'

'But she was born soon after I got here,' Anne exclaimed. John was amazed. 'I thought she was born this morning. The porter told me to ring after seven and they said then you'd had a daughter, 7lb 4oz.'

'You haven't looked at her,' Anne said reproachfully, and John looked in the cot. 'Very small, isn't she?' he said. 'What was Gerry like?'

Anne's expression softened. 'I forgot you didn't see him,' she said. 'He wasn't much bigger than her, but very blond. Blue eyes. Long limbs.' She smiled reminiscently. 'He was a lovely baby, but he cried a lot in the hospital. He was fine when we came home though.'

The hospital had less rigid rules on visiting than the one where Gerry was born, and the next night Cathy came with John, and the following night Maureen came. Anne quickly realised that although her mother-in-law knew that John had been out when Anne was admitted, Maureen and presumably the rest of her family knew nothing about it.

'John asked Dad if he'd like to come,' Maureen said. 'You know he's dying to see you and the baby, Anne, but he'd feel out of place here among all these women.'

Anne laughed. 'I know,' she said. 'I'll see him soon anyway. I'll be in for ten days.'

Maureen went to the foot of the bed to look in the cot, and Anne whispered, 'She doesn't know you were out, does she?' John shook his head and Anne said urgently, 'Don't say anything then.'

Maureen left the ward before the end of visiting time, to give Anne and John time alone, and he said in an aggrieved voice, 'Mum was tearing a strip off me all the way home last night about going to the meeting. The baby shouldn't have been born for weeks yet, should it?'

'Not until the tenth,' said Anne. 'But I should have known when I got the urge to clean.'

'I wish you'd warned me then,' he said. 'I would have come straight home.'

'The tenth was only an approximate date anyway,' she said sharply. 'And I didn't realise it was going to happen so soon or I wouldn't have been in such a panic.'

The bell had gone for the end of visiting and John kissed her. 'Never mind, love. I'm not blaming you.'

Big of you, Anne muttered to herself as he turned away, but as he began to walk out she called him back.

'The baby,' she said. 'Say goodbye to the baby.' John glanced in the cot. 'She's asleep,' he said, and with a smile and a wave he departed.

Anne was left fuming, and that night and during the following day she felt unsettled and the baby was unusually cross. Anne was pleased that John's grandmother came with him at visiting time.

They had decided to call the baby Laura Anne, and Sally was pleased. 'I think she's got a look of Lawrie,' she said.

'She's very good but she's been a bit cross today. I think that was my fault, though. I got worked up about something last night.'

'Aye, that could upset her. You won't have to let things worry you while you're feeding her. Just let them pass over you,' Sally said.

She smiled but before Anne could speak, John said, 'And even when you're not. I know you don't often quarrel with people, Anne, but you have a bad habit of brooding on some fancied grievance.'

'Thanks very much!' she exclaimed, her face growing red with anger. 'Now should I tell you some of your faults?'

John sighed. 'You see. You resent even a mild comment like that. I was only saying it for your own good.'

'Yes, and for *your* own good, you'd better shut your mouth,' Sally said. 'You were behind the door when tact was given out, that's for sure.'

'But I was only —' he spluttered.

'Yes, we know,' Sally interrupted. 'Go and see the sister. I want to talk to Anne.'

He went off obediently and Sally handed a handkerchief to Anne. 'Don't cry, girl,' she said. 'You'll only upset yourself and your baby.'

Anne dried her eyes. 'I'm sorry,' she said. 'I shouldn't have flown at him like that while you were here.'

'I'd have thought less of you if you'd let him get away with it,' Sally said. 'He's a good lad really, Anne, but he never thinks before he speaks. He'd go to Hell and back for you, girl, you know that, but he just opens his mouth too wide.'

'But to say a thing like that!' Anne said. 'You'd think after him being out when I needed him, he'd be keeping quiet about my faults. Of course, he thinks *that* was my fault too.'

'Your fault!' Sally exclaimed.

'Yes. I said I should have known I was near my time when I felt like cleaning, and he said, all bighearted, that he didn't blame me!'

Sally sighed and shook her head. 'I could shake him,' she said. 'I tell you, love, he was really upset about that. His dad was furious and they had a real row about it. John stood up to him but afterwards with his mam, he *cried* about the way he'd let you down. Now I haven't known him do that since he was a little lad, so don't ever tell him I told you.'

'I won't,' she murmured, almost speechless with amazement.

'Cathy was really upset but she said to me, "Anne's a good girl. She won't hold it against him. She knows it was only a mistake." And I'm sure you won't, girl, will you?' said Sally.

'No,' Anne said, feeling more warmly towards John as she thought of him weeping with remorse.

'And just think, girl, he wasn't out gallivanting or drinking that night,' Sally said. 'And when he puts his foot in his mouth, remember, actions speak louder than words.'

'Yes, he's been very good while I've been expecting,' she said.

'He shops with me on Saturday afternoons so I don't have to carry anything heavy during the week, and he's done a lot round the house too.'

She saw John hovering at the end of the ward and smiled at him. He came up to the bed and told them that the sister had said that mother and baby were doing well. 'She said the baby lost three ounces, but she's gained again and now she's two ounces over her birth weight.'

'Did she say when I can come home?' Anne asked eagerly.

'She said if you go on like this the doctor will let you come home in ten days.'

'But that's Friday,' Anne exclaimed, and Sally warned her, 'Don't get excited now, girl, and send your temperature up. Gerry'll be made up to see you, anyway.'

'I took him on the Overhead Railway yesterday,' John said. 'Then down to the Pier Head. You should have seen him on the floating roadway. He thought we could run right down and on to the boat we could see at the bottom.'

'We'll have to take him on the Ferry when I come home.'

'I took him yesterday,' said John. 'Only over to Seacombe and back, but he loved it. I told him about Grandad going to sea, and showed him the shipping in the river.'

No more was said about the quarrel, and even when Sally left them alone for a few minutes, Anne only spoke about returning home and John said how much he missed her and that Gerry missed her too.

Anne had greatly missed Gerry and they had a joyful reunion when she returned home. He was delighted with the baby. 'Is it ours, Mummy? Can we keep it?' he asked anxiously. He hung over the baby's wicker cot, chattering endlessly while Laura lay looking up at him with bright dark eyes.

Anne had continued to correspond with Kathleen and it had been arranged that she and her husband and son would come to visit. They came in November which was a slack time on the farm where Arthur Kilmartin worked.

All the family contributed items to make the third bedroom warm and comfortable for Kathleen and Arthur. John's parents sent two large rugs, an oil heater for background warmth, and a spare wardrobe. From Anne's old home came the double bed which she had once shared with Eileen (as she now had a single bed), a bedspread and eiderdown, and a Lloyd Loom chair.

Aunt Carrie contributed a dressing table and a pair of sheets, and Anne put Gerry's outgrown cot in beside the bed for the child.

John had grumbled about having to miss a meeting on the evening that the visitors arrived, but soon after they all met learned that Arthur was a member of the Peace Pledge Union. He was delighted and the two men were soon deep in conversation.

Meanwhile, Anne and Kathleen were catching up on their news, and the two children surveyed each other warily, with Gerry standing protectively before Laura's cot.

Arthur was a tall, ascetic-looking man wearing rimless spectacles. He was a few years older than Kathleen, and had a quiet voice though he was not afraid to voice his opinions. Anne was amused to see John look discomforted when Arthur told him that he was surprised to find that John as a Peace Pledge Member had joined the armed forces.

'I wasn't a member then,' John said, and Anne added jokingly, 'Someone said he couldn't join the Army, so he was absolutely determined he would.'

'You make me sound an awkward cuss,' John muttered.

Kathleen and Arthur were tired after their long journey so they went to bed early. As soon as they were safely upstairs John said angrily, 'What was the idea of saying that about the Army? Were you trying to make me look a fool?'

'It was only a joke, for Heaven's sake,' Anne protested.

'It wasn't my idea of a joke. You tried to make me look small.

You made Arthur uncomfortable too.'

'I'm sure I . . .' she began but John roughly interrupted her, 'Never mind. Forget it. I don't want to discuss it.'

'Then why did you . . . ?' Anne started, but again John interrupted her. 'I said I don't want to discuss it. I don't want to hear another word.'

He had been winding the clock and now banged it back on the mantelpiece. '*I* want to discuss it,' Anne said, but he said loudly, 'No. That's enough. I'm going up. Goodnight.'

She was left fuming, and even when she had completed her preparations for the morning, and was ready for bed, still raged inwardly. He starts something but won't wait for an answer, she thought. Everything always has to be on *his* terms. But she was very tired and soon fell asleep.

Because they had visitors, Anne was unable to keep up the quarrel with John and he seemed unaware how angry he had made her. All right for him, Anne thought, he said his piece and refused to let me give him an answer. But she was anxious to give Kathleen a good impression of her marriage so pushed her grievance to the back of her mind.

Greg had fitted bookcases on either side of the sitting-room fire and Anne lit the fire there every day during the visit, so although John was at work, Arthur was quite happy browsing among the books.

Anne and Kathleen could talk freely in the kitchen, while Laura slept and Gerry and Kathleen's child, Ben, played together happily.

Kathleen wanted to know all about Anne's family and was intrigued to learn what had happened when Terry returned home from prison camp. Anne showed her photographs that he had sent from Canada. 'He was homesick at first, I think,' she said, 'but he seems to be settling down now. My cousins Des and Dom Anderson are thinking of joining him.'

'The terrible twins?' Kathleen said, laughing. 'Do you think Canada can stand it?'

'I don't know how Aunt Carrie'll stand it,' Anne said seriously. 'Or Uncle Fred. He relies on Des in his workshop, and I think he was hoping he'd take over. But Dom's unsettled, and where he goes Des will go.'

'At least we've got years before we need to worry about anything like that,' Kathleen said, glancing at the two little boys.

As the week progressed the two girls grew closer, and Kathleen told Anne more about her unhappy years before she was admitted to hospital with the shrapnel injury.

'It's a good thing I didn't realise just how strange it all was,' she told Anne. 'I suppose I was caught up in it too. Ella saved me, I think she was sorry for me and was so determined to get me out on my own, away from the closed circle with Mother and Cormac.'

'I'm ashamed that I didn't do more to keep in touch,' Anne said.

'You couldn't have done anything, Anne. In fact when I look back it was really the teacher getting me the job that saved me. Mother needed the money for Cormac's clothes, otherwise she wouldn't have allowed it, but I was always less important to her.'

'A good thing you were as it turned out,' Anne observed.

'Yes, and of course I worked with Ella all day, and she opened up my mind. Poor Ella. When I think of what happened to her, *I* feel guilty.'

'Why?' Anne asked.

'Did you know she was attacked?' Kathleen asked. 'I don't know whether it was Mother or Cormac, but it was one of them.'

'But another girl was attacked and the police got the man,' Anne said.

'Yes, for the other girl, but they knew someone in our house attacked Ella. They *haunted* the house, Anne, but Mother swore that Cormac was at home with her all the time. They asked the neighbours and they said we never went out separately.'

Anne was silent, partly with amazement and partly because she was uncertain what to say. Before she could decide, Kathleen went on, 'Poor Cormac. His mind was warped, you know, Anne, with Mother's delusions. She should be pitied too though.'

'She worked terribly hard, didn't she?'

Kathleen sighed. 'Yes. She regarded herself as a bondwoman and us of Royal blood. She felt it was her duty to work and provide for us, but we mustn't soil our hands. Especially Cormac.'

'And he accepted that situation?'

'Yes. That's why the call-up papers were such a shock to him and he —'

'So that was why he did it?'

'Committed suicide,' said Kathleen. 'Yes. Some official had been to see him. I don't know what he said. Perhaps he told Cormac what to expect. I'll never know. I was in hospital, and Mother was at work, and the man won't admit that he frightened Cormac, will he?'

'God forgive him if he did,' Anne said, and Kathleen said fiercely, 'God damn him, I say. I hope he rots in hell. *I'll* never forgive him.' Anne was alarmed to see a fanatical expression on her face which reminded her of Mrs O'Neill, but the next moment it had gone and Kathleen said easily, 'All long ago and far away now, isn't it? Mother only lived six months after Cormac.'

'Have you kept in touch with Ella?' Anne asked.

'Yes. You know she got married soon after she came out of hospital. One of the detectives actually, but they split up soon afterwards.'

'But you still see her?' Anne said.

'Oh, no, and I don't want to,' Kathleen said. 'I mean, she must know what the police thought, but she wrote to me when I was in hospital and I replied. We send only Christmas and birthday cards now. She's living in London.'

They were interrupted by the children and Anne was not sorry.

Kathleen's past was not mentioned again but Anne often thought about it. So she had been right after all to suspect Cormac or his mother of attacking Ella. Perhaps I was lucky that I didn't get too involved, she thought.

The rest of the week passed quickly and pleasantly, and John seemed to enjoy Arthur's company. He also enjoyed showing Gerry off to the visitors. Ben was only a year younger than Gerry but was much less articulate and intelligent, and John constantly urged Gerry to recite nursery rhymes or sing the little songs that Anne had taught him.

She was pleased when one day Gerry refused to sing, saying, 'No. I want to play with Ben.'

She said quickly, 'Ben's teaching him how to tie his shoelaces. I don't know how often I've tried, but Gerry seems to have got the hang of it at last from Ben. Perhaps he will be a teacher.'

'He's certainly very patient,' Arthur said, looking pleased.

'*I* didn't know Gerry couldn't tie laces,' John said, 'or —'

But Anne interrupted him. 'Who dressed him while I was in hospital?'

'Mum, I suppose, or Grandma,' John said. 'Except Sunday. I dressed him on Sundays.'

'And I suppose you tied his shoelaces?'

'Maybe. I don't see that it matters,' John said.

'Not then, but the more he can do for himself the better now that I have Laura to look after,' Anne said. 'And when he starts school he'll need to be able to tie his own shoelaces.'

John said no more then, but later when the children were in bed, Arthur and Kathleen talked of their hopes for another child. 'More if possible,' Arthur said. 'I was an only child, and sometimes very lonely. I had to fulfil all the ambitions of my mother *and* my father too.'

'I had a brother, of course,' Kathleen said. 'But the less said about *my* childhood the better.'

'You weren't as fortunate as Anne then,' John said. 'The spoiled youngest of a large family.'

'I wouldn't say I was spoiled,' Anne said indignantly, but John hooted with laughter.

'Not spoiled?' he said. 'Why, they wouldn't let the wind blow on you. Not only your parents but all your brothers and sisters protected you too.'

Anne felt near to tears with anger and distress at John's jeering tone, but she swallowed and said quietly, 'I hope you're able to have more children, Kath. Helen and Tony can't, unfortunately, but there's a reason for that.' She avoided even looking at John, feeling that he was being spiteful because of the earlier disagreement.

Kathleen disregarded her words and spoke directly to John. 'Yes, I remember Anne at school. She was always the teacher's pet because her elder sisters had gone through the school before her and been such angels, it seemed.' She looked at Anne. 'Then you brought so much money for the Good Shepherd Fund, and flowers for the May altar.'

'But that was because Mum supported the Missions, and Tony and Maureen gave me money for flowers when they were working,' Anne protested.

'Exactly,' Kathleen said triumphantly, 'because you were the youngest and still at school while they were working. And in the playground . . . The way I was treated, but no one dared to touch you! Everyone had to be friendly with *you* because they were afraid of your Eileen. She watched over you even though she was in the other playground.'

Anne was tempted to reply that Kathleen's isolation in the playground was her own choice, but she had been taught never to be rude to a guest so she rose to her feet. 'Excuse me. I'll put the kettle on,' she said.

The walls of the house were thin and as she stood in the kitchen

Anne heard Arthur say, 'It's only an accident of birth that Anne's the youngest in her family, and I don't know why you say she's spoiled, John. Anyone less sweet-natured would have raged at you and Kathleen when you said things like that about her.'

Anne's hurt feelings were soothed but she heard John reply, 'Yes, but it's a fact, Arthur, Anne has always been shielded by her family from any unpleasantness, and they all still dote on her. She's been very lucky.'

'I think Anne would be happy whatever her circumstances,' Arthur said, and she heard John reply cheerfully, 'I'm sure she would. My grandma says Anne has a gift for happiness.'

The next moment he came into the kitchen, offering to carry the tray, and Anne was able to smile lovingly at him. I'm just too touchy, she thought as she followed him into the living room. I'll have to watch it.

Kathleen too seemed unaware of upsetting Anne and talked about her shock at seeing so many empty spaces in Everton where houses had stood before the Blitz.

'Whole streets gone without a trace,' she said. 'I just couldn't believe my eyes.'

'Never mind, dear, you laid a few ghosts today,' Arthur said, taking her hand.

The following day Kathleen spoke again about Anne's childhood. 'I remember you telling me that your uncle called you Happy Annie. I thought it would be strange if you *weren't* happy with a childhood like yours. I suppose even then I realised that there was something wrong with mine, although I couldn't recognise what it was.'

'But your mother loved you very much, didn't she?' Anne said. 'She was very protective.'

'*Too* protective,' Kathleen said grimly. 'I'm not making that mistake with my children. As soon as Ben's seven I'm sending him to Canley Prep school as a weekly boarder.'

'*Seven!*' Anne said. 'That's too young, surely, Kath? Won't you worry about him?'

'Rich children are sent as full boarders at that age,' Kathleen said firmly. 'Arthur's chosen to be a farm labourer, but my children are not going to suffer for his beliefs.'

'But surely it'll be very expensive?' Anne said.

'I'll manage,' Kathleen told her. 'I have a nice little nest egg towards it already. We don't pay rent, and we have a very big garden. I spend very little. We've got the chickens and plenty of eggs, and of course all the vegetables and fruit we need. Arthur's got a half share in a pig with a neighbour too.'

'That must make a difference,' Anne agreed. 'I spend a lot on food.'

'I sell eggs and chickens and vegetables and soft fruit to a stall in Canley market, and I do outwork for a firm in Canley. Dolls' clothes and bedding, y'know, sheets and eiderdowns for dolls' cots, and I do button sorting for another firm. It all helps.'

'You must work very hard,' Anne exclaimed.

'Why not? It'll be worth it,' said Kathleen. 'Ben will have a good education and learn to stand on his own feet, and I'll do the same for any other children we have.'

A disquieting memory flashed into Anne's mind, of Mrs O'Neill's three jobs, but she thrust it away.

'I just want to have a home like ours was,' she said. 'I'd like six children so they'd always have a good time together like we did, and plenty of company. "A nest of singing birds", in fact,' she said, laughing. 'But who knows what's in store for any of us? "Man proposes, God disposes", Mum always said.'

'And John isn't a doting husband and father like your own was, is he?' Kathleen sneered, but Anne made no reply.

Chapter Thirty-Six

She was secretly relieved when the time came for her visitors to leave, although they parted with many promises to keep in touch and thanks from Kathleen and Arthur. The two little boys clung together and cried loudly when they were parted.

Greg Redmond had offered to drive them to the station, and when Anne and John had waved them off and turned back into the house, John exclaimed, 'Well, I can't say I'm sorry that's over, although Arthur's a smashing fellow.'

He seized Anne round the waist and waltzed her about the room, singing, 'Just Annie and me, and baby makes three.'

'Four,' Anne said, laughing. She wished that he had done this while Kathleen could see them. Aware of her views on their marriage, Anne had tried to present a loving picture to her, yet she was unable to resist snapping at John sometimes, and he did the same.

Gerry began to cry again for Ben and John picked him up. 'I know, should we look under the stairs and see what we can find?' he suggested. Knowing that Gerry would be upset, John had bought him a Triang toy crane and concealed it under the stairs, and Anne had a small bag of Dolly Mixtures for him.

Gerry's tears were soon dried as he and John filled the bucket of the crane with Dolly Mixtures and wound it up. Anne happily hummed Tea For Two as she nursed Laura.

Laura was not as placid as Gerry had been as a baby, and Anne often thought of the sister's words about her determined little mouth. Anne had a bout of influenza in January which left her feeling weak and depressed, and unable to continue breast feeding the baby.

Laura refused to take the bottle, twisting her head from side to side and pressing her lips together as Anne tried to force the teat into her mouth. Mrs Rooney tried too without success.

'Four months old and she's got the better of the pair of us,' she exclaimed, and Anne worried that the baby would die of malnutrition.

Fortunately Sally came to see Anne, and she prepared a solution of honey and water for Laura. She walked up and down with the screaming child, and as Laura paused for breath slipped the teat into her mouth and let the honey and water dribble on to her tongue.

The baby sucked greedily at it until the bottle was empty, then slept, and when she woke took the bottle of milk without protest.

Mrs Rooney watched Sally with awe. 'How many did you have?' she asked respectfully.

'Only two of my own,' she said. 'But one of them was a real handful.'

'And Grandma was midwife, District Nurse and everything rolled into one,' Anne said. 'Everyone sent for her when there was sickness or trouble in the house.'

'I was more free to help,' Sally said, 'having only two children to look after.' But Mrs Rooney knew that that was not the real reason.

She had been a good neighbour to Anne while she was ill, and spent much time with her, but she told Anne that it suited her to be in her house instead of in her own.

Con had suddenly produced a girlfriend who was alleged to be pregnant and they were married within two weeks.

As it was impossible to find anywhere to live they were staying with Mrs Rooney who detested the girl.

'Says she must've made a mistake, or had a miss and never noticed, so she's not pregnant after all,' Mrs Rooney said to Anne later. 'A likely story! She says she's only twenty-two, but she's had a few years in her stockinged feet, the same one. Thirty if she's a day, I reckon.'

'How old is Con?' asked Anne.

'Twenty-eight, and never bothered much with girls. Always full of ideas, but I never thought he'd be caught like this. I can imagine the other feller, our Barty, getting caught. He doesn't know what day it is. Always got his head stuck in a book, but I thought my Con was smart. This crafty bitch has hooked him, though, bad luck to her. Going on the protest march, with him, pretending she's interested.'

The weather was bitterly cold and Anne was glad to stay indoors, especially as both children had coughs. John did the bulky shopping on Saturday afternoon and Mrs Rooney, who shopped every day to avoid her daughter-in-law, would always bring small items for Anne. In return Anne tried to have her washing and cleaning finished early so that she could be ready to welcome her neighbour and spend time with her.

Her thoughts often dwelt on her childhood and her happy home, and Mrs Rooney never tired of hearing about it. Her own childhood had been very different. 'I never had a shoe on me foot until I was nine,' she said, 'and then it was police clogs. Me da died when I was five and I'd never seen him sober, as God's me witness.'

'Were you an only child?' Anne asked.

'Sweet God, no, girl. Me mam had seven, one every year, but she buried four. Me poor mam. Me dad drank most of what he earned, but she always had something off him. When he died she had tuppence in her purse and didn't know where to turn. No widow's pension in them days, girl.'

She was silent for a moment, staring into the fire, then she sighed. 'We all had to turn to. Be the time I was six I was selling papers, and me brothers were picking up what they could. Carrying cases and holding horses' heads and that. The sister younger than me died the next year, then me mam.'

'What did you do? What happened then?' Anne asked.

'Just had to fend for ourselves,' Mrs Rooney told her. 'The parish buried me mam, and after that I just got knocked from pillar to post. I was terrified the coppers'd get me and put me in a home, so I kept out of the way. It was only when I was sick and some woman took me in that I went to school when I was nine. She never had nothing but she was a good woman.'

'And you've got a nice home now,' Anne said.

'Yes, and a bloody viper in it! But don't worry, I'll soon shift her. I learned to look after meself in a hard school, girl.'

A few mild days in February encouraged Anne to go out and she felt remorseful when she saw how much Gerry enjoyed himself on the swings in a little park.

'I should have made the effort to take him out,' she told John, 'even though the weather was bad and I felt so rotten. He shouldn't have been cooped up so long.'

'He's been out with me every weekend and all weekend,' he said, and she agreed. John had taken Gerry on a round of family visits every Saturday afternoon and Sunday, and then on to ride on the Overhead Railway or the ferries to the other bank of the Mersey.

Anne resumed her weekly visits to John's parents and grandmother, and he again came for his meal before they were driven home by his father. Laura was a delight to all the Redmond family. At six months old she was a pretty and well-behaved child, although still very stubborn.

'She must take after Cathy,' Sally said. 'She was a good child but stubborn.' Cathy raised her eyebrows and smiled at Anne who said quickly, 'My mum said I was stubborn too.'

'Then Laura's got a double dose,' Cathy said, laughing. Her eyes sparkled and dimples showed in her cheeks, and with a sudden rush of affection Anne flung her arms around her mother-in-law. How nice the Redmonds were, she thought.

Cathy hugged her but looked closely at her. 'You still look peaky, love,' she said. 'That 'flu's a very weakening thing.' And Sally agreed.

'You look after yourself,' she said. 'Never mind the house-work. Put salt on it until you feel better and make sure you get plenty to eat.'

Anne enjoyed being fussed over by Cathy and Sally and being given milky gruel to drink. 'It'll put a lining on your stomach,' Sally said, and they insisted that she had a rest on the sofa while they looked after the children.

She visited her own old home on another afternoon. Only Sarah was there, but they had plenty to talk about. Sarah was expecting another baby in March and many other changes were imminent in the family.

Stephen had become engaged at Christmas to a girl who had been in the same class as Sarah at school, Margaret O'Dowd. 'I only vaguely remember her,' Sarah confessed. 'Of course there were forty-eight in the class, but she's very nice. They don't want a long engagement.'

Pat Fitzgerald's business had been booming since the end of the war, and he had taken his foreman, Billy Joyce, and Billy's son, Freddy, into partnership with him.

'None of the lads want to carry on the business,' he told Fred. 'And Billy stuck to me in good times and bad. Freddy's always been very reliable and came back to me the minute he was out of the Army.'

Fred's business was also making money rapidly and it was

arranged that he would put some of his capital in Pat's firm so that he could expand.

'No use me thinking of expanding,' said Fred. 'I've got as much work as I can handle with the quality leather side, now that Des has gone to Canada. The shoe shop is the right size to bring me a steady return without me having to worry about it.'

'Aye, it's more a personal skill, like, with the leather work,' Pat agreed. 'It's a pity Des emigrated when he had such a flair for it.'

'Theresa's lad, young James, is shaping well, and he's got good ideas too,' Fred said. 'But he's not twelve yet, so I might as well let my money work with you, Pat, for the time being.'

There were many open spaces now in Liverpool, from which bombed houses had been cleared, and on one of these, near St Domingo Vale, Pat planned to build two pairs of semi-detached houses.

Sarah and Joe were still well down the waiting list for Corporation houses, and Helen and Tony had been warned that their house was due for compulsory purchase under a clearance scheme.

Pat had earmarked two of the houses for the two couples, and Sarah was excited at the prospect of a new house, and of having Helen and Tony as neighbours. She was worried that Anne might feel hurt that the house had not been offered to her and John, but Anne assured her that they were quite happy in their present house.

'We've got good neighbours, and it's handy for the church and school and the tram,' she said. 'The rent is as much as we can manage without worrying anyway.'

'It'll take us all our time to pay the mortgage,' Sarah admitted, 'but we won't worry about furniture and things when we first move in. We'll make do with what we've got, and neither of us are worried about posh clothes or fancy food. We'll be able to live very cheaply.'

Sarah had been interested to hear about Kathleen's visit. 'The way you used to worry about her, Anne,' she said. 'But that queer life doesn't seem to have had any effect on her.'

Anne looked doubtful. 'I'm not so sure,' she said. 'The more I think about it . . . just now and again she seemed really unbalanced. Talking about that doctor she had the craze for at the hospital – she must have nearly driven the man desperate. And the nervous breakdown was really because he was getting married.'

'I thought it was because of Cormac's suicide?'

'I suppose that came into it, but she seemed to have really gone over the top about that Doctor Boland. And sometimes she spoke so vindictively about people, but luckily Arthur seems a very calm and patient sort of man.'

'Yes, she seems to have put into a good harbour now, as my grandad would say,' said Sarah.

'She doesn't think I have,' Anne said. 'She envies my happy childhood, but she doesn't think much of my marriage.'

She tried to speak lightly but Sarah glanced at her shrewdly. 'I wouldn't worry about Kathleen's opinion about *that*,' she said. 'Wishful thinking, maybe, and a bit of jealousy.'

'Perhaps,' Anne said. 'I wanted to give her a good impression, Sar, but d'you know, John and I seemed to be picking at each other all the time she was there.'

Sarah laughed. 'Why worry? She'd probably made up her mind before she ever came, and anyway we all know you're happy even though our John was spoiled rotten at home.'

'I'll remember that,' Anne said, giggling. 'Turn the tables on him when he talks about *me* being spoiled. Have Stephen and Margaret fixed the date yet, by the way?'

'No, but no later than September,' Sarah said. Anne had begun to pack her bag with spare napkins, dusting powder, bibs, feeding bottles and a tin of dried milk.

'John's amazed at what we have to bring with us when we go

out with Laura,' she said. 'He missed all the early months with Gerry.'

'And he was out of nappies by the time John saw him, wasn't he?' Sarah said. 'I'll walk to the tram with you, anyway.'

Sarah was admitted to the Maternity Hospital on the morning of 15 March 1949 and her daughter was born at six o'clock in the evening. Clothes rationing had finished on that day and there were many jokes about the timing of the birth.

'It's an omen,' Anne told Joe. 'Your hand will never be out of your pocket buying clothes for her.'

'Yes, she'll be a fashion plate like Carmel,' Eileen said. 'I don't think I can stand it. I always feel so scruffy when Carmel arrives like a picture of elegance.'

'She can't wait to get into old clothes, though,' Maureen said.

'And that makes me feel worse,' Eileen retorted. 'Because she still looks like a million dollars.' Joe was oblivious, walking about with a beaming smile on his face.

The baby had reddish-brown hair and blue eyes and everyone agreed that she looked like Sarah and her grandmother. She was christened Rosaleen Sarah, and although her baby hair rubbed off, her new hair was even more red.

Gerry showed less interest in the new baby than he had in David, now that he had his own sister. Anne had taken him to the school to register him, and the headmistress had suggested that he should start school in September, although he would not be five until January.

'He seems very advanced for his age,' she said. 'And he'll have the advantage of starting before we have the children from the "baby boom" just after the end of the war.'

John still put Gerry to bed every night, except for the rare occasion when he went straight to a meeting from work. Anne was still excluded from these bedtime sessions, although Gerry told her about them the following day.

'Daddy taught me my letters,' or 'Daddy showed me how to do sums,' he would announce proudly.

Anne worried that John might be teaching the child by a different method to that used by the school, and confusing him, but John dismissed the idea. 'It'll give him a head start,' he insisted so Anne only shrugged and said, 'Time will tell.'

John never offered to take Laura to bed, or even to nurse her or give her a bottle. All his attention was still on Gerry, but Anne thought that this would change when Laura was older and more interesting to him.

He had resigned from the Catholic Young Men's Society committee as it clashed with the gardening club meetings on Sunday lunchtime, although he continued on the St Vincent de Paul Society committee, and was also involved with the local Labour Party.

John could take Gerry to the gardening club meetings and to some of the meetings at the Labour Club, and in both places Gerry played happily until his father was ready to take him home.

Anne and John and the two children still went as a family for Sunday tea at the Redmond house or to a gathering of the family for tea at the Fitzgeralds'. At his mother's house, if the weather was fine, John would take Gerry to a nearby park before tea to play ball or to watch the footballers.

At the Fitzgeralds' he would also take Gerry out before tea, making the excuse that he wanted to show his son the places where he had gone with his grandfather before they were all swept away.

Stephen's fiancée Margaret O'Dowd, and Eileen's boyfriend Martin Hanlon, were now present at the Sunday family teas, but not Chris Murray as Maureen was unwilling to explain her situation to the prospective new members of the family.

Chris still went to Llandudno once a month to see his wife and paid her the same large proportion of his wages, although she had now left the nursing home and was sharing a flat with the ex-Matron of the home.

'That sounds fishy to me,' Eileen said. 'Why did the Matron get the push? Chris is a fool to pay money to a set up like that.'

'She's still his wife and he has a moral duty to support her,' Maureen said quietly, and Eileen said no more to her. To Theresa she said that she was sure that Maureen had no idea what she meant about the set up.

'She wouldn't say any different even if she did realise they were lesbians,' Theresa said. 'Although she's so gentle, Maureen's as hard as a rock where her principles are concerned.'

In August work began on a factory at Capenhurst which was to produce enriched uranium, in spite of protests against it. John was furious about it and the meetings of the Peace Pledge Union seemed to last longer and longer.

At the weekend nearest the opening John and Con and his wife joined a protest against it, carrying banners made by Con's wife, Dolores.

'I wish you'd come and show as much interest as Dolores,' John said to Anne.

'And who'd look after the children?' she demanded.

Mrs Rooney was annoyed, although pleased to have Dolores out of the house for the day. 'She's a hardfaced bitch,' she told Anne. 'I only passed a remark about her name being funny and you should've heard her.'

'She wasn't pleased?' Anne said, smiling.

'She turned round and told me with names like Cornelius and Bartholomew and Isabella Mary in the family, I should keep quiet about her name.'

'Do you like long names?' Anne asked diplomatically.

'It wasn't me. It was Eddie what chose them. He said if they didn't have nothing else off us, at least we could give them important-sounding names.'

Although Anne resented the time that John spent at meetings, she was very happy otherwise. Both her children were healthy and happy, and John was a tender and loving husband. They were again using the safe period but only until Laura was about eighteen months old. Anne still hoped for a large family so that she could re-create her happy childhood home.

Laura was one year old on 2 September, and Sarah brought David and Rosaleen, and Helen brought Moira, to a little birthday party for her.

They left before John arrived home from work, but Gerry insisted that the small remaining piece of cake should have a candle stuck in it to be lit by his father.

They all sang 'Happy Birthday' again and Gerry applauded loudly. 'He's enjoying Laura's birthday even more than she is,' Anne laughed, and John said with satisfaction, 'Not a jealous bone in his body as my grandma would say.'

The following week Gerry started school and was happy there from the first day. Although the school was not far away, Anne found the walk there four times a day to take Gerry or bring him home very time-consuming. She still rose early and managed to do some housework or washing before wakening Gerry for school, then after leaving him she went to church for nine o'clock Mass, and then for her shopping. It was impossible now for her to travel back to Everton to shop.

After she had brought Gerry home for lunch and taken him back she sat with Laura on her knee to listen to 'Listen With Mother', then the little girl went down for a nap and Anne whirled about doing housework and preparing the evening meal before again collecting Gerry.

It was an orderly, happy existence. She met many of her friends as she walked about and Laura thrived on the fresh air

483

and the exercise as she often walked behind the pushchair instead of riding in it.

At the end of September Stephen and Margaret O'Dowd were married, and the family were convinced that this time he had found the right girl. Margaret belonged to a large and boisterous family, and several of her brothers and sisters were married with children so the reception was held in a church hall.

'I'll need the George's Hall for the next one,' Margaret's father told Anne. 'Our Josie's engaged to a lad with nine brothers and one sister.'

'You've just been unlucky,' Anne said, laughing. 'Plenty of only children around.'

'Aye, but not like Stephen,' Mr O'Dowd said. 'We all think the world of him. Maybe belonging to a big family has made him the lad he is.'

Eileen and Martin Hanlon waited until after the wedding to announce their engagement. Martin was a dark serious man, totally unlike Whitey as described by Eileen, but with a quiet determination which overcame all her doubt and hesitation.

They were negotiating to buy a house on the estate where Theresa and Jim lived, and would marry quietly as soon as the deal was completed.

Stephen and Margaret were buying a house on a nearby estate, and Anne was not surprised when John spoke again about finding a better paid job and owning their own house.

'I don't think we should move,' she said. 'This house is big enough for us, and Gerry's happily settled at school. I've got good friends at the church and the Clinic, and look at all you're involved in.'

'I haven't got the new job yet,' was all that John said, but Anne felt that she had not convinced him.

Gerry and Laura were a source of endless delight to them. Gerry had made good progress at school and at Christmas was chosen to be St Joseph in the Infants' nativity play. John got time off to accompany Anne to see it.

Gerry was also a member of the class band. The teacher played the piano and the group of children on the platform banged drums, clashed cymbals or shook tambourines with varying degrees of skill, but Anne and John had eyes only for their son. He stood at the edge of the group, his tongue caught between his teeth in concentration as he watched the teacher and struck his triangle at her signal.

After the concert Anne went into the cloakroom with other mothers to help the children to change into ordinary clothes and John waited outside with Laura. The headmistress paused beside him. 'Mr Redmond?' she said. 'Gerald is an excellent pupil. He pays attention. It gives a child a good start when he's been trained at home to be polite and obedient.'

John's eyes were shining with pride when Anne came out with Gerry, and he swung the little boy up into his arms. 'I'm proud of you, son,' he said. Gerry was not yet old enough to resent his father's show of affection, and flung his arms about his neck and hugged him.

As they walked home John told Anne about the teacher's words and she was equally delighted. Gerry loved Laura and played with her endlessly building up blocks which she knocked down with shrieks of delight.

John showed more interest now in Laura but he still gave Gerry most of his attention, taking him about and putting him to bed at night. Anne sometimes wondered whether she should point out to John that he was making a distinction between his children, which she was sure he was unaware of, but she put it off, hoping that time would rectify matters.

Mick came home for Christmas and told his parents that he now had a girlfriend named Gerda, but would bring her home later as she was spending Christmas with her family.

He showed photographs of Gerda and everyone agreed that she looked a nice girl, but Christmas was overshadowed for all of them by worry about Kate.

A letter from Mary, received just before Christmas, told them only that Kate had left her husband and was now staying with her aunt and uncle. 'Whatever can have happened?' Cathy wept. 'Gene seemed such a nice lad, and his family couldn't have done more to make her welcome.'

'Too much, maybe,' Sally said grimly. 'It'd do Kate good to have to rough it a bit.'

'Mary's letter told us nothing,' Cathy said. 'Except that she was pleased to have Kate staying with her.'

Anne had brought the children to see Mick and now she said hopefully, 'Perhaps it's just a storm in a teacup and Kate is back with Gene by now?'

'Let's hope so,' Cathy said with a sigh. 'She won't get much good advice from our Mary, though.'

'Don't forget Sam's there,' Mick said. 'He'll soon sort it out.'

Cathy managed a rather watery smile and Sally said briskly, 'These young ones talk a lot of sense, Cathy. Try to put it out of your head, girl, until we know more.'

Cathy tried to take her advice but it was clear to everyone that it was an effort and all the family found that their thoughts were often far away in America.

Chapter Thirty-Seven

Anne and John and the children were due to have Christmas dinner at her father's house but even there Anne felt sad. Before long, she thought, only her father and Maureen would remain in the house which had once been so full of their happy family.

She looked round the kitchen, trying to remember it as it was before it had been wrecked during the 'May Blitz'. Very little remained the same.

The dresser was still there but the Crown Derby dinner service, her mother's pride and joy, had been destroyed, and now only a few odd dishes stood on the shelves. Patrick's re-framed photograph still stood there, along with numerous others of weddings and grandchildren.

The long table, scrubbed white, and the wooden kitchen chairs had been replaced by a small polished wood table and upholstered chairs. Her father's wooden armchair had been mended, but her mother's chair had been smashed beyond repair. Tony had gathered up the pieces and taken them to his own house, Anne remembered.

She remembered too that they had brought a comfortable chair from the parlour for her mother to use, not realising that she would never again leave her bed. Tears filled Anne's eyes at the memories but she wrenched her mind back to the present.

They spent the rest of Christmas Day with John's family, and the children diverted their thoughts, at least temporarily, from the trouble in America.

A few days later a letter came from Sam in which he said that Kate was well, but she became upset if they suggested contacting Gene. He had contacted Gene's father, however. 'He was glad to know that Kate was safe with us,' Sam wrote, 'but at a loss to know why she left. Gene was very upset. I must confess that Kate's complaints seem trivial to me, but as I explained to Mr Romero, it must have been difficult for her at such a young age to adjust to being a married woman and living in what to her was a strange country, far from her family where she had always been cherished. He is a very reasonable man and took my point. I will let you know immediately of any developments.'

'Thank God Sam's there to look after her,' Cathy said. 'He's a rock of sense.'

'Yes, but it's not fair that he should be worried,' said Greg. 'I must write to Kate and to Gene.'

Later in January John received a letter from a factory in Long Lane, offering him an interview for a job.

'But you've just had your Christmas bonus,' Anne said in dismay. 'You can't leave Johnson's now.'

'Fifteen pounds?' John said. 'I might earn that in a week. You know yourself a factory is the place to make money.'

Anne was silent. She knew that it had rankled with John that he had been unable to save while a soldier, but Anne had had a nest egg when they married. She had never earned less than seven pounds a week in the factory and sometimes as much as nine, but her mother would take no more than three a week from her.

'Sure that's a man's wage, child,' she would say, 'I couldn't take more.' So Anne had put money in the Post Office Savings Bank or in National Savings Certificates. This money was collected in the factory, and she saved more because she had so little free time to shop.

'I'll offer to return the bonus if I get this job,' John said. 'But I can't turn down this chance, Anne.'

'But you might hate the factory job.'

'Not if it pays well,' he said with a grin, but added more seriously, 'You must see, Anne, that we can't go on as we are. There's always month left at the end of our money, and I know you keep dipping into your savings to make it up.'

'*Our* savings, John,' she protested. 'A lot of that money was saved when I lived off your allotment after we were married and saved my wages. The cigar box has only run out once or twice anyway.'

They were both easygoing about money, and their system was for John to put his month's pay into an old cigar box from which they each drew money as they needed it. Anne always felt pleased that they had never argued about money which she felt would be degrading.

She was afraid that John's father would be upset when he obtained the factory job and gave in his notice, but Greg only said quietly, 'He must do as he thinks best. I hope he won't regret it.'

John seemed to be in a state of permanent excitement throughout January. In addition to his elation about the job, he was constantly dashing back and forth to the Labour Club as the General Election approached, making speeches, delivering leaflets and canvassing.

America had announced that she would develop the hydrogen bomb, which would be much more powerful than the atomic bomb, and John was conferring with Con and his wife, dashing off to meetings and writing numerous letters of protest.

'I feel I should tie you down or else you'll take off like a kite,' Anne said.

'Or a hot air balloon,' he said with a grin. A self-deprecating remark like this could disarm Anne when she grew irritated with his efforts to reform the world single-handed.

In February Eileen and Martin were married very quietly and moved into the house they had bought in West Derby.

Anne had felt queasy during the ceremony but managed to conceal it, but on the following Sunday she fainted in church. She later found that she was pregnant and that the baby was due in October.

'Well, you found out in good time,' Mrs Rooney said. 'And Laura'll be turned two.'

'Yes, we're very pleased,' Anne said. 'It's a *little* bit sooner than we meant but very welcome all the same.'

'You'll soon have your six, girl,' Mrs Rooney said. 'That's if you don't change your mind.'

Anne soon found that this pregnancy was totally different from the two previous ones. She was sick every day, not only in the morning but throughout the day, and everything that she did required an effort. Milly, the war widow who had accompanied her to hospital when Laura was born, proved a true friend, quietly helping her in many ways.

She found a neighbour whose child attended the same school as Gerry and arranged for him to be taken to school and brought home. Mrs Rooney and other friends were also very willing to help Anne.

John stayed at home nearly every evening, but he was restless and Anne felt that he wanted to be elsewhere. The telephone had been installed soon after Laura's birth and Anne was irritated by the number of people who telephoned John. She grew tired of hearing him say, 'I'm sorry, I know, but it's not possible. I can't leave my wife alone at present.'

'I don't know why you don't go to the meetings,' she told him. 'Laura and Gerry never wake once they're asleep, and I'll be all right.'

'But you're sick so often,' he said.

'I know, but I'll go to bed early with a book and I won't be far from the bathroom.'

'Well, if you are sure you'll be all right,' John said. 'These meetings are important. We want to get a million signatures for the Stockholm Peace Appeal.' Twenty minutes later he had put a hot water bottle in the bed, banked up the fire, made Anne a cup of tea and was ready to go.

Like a hound off a leash, Anne grumbled to herself, but then she thought she was being unreasonable when she had urged John to go out. Laura was at a mischievous age but often when Anne rushed to the bathroom because she was sick, she found the little girl beside her, patting her leg and saying, 'Poor Mummy.'

Anne grew very close to her little daughter at this time, but Laura was not as well behaved with John. Anne had gone to the monthly Communion Sunday of the Women's Confraternity alone, and John had also gone alone to the CYMS Communion Sunday, but on the other Sundays they had gone as a family to Mass.

Now Anne went alone each Sunday to sit near the back and frequently to come out to be sick. After a few weeks the parish priest came to see her. 'There's no obligation for you to come to Mass while you are feeling so bad, Mrs Redmond,' he said. 'In fact I would say that it would almost be wrong if you did, while you have your duty to your family.'

'I keep hoping it will pass, Father,' she said. 'It's unusual to be sick for so long.'

'I'll say a prayer you'll soon feel better,' he said. 'But remember now, keep indoors and look after yourself and I'll bring Holy Communion to you. This is the coldest April for twenty-five years, the papers say.'

For a few weeks John took the two children, but he complained that Laura was very unruly.

'She won't keep still for a minute,' he said. 'Pulling the shoes off the woman in front and shouting and crying during the sermon, or climbing over the bench. She distracts everyone around us yet Gerry's as good as gold.'

'Leave her at home then,' Anne said. 'She's all right with me.'

The family were all worried about Anne, but everyone was busy with their own affairs. Sarah and Joe were preparing to move into their new home, but Helen and Tony had to defer their move because Moira was in the Isolation Hospital with scarlet fever.

Fortunately she made a good recovery and they were able to go ahead with the move. Anne attended the ante-natal clinic at the hospital and went to see Sarah for the last time in Magdalen Street.

Anne was very upset after one visit. 'I know students have got to learn, Sar,' she said, 'but I felt terrible. All of them standing round me and I had to ask one of them for a dish because I was sick.' She wept a little. 'I felt bad enough with them all there, even without that, but the nurse was very nice. She held the dish and stood in front of me to hide me.'

'You'd think they'd have the nous to go away,' Sarah said indignantly.

'I suppose they don't know what to do, and it was over in a minute, but then they started guessing what was making me sick and frightening the life out of me.'

'Take no notice,' Sarah said soothingly. 'Like you said, they were only guessing. You'll be all right soon.'

She hid her alarm at the sight of Anne's thinness and her white face with dark shadows like bruises under her eyes, but she told her grandmother about her. Sally came to see Anne the next day. 'I'm sorry I haven't been to see you, girl, with Cathy being ill,' she said.

'How is she? What's wrong?' Anne asked anxiously.

'Nothing but worry over that little faggot in America,' Sally said. 'A good hiding is what that one needs and I told Sam so when I wrote to him.'

'Is she back with her husband yet?' Anne asked. 'John said Sam had arranged it.'

'Aye, she's back on her own terms, but how long it'll last I don't know,' Sally said. 'She's insisted on leaving that lovely house and going to live miles away from Gene's family, and she's been trying to make him leave his father in the lurch in his business. The lad dug in his heels over that, anyway,' she said with satisfaction.

'But the Romeros have been so good to them,' said Anne.

'Yes, and the father relies on Gene as the only son. He's kept that business going all through the war, waiting for Gene to come back and take the weight off his shoulders. The lad drew the short straw with that madam,' Sally declared.

She made milky gruel sweetened with honey for Anne, and told her to take it slowly. 'If you can keep that down, I'll do you some fingers of toast,' she said. She told Anne that she thought that there was more to Kate's flight than met the eyes. 'I think she's been playing around,' she said. 'But don't breathe a word to John in case he lets it slip to his mother.'

As Sally had intended she left Anne with a lot to think about, apart from her own troubles, and promised to come to see her again in a few days' time. Milly came over before she left and Sally showed her how to make the gruel and sweeten it with honey.

'It's very strengthening,' she said. 'And for a cough a hot lemon drink sweetened with honey is soothing.' Milly told Anne that she would try the lemon and honey for her young daughter who had a persistent cough.

'Mind you, it's all right now when you can take the kids to the doctor without paying,' she said. 'But some of those old remedies are the best.'

'Grandma had some marvellous ones,' Anne said. She began

to laugh as she told Milly about the jollop that Sally made for 'women's complaints'.

'Sarah told me about it,' she said. 'The basis was Grandma's homemade wine which was very potent, so the husbands started to drink the medicine. Grandmas gave it free for women with growths and other painful things, but when someone told her about the men she didn't say anything. Just told women when she gave them the medicine that it would make men impotent.'

They both laughed heartily and Anne thought how different Milly looked when she laughed. 'I remember the day Sarah told me and the way we laughed,' she said. 'After that we only had to say "women's complaints" and we fell about.'

'Things are much better now,' Milly said seriously. 'I remember my poor mother and what she suffered with something wrong with her insides after my youngest brother was born.'

'Grandma's jollop would have helped her,' Anne said sympathetically.

'Yes, or a doctor,' Milly said. 'It was all right for men. They could go to the panel doctor if they paid the stamp but women just had to get on with it and dose their children the best way they could. Life's better for everyone now, isn't it?'

Anne felt very humble. Mrs Rooney had told her that Milly's life had been tragic. She had taken her children to the shelter during an air raid, and emerged from it to find her home demolished and her mother and father, two aunts and her grandmother had all been killed by a direct hit on the Anderson shelter in the back garden.

'She only went to the other shelter because the baby's crying was disturbing her grandma,' Mrs Rooney said. 'Then on top of that her husband died in a Jap prisoner of war camp. She's had more than her share.' Yet Milly could rejoice that life was better for everyone.

Anne felt that instead of feeling hard done by when John went out she should be thanking God for her happy life.

She hoped every day that the sickness would end but it persisted and she felt weak and drained. Before the school summer holidays started Bridie came to see her and suggested that she took Gerry and Laura to stay with her for a couple of weeks, or if Anne felt unable to part with them, that Monica came to stay with her to look after the children during the day.

Monica was now fourteen years old, as pretty and doll-like as ever, but Anne had seen her mothering the younger children at Fred's parties and accepted Bridie's offer gratefully.

'She wants to be a children's nurse so it'll be good training for her,' Bridie said. 'I know your neighbours are very good, Anne, but Monica won't step on anyone's toes.'

'I know, Bridie,' she said. 'I'll be able to rest easy though if I know the children are with Monica. Any news about Danny?'

He had been called for National Service, and when the American troops were landed in South Korea, Bridie feared that Danny might be sent there. Now she shook her head. 'They said on the news that General McArthur was Commander in Chief of all UN Forces Korea, though,' she said. 'That doesn't sound too good, does it?'

'Perhaps it will all be over before our lads have to go,' Anne said. 'Makes a change for us not to be the first anyway.'

Bridie had brought some books for Anne from the secondhand bookshop, and now she rose. 'I'll leave you to read now,' she said, 'but keep your spirits up. It'll soon be all over. I'll bring Monica next week.'

John was vigorously refusing to allow Bridie to take the children before Anne had finished telling him what she had proposed. 'Don't shout,' Anne said wearily. 'Let me finish.' Then she told him about Bridie's offer to send Monica. 'Sorry I went off half cocked,' he said contritely. 'But I wasn't shouting.'

'You were,' Anne began, but John said quickly, 'Never mind. Forget it. I don't want to discuss it.' Anne felt a familiar irritation and frustration, but was too weary to care and simply turned her head away.

Monica was a great success with the children and Anne foresaw trouble with Gerry when she went home. Anne enjoyed Monica's company too and John seemed to think that her presence freed him to go out whenever he wished.

He had found work on the production line very hard after his years of sitting at a desk, but he was earning much more money and was determined to show that he had made the right decision about his job.

Often he seemed exhausted when he returned home, but after a quick bath and a meal he was ready to dash out for his meetings and other activities.

The Labour Party had been returned with a narrow majority at the General Election, but John had now parted from the local party after a furious row.

The British Peace Committee had collected a million signatures to the Stockholm Peace Campaign against the atomic bomb, but it had been backed by the Communist-led World Peace Conference so the Labour Party had repudiated it.

They had also put the World Peace Conference on a list of proscribed organisations and John had sent off furious letters to London then had an angry confrontation at the Labour Club at which he had torn up his membership card and stormed out.

'John's always falling out, though, isn't he?' Monica said calmly to Anne. 'Mum says he's always out of step with everyone else.'

'Sometimes he's right,' Anne said indignantly. 'His grandma says his grandfather was out of step too but he was proved right in the end.'

'Was that Lawrie Ward?' Monica asked.

Anne was amazed. 'Yes, but how do you know about him?'

'My mum told me about him, and my dad knew him too and

Mrs Meadows often talks about him,' Monica said. 'But I don't think he fell out with people.'

'Of course, I forgot, you live in their old home in Egremont Street, don't you, Monnie?'

'Not in the Wards' house,' Monica said. 'Our house used to belong to the Redmonds, Sarah's family. The Wards' house used to be over the road from us but it was bombed and knocked down, and the kids play where it used to be. We call it the debbry.'

'The debris!' Anne said. 'Don't ever say that in front of Mrs Ward, Monica. She often talks to me about when she lived in that house. She was happy there.'

'Do you know Ethel Nickson? Her auntie has the corner shop,' Monica asked. And when Anne shook her head she said, 'She's bald. No hair at all, and she always used to wear a knitted hat when she was out, but she didn't go out much. Now she's got a wig through the National Health and she goes everywhere, even dancing. Mrs Meadows said to my mum that Lawrie Ward would have been made up about it.'

'I'm sure he would. The Welfare State was always his dream, John says,' said Anne. 'I must tell him that the old neighbours remember his grandad.'

Monica laughed. 'Yes, if you can catch him before he rushes off somewhere to have an argument,' she said. 'Still, he doesn't argue with *you*, does he?'

'Sometimes I wish he would,' said Anne, then added hastily, 'Only joking.' As she listened to Monica prattling on, artlessly revealing her mother's opinion of the rest of the family, Anne thought that she should be careful not to say anything which might be repeated and misconstrued. As she thought over Monica's comments about John, she realised how quickly the child had summed up the situation.

Monica went home for the weekend, but Anne had several visitors on Saturday. Eileen and Martin came, and Sarah and Joe, closely followed by Uncle Fred and Aunt Carrie.

'We left our children with Helen because we know you need to rest,' Sarah said when Anne said that John had taken Gerry and Laura to the park. 'Do you feel any better, Anne?'

'I'm not sick so often now, but I've got a pain in my back all the time. I get a lot of cramp too and headaches.' She gave a faint smile. 'Full of little troubles, aren't I? I sound like Aunt Minnie.'

'*Never*,' Fred said heartily, and Carrie said sympathetically, 'You're just going through a bad patch, love, but one thing about having a baby, you know there's got to be an end to it.'

'That's true,' Anne said. 'And everyone's being very good to me.' She told them about her neighbours and about Monica. 'She's lovely with the children, a proper little mother,' she said. 'And we get on like a house on fire. Sometimes though I feel as though I'm the child and she's the adult.'

'I think Bridie talks very freely to her,' Carrie said. 'You know she must have been over forty when those twins were born, but you see her and Monica walking round town, arm in arm, like a pair of sisters.'

'And yet another time, when Monica and Michael are fighting, she sounds like a child again,' said Sarah.

'Anyway, she's company for you, girl,' Fred said to Anne. 'While John's out so much.'

Before Anne could reply, Eileen stood up and began to adjust the pillow behind Anne. 'He hasn't lost his talent for putting his foot in it, has he?' she murmured. But Joe had started to ask about Fred's business and Anne only needed to smile.

On Sunday Maureen drove her father up to see Anne, bringing a jar of Benger's Food and calves' foot jelly. 'That was always reckoned to be good for a delicate stomach, chick,' her father said, but Anne felt that his loving concern did her more good than anything else.

They were pleased to hear that Monica was such a help to her, and Maureen told John that she could always get time off to stay with Anne if he was worried about her. 'I know it's not as easy for you to get time off in this new job, is it?' she said in her gentle voice.

John knew that there was never a hidden meaning in Maureen's words and she was always sincere so he agreed about his job and promised to call on her for help if it was necessary.

Monica returned on Sunday night to spend another week with them, but after that she was going with her family to a caravan at Moreton for the rest of the holiday.

Gerry was inconsolable until John promised to take him for the day to Moreton, on the other side of the River Mersey, to see Monica.

It was a warm sunny day when John and Gerry went to Moreton and Anne sat in the garden with Laura playing happily at her feet. Presently she saw Barty Rooney sitting in a corner of their garden and called to him. 'Thanks for the books, Barty,' she said. 'I enjoyed that Victor Canning. I'm trying a lot of authors I haven't read before since you've been changing my books.'

He came to the fence. 'I'll change it tomorrow if you've finished it.'

'Only if you're going to the library anyway,' Anne said. 'I've still got the Phyllis Bentley to read.'

'I'll be going,' Barty said quietly, smiling at her.

A few months earlier Anne had told Mrs Rooney that she was worried about her library books being overdue, and Barty had immediately offered to change them for her. Since then he had changed them regularly and Anne had enjoyed talking about books to him. He was a quiet shy man, totally unlike his brother, but Anne's friendliness had broken through his reserve.

All was not well in the Rooney household. Mrs Rooney had been unable to rid herself of Dolores as she had hoped. 'She's got our Con under her thumb,' she told Anne. 'If she goes, he'll go with her.'

'But I thought that was what you wanted?' Anne said.

'What! And take his wages? Not likely, girl. No, it was her I wanted out but she's as crafty as a barrowload of monkeys.'

Tremendous rows took place, which Anne tried to avoid hearing, but Mrs Rooney told her about them anyway.

'Did you hear what she called me last night? A bloody old bloodsucker! And our Con turned round and said all I cared about was money,' Mrs Rooney said. 'Barty told him not to speak to me like that.'

'It's a shame if he gets drawn in,' Anne said indignantly. 'It's got nothing to do with Barty.'

'That's what our Con said, and Barty told him he didn't like two on to one.'

They were in Anne's kitchen and she saw Barty, who was on shift work, walk down the garden. 'You'd never think they were brothers, would you?' Anne said, looking at Barty's thin face and body and brown wavy hair. She thought that Con looked very flashy with his black hair sleeked back and his pencil moustache but Mrs Rooney said, 'No, our Con's so smart and Barty goes round in a dream half the time. That one wouldn't have bothered to get her claws into *him*.'

Anne's sickness had stopped at last, but she found the hot weather very trying. She felt that her pregnancy had lasted forever, but there were still two months to be endured before the baby was due to arrive in early October.

Chapter Thirty-Eight

John seemed unable to talk of anything but the campaign against the A-bomb. Anne sometimes closed her ears deliberately to his conversation. She thought resentfully that he should be trying to avoid talking on subjects that worried and depressed her, instead of harping on the awful prospects for the future of mankind.

Bishop Barnes of Birmingham had demanded that Britain should not follow the example of America, in making a still more powerful bomb, and John talked at length about him, and about one hundred Cambridge scientists who had petitioned the Government on the same grounds.

'These are clever men, Anne,' he said. 'Men who know what they're talking about, and they are absolutely against it.'

'Then why don't you leave it to people like that?' she said wearily. 'Surely the Government will take more notice of men like them?'

'But we have to back them up,' he said. 'Votes are what count with politicians, and the three million signatures on the Stockholm Peace Appeal will have made them realise how many people are against the bomb.'

'What does Con think?' Anne said. Not that I really care anyway, she thought, but I wish he'd go and talk to Con.

'Oh, Con!' John said in a disgusted tone. 'He was so keen, and I thought Dolores was too, but I think it was only a means to an end with her and she wears the trousers there. Do you know they're planning to leave next-door on Friday? Dolores has found a flat.'

'Does Mrs Rooney know?' Anne exclaimed.

'I think they're telling her tonight.'

'The mean things! They should have given her more warning,' Anne said indignantly, but John said nothing. He stood up and wandered about the room, fiddling with ornaments and taking books from the bookshelves and putting them back again.

Finally he said suddenly, 'Listen, Anne. I've been asked to go to London on a demonstration march. Would you mind?'

'When is it?' she asked.

'August Bank Holiday weekend. It's the anniversary of the atomic bomb being dropped and this is a Hiroshima Day commemoration in Trafalgar Square. You're not so bad now the sickness has stopped, are you? And your Maureen would probably stay with you, wouldn't she?'

'I suppose so,' she said, thinking that he had made all his plans before he asked her. 'Is Con going?'

'No. Dolores has other plans for him, but never mind. We expect to have thousands there anyway.'

'*Thousands?*' Anne said in amazement.

'Yes. From various groups, religious and pacifist and others. I'm fighting for a future for Gerry and other children, Anne. There'll be none for them if atomic warfare starts – for anyone. Only a horrible death.'

Her face became even more pale. 'Oh, God, John,' she gasped. 'Surely it can't happen? No one would be so mad.'

She put her hand to her side, her face twisting with pain, and John fell on his knees beside her and put his arms round her, looking remorseful.

'No, it won't, love,' he soothed her. 'We won't let it. That's what these protests are for, to make sure that the men in power get the message. Do you feel bad?'

'No, I'm all right. It was just the baby moving,' she said. She thought John might change his mind about going to London, but he went ahead with his preparations and asked Maureen if she would stay overnight with Anne.

Maureen agreed, although Anne thought she looked surprised by John's request. She said nothing, however, except that she would arrange for her father to have his meals at Aunt Carrie's house.

Eileen was more forthright. 'A queer time to go away, isn't it?' she said to Anne. 'August Bank Holiday. You'd think he'd be taking the opportunity of getting out with you and the kids.'

'I don't want to go out,' Anne said. 'I'm happier in the house or the garden at present.'

'But he could take the children off your hands, and do things in the house to help you.'

'He does a lot to help,' Anne said. 'I've been able to do very little for months, and John's done washing and ironing and cleaning for me. He takes the kids out too, and does the heavy shopping. Anyway, he's asked Maureen to stay with me.' No matter how much she might secretly criticise John, Anne always flew to his defence if anyone else said something derogatory about him.

Eileen said no more but Anne wondered whether there had been some discussion within the family when Helen suggested taking Gerry and Laura for the Bank Holiday weekend. 'Moira would love to have someone to play with,' she said. 'And you and Maureen could talk in peace, Anne.'

Tony was with Helen and his manner towards Anne seemed even more tender and loving than usual. This seemed to annoy John who plunged in, 'You're in the Peace Corps, Tony. And you know how important this protest is. I'm surprised you're not taking part in it.'

Tony looked at him unsmilingly. 'I leave that to people without commitments,' he said curtly. 'I have a wife and child to consider.'

John's face grew congested with anger. 'All the more reason,' he said, his voice rising in temper, but Helen said hastily, 'Oh, Tony, I've left that bag of sweets and fruit in the car. Will you get it for me, please?'

Unseen by Anne Helen gestured towards her and looked pleadingly at the two men. Tony turned and went out and John went into the kitchen and drank a glass of water. The discussion was not resumed. Before Helen and Tony left, arrangements were made for them to collect Gerry and Laura on Saturday morning and keep them over the weekend.

On Saturday morning Gerry ran happily to meet Moira but Laura clung to Anne and cried when she realised that she was to go without her mother. Anne was upset too but Helen gently coaxed Laura away, telling her that she could ride on Moira's rocking horse and play with her doll's pram then come home to her mother.

Maureen and Anne sat in the garden for a while but Mrs Rooney came to tell them tearfully about Con and his wife moving out, and the rows that had taken place. They sympathised, then she started again to tell them the same details until Barty came out and told her that she had been standing too long and must sit down and have something to eat.

He drew her into her house and Anne and Maureen went indoors too. 'I'm sorry about that, Maureen,' Anne said. 'She isn't always like that. She's just upset about Con going off.'

'I know. I've talked to her before,' Maureen said. 'It's a good thing the other son is still there.'

'Barty? Yes, he's a smashing fellow,' Anne said warmly.

They had a simple lunch then Anne slept while Maureen cleaned the kitchen and did some ironing. In the evening they sat talking together and knitting baby clothes. Maureen talked about Chris. 'He insists that I keep up with my friends and with all my church affairs,' she said. 'I'd like to spend all my time with him and I know that's what he wants really. He says knowing me is his only reason for living, but he still says I should keep going to the Children of Mary and the Altar Society, and having nights out with Mona or Annie Keegan.'

'He must think it's best for you to have other interests,' Anne said gently. 'He's very unselfish, isn't he?'

Maureen agreed. 'He is, but I don't want to take advantage of his unselfishness like that wife of his.'

'What's happening with her?' Anne asked.

'She's still living in a flat with the ex-Matron. Another rock for that limpet to cling to,' Maureen said bitterly, then added, 'I shouldn't have said that, but it makes me mad. Beryl always seems to fall on her feet, yet she's still bleeding Chris dry for money.'

The conversation turned to family matters. 'Joe and Tony are made up with their houses, aren't they?' Maureen said. 'Anything Dad builds is well done. No jerry building for him.'

'No. Sarah said that – how well the house was built,' Anne agreed. 'Eileen's house is much shoddier. Flimsy little skirting boards and gaps round the window although it's a new house, too. Joe's making a good job of the garden at their house.'

'Yes, he must have green fingers,' Maureen said, smiling.

'They're very happy, aren't they?' Anne said. 'Still absolutely wrapped up in each other.' She spoke more wistfully than she realised and Maureen glanced at her and said gently, 'They've a lot of time to make up, Anne. All those years when they had to hide how they felt about each other.'

'Yes, I suppose so,' she agreed.

Maureen laughed. 'When the children start growing up, Sarah and Joe might start arguing. Theresa says children are a fruitful cause of disagreement, and she should know. The rows she has with Jim.'

Anne chuckled. 'At least Theresa doesn't throw things at Jim like Aunt Carrie used to do at Uncle Fred.'

'Tess said that to Eileen,' Maureen agreed. 'She said it was because of the shortages after the war, but she might start now that things are coming back in the shops.'

Anne went to bed feeling cheerful and happy after her talk with Maureen, but spent a restless night, troubled by pains in various parts of her body. She was woken by a searing pain to find herself lying in a pool of blood.

'Maureen, Maureen!' she screamed, and her sister came running into the bedroom.

'What's wrong? What's happened?' she exclaimed.

Anne closed her eyes and turned back the bedclothes and Maureen gasped in horror. She looked wildly at the clock. Five o'clock and not a sound outside.

'Get Mrs Rooney,' Anne gasped. Her face was contorted with pain and Maureen ran and hammered on the door of the next house.

Barty opened the door, a coat flung over his pyjamas, and Maureen shrieked: 'My sister! The baby! Your mother . . .'

He understood instantly, and said, 'All right. Go back to her. Ma'll be in in a minute. I'll come to ring the hospital.'

Mrs Rooney was on the stairs and had heard. In spite of her bulk within minutes she followed them into the house. She bent over Anne and said reassuringly, 'You're all right, girl. It's coming early, that's all. Barty's getting the ambulance.'

He had got through to the hospital and called to Maureen, 'What date is it due?'

'About the fourth of October,' she said, and he repeated this, then Maureen heard him say, 'No, it's a third child. Yes. Normal births. How did it start?' He looked enquiringly at Maureen and she said, 'She woke up. The bed was full of blood. She's in awful pain.'

Barty repeated this and then he said, 'No, I'm just a neighbour. Her husband's away and her sister's staying with her. Thank you.'

He replaced the receiver and looked at Maureen. 'The ambulance is on its way and the hospital has got all the details now,' he said. She sat down suddenly as though her legs had given way. She looked about to faint and Barty pressed her head forward between her knees.

After a moment she sat up then rose to her feet. 'I'm sorry. I'm not much use,' she said.

'You've had a bad shock,' he said calmly. 'The ambulance will be here soon. Will you go up and tell them?'

Maureen went up to the bedroom to find Anne still curled up in pain, sweat running down her face, and Mrs Rooney getting out a clean nightdress for her. Together Mrs Rooney and Maureen removed Anne's bloodsoaked nightdress and Mrs Rooney wrapped a bath towel around her like a napkin before they put her into the clean nightdress.

'Go and get your clothes on quick so you can go with her,' Mrs Rooney said, and Maureen quickly flung them on. The next moment the ambulance arrived and the ambulancemen spoke reassuringly to Anne before taking her downstairs.

As she was carried past Barty on the stretcher she tried to smile at him and mouth 'Thanks' and he said gruffly, 'Don't worry. You'll be all right.' The next moment they were gone and Barty and his mother were left looking at each other.

'I wonder if anyone else in the family is on the phone,' he said. 'It's too much responsibility for her sister.'

He looked at the notebook beside the telephone in which numbers had been written. Most were connected with John's various activities but there were numbers for Tony and for John's father.

'Tony and Helen, they're the ones what have got the kids,' Mrs Rooney said. 'Better ring *his* father.' By this time several neighbours had been drawn to their windows by the sound of the ambulance, and Milly had come over to see what was happening.

'History repeating itself,' Barty said grimly, 'but at least her sister was with her this time.'

'Of course he's away, isn't he?' Milly said. 'Some march or other, Anne told me. At least last time he was working and couldn't help not being here.'

Before Barty could stop her his mother exclaimed, 'Working! Don't you believe it. He was out then at one of his poxy meetings. Poor girl.'

'But Barty said . . .' Milly began, and he interrupted her. 'I know I said he was working. I thought she would prefer people to think that. I'm going to ring John's father now.'

'Will you give me a hand with the bed, Milly?' Mrs Rooney asked, leading the way upstairs. 'Good job them poor kids are at her brother's.'

Greg Redmond answered the telephone, obviously newly roused, but all trace of sleepiness disappeared when he heard the news. 'Which hospital?' he asked, and when he was told said immediately, 'My wife and I will go there right away. May I ask your name?'

'Bartholomew Rooney. My mother and I live next door to Anne. Her sister went with her in the ambulance, but I think she's in a state of shock too.'

'We'll be with them within half an hour,' Greg said. 'Thank you for letting us know, and we appreciate very much the help you and your mother have given them. I'll keep you informed. Thank you again.'

Very different to his blasted son, Barty muttered as he replaced the receiver.

Neither Anne nor Maureen could afterwards remember much about the journey to the hospital, nor what happened immediately afterwards. For Anne it was just a blur of pain, but at one point she remembered a doctor bending over her and saying, 'You have a little girl, Mrs Redmond, but she's very small.' Then she slipped into merciful unconsciousness.

A nurse brought a cup of tea to the waiting room for Maureen, and she asked eagerly about Anne. The nurse could only tell her that everything possible was being done. She went away, but Maureen found that she was shaking too much to hold the teacup. She kept going into the corridor but everywhere seemed deserted.

When Cathy and Greg appeared Maureen fell into Cathy's arms, weeping uncontrollably. 'Has something —?' Cathy asked fearfully, but Maureen managed to say, 'No. I don't know what's happening. I can't find anyone to ask.'

Greg went out of the room immediately and Cathy held Maureen close, weeping with her. Greg was back shortly.

'I managed to find a doctor,' he said. 'Anne's had the baby and they're both holding their own, he said.'

'Thank God,' Maureen said fervently, but Cathy looked searchingly at Greg. 'What else did he say?' she asked.

'Anne's been given a blood transfusion, and the baby's in an oxygen tent. It's very small, but of course it's two months premature. It's perfectly formed.'

'And Anne's going to be all right?' Maureen said anxiously.

'Yes. She's weak at the moment and very shocked, but the blood transfusion will help, and she has youth on her side,' Greg said.

'And the baby? What is it?' Cathy asked.

He looked confused. 'I don't know. The doctor just said the child and I didn't think of asking.'

He went out again and a sister came to the waiting room and beckoned to Cathy. 'Are you the grandmother?' she asked. And when Cathy said she was, the sister asked if a name had been chosen. 'Julie Anne for a girl,' Cathy began, and the sister whispered, 'I'm giving her conditional baptism, but don't despair. While there's life there's hope.'

'It's a girl,' Cathy said when she went back to Maureen, but told her nothing more. Greg had been allowed to see the baby but the doctor advised against letting Cathy or Maureen see her. 'If she survives she'll look better in a few days,' he said. 'No use distressing them now.' And Greg agreed.

He had been shocked at the sight of the baby, tiny and wizened, dark blue in colour, and could see little hope for her.

They were allowed to see Anne very briefly, but she was asleep with a tube in her arm and a bottle of blood suspended above her.

They left and drove to Anne's house to tell Mrs Rooney and Barty what had happened. 'She'll need plenty of blood, God help her,' Mrs Rooney said. 'I nearly dropped dead when I seen what she'd lost. I've got the sheets in soak but I can't do nothing with the mattress.'

'I'll arrange for a new one,' Greg said quietly, and Cathy protested that Mrs Rooney should have left the sheets to her.

'No trouble to me,' she said. 'Just so long as Anne's all right. I love the bones of that girl.' She dabbed her eyes and Cathy said gently, 'She'll be all right, I'm sure. She was asleep when we left and my mother always says sleep heals.'

She spoke as much to reassure herself as Mrs Rooney. She had seen that Anne was in a drugged sleep, and had been terrified by the sight of the girl's paper-white face and shallow breathing. John will never forgive himself, she thought, if anything happens to her and he is not here.

Maureen had collected her clothes and they took her home then returned to their own house. 'If John tries to ring and doesn't get an answer, he'll try here,' Greg said. And later John did telephone. Greg could hear his voice but John evidently could not hear his father's.

'I can't get through to Anne either,' Greg could hear, then there were crackles and clicks before the line went dead. On Monday

John tried again, and after some delay managed to get through.

'Dad,' he shouted, 'can you hear me? I can't get any answer from our phone. Is everything all right?'

'No, it isn't,' Greg said. 'Where are you?'

'In Cheshire. The van broke down. What's happening?'

'Anne went into hospital early yesterday morning,' Greg said curtly. 'The baby was born prematurely.' Cathy was standing beside him and she could hear John's agitated voice.

'Tell him they're all right,' she whispered, but Greg shook his head.

'Yes, she's had blood tranfusions. The baby's in an oxygen tent. She's been conditionally baptised, Julie Anne.' There were more agitated questions from John and his father relented. 'No, I think Anne's out of danger now,' he said. 'But get yourself home as soon as you can.'

The telephone went dead and Cathy said indignantly, 'Why did you tell him all that? He'll be worried to death now, stuck somewhere trying to get home.'

'He should never have been away,' Greg said. 'And he's overdue for some worrying.'

Sally stood up. 'It'd be no kindness to tell the lad everything's fine, Cathy, when we know what he's got to face when he gets home. It'll be a long time before Anne gets over this, no matter how it goes with that poor little baby.'

John returned home on Monday evening and dashed off to the hospital, still dirty and unshaven. Anne was again in a drugged sleep, her right arm attached to the transfusion bottle and a drip attached to her left arm.

John sat beside the bed for a while but Anne still slept and a nurse offered to take him to see his daughter. He was shocked at the sight of the baby in the oxygen tent. 'Why is it blue?' he asked. 'Will it live?'

'She has a chance,' the nurse said cautiously. 'I don't want to raise your hopes, laddie, but she's survived for over twenty-four hours.'

John peered again at the child. 'It has no nails,' he exclaimed, but the sister told him that was normal. He turned away, visibly upset. 'My wife will go mad,' he said, but the sister said kindly, 'Don't give up hope. We've had even tinier babies who survived. One less than two pounds.'

'What weight is it – she?' he asked.

'Three and a half pounds,' the sister said. John went back to sit beside Anne's bed until he was told to go while she received treatment.

Greg was waiting outside and drove John back to his house where his mother and grandmother waited anxiously for news. 'Anne was asleep all the time I was there,' John said. 'But the nurse said she was improving.'

'Thank God,' both women said together, and Cathy asked about the baby.

Greg had warned John that his mother only knew that the baby was small so he said briefly, 'It's very tiny, but the sister said smaller babies have lived. It hasn't got any nails.'

'That's not unusual,' Sally said. 'Remember Duggan's lad who was in the Air Force? He was born at seven months. I wrapped him in cotton wool soaked in olive oil and we fed him with a fountain pen filler at first. Nobody thought he'd live but he made a big strong lad in the end. He was born without nails, but they grew.'

John seemed scarcely to be listening. 'I wonder will they tell Anne I've been when she wakes up?'

'I'm sure they will,' his mother said soothingly.

There was a message from Helen that she would keep the children for as long as John wished. He wanted to go to see them, but his mother pointed out that they would be in bed and persuaded him to go to see Maureen instead.

'She and her sister went to see Anne this morning,' Cathy said.

'But you can tell them how she is now, and the baby, and thank her for all she did for Anne. Poor girl, it was a terrible shock for her.'

'And don't forget to thank Mrs Rooney and her son too when you go home,' Greg said. 'I don't know what would have happened without their help.'

John was received coolly at the Fitzgerald house where several of the family had gathered, but they were relieved to hear that Anne was improving.

'What about the baby?' Eileen asked brusquely.

He hesitated. 'It's very small,' he said. 'But the sister said it's hopeful that it's lived for over twenty-four hours, and smaller babies had survived.'

'How big is she?' someone asked, and when John said, 'Three and a half pounds,' Aunt Carrie said immediately, 'Then there must have been something wrong all along. The child should have been bigger even at seven months. No wonder Anne was bad all the time, poor girl.'

John felt that she looked at him reproachfully and was glad to escape from the house. At the hospital he was told that Anne was still sleeping so he went home.

He was glad to see that the Rooney house was in darkness and went into his own house and wearily up to bed. He had a fresh shock when he walked into the bedroom. He had been warned about the mattress but the reality hit him like a blow.

The bloodstained mattress was still on the bed and the room reeked although the window was open. John stood looking at it, his thoughts in chaos, then went into the third bedroom and fell fully dressed on to the bed. He fell asleep instantly, worn out by the events of the day.

The following morning he saw Mrs Rooney before he left for the hospital and thanked her, and she gave him a graphic account of all that had happened when Maureen called her. Barty was at work and managed afterwards to evade John so skilfully that he was unable to thank him. John felt sure that it was done deliberately and wondered if it was Barty's way of showing disapproval.

The first time that John saw Anne awake he said quietly, 'I'm sorry I was away when all this happened,' but she was only concerned about the baby.

'They won't let me see her,' she said. 'They won't let me up, and they say she's in an oxygen tent as a precaution. Have you seen her?'

'Yes, she's in an oxygen tent, but only because she's premature.'

'Who is she like?' Anne asked eagerly. A phrase of his grandmother's flashed into John's mind: 'Like a fourpenny rabbit.' But aloud he said, 'It's hard to tell yet.'

'I wish they'd let me see her,' Anne fretted. 'Another woman from this ward goes in a wheelchair to see her baby in the prem ward.' She fell asleep again.

Anne was in a large ward with beds close together, and although she was awake when John visited her every day after that, there was no privacy to discuss the subject of his absence when Julie was born. It lay between them like an unexploded bomb.

Anne was in hospital for a month, and the baby remained in hospital when she was allowed home. Laura had remained with Helen, but Gerry was back attending school and sleeping with his father in the third bedroom. The mattress had been replaced and the main bedroom made ready for Anne's return.

She had been longing to see the children and Helen brought Laura home soon after Anne returned. Gerry had been shy and withdrawn at first with his mother, but Laura clung to her as though she had never been away.

Laura slept with Anne as she refused to be parted from her, and Gerry continued to share his father's bed. It was meant to be a temporary arrangement but it was never discussed and they drifted on like this.

The matter of John's absence at the birth was never discussed either. Both were unwilling to broach the subject, and as time went on it was overlaid with other matters, but not forgotten.

Anne had visited the hospital every day to see Julie, accompanied by John at the weekends. The baby continued to gain weight and at the end of November she reached five pounds and was discharged from hospital.

Greg drove them to collect her while Cathy waited at home with Laura and Gerry. They were delighted with the baby, and Greg said quietly, 'I can't believe the change in her. I never thought she'd make it, when I saw her first, and neither did the doctor.'

'I felt the same,' Cathy said, 'when the sister asked me for her name for conditional baptism, but thank God, she's fine now.'

'Why did the sister ask *you*?' John said to his mother.

'Because you weren't there and Anne was too ill to ask,' Greg said sharply. For a moment the words seemed to hang in the air, as Anne and John looked at each other, but Cathy said brightly, 'Her name suits her, doesn't it?' and the moment passed.

Chapter Thirty-Nine

Maureen and Anne had grown even closer after Julie's birth and Maureen came frequently to see her and the children. She was particularly fond of Julie, who was becoming more and more like their mother.

'I know you and Joe and I take after Mum,' Maureen said, 'but there's something more with Julie. Her expression sometimes, or the way she turns her head. I don't know what it is, but she reminds me so much of Mum.'

'I think she'll be like her in character too,' Anne said. 'She's so good and even when she cries it's a sort of ladylike little cry. Not a roar like Gerry or even a loud cry like Laura.'

They were both smiling and Maureen said impulsively, 'You look better, love.'

'I feel fine,' she declared. 'Except that my hair is still coming out.'

'Yes, but it's growing again quite strongly.'

'I know. I'm thinking of going in Bridie's perm club,' said Anne.

Bridie ran several clubs, for a hairdresser, a photographer and a crockery shop. Members contributed a shilling a week for twenty weeks and drew lots to determine in which order they received their share.

Anne's hair grew quickly and at the end of December she had a permanent wave. 'A perm will do you good,' Bridie told her.

'Make you feel better to have a change, and you won't miss the shilling a week for it.'

It was true, Anne thought, that she felt quite different with her straight hair now in rather fuzzy curls. John's only comment had been 'Very nice' but Barty had told her that she looked smart and fashionable.

Anne had also joined Bridie's photography club and in early January a photographer came to the house. He arranged Anne and John sitting on the settee, with Julie on Anne's knee, and Laura on John's, Gerry standing beside his father.

'Smile, please,' the man said. He produced a Mickey Mouse voice to amuse the children, and all the family were smiling when the photograph was taken. It was framed and placed on the sideboard and sometimes when Anne looked at the smiling faces, she thought what a false picture it gave of their family.

She and John seemed to be drifting further and further apart. They spoke only about household matters, or necessary words about the children, and the sleeping arrangements persisted. Anne talked to Barty more than to John, and sometimes thought he took more interest in the children than her husband did.

Julie was now over six pounds in weight but still seemed tiny and fragile. John seemed afraid to touch her yet Barty nursed her quite confidently.

John always switched the wireless on when he came in from work, so there was no need to talk while they ate their meal, although Gerry and Laura usually chattered. After the meal Anne washed the dishes and John dried them, but they had little to say to each other.

Afterwards he usually sat with Gerry while the child told him details about his day which he had already told his mother, and John helped Gerry with reading and writing and simple sums.

Julie needed frequent bottles and Anne was kept busy looking after her and preparing the younger children for bed. Laura still clung to her, and Anne thought sometimes that they were like two separate families in the same room.

John was still interested in the Peace Movement, and now he was also involved with his trade union at the factory. When the children were in bed he went out on several evenings a week to meetings, but he was always home early.

On the surface all was well. Anne seemed happy, proud of her children and enjoying visiting or being visited by her family. And on one level she *was* happy. On a deeper level she felt only misery and loss, a feeling that her life had taken a wrong turning and that it was empty and without meaning. Nothing in her happy life so far had prepared her for the bitter feelings of desolation which swept over her. She struggled to crush them and to turn a bright face to the world. She tried to convince herself, as well as other people, that she had the happy family life she had always wanted, and with most people she succeeded. Only John sometimes looked at her doubtfully, and Mick seemed to see below the bright surface.

'Everything all right?' he asked her once, and she said brightly, 'Yes, of course.'

He patted his shoulder. 'Anytime you want a shoulder to cry on, here it is.'

'I'll remember,' Anne said with the same forced cheerfulness. 'Gerda's a lovely girl isn't she?'

Mick smiled at the obvious change of subject, but agreed. 'I think so,' he said. 'I'm glad you do too.'

Anne had been nervous about meeting Gerda when she heard that she was a qualified accountant, but Mick and Gerda had visited Liverpool several times during the year and Anne found her a pleasant and friendly girl.

The dark gloomy days of January 1951 ended but February was as bad. An influenza epidemic swept Liverpool and the Fitzgerald family were saddened by the death of their old friend Mrs Bennet. Worse was to come.

Chris Murray was sent home from the shop on Saturday morning and his landlady sent a message to Maureen who went to the house immediately.

'He shouldn't never have gone in,' the landlady said. 'But you know what he is. Worried because it was their busy day.'

'It's only a cold,' Chris protested when Maureen went to his room. 'But don't come too near me, love, in case you catch it.'

'Doesn't seem like no cold to me. More like 'flu,' the landlady, Mrs Stopes, said to Maureen. 'I'm sending for the doctor anyway.' Maureen agreed. It was several hours before the doctor arrived and by that time Chris was delirious.

He was admitted to hospital on Saturday evening, and early on Tuesday morning he died. Maureen had been allowed to stay with him, and in a brief moment of lucidity he said sorrowfully, 'I've been selfish, Mo. You made my life worth living – made me happy – but it wasn't fair to you.'

'Oh, Chris, I wish we'd gone off together, not worried about anybody. I love you so much,' Maureen said, cradling his face in her hands and kissing him.

'Wouldn't have worked,' he murmured. His voice was fading but he gripped her hand. 'I love you, Mo,' he said. She pressed her face against his and heard his faint whisper, 'Better this way,' before he slipped back into unconsciousness.

Those last three words were to trouble and puzzle Maureen for many years. Did Chris mean it was better that he died, or better that he had lived faithful to his marriage vows though at such cost to himself and Maureen? She would never know.

She was still holding Chris's hand when the night nurses came to the bed. They seemed cheerful and uncaring to Maureen as they told her, 'He's gone, love. You'll have to go now while we see to him. See the Almoner.' She realised later that the girls could only cope in this way with the many deaths they saw.

Tony was waiting outside the ward when she went out. 'Come

on, love, I'll take you home,' he said, putting his arm around her. 'They said see the Almoner,' Maureen said in a dazed voice, but Tony gently steered her to the lift. 'Don't worry about that, pet,' he said. 'I'll see Mrs Stopes and attend to all that. It's half-past three in the morning now.'

When they returned home her father and Helen were waiting for them and Pat took his daughter in his arms. 'There, there, queen,' he said, as though she was still a child. 'There, there,' as Maureen's tears came.

Helen had a bright fire burning and quickly made tea. Pat had sat down in his chair, still holding Maureen, so that she sat on his knee with his arms around her to drink the hot, sweet tea which Helen gave her.

'You've had a shock, love. This will help,' Helen said gently.

Never before had Maureen felt the strength and comfort of her family as deeply. All the family rallied round her, and Tony and Joe took charge of the arrangements. Pat Fitzgerald offered to meet all expenses.

Tony telephoned the flat in Llandudno to inform Chris's wife of his death and the ex-Matron answered.

'What a nuisance,' was her reaction to the news, and Tony was thankful that Maureen had not heard her. He introduced himself as a friend of Chris's and offered to arrange the funeral if Beryl wished, adding that the expenses would be taken care of.

'That would be kind,' the ex-Matron said graciously. 'It would all be too much for Beryl. Yes, go ahead with the arrangements.'

'You're sure Mrs Murray will agree?' Tony said, but the woman assured him that she could speak for Beryl. The funeral was arranged for Friday and Tony notified Beryl, but a reply came that her health would not permit her to attend.

Maureen was relieved. Now, she felt, only those who had loved Chris would attend him to his last resting place. At the Requiem Mass Maureen's father knelt on one side of her and Tony

521

on the other. It was a working day but he, Joe and Stephen had arranged for time off. Eileen and Anne were there, and Sarah, Helen and Margaret. Bridie and Theresa knelt with Aunt Carrie and Uncle Fred.

The only sign of Beryl was an ornate wreath of artificial flowers with a card signed 'Beryl and Agatha'. There were many other wreaths, from all the Fitzgeralds and their relations, from the Redmonds and Mrs Stopes, and from Chris's workmates, some of whom were in the church. Maureen's simple tribute said only: 'All my love. M'.

She was comforted by the number of people who had come to pay their last respects to Chris, and by the fact that they acknowledged her loss. The priest came to her to offer condolences, followed by men who worked with Chris and who told her how much they had liked him and how sorry they were for her loss.

At the graveside the undertaker came to her first with soil to be cast on the coffin, and later Uncle Fred said, 'Quite right too. You were more his wife than that one in Llandudno.' Aunt Carrie hustled him away, looking at Maureen apologetically, but she found comfort in his words.

It was only weeks later that she felt the reality of Chris's death and the magnitude of her loss. Never again to hear his quiet voice or to exchange their own private jokes or even to sit together, not speaking but knowing they were totally in accord.

It was to Anne that she turned at this time. She spent hours with her, nursing the baby and talking, mostly on trivial matters. If John had not already left for a meeting when Maureen arrived, he went soon afterwards and the two girls could sit quietly together while the children slept.

Anne wondered sometimes if it was her own unhappiness which drew Maureen to her. Whether the dark current which flowed beneath her surface cheerfulness answered her sister's own despair.

One night Maureen suddenly looked down at the baby she was

nursing and burst out, 'Oh, Anne, she's so like Mum. Oh, God, I miss her so much.' They both cried for a while and then Maureen went on, 'Poor Dad. He's so good. He tries to help and I know I worry him. He brings me little treats and I just cry like a fool.'

'He's better going for a drink with Fred and you coming here,' Anne said.

On another occasion she knew as soon as Maureen arrived that her misery was overwhelming her. She was earlier than usual and John was still in the bedroom with Gerry, but he went out shortly afterwards and Anne put her arms round Maureen. 'Do you feel bad, Mo?' she asked quietly.

Maureen burst into tears. 'What's it all about, Anne? What's it all *for*? Why were we such fools, Chris and I?'

'What do you mean?' Anne said in bewilderment. 'You made Chris happy.'

'Did I?' Maureen said bitterly. 'Why did we live like that because of a farce of a marriage? Because of my stupid scruples, that's why, and what did it matter? We could have been really happy, living our lives together. We only have one life, and now his is over and I wish mine was too.'

'Don't say that. Don't even think it,' Anne cried. 'You did what was right. You can still feel close to Chris, still pray for his soul.' But Maureen only cried more bitterly.

'How do we know?' she said. 'What if it's all a swizz – if when we die that's all there is? Nothing. And we've denied ourselves all our lives for nothing, for a dream, an idea, a falsehood.'

Anne held her sister close, her mind racing. How could this happen to Maureen of all people? But she was speaking again. 'There's nothing, Anne. Nothing to live for, nothing after death. I just want to be finished with the whole stupid business.'

Anne felt frantic. Thoughts tumbled about in her mind, phrases from half remembered religious lessons. Occidas – was that it? The ultimate sin, the sin of despair? Was this what Maureen was experiencing now? She whose faith had meant everything to her. If she lost that, she truly lost her reason for living, thought Anne.

She pushed her sister into an armchair and snatched a handkerchief from the sideboard drawer. 'Dry your eyes, Mo,' she said. 'I won't be a minute.' She dashed next-door and when Barty opened the door she could see Mrs Rooney asleep in an armchair.

'My sister's upset. I have to take her to church. Will you mind the kids?' she said breathlessly. And Barty said, 'Sure. I'll leave a note for Ma.'

Anne went back to Maureen, taking their coats from the hall cupboard on the way. 'Come on, Mo. We're going out,' she said firmly. Barty had followed her and he held Maureen's coat for her, then Anne handed her her scarf to tie over her hair.

She slipped her own coat and scarf on and said to Barty, 'There's a bottle ready if Julie wakes. We won't be long.'

Maureen seemed bemused and walked docilely beside Anne as she gripped her arm and walked quickly towards the church.

At the door Maureen hesitated but Anne whispered, 'Please, Mo,' and drew her inside and into a bench near the back. Benediction was nearly over and the smell of incense hung in the air. As they knelt down the priest's voice rose: 'For those who have gone before us in the sign of faith and sleep in the peace of Christ, have mercy on them, O Lord, and on us thy poor pilgrims here below. Strengthen us in faith and love, and bring us to our everlasting home.'

Anne glanced anxiously at her sister. Maureen's face was hidden in her hands, but when the Blessing was given Anne was relieved to see that she made the sign of the Cross. They sat down and remained there after the congregation had gone and the church was in darkness except for the sanctuary lamp, both silent and immobile, until finally Maureen stirred and whispered, 'Shall we go?'

They walked along, arm in arm, without speaking until they had almost reached the house, then Maureen sighed. 'Thanks, Anne,' she said simply. 'I don't know what happened to me, but I'm all right now.'

'"The dark night of the soul",' Anne said. 'I know it well.'

Maureen's head jerked round and Anne said hastily, 'Only dramatising, Mo. I mean, I just feel miserable at times and wonder what I'm doing here, but I'm always quite sure I'll get to Heaven eventually. Meet up with Mum and Patrick, and now Chris and Mrs Bennet.'

They went into the house and Barty reported that none of the children had wakened. Anne was alarmed to see how white Maureen looked in the light, and how she almost collapsed into a chair.

'You'll have to stay,' she said. 'I'll ring Fred's and tell Dad it's foggy up here.' Maureen seemed too tired to protest, and Anne swiftly filled a hot water bottle and put it in Laura's bed, then lifted the sleeping child into it.

'Would you like a drink or would you rather go right up?' she asked Maureen. Her sister slowly rose to her feet and said she would go right to bed.

Anne went up with her to lend her a nightdress and tuck her into the double bed, still warm from the child's body. She heard John come in, and as she walked down the stairs could see through the open door of the living room as though it was a stage set.

Barty had been sitting in John's chair and was rising to his feet, his finger marking the place in his book, while John stood inside the door, glaring at him. Anne went quickly into the room.

'Thanks, Barty,' she said. 'Sorry to call on you so unexpectedly.'

He smiled at her. 'Anytime,' he said. 'I can read just as well in here as at home. Goodnight. Goodnight, John.'

'Goodnight,' he muttered, still looking vexed.

'Maureen was upset,' Anne said when he had gone. 'I took her to church and asked Barty to mind the kids. I've put her to bed. She's not fit to go home, and I'm going to ring Dad now.'

'I could have looked after the children,' John said, and Anne said, 'Yes. But you weren't here, were you?'

'I could have been. I only went out to be out of the way. I've been nursing half a pint in the Dog and Duck all night. You should have said about church.'

'I didn't know when you went out. I thought it was a meeting as usual anyway.'

'I don't have a meeting every night,' he said angrily. 'You don't need *him* as a baby sitter. For your information I've spent quite a few nights in the Dog and Duck recently, to be out of the way.'

Anne walked into the hall. 'I'm going to ring Fred's,' she said, over her shoulder. She spoke to her father and reassured him that Maureen was quite well but the weather was too bad for her to go home. John had been into the kitchen. He came past her as she stood at the telephone. 'I'm going up. Goodnight,' he said curtly.

Anne put the receiver down and went into the living room, collapsing into a chair as Maureen had done. She felt completely drained and her thoughts wandered vaguely through the events of the evening. John's angry words drifted across her mind without really registering with her.

She thought of her sister's anguish at her loss of faith, all the deeper because it had meant so much to her, and of her own fervent prayers that Maureen's faith would be restored and with it her reason for living.

Gradually Anne's strength was returning and she dragged herself to her feet and went into the kitchen. A rinsed mug stood on the draining board and it reminded her that Barty had been there earlier. Dear Barty, I can always depend on him, she thought.

She collected Julie's bottle and other items she might need if the child woke and went wearily to bed. Maureen still slept and Anne fell asleep quickly but wakened some hours later and lay thinking again about the evening, but less about Maureen and more of herself and John.

Was it true, as he said, that he had only gone out to leave her alone with Maureen? That was the longest conversation they had for ages, she thought. Perhaps she should have taken the opportunity to have things out with him, but she had been too weary. Probably, anyway, he would only have rushed away, saying he had nothing more to say.

Anne thought of the time in the quiet church when she had prayed not only for Maureen but for herself. Only her children gave her a reason for living. My marriage is as good as over, she thought bitterly. John and I are like strangers living in the same house. He has no interest in me or the girls, only his stupid meetings where he can be the big fellow telling everyone what to do.

It hasn't all happened since Julie's birth, either. Things have never been right between us, she thought, dredging up every grievance from the time when John had insisted on secrecy about their meetings before they were married up to his behaviour a few hours earlier.

She deliberately ignored all the good times, all John's care for her and the fun they had had together setting up their home, the joy their children had brought, and most of all she refused the memory of the nights when they had lain in each other's arms making love.

Instead she thought of Barty and how he cared for her. The way that more and more he made his feelings clear to her, looking deeply into her eyes and holding her hand as they sat together. He loves the children too, she thought. *All* the children, not just Gerry.

She fell asleep, smiling as she thought of him, until she was wakened by Laura climbing into the bed. She was surprised and almost disappointed to find that John had left for work as she was in the mood to confront him with her grievances while they were uppermost in her mind. Maureen still slept beside her.

When she woke she telephoned her office then went home, after thanking Anne for helping her over a bad patch. That night Laura returned to her mother's bed. John maintained an offended silence, and so did Anne.

Stephen and Margaret had bought a house in the south end of the city, near to his present job, but were unable to take possession immediately. Their own house was sold so they returned to live in Magdalen Street where they could be with Pat while Maureen went to a convent in Wales to spend a week on retreat.

Shortly after Chris's funeral Des and Dom had written from Canada to condole with Maureen, and to ask her to tell their parents that they intended to return. Des added a postscript asking if he still had a job with his father.

'Why couldn't they write straight to Fred?' Pat said, and Anne explained that giving Maureen the task of telling the good news was the twins' way of cheering her up.

'Pair of headcases,' Pat said, but Anne thought the twins had shown imagination and kindness. Terry had arranged for flowers to be delivered to Maureen a few days after the funeral with the message, 'Sorry to hear about Chris. Chin up, Sis. Thinking of you, love, Terry.' The flowers and the message had meant a lot to Maureen, but Terry said nothing about coming home.

Fred had been uncertain about his Easter party but Maureen urged him to go ahead with it. 'I'm all right, Uncle Fred,' she said. 'And the children look forward to it.' Fred thankfully agreed.

As usual the party was a success and Anne enjoyed it, though she was secretly hurt that once again John was absent on his own affairs. All the children who were old enough performed a party piece. Theresa's son James played the flute and Monica accompanied him on the piano. Theresa's twin girls recited nursery rhymes, and Laura sang Twinkle Twinkle, Little Star.

'I thought that was your song, lad,' Uncle Fred said to Gerry, and he replied sturdily, 'It used to be but I'm too old for it now, so I gave it to Laura.' The adults smiled and Gerry sang next. He sang Eileen Aroon and several verses of The Mountains of Mourne, then at the special request of his grandfather, The Lark in the Clear Air.

Gerry's voice was strong and sweet, and he was heartily applauded and praised. 'Do you know The Spanish Lady?' one of the guests asked, but Anne said quickly, 'I think David should recite now. He knows Jack and Jill, don't you, love?'

She was afraid that her father would be upset by the words of The Spanish Lady but Fred said, 'Yes, then Gerry can sing again. I think we've got another John McCormack here, Pat, and he remembers all the words even at *his* age.'

Joe sat his young son on his father's knee. 'Say Jack and Jill for Grandad, David,' he said, and the child recited it, then turned and buried his face in his grandfather's shoulder. 'He's shy like you and Sarah, Joe,' Uncle Fred said. 'Gerry's like his dad, fond of the limelight.'

Several people spoke at once and no one mentioned Fred's comment but for Anne it was another item in the case she was mentally building against John. It's not just me, she thought, other people think he's a big head too. Later she felt a bittersweet pleasure when she heard Gerry telling John about his triumph, and saw the regret in John's face that he had missed it.

She and John scarcely ever went out together now, with or without the children. Even for Mass it seemed more convenient for Anne to take Gerry and Laura to nine o'clock service leaving the baby with John, and for him to go alone later then on to a meeting.

Anne was not able to visit John's family as often now. While

Gerry was at school she was not free to go out for the day, and when he was on holiday she was unable to manage the three children and a pushchair on the tram.

On Sundays Greg sometimes drove his wife and her mother to see Anne and John and the children, and Anne felt that the company of the children helped John's mother who was worried and distressed about Kate in America. Kate had again left her husband and was staying with Mary and Sam, and Mary had hinted in her letter that other men were interested in Kate.

Anne never discussed this or anything else with John but she felt that she should try to see Cathy more often. 'I think we should all go to your mother's on Sunday,' she said abruptly to John.

He said only, 'All right. What time?'

On the tramcar Anne held Julie on her knee and Laura sat on John's knee with Gerry firmly anchored beside him on the long seat. Anne still worried about the baby and had wrapped her in so many layers of blankets and shawls that only her face peeped out from them.

'Are her nails growing?' John asked. Anne resented the question which she thought showed how rarely he examined the baby in her cot and said briefly, 'Yes.'

Laura leaned forward. 'Mrs Rooney said it was bad luck to cut Julie's nails,' she announced. 'Mummy said it was sup – sup – what, Mummy?'

'Superstition,' Anne said. 'And so it is.' John began to explain the word to Laura and Anne turned her head and looked out of the window, ignoring him.

Cathy and Greg and Sally were delighted to see them. The children were hugged and kissed, and Laura gave her grandmother and great-grandmother the sweets she had brought for them. Gerry presented them with a card and a paper basket he had made in school, and then produced a marble for Greg.

'You shouldn't be left out, Grandad.'

'Bless him,' Cathy said fondly, giving him a hug. 'You're a good lad.' The baby was unwrapped and exclaimed over, and Greg carried Laura out on his shoulders to see his garden.

Everyone was happy until suddenly a disagreement began between John and his father. There had never been a union in the timber merchant's where John had worked in the office, and where his father was still a partner with Stan Johnson.

John argued that the workmen should belong to a union and Greg said, 'Nonsense. They couldn't have better conditions if they belonged to half a dozen unions. Stan's an excellent employer.'

'Yes, but what if Stan dies?' John said, and his father snapped, 'Then I'd take over. I think you can trust me to be fair.'

'Have you seen Stan's will?' John said. 'What if someone else comes in who has the whip hand and doesn't play fair, as you call it? Anyway, good conditions should be the men's right and they should have a union to fight for them, not have to depend on someone's benevolence. You're living in the past.'

Anne had never seen her father-in-law so angry. His face was red and congested and a pulse beat in his temple. He seemed almost too angry to speak but he snarled at John, 'Don't you lecture me? You chose to leave a good respectable berth to work with the rabble you're with now, so leave us alone. Live the way they live, fighting and brawling with you leading the pack.'

John's face was as red, and he turned on his heel and dashed into the hall. Anne put down her cup. 'Just going to the bathroom,' she said to Cathy, and followed him.

He had taken his hat from a hook and Anne said cuttingly, 'Going walkabout? Can't you stand your ground like a man?' She had passed him and started up the stairs but she leaned over the banister. 'You had *your* say, then as usual, as soon as someone tries to answer you, you run away. Think about someone else for a change. Your mum has enough on her plate.' John was staring at her open-mouthed and she said with contempt, 'And shut your mouth,' then continued up the stairs.

He stood for a moment then replaced his hat and went back into the living room. Anne found that she was trembling but she stayed in the bathroom until she felt calmer then went downstairs.

All was peaceful. Photographs were being passed round of the party in York, Gerda's home city, to celebrate her engagement to Mick at Easter. The quarrel was not mentioned and later Greg drove the family home. Gerry had fallen asleep and he carried him indoors and helped Anne and John to put the children to bed.

Before Greg left he kissed Anne warmly and she said, 'You're very good, coming out to drive us home and using all your petrol.'

'No problem now that rationing's finished,' he said, smiling at her and clapping John on the shoulder. Anne knew that Greg knew what she really meant, that she was sorry for John's outburst and appreciated the fact that he had overlooked it.

Do we ever say what we really mean? she wondered. She knew that the quarrel between John and his father had less to do with the unions than with John's contempt for the job he had been glad to take after the war and Greg's resentment of his ingratitude. Neither would ever have admitted or indeed recognised the true reason for their anger with each other.

And my tirade in the hall too, Anne thought ruefully. I talked about John not letting his father answer, but really I was talking about the way he refused to let me answer him. I said my piece then though, she thought with satisfaction, but almost immediately depression settled on her again.

What does it matter? she thought. What does anything matter? The brief euphoria of her visit drained away, leaving her even more miserable than before.

Chapter Forty

The factory was now very busy and John was working extremely long hours. He took every opportunity of working overtime, and the money in the cigar box increased rapidly. Anne's depressed moods when she spent scarcely anything were balanced by 'up' moods when she spent recklessly on clothes and household goods.

Everyone seemed to be looking forward to the summer of 1951 when the Festival of Britain was to take place, and many events were planned for Liverpool.

Anne went to only one event with John. River pageants followed by firework displays had been organised for three evenings, and a family party was arranged for one of them. Maureen had already been to one with friends and she offered to look after Julie and Sarah's baby, Rosaleen.

Anne and John, Sarah and Joe, Helen and Tony, Stephen and Margaret and Eileen and Martin, accompanied by their children, made a happy and noisy group. In such a large gathering no one noticed that Anne and John kept apart from each other.

As the group shifted about Anne found herself beside Eileen. 'Hello, Eil,' she said. 'I haven't seen you lately. How are things?'

'Fine,' Eileen said. 'You look better. You had us worried last year.'

'I know,' said Anne. 'But Julie was worth it all. She's

smashing. So good, and growing more and more like Mum.'

Impulsively she took her sister's arm. 'What about you? Are you happy, Eil?'

Eileen smiled. 'Yes, we are,' she said. 'Of course I know ours wasn't a love match, not like mine with Whitey or you with John. Nothing romantic about it. But Martin and I suit each other and we're very happy in our own way.'

John and I – a love match! Anne thought. A familiar cloud of depression settled on her but she pushed it away and said warmly, 'I think yours *is* a love match. Martin must have loved you to persevere when you kept handing him the frosty mitt.'

Eileen laughed aloud and hugged Anne. 'You're a scream,' she said. 'I must tell Martin that one. The frosty mitt!' She laughed again, but looked thoughtfully at her husband.

Anne watched John. The warm summer night was not really dark but the fireworks lit up his face even more clearly and it seemed grim and unsmiling. He looks as miserable as I feel, Anne thought in surprise, but then he bent and lifted Laura up in his arms and his face was hidden.

Laura caught sight of Anne and shouted, 'Mummy, Mummy,' so Anne had to go to them. She took Laura from John and he lifted Gerry up to see the brilliant display. They both spoke to the children, but neither of them spoke to the other, and Anne stood among the happy crowd engulfed in misery.

Barty's work as a hospital porter often left him free while John was at work, so he attended some daytime events with Anne and the children. He was solicitous with her, taking the baby from her if she seemed tired and protecting all the family in crowds. People probably think he's my husband and a model father, thought Anne.

During the outings with the children Barty was circumspect, contenting himself with gazing at Anne and holding her hand, but it became obvious that he was falling in love with her.

Anne, so deeply unhappy beneath her surface cheerfulness and becoming more and more estranged from John, was at her most vulnerable. She was soothed and flattered by Barty's tender care for her, and his affection and admiration and turned to him with growing fondness.

He began to slip in to see her in the early evenings when the children were in bed and John still at work, ostensibly to discuss the books they borrowed from the Public Library. It was quiet and peaceful as they sat together on the sofa in the comfortable room, with the children asleep upstairs.

Barty often brought volumes of poetry and read aloud to her, making his undeclared love more evident by pressing close to her and gazing at her passionately. One night he read several short love poems, then looked deeply into her eyes and quoted, '"How do I love thee, let me count the ways".' He drew her into his arms and kissed her tenderly.

For a moment Anne resisted but as he kissed her again she pressed her lips against his, and slipped her arms round his neck. 'Oh, Barty, I'm so unhappy,' she murmured.

'I know, darling,' he said lovingly. 'He doesn't deserve you. I love you so much, Anne. It breaks my heart to see the way you are neglected.' He held her closer and kissed her again ardently. 'I'd like to take you away from all this, darling. Love you as you should be loved.'

'Oh, Barty, I couldn't,' she gasped.

'Why not, darling, he wouldn't care,' he said.

He's right, Anne thought, snuggling into his arms and turning up her face for his kisses. John doesn't care about me. Not like Barty, who's always kind and considerate and really loves me.

Barty stroked Anne's hair. 'I could make you happy, darling,' he said tenderly. 'He wouldn't miss you.'

'I don't suppose he would,' Anne said sadly, 'Not now, and

he wouldn't miss Laura or Julie either. But what about Gerry? I couldn't leave him, yet it would kill John if I took him away.'

Anne still lay in Barty's arms, and for a moment there was silence as he sat without moving, seeming scarcely to breathe. With her face pressed against him, Anne was unable to see the look of dismay on his face, as her practical approach broke into his romantic outpourings.

After a while he said pensively, 'You're right, Anne. It wouldn't work.' He kissed her forehead. 'I'll always love you though, darling, and we can still have our lovely evenings together, can't we?'

Anne sat up. Inexperienced though she was personally, she had known of many love affairs among her wide circle of friends, and her practical good sense told her that she had made a mistake. Barty had never intended his attentions to be taken seriously. The haste with which he had seized on the excuse of the children had proved that.

All his sentimental speeches and languishing glances, which she had seen as a sign of true love, were only his romantic fantasy, a substitute for a real love affair with someone who was free, which he was unable or unwilling to embark upon.

All this flashed through Anne's mind as she smoothed her disordered hair, then she realised that Barty was saying again, 'We can still have our lovely evenings together, can't we, darling?'

He was gazing at her soulfully and as Anne looked at his large brown eyes and weak mouth, and the lock of brown hair falling artistically over his forehead she was irresistibly reminded of a spaniel.

An hysterical giggle rose in her throat but she quickly swallowed it. Poor Barty. I must have given him a fright. I must let him down gently, she thought. Aloud she said regretfully, 'No Barty, better not. Better for both of us. We mustn't see each other again like this, but we can still be friends, can't we?'

She stood up. 'John will be in soon. You'd better go, love.' She kissed his cheek and he moved with alacrity to the door, then turned and said sentimentally, 'Thank you, Anne. I will always treasure my memories of you, darling.'

She smiled vaguely and escorted him to the back door. As she closed it behind him she thought that she must slip the bolt on the door the following night, although it seemed unlikely that it would be necessary. Her pride had sustained her through the scene with Barty but now she went in and sank down onto the sofa, covering her face with her hands.

She burned with shame. What a fool I've been, she thought, believing that he really loved me, and meant all he said. For a moment she felt angry with Barty, but honesty made her admit that he was not really to blame.

He probably thought I realised that it was all a romantic fantasy. He would never for a moment expect that I would seriously plan to leave John.

I can't believe it myself, she thought, sobbing with shame and distress. What would the family think if they knew? And the Redmonds? I feel so ashamed. I must be going out of my mind.

And John? I can't face him. She sprang to her feet and fled upstairs. As she slipped into bed Laura cuddled up to her, and Anne took the child in her arms. Laura slipped her arms about her mother's neck, and soon in spite of her guilt and misery Anne felt comforted and slipped into sleep. John returned home while she was asleep and left again for work before she wakened.

In the rush of dressing the children and making breakfast for them, Anne was able to crush thoughts of the previous evening. But after she had taken Gerry to school and returned home with the younger children, memories flooded back again. As she recalled her behaviour Anne wept again and Laura came to lean against her knee. 'Have you got a pain, Mum?' she asked anxiously.

Anne hugged her. 'Yes, pet, but it's gone now,' she said. She wiped her eyes and stood up. The children are not going to be upset because I've been a fool, she vowed.

She smiled at Laura. 'Are you and Julie going to have a dolls' teaparty?' she said, and helped the child to set out her dolls' teaset, and place Dolly Mixtures on the plates. Tears threatened to over-whelm her, but she swallowed determinedly and forced herself to smile at the children.

She hung out her washing when she knew that Barty would be at work, and during the next few days went only back and forth to the school, and for one essential visit to the shops. She wondered how Barty would behave if they met, but the situation never arose.

As the days turned to weeks she heard his voice, but never saw him, and Mrs Rooney never came to speak to the children as they played in the garden, as she had done previously.

The climbing roses which John had planted along the fence had now grown to form a screen between their flower garden and the Rooneys' and Anne wondered whether Mrs Rooney was offended by this, or whether Barty had confided in her.

I hope he hasn't, Anne thought. I wouldn't like anyone to know I've been such a fool.

She had returned her library books and had not withdrawn others, partly to avoid meeting Barty, and partly because she felt too restless and unhappy to read.

The weather changed, and the grey skies and heavy rain seemed more in tune with Anne's mood. Now that she had lost Barty's company, she realised more and more how much his care for her had helped her. Deprived even of that, she found it hard to fight against her almost constant feeling of misery and hope-lessness.

Only the children provided brighter moments. She worried sometimes that John might be talking about causes to Gerry, when she heard them chatting in the early morning, and perhaps make the boy too serious, but she soon found that her fears were groundless.

As she waited at the school gates one day, his teacher came out immediately after Gerry. 'Ah, Mrs Redmond,' the teacher said. 'Gerald is making good progress. He's a bright, attentive boy, but he'd do better still if he didn't feel called upon to be the class comedian.'

They both looked at Gerry. He had grown tall and sturdy, with clear skin, blue eyes and thick, fair curls and Anne felt proud of him.

'He's always had a very happy disposition,' she said, and the teacher smiled. 'Yes, and I must admit he can be very funny, but it's important that his schoolwork doesn't suffer,' she said.

'I'll have a word with him,' Anne promised. Gerry had flung himself on his knees by the pushchair with his duffel coat trailing on the muddy ground, and the baby crowed with delight as he made faces to amuse her.

With one of her sudden swings of mood Anne felt happy again. She had three lovely healthy children who loved her and each other. She should count her blessings.

She looked at them proudly. It was a bitterly cold day but they were all well and warmly dressed. Gerry in the duffel coat which she was now fastening for him, Laura in a red coat with a velvet collar and matching bonnet, and Julie in a pram suit knitted by Maureen and a fleecy lined siren suit.

Anne had taken Julie back to the hospital for her first birthday in August, and had been told that she was a 'miracle baby'. She certainly is, Anne thought, remembering her as she had first seen her. Now she was still tiny for her age but with bright dark eyes and clear pale skin uncannily like Julia, the grandmother she had never seen.

They set off for the shops where Anne bought extravagantly. Fruit, sweets and cakes, and a toy for each of the children. Her happy mood lasted until they were in bed then depression came down like a weight upon her, and great weariness.

She had ironing to do but felt too tired to move. She was still there when John came in. He was carrying a folder of papers and looked surprised to see her still up. Lately she had been in bed when he left in the morning, and there again when he arrived home at night.

He had his evening meal in the canteen and Anne ate with the children, although often she felt too tired to eat. It was now ten o'clock and John said quietly, 'I thought you'd be in bed. Everything all right?'

'Yes, fine,' Anne said listlessly. 'I'm just going. Goodnight.' With an effort she stood up and moved to the door and he said, 'Goodnight. I've work to do.'

He had picked up two bulky letters from the sideboard and opened them and Anne thought scornfully, more Peace Pledge stuff, but at least it was mostly only correspondence now. She felt too weary to care. These dark moods seemed to make her physically exhausted too.

John had worked for several Sundays and Anne made this an excuse for not visiting her family or his. If anyone suggested coming to see her she managed to fob them off with excuses of being invited to friends or some festivity connected with the church.

She was determined that no one should know how things really were between herself and John, and had always managed to present a cheerful face to everyone. Now she began to feel resentful that no one had realised how unhappy she was. Too wrapped up in their own concerns, she thought bitterly. I'm the odd one out.

Helen and Sarah were next-door neighbours, and Eileen and Margaret lived within walking distance of them. All the young wives visited each other frequently, and Joe and Tony, Stephen and Martin, went together to watch Everton Football Club when they played at home on alternate Saturdays.

Anne needed to take two tramcars to reach the area where they all lived, and with three children and a pushchair it was too difficult. John had no interest in football. The other men often met for a drink, too, and he was asked to join them but was always working.

Even Maureen had other interests now. The house in Magdalen Street was too large for her and her father, but neither wished to move. Their problem was solved when Maureen's two friends, Annie Keegan and Mona Dunne, moved into the rooms vacated by Joe and Sarah.

Annie had lived in a bedsitter since she had been driven from her home by her brother's wife after the death of her parents. Mona had lived with her mother until she died shortly after Chris Murray.

They were delighted with the rooms which had been made into a completely self-contained flat and were careful not to intrude on Maureen and her father but were often invited into the living-kitchen. Pat enjoyed their company and they fussed affectionately over him.

The Christmas of 1951 was expected to be a good one for everybody, with the war now firmly in the past, more goods in the shops, and optimism about the future. Anne dreaded it.

Her black moods seemed to be becoming more frequent, and to arrive without warning for no specific reason. It never occurred to her to link them with the traumatic events of Julie's birth, and while she successfully concealed them from her family no one else could suggest the possibility to her.

John might have realised if he had not been so absorbed in his own problems. The doctor at the hospital had told him that Anne had come very near to death and only prompt treatment had saved her.

He warned John that another pregnancy, or at least one within the next three years, might prove fatal for her. Anne was still too ill to be burdened with this knowledge and John, feeling guilty and ashamed, confided in no one.

At first it was easy for him to forgo lovemaking, as Anne only slowly recovered her strength. The sleeping arrangements helped too. But now he was finding it more and more difficult. The doctor had asked which form of contraception he used, and when John told him the 'safe period', he had shaken his head.

'Not safe enough,' he said. 'In fact at present no form of contraception is one hundred per cent safe.' He shrugged. 'It's very hard, I know, but if you don't want to risk your wife's life . . .'

John loved Anne too much to take any risks and dealt with his problem in the only way he knew, by flinging himself into his work and his union activities. This had the double advantage of exhausting him and keeping him away from temptation.

He rose rapidly in his union as he was always available to act as spokesman for the men. And as an important union official and an influential member of the Peace Pledge Union, he felt that he was fulfilling his grandfather's hopes for him, and carrying on the fight.

This belief and his early morning talks with his son were all that made his life tolerable.

Anne and John were invited to his parents' house for Christmas dinner. Sarah and Joe were there with their children, and Mick and Gerda, and amid all this Anne's silence went unnoticed, but she thought that John's father was extra solicitous towards her, pressing her to have more turkey and to eat more. His grandmother, too, seemed to look at her keenly, and Anne made an effort to smile and join in the conversation.

The attention was all on the children after the meal until Sarah and Joe with David and Rosaleen and Anne and John and their children left to go to Magdalen Street.

All the family were there, including the four-year-old girl adopted by Helen and Tony. Helen had told Anne earlier in the year that she and Tony had given up hope of more children and decided to adopt. 'I'd like a newborn baby,' she said, 'but the age difference with Moira would be too much for both of them. We've asked for a girl about four or five.'

The child had been in the orphanage since the death of her mother a year earlier. She had been known there by her correct name of Dorothy but had told Helen that her mother called her Dilly, so Helen introduced her to everyone by this name. Already she was happily at home playing with her cousins, watched over by Moira.

Anne was warmly welcomed by all the family but especially by her father. He hugged her and looked with concern into her face although she was smiling at him. 'Good God, girl, there's not a pick on you,' he said. 'I can feel your ribs. You'll have to get more food down you.'

'I'm fine, Dad,' she assured him. 'It's just that some people put on weight after having a baby and some lose it.'

'Aye, but Julie's eighteen months now, queen. You should be picking up,' he said.

Anne had a disquieting encounter before they left. Maureen's friend and lodger Mona Dunne prided herself on speaking her mind and now sat down beside Anne.

'I think you should show more consideration for your family,' she declared. 'It's all very well making new friends and getting involved in things where you live now, but not if it means snubbing your own family.'

'What do you mean?' gasped Anne. 'I don't snub my family.'

'Well, I don't know what you call it, but you don't visit them, and if they want to visit you you've always got something more important on. I don't like to see Mr Fitz hurt and you're the apple of his eye, you know,' Mona said.

'I wouldn't hurt Dad for the world,' Anne said angrily. 'He's known me all my life and we understand each other. We don't need *you* to interfere.' She was flushed and breathless with indignation, but Mona only shrugged.

'I see what goes on, and I know none of them will say anything in case they upset you, but it needed to be said and now I've said it,' she declared, standing up and striding away.

Anne was furious, but soon her anger was replaced with the familiar depression.

After Christmas her depression was deep and constant. She struggled to get through each day, wondering despairingly why she bothered. I've been miserable for a long time now, she thought, but never as bad or for such a long time as this. It seems to be draining all my strength.

She did only what was absolutely essential for the children, and scarcely any housework, yet she was always exhausted. She never went out. Milk, bread and groceries were delivered, and now she paid an older girl to take Gerry back and forth to school. She never even answered the telephone, hoping that the caller would believe she was out.

She lay on the sofa one dreary day in February. The wireless was on to distract the children but Anne paid little attention to it until she heard an item about an anti-nuclear protest in London, code-named Gandhi. Eleven people had been arrested outside the War Office, and suddenly Anne thought of John's march to London when Julie was born.

That's when it all started, she thought. Lately she had felt that she couldn't think, she could only feel, but now as images of her happy life before that time crowded into her mind, she wept bitter tears. Oh, John, she cried silently, what happened to us? What went wrong with our marriage?

She pressed her hand to her chest, feeling her sorrow like a physical pain, when suddenly there was a loud knock on the door. She held her breath and the knock was repeated. She made no attempt to get up. Then there was a knock on the window and she raised her head to see John's grandmother looking through it.

Hastily she dried her tears and went to the door. 'Grandma, and on a day like this!' she exclaimed.

'Well, if the mountain won't come to Mahomet, Mahomet must come to the mountain,' Sally said calmly. Anne led the way into the untidy living room, feeling ashamed.

Julie was still in her nightdress, her face smeared with chocolate, and Laura's face was even dirtier and she wore a crumpled, stained dress. Anne caught sight of herself in the mirror and recoiled in shock at the reflection of her red-rimmed eyes in her pale face, her lank hair and grubby jumper.

Sally had taken off her coat and handed a small doll to each of the children. Now she drew Anne down beside her on the sofa. 'If I'd known,' Anne began, and Sally interrupted, 'Yes, if you'd known I was coming, you'd have cleared up and pretended everything was fine. Never mind the place. It's not important. What's wrong, girl?'

Anne looked down, twisting her hands together, and Sally said, 'Don't say nothing's wrong. We're all worried about you, child, but the rest of them are afraid of butting in where they're not wanted. I'm too old to care about that, and too fond of you. Tell me, girl.'

Quite suddenly Anne burst into tears and Sally put her arms around her, saying nothing until Anne was calmer.

'You're not well, are you?' she said finally, and Anne began to pour out her feelings of despair and exhaustion. Sally listened in silence, then when Anne finished she said, 'What time does your doctor's surgery finish?'

'Half-past eleven,' Anne said. 'But the doctor can't do anything. It's my mind. I think I'm going out of my mind.'

'No, you're not, girl. It's all to do with Julie's birth. I've seen it before, worse than this. A poor girl in Rupert Hill murdered her newborn baby. Infanticide, they called it, but she wasn't responsible for her actions.

'You go and have a bath and I'll have a cup of tea ready when you come down. Then you can get yourself off to the doctor and tell him what you've told me. I'll mind the children.'

Before Anne had time to realise what was happening she found herself sitting in the doctor's surgery. 'Tell him exactly what you told me,' Sally said as she speeded her on her way and Anne took her advice.

Haltingly at first, then with more confidence as the doctor listened with interest, Anne told of her swings of mood, her exhaustion and the spells of depression when she felt that she was smothering under a black blanket.

The doctor asked about Julie's birth and Anne told him all she could remember about it. He consulted her card which lay on his desk with letters from the hospital pinned to it, then leaned back and looked at her.

'I would say you are a classic case of post-natal depression,' he said. 'And now I'll examine you and see what we can do about it.' After the examination he weighed her and asked about her eating habits. 'I'm too tired to eat,' Anne confessed. 'But I see that the children have enough.'

'And what about your husband?'

Anne blushed. 'He works late every night, seven days a week, and eats in the factory canteen.'

'You are seriously underweight so we must build you up then deal with your other problems,' the doctor said. He wrote a prescription. 'The small white tablets will steady your moods a little. Two three times a day. And I'll arrange for you to see a consultant at the hospital clinic. The yellow tablets will give you the energy to eat. One every morning, but if you haven't taken it by one o'clock, don't take it.'

He smiled at Anne. 'I'll only give you fourteen tablets because they can be addictive, but come back to see me in two weeks' time.'

Anne left the surgery feeling as though a weight had been rolled away from her. Post-natal depression. All she had gone through, and all the time it was an illness that could be cured.

When she reached home she found Laura and Julie bathed and in clean clothes. Sally had swept the hearth and tidied the room, and had a pan of scouse on the gas stove. 'I brought the makings in my basket,' she said. 'I knew you hadn't been feeling like cooking.'

Anne told her what the doctor had said and Sally said, 'Yes, and if you hadn't been so stiff-necked, hiding it from everyone, you'd have got help sooner. Why didn't you tell John at least?'

'He should have known,' Anne muttered. 'He wasn't interested.'

'Now that's daft talk if ever I heard any,' Sally said. 'He knows there's something wrong. You've only got to see how unhappy he is to realise that, but how could he know what it was if you didn't tell him?'

'He's never here,' Anne said. 'He works all hours. He hardly knows Laura and Julie.'

'And why does he work himself into the ground? Because he's not happy. I'm not sticking up for him, Anne, I know he's pig-headed, but there's a pair of you. Too proud for your own good. But I'll say no more. You'll have to work it out yourselves. You'd better take the yellow tablet, hadn't you?'

She stayed to have some scouse with Anne but said no more about her problems, only talked about the family.

Minutes after Anne took the yellow tablet she felt a surge of energy through her body. 'It's amazing,' she told Sally. 'I can't describe it. As though I've had something injected into me.' She enjoyed her meal, and jumped up to wash the dishes as soon as she finished.

'Don't overdo it now,' Sally warned. She soon left, telling Anne that she was due to go to the pictures with her old friend, Peggy Burns.

'We have the time of our lives now,' she said. 'Pictures twice a week, and our tea in the Kardomah afterwards. Peggy says she used to want to live to look after her granddaughter who's backward, but now Meg has a good husband to look after her, Peggy says she wants to live to enjoy herself.'

'And you both deserve to,' Anne said warmly. 'I'll never be able to thank you enough, Grandma.' She kissed Sally and the old lady patted her arm. 'You're a good girl, Anne,' she said. 'I'm just sorry you've had all this trouble. Sort it out with John now, love. Ta ra.'

Anne watched her fondly as she walked briskly down the road, and turned back to her children, smiling.

Chapter Forty-One

Anne could still feel energy surging through her body and marvelled at the power of the small yellow tablet. She found that she could think more clearly too.

She took the children upstairs for their rest and began to clean the house, surprised to see how dirty it had become after the months of neglect, but she enjoyed making it clean and bright again. As she worked she looked back over the months, trying to see why she and John had drifted so far apart.

He's been too busy chasing his dreams, she decided. Trying to solve the world's problems and to be the crusader his grandad wanted him to be. I've been to blame too, she thought honestly. I couldn't help this illness but I should have asked for help sooner, particularly from John. Grandma was right. I'm too proud for my own good.

She sang as she cleaned the stairs, and when she went up for the children, Laura said, 'Mummy, I heard you singing.'

'I know, pet,' she said, hugging her. 'That's because I feel happy.' Or I will when I've talked to John, she thought.

Laura slipped off the bed and stood beside her mother as Anne lifted Julie from the cot. 'When I'm calling you hoo,' she sang, and the baby echoed 'Yoo hoo'.

'Me and Julie can sing too,' Laura said. 'Like the man on the wireless.' Anne kissed them. My poor kids, she thought. They must have had a rotten time with my moods.

I must have hurt Dad and the family too, she thought with remorse as she remembered Mona Dunne's reproaches. I suppose they didn't know what to make of my yarns. I must be a better liar than I thought.

Gerry arrived home from school and Anne felt that he looked nervously at her. I suppose the poor kid doesn't know what to expect. I've either been screaming at him or lying on the sofa whingeing, she thought.

After the children were in bed she took out a red dress which had been a favourite with John. Freshly bathed and with her hair shining, she looked very different to the reflection in the mirror twelve hours earlier. She was dismayed to see how the dress hung on her now but left it on.

She could still feel the effect of the yellow tablet, but she was nervous and excited as she waited for John, determined to discuss things with him but uncertain how to do it.

When he opened the living-room door and she saw him, thin and haggard with lines of strain and unhappiness on his face, her uncertainty vanished. Impulsively she went to him and kissed him, and he said in a bewildered voice, 'I thought you'd be in bed. What – what's happened?'

'Take your coat off. Come to the fire,' she said gently. He threw off his overcoat and they sat together on the sofa. She kissed him again and involuntarily his arms went round her. 'God, Anne, you're thin,' he exclaimed.

'I know,' she said. 'Grandma came this morning and made me go to the doctor's. He said I've got post-natal depression.'

'And that's why you're thin?'

'I'm thin because I've been too tired and too miserable to eat,' she said. 'But the doctor's given me some marvellous tablets that made me feel full of energy, and some others to help with the depressed feelings. I'm going to see a specialist at the hospital too.'

'But what is it – this illness?' John asked.

'It's just what it says. Depression after having a baby. The doctor said something about hormones. Grandma says it happens to lots of girls, often worse than me. She knew a girl who murdered her baby because of it.'

John cradled Anne in his arms. 'Good God! And I didn't know. Why didn't you tell me?' he said. Anne sat up.

'You should have seen it for yourself,' she said indignantly, but then she lay back again in John's arms. 'I don't want to quarrel,' she said more gently.

'I thought you were eating with the children,' he said.

'It wasn't just not eating. That was only part of it,' Anne said. 'It was these terrible despairing moods when I didn't want to go on living.'

John was silent, thinking, then he said quietly, 'How long has this gone on? When did it start?'

'I'm not sure,' she said. 'I think it might have started right away, but I thought I felt rotten because I was just getting over the birth at first. Then when we got Julie home, there was so much work and worry I thought it was that.'

'I should have done more to help,' he said.

'I think I shut you out,' Anne said honestly. 'And then you were always wrapped up in Gerry, and Laura seemed to cling to me. I used to think we were like two separate families in one room.'

'But why? Why did you shut me out?' he asked.

'I don't know. Partly because I was still mad at you because you were away that weekend, I suppose.'

'You don't know how bitterly I've regretted that, Anne,' John said in a low voice. 'Tony was right, I should never have gone.'

'But you thought you were fighting for a better world for our children,' Anne said.

'Yes, but I could have done it without going off like that,' he said. 'I did honestly think you had two months more to go, Anne. That's my only excuse.'

'Never mind, it's all water under the bridge now as Grandma would say. Gosh, John, I can't tell you how glad I was to see her this morning. I was just about as low as I could be, wishing I could die . . .'

'As bad as that?' John said quietly. 'And I didn't even suspect. I must have been blind.'

'We hardly saw each other,' Anne said. 'I was always so tired and you worked so late. Nobody else knew, not until just lately anyway. I didn't go to see the family, and if they wanted to come here I said I was going out. Mona Dunne told me off at Christmas for getting too involved up here and dropping the family. If she only knew!'

'I should have spent more time at home,' he said. 'When I wasn't working I was there doing union work or going straight on to a Peace Pledge meeting. No wonder we had no chance to talk.'

He said nothing about the other reason, the fact that they slept in separate beds. Anne would have liked to lie safe at last in his arms, not bothering to talk any more, but felt that now that they had started they should talk out all their problems.

She still felt full of energy, but was uncertain how long the effect of the tablet would last. She was afraid that if it wore off she would be too tired to talk as they needed to.

'If we'd been sleeping together we could have talked in bed,' she said. 'It was supposed to be a temporary arrangement, but it's just gone on and on.'

'I thought it suited you,' John said. 'You seemed quite happy with it.'

There was a trace of bitterness in his voice and Anne said defensively, 'It certainly seemed to suit *you*, and you were the one in a different bed.'

'I know. But I wasn't just drifting, I had a reason. It was better for us that way, but never mind about that.'

'What do you mean, never mind? If it concerns me, I've got the right to know.'

'Just leave it, Anne. I think you can trust me to do what's best for us.'

'For *us*? So that means it concerns me?' Anne said.

'For me, then. Really, love, it's better that you don't know,' he said.

'Don't patronise me,' she said indignantly. 'That's the trouble with you. You think you should decide what's best for us, but it's *my* life too. I should have some say.'

'But you do,' he protested. 'You make all the decisions about the house and the money and everything.'

'That's not important,' Anne said. 'It's other things. But you've always been the same. When we went out together *you* decided that people shouldn't know we were courting. You didn't ask me what *I* wanted to do.'

'But that was to protect you, because I was taking flak about fighting in Spain.'

'But I didn't care about that,' Anne said. 'Helen said she felt guilty because she and Tony had courting days and we didn't, but we could have done. We could have had a proper courtship, but *you* decided that it had to be a few furtive meetings as though we had something to be ashamed of. I hated it.'

'And you've kept this in your mind all these years, and never said anything,' he said slowly.

'I often meant to but it didn't seem the right time,' she said. 'But now you're doing it again. Making decisions for me. We should discuss things and decide together what to do.'

'I still don't think I should tell you, but you're forcing my hand,' he said. 'I hope you won't be sorry. The doctor at the hospital told me that you nearly died from loss of blood. Only prompt treatment saved you, and you shouldn't risk another pregnancy for years, possibly for ever.'

'And that's the big secret?' Anne said scornfully. 'I knew I was very ill when Julie was born. I was Anointed, remember.'

'But you didn't know what the doctor had told me.'

'No, but the sister told me she didn't want to see me back there. I don't worry about things like that. Nurses and doctors don't know everything and new things are being discovered all the time,' Anne said.

'But we daren't risk another baby, love. I know the safe period seemed to work for us but the doctor didn't seem to think much of it. He said no form of contraception was one hundred per cent safe except complete abstinence. So you see why it's easier for me if we sleep in separate rooms, don't you?'

'I thought you'd stopped loving me,' she said in a low voice.

'Oh, Anne, you didn't. You couldn't,' he exclaimed, holding her close and kissing her fiercely. 'It's because I love you I daren't take any risks, sweetheart.'

She clung to him and murmured, 'And I love you, John, and I don't think it's right for us to go on living like this.' They kissed again then she said quietly, 'I'm not worried about the risk, John. There was something different from the beginning about the third pregnancy, but I was all right for the other two. Once I get over this business I'll be perfectly healthy again.'

'Don't, Anne,' he said. 'I want you so much but we daren't. Not yet. I'll have to sleep in a different room. It's the only way I can manage. And you're still ill anyway.'

He stood up, drawing her to her feet with him, and kissed her again. 'This time I *am* making the decision, love, and you know why, don't you?'

'Yes. I know I'm not out of the wood yet,' she said quietly. 'But another few months – and then we'll reconsider.' She smiled at him. 'I think we've talked enough for now. You've got work in the morning.'

They went upstairs and kissed goodnight on the landing before going into their separate rooms. There was still much to be discussed, Anne felt, but she was happy that so much had been cleared up and the barrier between them had fallen so easily.

She still felt energetic and found it difficult to sleep at first but was woken next morning by John putting a cup of tea beside her. 'Goodbye, love,' he whispered, slipping quietly out of the bedroom after kissing her ardently.

Anne lay feeling confused then memory returned but she was dismayed by the lethargy she felt. I must have done too much yesterday, she decided. Fortunately she still kept to the wartime habit of carrying her handbag upstairs with her, and groped in it for the yellow tablets.

She took one and was immediately filled with energy as on the previous day. She decided that her first priority must be to put things right with her family so she sent a note to the school asking for Gerry to be excused and kept him home. They set off. Maureen and her father would be at work so she went first to visit Sarah and Helen, finding no difficulty in managing the three children and the pushchair on and off tramcars.

Sarah was hanging out washing in the garden and welcomed her warmly, then called Helen who came in with Dilly. The little girls played happily with Rosaleen's toys and Gerry was given paper to draw on while the mothers sat round the kitchen table with cups of tea.

Anne said immediately, 'I've come to apologise. I've been a fool trying to keep up appearances, but I've been to the doctor now and I know what's wrong with me.'

Helen and Sarah looked at each other and Helen took Anne's hand. 'What is it, love?' she said gently.

'The doctor called it post-natal depression,' Anne said. She was amazed when Helen and Sarah said simultaneously, 'Thank God.'

'We were afraid that you had the same as your mother,' Sarah said. 'You'd gone so thin. I think everybody thought it, but it was only the other day that Helen and I admitted it to each other. We haven't said anything to anyone else.'

'I'm sorry I've worried people,' Anne said. 'I was just in a world of my own with these awful moods. I was thin because I was too tired and miserable to eat.'

'I know it must have been terrible,' Sarah said, 'but it's such a relief that it's not that other thing. We haven't known what to do. We didn't know whether you'd been told or not.'

Later Eileen and Margaret called in on their way to the shops, and Anne felt humble and grateful at the generous welcome she received from everyone.

'I thought people would have fallen out with me,' she said. 'I know I've offended everyone. Mona Dunne told me my fortune at Christmas.'

'Take no notice of Mona,' Eileen said. 'She tried some of her straight talking with me but she didn't get very far.'

'The irresistible force met the immovable object,' Margaret said, laughing. She and Eileen left, promising to call back later, and Helen and Sarah organised lunch. Helen spoke about the death of King George VI, and Sarah reminded Anne about Mabel, the ardent Royalist they had worked with.

'I wonder if she's crying about this the way she cried about George V,' Sarah said.

'Or about the Abdication,' Anne reminded her. 'Poor Mabel. I wonder what happened to her?'

'Probably still nursing,' Sarah said. 'What about Kathleen O'Neill? How's she going on?'

'I don't know,' Anne confessed. 'I couldn't be bothered answering her letter, and she didn't send a Christmas card. I'll have to write and explain. God knows how many people I've offended, Sar.'

'Don't worry,' Sarah comforted her. 'Those who care about you will just be glad you're all right again, or on your way anyway.'

Eileen and Margaret came back and the conversation was general. No one dwelt on Anne's illness, but she was comforted by their affection and enjoyed their company.

Sarah walked with her to the tramstop. 'It's only one tram to Mum's,' she said. 'I go nearly every day.'

Sally was out at the cinema with Peggy, but Cathy was delighted to see Anne. She knew all the details of her troubles so no explanations were needed. Cathy took Anne in her arms and kissed her warmly. 'You've had a bad time, pet,' she said. 'But you've just got to take care now and get really well. You mean so much to all of us, and of course John most of all.'

Anne managed without being too specific to make it clear that she and John were united in dealing with the illness, and although Cathy said nothing plainly either, Anne knew that she was relieved.

They talked about Mick's wedding and about Cathy's daughter Kate in America. Sarah had told Anne that Kate had been divorced and was planning to re-marry and Cathy said with a sigh, 'I never thought there'd be a divorce in our family, but Grandma says she's not surprised.'

'I think divorce is quite common in America,' Anne said. 'With people who are not Catholics anyway.'

'Yes, but Gene was such a nice fellow. I'm ashamed that our daughter brought such trouble to him and his family. I never thought she'd do this. Our Mary was flighty when she was young like Kate was, but she's been a good faithful wife to Sam. I hoped Kate would be the same.'

'I know two girls who are divorced,' Anne said. 'I think it was almost impossible for people like us, before the war, and they both said it's still difficult, but women can get Legal Aid now and that helps.'

'Money's not the problem with Kate,' Cathy said. 'Still, as Grandma says, at least she isn't making a mess on her own doorstep.'

'Grandma was great,' Anne said. 'So kind yet so practical.'

'She always is,' Cathy said. 'She's had a hard life, Anne, but a happy one. But then, we all have our ups and downs, don't we? Let's hope it's going to be plain sailing for you and John from now on, love.'

Anne and the children had tea with her, then they went on to see Maureen and her father who would now be home from work. Anne still felt energetic and marvelled at the power of the small tablet.

Maureen opened the door and hugged Anne but she said nothing. Anne realised that she was crying.

'Mo, what is it?' she said fearfully, but Maureen released her and took out her handkerchief. 'I'm sorry, love,' she said. 'I know what's been wrong with you. Sarah's grandmother has just been here.'

She took the baby from the pushchair and led Anne and the other children into the kitchen. Anne's father was standing on the hearthrug and she went into his arms. 'Anne, my chick, why didn't you tell your old dad?' he said, and she burst into tears.

'I didn't know, Dad,' she sobbed. 'I thought I was going mad.'

There were tears in Pat's eyes too, but he took out his handkerchief and blew his nose vigorously. 'Never mind, queen,' he said. 'We'll just have to get you right. Get some flesh on your bones. It must be the poor food. Women never had troubles like this in my day.'

'You just never heard any women's talk, Dad,' Maureen said. 'Do you want to hold Julie?' He took the baby, and Laura and Gerry went to stand beside him and talk to him.

Anne and Maureen sat down together and Maureen told Anne

that Grandma Ward had called on her way home from the pictures to tell them what had happened.

'I wanted to go to see you,' Maureen said. 'I knew there was something wrong but I thought you didn't want us to interfere.' She looked embarrassed. 'I wondered, well, I thought – it might be something to do with you and John.'

Anne said nothing and Maureen went on, 'I thought he might have talked to his mother, so I went there to see her. I just said we were worried and they said they were worried too, and Mrs Ward said she'd go to see you.' She smiled. 'I said I didn't want to interfere if you didn't want to tell us, and she said, "Don't worry, girl. I've got a thick skin."'

'Anything but,' Anne said. 'She's very kind and very tactful. I wasn't glad to see her at first, I must admit, Mo, because I was so down and the place was a mess, but afterwards I was so glad she came.'

'I should have grasped the nettle,' Maureen said ruefully, 'but we've never been a family for interfering. Not that I think Mrs Ward interfered,' she added hastily.

'I was to blame,' Anne said. 'I hid it from everyone, even John, and it wasn't fair. Especially with him. He'd have realised but he was working such long hours seven days a week, and I was always asleep. I was going to bed at eight o'clock. I couldn't get enough sleep!'

'Are you tired now?' Maureen asked.

'No, I've got these amazing tablets. They're like monkey glands,' she said. 'I still feel I could clean a house.'

Julie had fallen asleep and Laura and Gerry were tired so Maureen drove them home. John was there and helped to put the children to bed, then he and Anne sat together on the sofa while she told him of her visits.

'I felt guilty because people were worried,' she said. 'Helen and Sarah thought I had the same disease as Mum but I wanted to keep quiet about it. Maureen thought there was something wrong between us.'

'Maureen was near the mark,' he said.

'Yes, but the main reason I tried to bluff them was because I didn't want anyone to know about us. I was all mixed up.'

'Never mind, everything's all right now,' he said. 'Do you know what happened to me today? I went in to see the manager and he said the Board had decided to offer me a job. A new thing. Personnel relations, they call it. It's a salaried position.'

'And what will you do?'

'It'll be like union work. You know I've been the spokesman for fellows with problems, and I've been representing them at the management meetings? It'll be official now.'

'Your grandad would be pleased,' she said.

'I'm sure he would,' John said eagerly. 'I've tried to carry on his work, Anne, although it's different now. The problems are different. We've got what he fought for, security from the cradle to the grave, but there are other things now that need to be put right.'

'Will it mean very long hours?' she asked, but John shook his head. 'No. The hours should be regular.'

'And no meetings?'

'Only very occasionally,' he said. 'I must have been mad to work those hours. I think I was making it a sort of substitute because I'd made such a mess of things here. And keeping myself out of temptation,' he added wryly.

'It certainly wasn't because we needed the money,' Anne said. 'That drawer's full of wage packets. I'll have to sort it out and take it to the bank.'

John kissed her. 'Practical Anne,' he said. 'You don't want to discuss my motives?'

'No. We'll look forward, not back,' she said firmly.

Anne continued to take the yellow tablets, but she soon realised that the energy they released had to be paid for with exhaustion the next morning. It could be cured by another tablet but she thought of the doctor's words about addiction so put the remaining tablets away for emergencies and managed without them.

This was easier because the family closed ranks around her. Every day she was visited by or visited one of her own family or John's, and everyone prepared delicacies to tempt her to eat.

'I feel like a turkey being fattened for Christmas,' she joked to John, but she appreciated the affection and concern shown by everyone.

Anne heard Barty's voice occasionally but only caught glimpses of him until she was out walking one day with John and the children. They saw Barty with a woman and a small child, and John said, 'I think Con's right. He calls Barty the married woman's friend. Says he never has a girl of his own, but always has a married woman friend. Probably feels safer that way.'

'Barty was very good to me when the girls were born, and very competent,' Anne said.

'Yes, I think he's a good fellow, but Con thinks he lives in a fantasy world,' John said. Anne said no more but thought ruefully, I probably gave him the fright of his life that night, getting down to details when he probably wanted a grand romantic scene and the great renunciation. She still felt grateful for his friendship which had helped her through her dark days.

John was best man at Mick's wedding in March, and Anne and John, Sarah and Joe, and Mick's parents and grandmother all travelled to York for the wedding. It was a bright, sunny day and Anne felt that it marked the end of winter and of her months of misery.

At Easter Fred held his usual party and Anne felt that she had never enjoyed it so much. I suppose you have to know sadness before you can really appreciate being happy, she thought.

Bridie was there with her family, and two additions. Danny and Teddy had both brought girlfriends and Bridie whispered to

Anne, 'Just think. I could be a grandmother in a few years' time!'

Dom and Des were now courting two sisters who were at the party. 'You've got the hearts of lions taking these two on,' Fred told them. Anne thought her father looked sad and guessed that he was thinking of Terry who was still in Canada so she carried Julie to him. His face brightened as he took his favourite grandchild.

'By God, she gets more like your mum every day,' he said.

'She's like her in character too, Dad,' Anne said. She often thought of her mother singing as she went about her housework as Julie sat playing with her toys and crooning softly to herself.

Bridie and Carrie both urged Anne to visit them and she promised that she would. 'I'll be able to get round to see everyone now the weather's better,' she said. 'And Gerry stays to school dinners.'

'It's a pity you live so far away from everyone,' Carrie said. 'Especially with the others living near each other and not far from your dad and us.'

Pat, who was sitting near her, agreed. 'Aye, you wouldn't have got so bad if you lived near. But we'll be keeping an eye on you from now on, girl.'

'I'd better watch my step then, Dad,' she laughed.

'That's more like it,' Fred exclaimed. 'That's the way. Happy Annie. Not crying and starving yourself. Dwindling away.'

Theresa took his arm. 'And that's like you, Dad,' she said with a grimace at Anne. 'Come and pour beer. The fellows are dying of thirst.'

Anne and John laughed later about that conversation, not knowing it would bear fruit that would change their lives.

They still slept in separate rooms but otherwise they were close and loving, frequently kissing and embracing. Anne often longed to make love and knew that it was even more difficult for

John to resist the temptation, but fear held him back.

She visited the doctor regularly and one day plucked up the courage to talk about the hospital doctor's warning that another pregnancy would risk her life and only total abstinence was one hundred per cent safe.

'I think there was a misunderstanding,' the doctor said discreetly. 'You would be given different advice now.' He told her that sometimes such pregnancies were part of a pattern but Anne's troubles had been caused by special factors that would not recur.

'I see no reason why you and your husband cannot resume normal relations,' he said. 'Your cycle is regular and you understand the "safe period".'

'And if I started with another baby?' she asked.

'Should be quite straightforward,' he assured her. 'You're a perfectly healthy young woman.'

John heard the news with joy especially when Anne told him that it was now the time between her periods when she was unlikely to conceive. The children were moved into their own beds and that night Anne and John lay together, making love as though for the first time.

'And to think this might have been possible months ago,' he said. He kissed her again ardently and held her close. 'We must make up for lost time.'

To crown their joy, Anne's father came to see them a few days later. 'You know them old houses in Norton Grove, near them I built in Domingo Vale for Joe and Tony?' he said. 'They were built in 1906 but they're good solid houses. I've bought four, and I'm going to do them up. Will you have one? Rent or buy, I'll fix you up.'

Anne and John looked at each other with delight, then Anne flung her arms around her father. 'Oh, Dad, thanks,' she said fervently.

He hugged her. 'You've got a bit more flesh on your bones,

chick,' he said gruffly, 'but I worry about you, stuck out here.'

'What are the houses like?' John asked eagerly.

'Four bedrooms and bathroom, kitchen, scullery and two parlours. No attics or cellars. Little garden at the front and a big one at the back. Some war damage, cracked walls, broken slates. They've been patched up but I'll do them up properly,' Pat said.

Anne and John were delighted with the house in Norton Grove even before Pat's improvements were made. They had both lost all their earlier joy in their present house. Their new house had large rooms with delicate moulding round the high ceilings and the fireplaces, and the family helped to decorate the rooms and hang curtains and pictures.

The two parlours later became a dining room and a sitting room, but the large kitchen was the heart of the house. 'I feel at home here,' Anne said, looking round it.

It was similar to the Magdalen Street kitchen except that there was an Aga stove instead of an open fire and the wide window looked out on to a large garden. A sycamore tree at the bottom provided hours of pleasure for Gerry as he climbed it, and for Laura and Julie on the swing which John hung from a branch.

He had more time at home in his new job and was happy in it, although Mick told Anne that he thought John had been bought off. 'He must have been too good as a union man,' Mick said with a grin. 'But they haven't reckoned on John's obsession with living up to Grandad.'

Anne said nothing about this to John, and when he was down-hearted because Britain tested her first atomic bomb in Australia in October 1952, she cheered him by joining the Peace Pledge Union.

'I've read all the literature and I really believe in it,' she told him. 'We'll win in the end, you'll see.'

Their joy in the house, and their feelings of hope and happiness, seemed to be shared by everyone as preparations were made for the Coronation of the new Queen. 'The New Elizabethan Age' the newspapers were proclaiming.

Coronation Day, 2 June, was wet, but everyone was in high spirits especially when the news came of the successful ascent of Everest.

Anne and John moved into Norton Grove on a sunny day two days earlier and for Anne the national rejoicing would always be associated with the start of her happy years in that house. Flags and bunting were everywhere and Laura exclaimed, 'Look, Mummy, the flags are out for us.'

Carrie and Fred, and Bridie and Jack, came to see the house, and Fred exclaimed, 'This is a good house for a party, Anne. Good big rooms, much better than those modern boxes.'

'We'll have lots of parties, Uncle Fred,' she promised. 'A big one in September when Laura will be five and we'll have been married ten years, please God.'

'Ten years,' Bridie sighed sentimentally. 'It's hard to believe. And a perfect marriage too.'

Anne looked embarrassed and Carrie said briskly, 'Well, I suppose you've had your ups and downs like everyone else, Anne, but you've been happy together, that's the main thing.'

'That's true,' she said, smiling at John as he gave her a quick hug.

'You know, standing here in this kitchen you could be your mother over again, Anne,' Carrie said. 'Julia as I remember her when she was young, with her children round her. I was the same.' She sighed. 'Happy days . . . Make the most of yours, love.'

'Oh, I *will*,' Anne said. 'This is what I've always wanted, Aunt Carrie. A home and a family like ours. We were always so happy.'

'Aye, like that feller said: "A nest of singing birds",' Fred said.

They went home a little later, and Anne and John sat round

the table with the children for their evening meal. Gerry had a mug with a Union Jack on it.

'I know a song about this,' he announced. He began to roar out the words of Land of Hope and Glory and Laura joined in, singing her own words. Julie sang tunelessly and beat her spoon on the tray of her high chair.

Anne pretended to cover her ears, but when John stretched his hand over the table to her she took it. As they laughed together he raised his voice to be heard over the happy noise their children were making.

'Here you are, love,' he said. 'What you always wanted – a nest of singing birds.'